# Life Lines

# Frontispiece

**BILL AND ROSE WEDDING PARTY**

Front: Doris Graybeal, Rose Moore and Bill Ramsay, Gwen Lanier

Back: Norman Aich, Dick Ramsay, John Ramsay, Ken Moore

**THE RAMSAY FAMILY: BEREA, DECEMBER 1970**

William Edward, John Robert, Laura Elizabeth

James Moore, Jennifer Rose, Rose and Bill, Stephen Gates

Rose

Life Lines

Bill

# The Chronicle of a Marriage and Family

## Bill and Rose Ramsay

# LIFE LINES
## THE CHRONICLE OF A MARRIAGE AND FAMILY

New Revised Standard Version Bible, copyright © 1989, Division of Christian Education of the National Council of the Churches of Christ in the United States of America. Used by permission. All rights reserved.

iUniverse books may be ordered through booksellers or by contacting:

iUniverse
1663 Liberty Drive
Bloomington, IN 47403
www.iuniverse.com
1-800-Authors (1-800-288-4677)

ISBN: 978-1-5320-4394-9 (sc)
ISBN: 978-1-5320-4393-2 (hc)
ISBN: 978-1-5320-4395-6 (e)

Library of Congress Control Number: 2018902366

Print information available on the last page.

iUniverse rev. date: 04/06/2018

# DEDICATION

We dedicate this book to marriage and family as God has established them from the beginning. We wish to memorialize the marriages and families of our ancestors which gave us our lives and our heritage. We wish to honor the marriages and families of our generation and, in particular, our children and grandchildren. Finally, we wish to dedicate our "Life Lines" to the marriages and families of the future, praying that they will be rich in heritage, secure in faith and strong in commitment to live and serve as Christ has called us, and as our heavenly Father would have His children live and serve until His kingdom comes.

**Bill and Rose Ramsay**

THIS COPY OF <u>LIFE LINES</u> IS ESPECIALLY FOR

_____

_____

_____

_____

Bill and Rose Ramsay

# CONTENTS

## PART III: COLLEGE YEARS AND MARRIAGE

# PART VII: BEREA, 1970-1995

## PART IX: BACK HOME IN BEREA

## PART X: THE LAST CHAPTER

## APPENDIX

# PREFACE

One of our art teachers used to draw a line on the blackboard and then pretend to go on past the board to the wall and indicate that the line went on and on forever. The image of not being confined by walls or space or time stuck with us. We see the lines of our lives having begun before we were born and going on beyond our earthly existence. During our years we have been given roles to play on the stage of our times. In this chronicle we have tried to provide a record of our two lines of life as they were twined together to become one and then woven with others to compose the fabric of family and community. Our lives have spanned a time of great changes. When we were born, many homes had no electricity or plumbing. Radios and telephones were novelties. Now, 86 years later, we are accustomed to surveillance cameras, and children carry the world in their pockets through devices half the size of a peanut butter and jelly sandwich.

In our attempt to write a narrative of our lives we are aware that our memories are selective, frequently confused and sometimes faulty. Nevertheless, we have been as faithful to facts and events as our minds allow. We have tried to provide a record as well as tell a story so many names are included, which may not be significant for the narrative, but are included for the record. And we know that names of others have been forgotten or passed over even though they may have played an important role in our lives. As we read old letters, names and events are brought back to mind which we had forgotten. A letter written to John and Winona who were at Celo, NC, in the 1950s, for example, mentions an enclosed check for $220 to buy a cow. We have no recollection of this matter. In another letter the name Hilda Brautegan is mentioned and we had forgotten this dear friend of our family who had been a member of Hitler's Youth Brigade and after World War II became a Christian and American citizen, teaching German at a college. We have known so many wonderful people.

In writing this account we have chosen the form of a third person narrative providing a continuing account of our lives, alternating with first person recorded memories of specific events and times that fit the narrative and round it out. At the end of each part of the chronicle we have inserted time-lines of the events of our lives alongside events in the wider world to give a context to the times. We have added some pictures from the time period of the narrative. Finally, we have indulged in reflections that give our thoughts on issues that have arisen over our lifetime. All of this is done to give our children, grandchildren, great grandchildren and future generations a sense of their heritage as they live their stories, which are really just a continuation of ours. The drama goes on.

Bill and Rose Ramsay
Berea, Kentucky
September, 2017

# ACKNOWLEDGEMENTS

We can't begin to recognize all the people who have been important to the forming of our "life lines." Letters from friends and family, as well as letters we wrote to each other, albums of pictures, journals, guest books, calendars, special books, phone calls and visits, and. more recently, e-mails, have all been channels of influence by others to the story of our lives. During the nitty-gritty of writing and remembering and checking and revising, some have been especially helpful. Our daughters, Laura Compton and Jennifer Escobar, have been of constant assistance and encouragement. Our son, Bill has helped untie knots in our relationship with our computer numerous times, for which we are grateful. Our granddaughters, Lydia and Isabel Escobar, with their keen eyes and quick hands, have been invaluable in going through albums and other material. Lydia Bauler, a graduating Berea College student, performed careful editing, finding typos and punctuation problems. We also depended on the rich lodes of Wikipedia and the omniscient Google for historical information and fact checking. For the book cover, our artistic granddaughter, Melissa Rinaldi created the sketches of us as we were in our younger years. All of our family and friends have given encouragement and support. We thank them all.

# PART ONE

*Introduction*

# CHAPTER 1

# WHO ARE YOU?

*"… and they became one flesh." (Genesis 2: 24, NRSV)*

It was September 7, 1952. They stood together in the chapel filled with family and friends with the minister before them and said their wedding vows. "Do you take this woman…? Do you take this man…?" Finally the minister said, "I now pronounce you man and wife!" So Bill Ramsay and Rose Moore were joined in holy matrimony. That was more than 65 years ago and they are still learning about "this woman" and "this man." They didn't know much at that time but they were in love and confident in a future that was meant to be spent together. They still have that love and that confidence but a much broader perspective on who they are.

What threads of history and lives went into bringing these two into life and brought them together? What patterns continue to be woven as their lives touch lives of others and the generations go on with children, grandchildren and great grandchildren? The lives of family and friends, a radically changing world, opportunities, difficulties, achievements, failures joys and sorrows, and faith, all intertwine in the ever changing fabric of life.

Where did it start? *"In the beginning was the Word…!"*
Where will it end? *"I am the alpha and omega!"*

Our short lives are but a breath. And yet we live and love and search for meaning. Who are we? Tom Bombadil in JRR Tolkien's <u>The Fellowship of the Ring,</u> when asked who he is, replies, *"Tell me who you are, alone, yourself and nameless."*

"Who we are" is often expressed in relationships like "John and Gertrude's son" or "Patty's little brother" or "Rosalba's man" or "Jennifer's dad," all meaning the same "Bill." The relationships change over time. "Eddie and Lochiel's daughter" meant "Rosalba" seventy years ago in rural Greene County, Tennessee and "Lydia's and Isabel's grandmother" would be identifying of Rose in Berea, Kentucky in 2017. Yet it is the same person. Sometimes we are known by occupation – doctor, lawyer or preacher. Or by position: "She is the reading teacher." "He is the president of the board." Identity may be associated with some special talent or contribution: "She's the woman who teaches literacy" or "the one who makes that great cherry dump cake." "He's the one who taught me to waltz," or "the guy who comes in for coffee every morning." But who we are in this place and in this time is the culmination of the choices and actions of countless ancestors. How did we happen to be born at a certain place and time into certain families? One needn't go back in time very far to see the awesome complexity of the answer.

# Chapter 2

# Family Roots

## Threads of Heritage: Rose

### The Kildays

Ephram Kilday was born in Ireland, of the Scotch-Irish people who had settled in Ulster decades earlier, and he died in Virginia in 1815. How he got to America isn't known but the Kilday family eventually migrated to East Tennessee sometime before Tennessee became a state in 1796. Ephram's great grandson Elijah married Amy Conkin in 1858. Amy's mother Barbary, according to family lore, was of Cherokee Indian descent, which may account for her great granddaughter Rose's beautiful high cheekbones which also show up in some of Rose's own granddaughters. Amy and Elijah had 14 children, one of whom was Eliza who married James Moore in Greene County, Tennessee. The Moores had one son named Edward (Eddie) Syril Moore who, after serving in World War I, married Lochiel Riggs. Their first child was named Elva Rosalba, later to be known as Rose. It was she who was the bride at the wedding ceremony in the chapel 21 years later.

### The Moores

The Moore family had been in East Tennessee at least since the 1830's, probably having come from North Carolina or Virginia, perhaps to harvest the plentiful lumber in those parts. They purchased a small piece of land and settled in. James Moore, married Eliza Kilday in 1892. James and his father-in-law, Elijah Kilday, were founding members of the Oak Dale Missionary Baptist Church in 1895. Later, with his son Eddie, James built

3

the small frame house in which Rose was born to Eddie and Lochiel in 1931 and from which she went to Berea College in 1948.

## The Riggs

Willie Lochiel Riggs was born in 1906. She was named "Lochiel" (the name by which she was known) for a local woman whom her mother admired, but it is Scottish for "White Lake" (loch hiel). Little is known about the Riggs family ancestry. Gravestones in Rock Springs cemetery near Kingsport, Tennessee show Samuel Riggs, 1855 – 1914 was married to Matilda Ann Fitzgerald, 1855 – 1920, but don't reveal the places of birth or place and date of marriage. Their son, William Garrett Riggs, lived on the family farm near Kingsport, married Laura Fleenor and died in 1948. Lochiel, their second daughter, married Eddie Moore in 1924 in Greene County and moved to the Moore farm where their daughter Rosalba was born.

## The Fleenors

A century before Samuel Riggs birth, Laura Fleenor's great, great grandfather Johannes Fliener and his wife Anna fled Germany seeking religious freedom in America. They sailed via Amsterdam, Netherlands and then Portsmouth, England on the *John and Elizabeth* arriving in Philadelphia on November 17, 1754. The Fleenors migrated from Pennsylvania to Maryland, then Virginia. John Quincy Fleenor in 1858-60, having five children from a previous marriage, married Sarah Adaline Gobble. They moved to Tennessee near Rock Springs in 1878 where the last of eight additional children, Laura, was born in 1879. Laura and William Riggs were married and had three daughters and a son. The second daughter, Willie Lochiel born on January 1, 1906, married Edward Syril Moore and had three children. Their first child, a daughter, born on July 5, 1931 was named Elva Rosalba. Lochiel died on March 29, 1952 so her daughter's wedding on September 7 of that year had no "mother of the bride." Grandma Laura Fleenor Riggs lived until 1959.

So the Kilday, Moore, Riggs and Fleenor lines converged with the marriage of Eddie and Lochiel followed by the births of Rose and her two brothers, Kenneth and Wayne. Back beyond these ancestors are countless other generations of mothers and fathers all of whom played a part in preparing for the birth of this new child in 1931 named Elva Rosalba Moore and weaving the threads that led to her being the bride in the chapel in 1952. While these families were unknowingly cooperating in the design that produced the bride, others were weaving threads in disparate places that would lead to the groom at the wedding, whose very name, William Romig Ramsay, reflects his history.

## Threads of Heritage: Bill

### The Ramsays

The Ramsays, of Lowland Scottish Presbyterian descent, are part of a clan with its own coat of arms and tartan. The scientist, William Ramsay, who discovered neon, and the theologian, William Ramsay, who became the world's authority on the Gospel of Luke, were both part of that clan. In 1852 another William, a miner from a poor branch of the family and his wife Elizabeth Sharp and their four children came to America to escape the hard times in Scotland. But times in America were hard also and after several children, born in the new land, died they went back to Scotland in 1853 preferring to "starve at home rather than in a strange new place." In 1863 they returned to America on the ship "Tuscarawa" landing in Philadelphia, now with three more children, a daughter-in-law and a couple infants. They found work in Pennsylvania. One of their older sons, Morris Ramsay, who had been born in 1848 in Fordell, Fife, Scotland, married Sadie Greer in 1870. Sadie had been adopted by the Greers when her mother Maria Long Helman died in childbirth. Maria's birth mother, Catherine Ludwig Long, was from the same Ludwig family that a century earlier included Mary Ludwig Hayes, better known as the Revolutionary War's "Molly Pitcher." Morris and Sadie's first of thirteen children, a son born in 1870, was named William. William became a mining engineer and married Jesse Thompson in 1891. His father, Morris Ramsay, died in

Morewood, Pennsylvania in 1892. William and Jesse, after several infant deaths, had two sons and eight daughters who lived to adulthood. The first son was John Gates Ramsay, born in 1902 in Indian Territory that is now Oklahoma. The family moved to Bethlehem, Pennsylvania. John worked in the steel mills and married Gertrude Eleanor Martin in 1926. They had four children. Child number three, born in 1931, was named William carrying on the long Ramsay tradition.

## Flennikens and Thompsons

John A. Flenniken was born in Ireland in 1719 and came to America in 1738 settling in Pennsylvania. His son Elias Alexander Flenniken was a Revolutionary War soldier and was buried in the Glades Cemetery near Carmichael, Pennsylvania in 1834. Elias had a grandson with the same name who in turn had a daughter Sarah Jane (1849-1919) who married Joseph Byers Thompson in 1871. Their daughter Jesse married William Ramsay in 1891 and their eldest son was John Gates Ramsay who married Gertrude Eleanor Martin setting the stage for another William Ramsay, with the middle name "Romig," who stood in the marriage chapel in Berea, Kentucky on September 7, 1952.

## The Romigs

The Romigs settled in Pennsylvania during the same period as the Thompsons and Flennikens. Moving back in time and over to Germany and Poland, records show John Adams Romig being born in 1689 in Germany and dying in 1768 in Pennsylvania. The Romigs were Moravians who sprang from a church reform movement that began long before the protestant reformation and was called the *Unitas Fratrum* in the mid 1400's. John Adam Romig was followed by a son and grandson both named John Frederick; then the next generation's John Romig married Elizabeth Bickle and became an early settler in the Tuscarawas valley in Ohio, where there are still many Romigs. One of their six children, Samuel, married Elizabeth Minnich and became a noted innkeeper in the valley. One of their sons, Benjamin, was called to the Moravian ministry and missions. He married Cornelia Wolle and they went to the Caribbean. Cornelia died

6

at age 24 leaving Benjamin with two sons and two daughters. Benjamin then married her older sister Maria Elizabeth who took her sister's place in the mission field and raised six additional children. The Wolle sisters' father was Frederick Wolle of a royal Polish family and their mother was Sabina Henry, daughter of William Henry, a noted figure in the early development of the United States. Benjamin was named a bishop and moved to Herrnhut, Saxony (Germany), the headquarters of the Moravian Church. Their daughter Elizabeth Beatrice married Johannes Theopholis (Theo) Martin and they served among the Miskito Indians on the coast of Nicaragua. Theo and Lizzie's second daughter, Gertrude was born in Bluefields, Nicaragua in 1904 and, after the family had returned to the USA due to health problems experienced by Theo, they ended up on a farm they named "Hidden Paradise" near Bethlehem, Pennsylvania. Gertrude completed Moravian College and met John Ramsay, whom she married in 1926. They had four children during the difficult depression years, the third of whom was known as "Billy."

## The Martins

Johannes Theopholis (Theo) Martin's family traces back to Auerbach/Vogtland (Germany) where in the late 1600s they were bakers. Theo's father Christian August Martin (1837-1909) married Hanna Lydia Renkowitz (1838-1905) and, instead of following the family's baking profession went to the Moravian mission field in Nicaragua. Christian and Hanna's son, Theo, married Bishop Benjamin Romig's daughter, Elizabeth, in 1898. They continued to serve in missions as their parents had. Theo translated scriptures and hymns into the Miskito language and Moravian churches are still found in the area more than a century later. Theo's brother, Frederick, settled in the Moravian community of Christiansfeld, Denmark where he founded the Martin Printing Company. Life in the mission field was hard and the first babies died at birth but then nine children survived and grew to adulthood. Theo's tuberculosis required a move first to Minnesota and then to a farm near Bethlehem, Pennsylvania, which originally had been established as a Moravian settlement. Martin descendants can be found in the Emmaus, Macungie and Old Zionsville area and the farm, "Hidden Paradise," is still in Martin's hands. Gertrude Eleanor was the first of the

Martin children to be married. She and her husband John Ramsay had four children. Gertrude's mother Lizzie died in 1930 so only lived to see the first grandchild, Patricia. Theo died in 1933, two years after grandson William Romig was born.

The names of the three Ramsay boys (Patricia, the only girl was the oldest child) were known as Johnny, Billy and Dicky, but their full names, John Martin, William Romig and Richard Morris, reflect the family history from Ireland, Scotland, Germany and Poland. Add these to the bride's family heritage and what a genetic, cultural and religious conglomeration was represented at that marriage ceremony in Berea on September 7, 1952. Who in the world could have planned all these intricate designs?

*"God gives to all men life and breath and everything else. And He made from one every nation to live in all the earth, having determined allotted periods and boundaries of habitation…. (Acts 17:24-26, NRSV)*

*"Before I formed you in the womb, I knew you…." (Jeremiah 1:5, NRSV)*

# SCOTLAND GERMANY ENGLAND IRELAND POLAND

## AMERICA

Morris Ramsay - Sadie Helman Greer
1845-1881        1853-1892

Benjamin Romig - Maria Elizabeth Wolle
1834-1903              1837-19061

Joseph Thompson - Sarah Jane Flenniken
1845-1881              1849-1914

Christian Martin - Hanna Renkewitz
1837-1909              1838-1905

William Ramsay – Jessie Thompson
1870-1943        1872–1944

Johannes Martin – Elizabeth Beatrice Romig
1869–1933              1875–1930

John Gates Ramsay – Gertrude Eleanor MartIn
1902 – 1991              1904 – 1984

William Romig Ramsay  1931
Married 1952
Elva Rosalba Moore  1931

Edward Syril Moore – Willie Lochiel Riggs
1893-1961              1906-1952

James Moore – Eliza Jane Kilday
1867-1945        1869-194

William Garrett Riggs – Laura Margaret Fleenor
1886-1948              1879-1959

Elijah Kilday - Amy Conkin
1842-1894 1838-1896

Samuel M Riggs - Matilda Fitzjearold
1855-1914        1855 -1920

Alexander Moore - Nancy Dobbins
1836-1900        1835-1903

John Q Fleenor - Sarah Adaline Gobble
1821-1861              1841-?

## AMERICA

## ENGLAND IRELAND CHEROKEE NATION GERMANY

9

# BILL AND ROSE RAMSAY TIME LINE

## PARENTS: 1893 - 1931

| YEARS | FAMILY AND RELATED EVENTS | WORLD EVENTS |
|---|---|---|
| 1893 | Edward Syril Moore born Jan 12 in TN | President: Grover Cleveland |
| | | First women's vote in New Zealand |
| 1902 | John Gates Ramsay born June 12 in Indian Territory (Oklahoma) | President: Theodore Roosevelt |
| | | Cuba gains independence from Spain |
| 1904 | Gertrude Eleanor Martin born Dec 28 in Nicaragua of missionary parents | Panama Canal construction begins |
| 1905 | | Russian revolution begins |
| | | Einstein's theory of relativity |
| 1906 | Willie Lochiel Riggs born Jan 21 in TN | Women get vote in England |
| 1912 | | Woodrow Wilson president |
| 1914 | | World War I begins |
| | Edward Moore served in US Army but did not go overseas | |
| 1918 | | World War ends |
| 1924 | Edward Moore & Lochiel Riggs marry Nov 27 In Greene County, TN | President: Calvin Coolidge |
| | | Lenin dies and Stalin becomes dictator |
| 1926 | John Ramsay marries Gertrude Martin Nov 22 in Bethlehem, PA | |
| 1927 | Patricia Gertrude Ramsay born | |
| 1929 | | Stock market crash, depression |
| 1930 | John Martin Ramsay born | Gas costs 19 cents a gallon |
| 1931 | Elva Rosalba Moore born | |
| | William Romig Ramsay born | |

LOCHIEL RIGGS MOORE

EDWARD SYRIL MOORE

ELIZA MOORE, ROSALBA, JAMES MOORE, KENNETH

LOCHIEL WITH MOTHER, LAURA RIGGS

JAMES &ELIZA MOORE ,EDDIE & LOCHIEL, LAURA & BILLY RIGGS    c.1927
LUCILLE RIGGS                        GUY RIGGS

## ROSE'S PARENTS AND GRANDPARENTS

## MOORES AND RIGGS

EDWARD SYRIL MOORE SERVED IN THE US ARMY DURING WORLD WAR I. THE WAR ENDED BEFORE HE WAS SENT OVERSEAS.

EDDIE MOORE WAS A FARMER ON THE FAMILY FARM IN GREENE COUNTY, TENNESSEE WITH HIS FATHER JAMES, MOTHER ELIZA AND HIS WIFE LOCHIEL. THIS IS WHERE ROSALBA, KENNETH AND WAYNE GREW UP

MORRIS AND SADIE RAMSAY

BISHOP BENJAMN AND MARIA ROMIG
ELIZABETH AT FRONT LEFT

THEO AND ELIZABETH MARTIN AND CHILDREN
ED, GUS, FRITZ, GERTRUDE, PEARL, GRACE (LYDIA ABSENT)
JOHN, CLARENCE

WILLIAM AND JESSE RAMSAY WITH GRANDCHILDREN (BILLY FRONT RIGHT)

JOHN AND GERTRUDE RAMSAY

JGR WITH CAKE FROM SWITZERLAND AFTER PEACE CONFERENCE (c1940)
WITH HAT (c1982)

GERTRUDE WITH BUFFY

12

# REFLECTIONS 1

## <u>THE LAND OF THE FREE</u>

After recording our history and memories in chronological order, we wanted to reflect on our lives from the perspective of more than eighty years. What have we learned? What do we see as important? What thoughts might we want to pass on to the following generations? So we have indulged in interrupting the narrative and memories at the end of each section with the ramblings of the elderly. Maybe it will help answer the question of who we are. The pronoun "we" is used because, after more than 65 years together, we share each other's thoughts, spoken or unspoken, and speak as one.

We have been blessed to have been born, raised and lived long years in America. Too often we take our blessings and our freedom for granted. Many before us risked much and sacrificed so we might be free. Fundamental to our freedom are the freedoms of religion and speech. We emphasize "freedom of religion" and "freedom of speech" not "freedom from religion" or "freedom from speech."

Every person must choose what gods he will serve. There is no escape from that choice. Not choosing is a choice as well. Our Fleenor ancestors fled their homes in other lands because of religious persecution. The Ramsay's were Scotch Presbyterian. The Romigs and Martins were Moravian missionaries. The Moores helped establish the Baptist church in east Tennessee where Rose's parents and other ancestors are buried. Some ancestors were soldiers in the American Revolution. We have not had the struggles they experienced in their efforts to be true to their faith and find freedom. But much of the world is still having such struggles and people are being persecuted if they express their faith or don't accept the faith prescribed by their rulers or their culture.

America is not immune to such problems and citizens must be wary of the encroachment of government or the pressures of a media culture or the attempts of an educated or propertied elite, to restrict their freedoms. America was founded on the principles expressed in the Declaration of Independence, written in the Judeo-Christian tradition, asserting that all are created equal in terms of their worth as human beings and derive their rights, not from government, but from their creator. Beware those who would try to tell you what you may say or what you must think, be they government officials, judges, advertisers, media stars, professors, the financially powerful, religious figures or protest leaders.

It is wrong when people are fined or threatened with other penalties when they decline to perform a service because of matters of their faith or conscience. Back in the early days of struggle for equal public services for black citizens, we worried that allowing the government to dictate to businesses who they must serve could lead to abuses. Removing laws that legalized or required racial discrimination was necessary and passing laws supporting the civil rights of all citizens was necessary, but allowing the government to intrude into the business of individual choices is dangerous and fraught with potential for misuse. A law shouldn't tell us who we are not allowed to sit with on a bus, but neither should it tell us with whom we must sit.

# REFLECTIONS 2

## THE HAND OF GOD

We don't know how anyone can ignore the evidence of creation all around them, the history of human beings in all parts of the earth, the revelations of the Bible, their own experiences of life and love, or the inner senses of their hearts, and come to the conclusion that there is no God. Without that fundamental truth, all is chaos and meaningless. Are our lives meaningless? Ask that question of your children and their children. Looking back on our lives we see the hand of God much more clearly than we saw it along the way. We did not follow a life of our own careful planning, nor were we tossed to and fro like flotsam and jetsam on a restless sea. No, a higher power guided us, whether or not we knew it at the time– and sometimes we did know. Our families, our marriage, our children, our work and our welfare were not simply our own doing, although we had a part to play.

Someone once asked us how to have good health and a good life. We answered, somewhat facetiously, that the first key was to choose the right parents. Our parents and our heritage were given to us through no choice or merit of our own. We were blessed with wonderful parents and ancestors and have reaped the benefits of a goodly heritage. It reminds us that we are not just our own, but part of generations before and after our short lives. The Bible often records that the Israelites were blessed because of God's covenant with their ancestor Abraham or because of His love for His servant David many generations earlier, and not because the people had earned or deserved His blessing. Likewise scripture tells us that the sins of parents are visited upon their children as well as the blessings. What our ancestors did produced consequences for us and what we do has consequences for our children, grandchildren great grandchildren and on and on. In Deuteronomy 5:9-10 we are told that the Lord is a jealous God…. *punishing children for the iniquities of their parents to the third and fourth generations of those who reject me, but showing steadfast love to the thousandth generation of those who love me and keep my commandments.* This is a sobering fact. It may not seem fair, but we all know too many examples of friends and family who suffer or who are blessed because of what parents did or didn't do, to deny the truth.

*"No Man Is an Island,"* That quotation from a poem by John Donne goes
on to observe,
  *"Any man's death diminishes me*
  *Because I am involved in mankind*
  *And therefore never send to know for whom the bell tolls*
  *It tolls for thee."*

In more down to earth terms we recall Martha Washington's words through an impersonator at Williamsburg, when asked about her dress. She said how you dress is important, "After all you are part of someone else's landscape." That sentiment seems far from the current emphasis on self. "It's my life!" or "It's my body!" is heard often to justify behavior that is detrimental to others and, ultimately, to one's self. We do have free choice, but oh what consequences our choices have for ourselves and for others. We did not create ourselves and we are part of something bigger than ourselves.

We constantly thank God for our wonderful heritage and for our family and we pray for all the new lives that are just beginning their journeys in this alien world. For our part, we will try to remember that our choices have profound consequences for our family, our friends, and our world, now and in the future. We want to be part of our descendants' "goodly heritage."

# PART TWO

*The Early Years*

# Chapter 3

# Growing Up Rose

Surrounded by loving family and community Rose spent her early years living with her parents, grandparents, and then, younger brothers, in the little house built by her grandfather and father at Afton, Tennessee. She knew from the beginning that she belonged to an extended family that had a history. Even as a child she was interested in that history. In 1944, the year she turned 13, she wrote a handwritten "autobiography," probably as a school assignment, drawing from family records and stories passed down. A printed copy is included here, although it repeats some information already recorded, because it adds detail and gives a perspective of family history seen through the young girl's eyes.

### *MY AUTOBIOGRAPHY*
#### *Rosalba Moore*
#### *(Handwritten copy dated 1944)*

*My great grandmother on Daddy's side was Amy Conckin. She was born on June 27, 1838. She married Elijah Kilday on February 23, 1859. They had fourteen children – Amos, Thomas, Johnson, Hagan, William, Sarah, Eliza, David, Barbara, George and James, Nathan, Joseph and Cordie.*

*My great grandfather Kilday fought in the Civil War with the Union army. He came home for a few days and took typhoid fever. He was just taking it when the Confederates came, captured him and took him to a man named Barnes' house. They intended to take him on next morning. My great grandmother went with them and that night, while the soldiers were asleep, she helped him through a window and followed him. He was too weak to walk so she carried him a long way to her mother's house and took care of him until he recovered.*

*He went back to the army and a while before the war was over, he was wounded in the arm. It was stiff the rest of his life. He died in 1894 at the age of 56. My great grandmother died almost three years later with typhoid.*

*My great grandfather on Daddy's side was Alexander Moore. He was born in 1836. He married Nancy Dobbins. They had six children – Jessie, Martha, Sarah, Charlotte, James and Drucilla.*

*My great grandfather got both legs broke during the Civil War and didn't have to do any fighting. He died at the age of 65 and my great grandmother died at the age of 72.*

*My great grandfather Riggs on Mother's side was Samuel Riggs. He married Matilda Fitzgerald. They had seven children – William, Thomas, Ade, Alfred, Adelaide, Coy and Lannie. My great grandfather was too young to fight in the Civil War. My great grandmother was just a little girl during the Civil War. She told Mother that she could remember when the Confederates came in their house and took their bed clothes. My great grandfather and great grandmother had a very good education. My great grandfather died in 1915 and great grandmother four years later.*

*My great grandmother Fleenor, on Mother's side was Sarah Gobble. She married George Fleenor. They had seven children – William, Jennie, Abe, Ellen, Pauline, Bob and Laura. My great grandfather fought in the Civil War with the Union Army. He was not wounded in the army and returned home after the war was over.*

*I don't have the exact date of my great grandfather's death, but he died many years before my great grandmother did. She died March 10, 1912.*

*My grandfather on Daddy's side is James Marion Moore. He was born on May 8, 1867. His mother made all his clothes and his father made his shoes. He had to help cut wood and work in field and garden. They tapped sugar trees and got sugar water to make sugar.*

*The schools in those days just lasted two or three months. He didn't get to go very much and only completed fifth or sixth grade. When he was eighteen, he went to work at a saw mill for $15.00 a month.*

*April 17, 1892, he married Eliza Jane Kilday. She was the daughter of Elijah and Amy Kilday. They had one child, Edward Syril, who is my father. They are both still living and are living with us. Grandfather is 77 and Grandmother is 75.*

*My grandfather Riggs is William Garrett Riggs. He was born February 17, 1877. His father was a farmer and Grandfather Riggs had to help him on the farm. He didn't get to go to school until the fall work was finished, and only completed the sixth grade.*

*When he was about 20 years old, he and his brother Ade went to the West. He visited Louisiana, Texas and a few other states. Almost two years later he returned and married Laura Fleenor. They are still living. They had four children, Lola, Lochiel, Lucille and Guy.*

*Lochiel, my mother, was born January 21, 1906. She started to school when she was six and completed the eighth grade when she was fourteen. About that time her family moved to Kingsport and she started to high school. She found it hard to learn what all the bells meant. One day when the fire alarm rang, she didn't know what it was for so she asked another girl. The girl explained that it was the fire alarm. Thinking the school was really on fire, Mother took her books with her. After they were outside, the other students explained that it was just a drill and they weren't supposed to take anything with them. She never made that mistake again. She quit school during the second year and started working at the Kingsport Press.*

*While visiting her uncle, she met Edward Moore. They went together for about one and a half years and were married November 12, 1924.*

*Edward, my father, had been in the army during the World War, before they were married. He was a Military Police. He was in the army eight months, but never had to go overseas. He was stationed in Alabama. He was fixing to go overseas when the Armistice was signed. While he was in camp an epidemic of flu swept the camp. Many of his company died. He was lucky and happened not to take it.*

*He returned home in January, 1919, and started working on the farm as he did before the war. When he and Mother married, six years later, they moved in with his parents.*

*They had been married almost seven years when I was born. I was born July 5, 1931. Three years later, my brother Kenneth Harold was born. He was a strong, healthy baby and was walking at the age of eleven months.*

*When he was small he was very mischievous. One day he threw a toy pistol at me. Barely missing my head, the pistol went through a window.*

*When I was ten years of age my brother, Wayne was born.*

## Life on a Small Farm

The Moores' small farm was in the Oak Dale community in Greene County, Tennessee between Greeneville and Kingsport. Eddie, the only child of James and Eliza Moore, lived with his parents and helped with raising wheat, corn and tobacco and taking care of the horses, cows, pigs and chickens. He served in the army during World War I and had purchased an automobile, likely with discharge pay. Car ownership in the area at that time was not common and Eddie was often called upon by others for trips to the doctor or other services.

James, Eliza and Eddie belonged to Oak Dale Missionary Baptist Church, about a mile from their house and walking to the church on Sunday was a regular event. The Reverend Alfred Riggs was minister of the church and when his niece, Lochiel Riggs, came and spent a few weeks with him, the Moore family became acquainted with her. Her father, William Garrett Riggs, and mother Laura Fleenor Riggs, lived on the family farm near Kingsport. Lochiel, had completed two years of high school and gone to work for The Kingsport Press. Eddie was past 30 and when Lochiel went back home he drove his Model T Ford to Kingsport on weekends to "call on" her. In those days, on those roads, the trip could take several hours and involve tire patching. In November, 1924 they were married at Uncle Alfred's home. Uncle Alfred officiated and two good friends stood with them. Lochiel was 18 and Eddie was 31 that year.

For a few months after the wedding, they had their own place, a small house on the farm next door. Then, they moved to the Moore farm with Eddie's parents and all worked together to make a living. They had been married seven years when Elva Rosalba was born in 1931. Rosalba was named after the daughter of Dr. Hawkins, who attended her home delivery and it was not until college years that she became known as "Rose" by everyone except family and home folks. Three years later Kenneth Harold was born and then in 1942 another brother, Randolph Wayne, completed the family. Rose has recollections of living together with this family of four adults and three children in rural East Tennessee.

## Memories

*Our house was small, but to me it was a fine place. We had four rooms - kitchen, living room, bedroom and a screened back porch. There were two beds, a few chairs and the coal stove in the living room. My grandparents slept in the living room and that room was the central area where we gathered to talk, to read, to do hand work, to shell corn, to pick kernels out of walnuts and to have visitors. For a few years I slept in that room with my grandmother. My parents and my brother, Kenneth slept in the bedroom. The quilt Mama was currently working on usually hung in that room. Shortly after Wayne was born, Daddy, with some help from neighbors, built two small rooms on to the bedroom side of the house for Kenneth and me, now approaching our teen years.*

*Our day began early. Mama made light, fluffy, delicious biscuits in her wood stove. We cooked and ate in the kitchen, except in summer, when we ate on the back porch. After breakfast, she might have gardening to do, or help with hoeing in the fields, or take Kenneth and me and go pick blackberries. We had a garden and lots of fresh vegetables. Our orchard had apple trees, peach trees, cherry trees and a pear tree. We would can beans, corn, tomatoes, and other vegetables or fruit. We also made jams and jellies. We might gather walnuts or pick some cotton to be carded for use in a quilt. There were always delicious smells coming from the kitchen - chicken frying, vegetables cooking, bread dough rising atop the warm water reservoir on the wood cook stove, maybe a cake baking in the oven. My mother was a wonderful cook and we had plenty of food. We had a strawberry patch and sometimes we also picked wild strawberries. We made pies, cobblers and shortcake. Since we had our own cows and milk, we had real whipped cream.*

*No one in my community had a freezer because we had no electricity. Some people had ice boxes. Once each week, a man came by and sold big blocks of ice for the boxes. Eventually we got an ice box, but, before that, I remember keeping milk cold by setting the crocks in well water. We drew the water from a well in our yard. We put fresh cold water around the milk every hour or so. If the milk soured we used it for buttermilk or for the pigs. Pigs were a source of food. We always had two, and we fed them well. They grew large and fat by November every year. Usually in late November, they were killed and the meat was preserved in various ways. Hams and shoulders were preserved with salt and brown sugar and hung in the "smoke house," in back of our house. We ground some of the meat and made sausage, which we canned. We also canned cubes of tenderloin, a very good cut of the hog. Mama made a head cheese, which she called "sauce meat." It was made into loaves and left in a cold area to be sliced for sandwiches.*

The Moore house was heated by a coal stove in the living room and the wood cooking stove in the kitchen, the rest of the house was cold in the winter. Of course the outhouse was always cold in the winter but it was an improvement on the days before the family had one and used a "slop pot" or the woods. The canning shelves were in the bedroom, which was cool. The back porch, screened and later closed in with windows, was very cold in the winter. It was good for storage. Unlike many homes the house had no cellar for storing potatoes, pumpkins, and apples for the winter. The men would dig a deep hole in the fall to store potatoes and a hole for dahlia bulbs. The potatoes were covered with straw and boards that could be removed as needed to get potatoes for cooking. Always some were saved as seed potatoes for spring planting. Dahlias were covered with boards and soil until spring, when they would be uncovered and planted long rows in the garden. Later everyone would enjoy the beautiful blooms.

Chickens provided eggs, and a few became fried chicken. In the winter, older chickens provided chicken and "dumplin's." Some eggs were left with a "settin' hen" which hatched out ten or twelve chicks.

*We had to watch for hawks that came to prey on the chickens. One time Mama shot a hole in the porch floor trying to shoot a hawk. Hot cereal or sausage and gravy, eggs, and biscuits for breakfast were wonderful and fortified us for the long bus ride to school. Sunday dinner usually featured fried chicken, mashed potatoes, and always beans--green beans and pintos. We had pinto beans every day. On weekdays, we had some kind of pork, vegetables, biscuits and cornbread for dinner. Supper would be soup and cornbread or the leftovers from lunch (dinner).*

*I realize now how hard my parents and grandparents worked to keep the farm going. We were expected to work and we did. There was very little money, but we didn't need much. We bought sugar and coffee, which Mama often "traded" eggs for. We bought material or used material from feed sacks for shirts and dresses. Shoes and coats, and overalls for the men, had to be purchased. The women made quilts from old clothes and scraps. We seldom had a "ready-made" dress. Mama made dresses, shirts, curtains, bedspreads, tablecloths, sheets, pillowcases, and most any item of that sort that we used. She had a treadle sewing machine and was a very good seamstress.*

*One Christmas I found a doll under the tree, dressed in clothes Mama had made. She was baby size and I thought she was beautiful. I named her Elizabeth. That was the name of Lizzie McAmis, our neighbor who held me on her lap and told me stories. I thought she was beautiful too. I could hardly be parted from my baby Elizabeth, and still have her almost 80 years later. I know now that it must have taken a lot of egg money to give me this present. We always had a Christmas tree. It was a cedar because they are plentiful in east Tennessee. I could hardly sleep the night before Christmas for excitement of what would be under the tree. Elizabeth was the best present ever. We had no Christmas stockings. Most gifts were hand made.*

Neighbors worked together and helped each other. They shared what they had. No one felt poor. They owned their land and could grow or make most of what they needed. Doing things together as a family was the norm and expected. They didn't have to *make family time* in a busy schedule of separate activities. Families were always together, doing the same things, keeping the farm going.

*When we made apple butter, we peeled the apples in the evening, quartered them, put them in tubs, and covered them with clean cloths made from feed sacks. The next day, Daddy would build a fire under our big copper kettle. Most of the apples, a little water, and sugar would be put in the kettle and a day of work began. My grandfather liked to stir the apples as they cooked. The "stir" was a flat paddle attached to a long pole. He sat in a chair and stirred steadily, back and forth. We thought that a great job and he would give us a turn. Our arms tired quickly, however, and we were glad to hand the pole to him. As the apples cooked down, more apples were added. Gradually, the light colored apple slices cooked into a dark brown-red, thick sauce. When it was the proper thickness, the kettle would be moved from the fire and the delicious apple butter put into jars. We always had fresh bread and biscuits for sampling the new, warm apple butter.*

## Daily Routines

Work on the farm was a daylight-to-dark effort for the Moore family as it was for other families on small farms. They were up by 5:30 AM to get a wood fire going in the cook stove and, in winter, to add coal to the living room pot bellied stove. While Mama got the kids dressed and started breakfast Dad would be off to the barn to care for the livestock. Then all would go to the barn and while the parents milked and took care of the larger animals the children fed the chickens and pigs and gathered eggs. Then the children went back to the house with Mama to strain the milk and put it in the proper containers - some in crocks for the family and the rest went into a large metal milk can which would be picked up by a "milk truck" and carried to a processing plant in Greeneville. "Mammaw," the grandmother, then helped Mama finish breakfast. By 6:30, everyone was gathered around the table and enjoying a very good and very large breakfast. During the school year, children left for school by 7:00 AM. The bus ride was half an hour to the elementary school and an hour to the high school. After breakfast the men would go to the barn, harness the horses, and head to the fields to plow, cut hay or grain, or plant hay, tobacco, or wheat. Sometimes they would go to the woods and bring in logs to be cut, split and used for firewood. Water had to be drawn from the well out back or from the rain barrels at two corners of the house and placed in containers for washing hands, clothes, dishes, cooking and drinking. After the house chores were finished, Mama often helped in the fields or worked in the garden. Mammaw washed dishes, cleaned house, and often swept the porches and the path through the front yard.

*I remember that Monday was wash day. Daddy would build a fire in the yard and put the wash kettle on. Mama would add lye soap she had made and then put the white clothes, sheets and towels in to boil for a few minutes. Then the fire would be put out, the clothes removed and put into a large tub, cool water added, and the clothes scrubbed on a wash board. Then they were rinsed and put on the line to dry. Dark clothes were washed in warm water and scrubbed on the wash board. In about 1945 an electric line was run to the house. A washing machine was added. There was nothing automatic about it. With no plumbing, water had to be brought in pails from the rain barrels and heated, but it was still a luxury with a big tub and an agitator and a wringer. Wash day became easier. Then a refrigerator was bought which kept the food cold and prevented spoilage. Ironing, before electricity, was difficult. The irons were heated on the stove. One had to grasp the handle, using a hot pad and press the clothes until the iron cooled. Then that iron was returned to the stove and another hot one was used. A careful check was needed to be sure the iron was not too hot or you might scorch the garment or burn your hands.*

## More Memories

*Mama loved flowers and had lots of roses, peonies, gladiolas, dahlias, lilacs, sweet peas, bridal wreath, spirea, and petunias. I remember a large climbing rose bush she had in the back yard. Daddy said it was taking over the yard so she moved it to a gully which ran the length of a steep area of the farm. It grew and spread along the gully and was a mass of red roses in the spring. It probably helped prevent erosion as well!*

*I remember some special things about my grandparents. Mammaw Moore was small and dark. Her hair was long and she brushed it back and twisted it into a circle at the back of her head. She held it there with 4 long hairpins. She always wore ankle length dresses. She worked in the house but did very little of the cooking. She had strong opinions and didn't mind expressing herself.*

*Grandpap Moore was tall and gentle with a kind smile. He loved the farm and the outdoors, and birds and animals. He took great pride in his work--hoeing a row of corn, plowing a straight furrow, splitting shingles so all were even in size. He liked to carve and made tiny doll furniture for me when I was seven or eight. He and Mammaw had not gone to school and could read very little. They loved having me read to them, especially from the Bible. They attended the Baptist church every Sunday, both morning and evening services.*

The church was a central part of community life. Not only on Sundays but whenever there was a church event families attended. The preacher often had more than one church so the church at Oak Dale didn't have a regular "sermon" every Sunday, but they gathered for worship and a member would give a message or testimony. As she got older Rose sometimes played hymns on the piano while the people sang. The choir was anyone who would gather around the piano and a local man led the singing. When the preacher was there he took his Sunday meal with local families and often at the Moore home. Every spring each church had a "decoration" when flowers were put on graves and those who had loved ones buried there gathered for fellowship and shared memories. The Moore graves were at Oak Dale. The Kilday ancestors were in a graveyard further down the road so the family went to at least two "decorations." Flowers were from their gardens and others came to pick some of the abundant roses growing in the gulley for their floral offerings. A couple times a year the church would schedule "dinner on the grounds." Planks would be set on sawhorses to make tables and covered with cloth. Wonderful food was supplied by all who came. There would be prayer and singing.

Once every year a revival was held with meetings every night for a week. An evangelist gave the sermons and there were prayers, testimonies and music. People were invited come to the altar, be forgiven of sins and make a commitment to Christ. There were tears and expressions of joy and support from each other. Also once a year a baptism by immersion was held at a pool on Lick Creek a mile or so down the road from the church. Those who had offered themselves up for baptism would wear some light clothes and the preacher, standing in the creek with the one to be baptized, would say the ritual words and then ease the person over backwards under the water for just a moment. After immersion the boys would go to the nearby barn and the girls to the house to change to dry clothes. Rose remembers being a little scared about going under the water and had practiced holding her breath. Baptism was a big event and many people, not just church members, attended.

In the summer the church had Vacation Bible School and children would sing songs, do crafts and learn Bible stories and verses. One time a college student from Carson Newman College in Jefferson City, TN came to help and stayed with the Moore's. Rose looked to her with admiration and decided she'd go to Carson Newman when she was finished with high school.

## Daddy, Mama and Riggs Grandparents

*My Dad was a friendly, outgoing person. He was always ready and willing to help anyone who needed him. Since he was one of the few in my community who had a car he was often called to drive some one to see the doctor. Our community had one very busy doctor who lived about 10 miles from us. Daddy loved to read, especially Zane Grey books. He often read aloud to us. I liked to stand in back of his rocking chair and follow the words. I think I learned to read this way. Many homes had no books except the Bible but we had books, mostly classics that Mama got when she had worked at The Kingsport Press, and we learned to read early.*

*Mama was always busy; her hands were never still. If she sat down, she mended our clothes, put together quilt pieces, did some tatting, embroidered a table runner or pillow case, or brought in a pan of walnut halves to pick out the kernels. The walnuts could be used in baking or sold for much needed cash. She liked to sing and often sang with us. I remember many hymns and a few folk songs. Some of her favorites were "Just as I Am," "When the Roll is Called Up Yonder," The Old Rugged Cross," "On Top of Old Smokey," and "The Little Mohee."*

*Mama was a care giver in the community. She often went to someone's home to help care for a child, or an ill grandparent. She took food to families who were in need, due to illness or work conditions. She sometimes helped deliver a baby. Both she and my grandmother Riggs knew a lot about herbs that could be used for tonics or for healing. Mama was the recipient of community caring when Wayne was born. I was almost 11 and Mama had a hard time, both during pregnancy and after the birth. They didn't think she'd live and weren't sure about the baby. I prayed hard. He was born healthy but she was not doing well and needed a blood transfusion. There was no blood bank. Blood donors had to give blood directly and Mama had a blood type hard to match. The word was passed in the community probably by the unofficial news carriers – the man who collected the cans of milk from the farms and the mail carrier. Around 50 relatives and friends came forward to offer their blood. Only two had matching blood types and they were not relatives at all but our closest neighbors. They gave blood and she lived.*

The Riggs grandparents grew vegetables and beautiful flowers on their farm near Kingsport and sold them in town. They had customers and delivered produce weekly. Ma Riggs had rows of gladiolus and dahlias along her garden, which were beautiful to see. She made lovely bouquets for her customers. Often people came to the house to buy flowers. The children loved to visit Ma Riggs and Daddy Riggs. The house was lovely, roomy, cool, and quiet. There was a white picket fence around the yard. Underneath the house was a cellar, Its shelves were filled with Ma Riggs' canned fruits and vegetables, The spring house, which was a short distance from the house, was a favorite place. The milk and butter and buttermilk were kept there in the cold spring water. The walls of the spring house were thick and it was very cool inside.

*I loved to stand inside the spring house and listen to the bubbling spring and look at the clear water. Ma Riggs was tall and slender, active, and full of fun. She loved to tell ghost stories and we loved to listen. Daddy Riggs was short and stocky and quiet. He worked hard and did not seem very friendly to people. We knew he liked us, but he didn't pay us much attention. These grandparents did not go to church. Daddy Riggs was very negative about church and church people. I always wondered about this since his brother, Alfred, was a preacher. I know Ma Riggs was a believer, but she didn't talk about it.*

## **Work and Play**

Tobacco was the major cash crop and the cash received for it in the late fall had to last for a year. Raising tobacco was hard work. In early spring all the fields, including the tobacco beds would be plowed. First the stables would be cleaned and the manure scattered over the fields to be plowed under. The Moores did not have a tractor so a horse, or sometimes two, would pull the manure wagon, plow and harrow. Finally a heavy "drag" made of wood was used to smooth the soil in preparation for planting. Brush would be piled on the tobacco beds and burned to kill weed seed and provide ash. Then the area would be raked and seeded and tobacco cloth stretched over each bed. When the seeds sprouted and the plants had grown enough to move they were planted in the tobacco field. During the summer the tobacco had to be hoed to keep out weeds, and suckers were pulled off to assure good growth. Tobacco worm dust had to be spread and even then some big green juicy worms would grow and have to be picked off by hand and destroyed. Rose and Ken remember sometimes playing with them first in little dirt-and-stick-made "houses" before they were destroyed. When the tobacco plants were mature the seed clusters were broken off, saving enough seeds for the next year's planting. When the long leaves were turning yellow the stalks with the leaves were speared on a tobacco stake for hanging in the barn to cure. In late fall the now dry hanging tobacco would be taken down, stripped off the sticks, and the leaves individually sorted into several grades – "bright" being the best leaves which would bring the best price. The leaves were bundled into "hands," and taken to market.

The whole family helped in the tobacco and also in the fields of wheat, corn, sorghum, rye or alfalfa hay and sometimes cotton for home use. Also a large vegetable garden was tended. There was always work to be done.

Not everything was work. Sometimes the men would go hunting and going on a fox hunt was a special time for them. They would go out with their hounds and find a scent and turn the hounds loose. The hounds would follow the scent baying when they were hot on the trail while the men built a fire and sat around listening to the hunt, talking about the dogs and swapping stories. They never seemed to catch the elusive fox.

*We children had time to play too. Drawing from the wonderful books we had at home or got from the school with stories about heroes and heroines, damsels in distress, fairies and adventures, we could live in an imaginary world we called "play like." Kenneth would do or be whatever I asked him when I said "play like." The gully in the field not far from the house became our castle, fort, secret garden or whatever we needed in our imagination. The creek with moss among the tree roots and rocks became the abode of fairies and a magic place. When Wayne was born and I was thrilled to have a real baby to play with and be responsible for, Kenneth complained to Mama that "Sister" never does "play like" with me anymore. Mama spoke to me and I took time to go with him into our world of make believe again until we both grew older.*

## Dealing with a Bully

Kenneth called Rosalba "Sister" until his school years and depended on her not only for play but for protection. Rose was always protective of anyone or anything in distress and couldn't stand anyone being hurt. When Kenneth was due some punishment, she would try to intervene and sometimes bodily get between him and the impending switch. One day when Kenneth had just begun school a bigger boy grabbed his lunch box and held it out of the little boy's reach, teasing him and laughing, while Kenneth cried. "Sister" was furious and told the big boy to give Kenneth back his lunch box. When the older boy, who was much bigger than Rose, continued to laugh and tease she went to the storage area where equipment was kept, picked up a baseball bat and proceeded to attack the boy. He was large enough that he was in no danger of serious injury but decided the teasing was not worth the fury of the small girl defending her little brother and he gave the lunch box back. Sixty years later in her church in Berea, Kentucky, at the "children's time" the question was "What do you do about bullies?" and one of Rose's grandchildren, Lydia, raised her hand and said "My Grandma... and went on to share this piece of family lore to the delight of the entire congregation. Rose tried to sink out of sight in the pew. After the service a young man came up to Rose and said, "Mrs. Ramsay, if I've ever done anything to offend you, I'd like to apologize now!" The family joked that they always kept all the baseball bats in the house hidden.

The family's life centered around the farm, school, church and the neighbors. Communication with the outside world was very limited.

*We traveled very little in those days. When I was small, there were few cars and the roads were mostly graveled, narrow and rutted. Occasionally, Mama, Kenneth and I would go by bus to visit our Riggs grandparents. We could catch the local bus at Union Temple, about two miles from our house, and ride to Kingsport to the Tennessee Eastman where my Uncle Guy worked. When he got off work, he would take us to Ma Riggs' house, near Blountville, Tennessee. Uncle Guy and Aunt Ruth lived there also. Usually we would stay several days, then Daddy would come and pick us up or we would go back by*

33

*bus. Sometimes we would ride with my Uncle Alfred to visit Ma and Daddy Riggs. At that time Uncle Alfred pastored a church near their home. Aunt Lola, Mama's sister, lived nearby and we would visit her and her family.*

*What food items we bought came from a little store about a mile from our house. When I was a small child, we seldom went to Greeneville, our nearest city, to shop. Daddy and Grandpap would go to sell the tobacco and to buy a few things. I remember going to Penney's for shoes and coats or for fabric. It was very exciting to go to the "big city!" Later there were better cars and roads, so there were more trips to town.* Another special occasion which happened every year was the Kilday Family Reunion. It was held at Uncle Joe's most years but once it was at Eddie's and Lochiel's. Scores of Kilday relatives attended. A baseball game was organized in the mowed field near the house. Children would run and play while older folks talked and remembered and laughed. Enormous amounts of food covered the tables made of sawhorses and planks and covered with sheets. Almost everyone lived on a farm so there were all kinds of meats, vegetables, fruits and desserts. The Kildays had a strong sense of family and since Mammaw Eliza had 13 brothers and sisters there were lots of aunts, uncles, cousins, second cousins and in-laws. The Kildays seemed to have more books and more pictures than was usual and must have had property and education in their background. One framed picture of Mammaw's father and mother, Elijah and Amy, taken before his death in 1894 has continued to be handed down from generation to generation. In the style of the time, they both look very serious –even stern- but with lines of strength and character.

## The Outside World

The world outside East Tennessee seemed very remote. In the aftermath of the great depression government programs reached into the rural Appalachian mountains and the people were grateful for help in constructing safely placed outhouses and the addition of electric lines. Other programs were resisted by the people who didn't much trust government, were self reliant and carried forward their support of the Republican Party from Civil War times. The intrusion of World War II in December of 1941 began to make larger changes. Some relatives and friends went off to war and news from outside became important. Others went to work in new jobs for the war effort. A few went to a mysterious place near Knoxville to work on a secret project that they couldn't talk about but at the end of the war was known to be the atomic bomb. The adults would cluster around a radio at someone's house and then spread the war news. Patriotic sentiments were shared in homes, schools and work place.

*I remember signs in windows supporting the soldiers and going out from school to collect scrap items for the war effort. One of my older cousins was in the Philippines when the Japanese invaded and was missing in action. I remember his mother crying and the other women comforting her. It turned out he was hidden by natives until liberation and he came home. His mother said it was a miracle. The church prayed and the women sewed and everyone was anxious to do something to help. My Dad, having been in uniform in World War I, was of the opinion that we should never have let the Germans become a nation again after defeating them back then.*

## **School Days**

Rose attended school first at Union Temple. It was a two room school with the first three grades in a small room and grades 4-8 in a larger room. One teacher managed each room and taught all subjects offered. Her father drove her to school with some classmates.

Because she could already read when she arrived at school she spent only two years in the small room at Union Temple.

*For my first few days at school, my Mammaw Moore went with me. She wore her long dress and had her long dark hair wrapped up in a bun at the back of her head. We sat in a bench attached to a double desk and no one thought it odd. Families were expected to be close. Looking back, mine was especially close. I was Eliza's and James' only granddaughter. I had suffered some illness, including pneumonia, as a young child and they were very protective of me. I realize now how treasured I was and how much devotion there was in the family for each other.*

35

The students sat at desks divided into sections by grade level and in turn each grade would come forward to a bench at the front of the room to do their lessons with the teacher. Rose first sat with the first graders but was moved to the third grade section because she could read and write. Mother Lochiel wasn't satisfied with this and Rose was moved to the second grade section with those closer to her age, so she was ready to move to the larger room after two years. When school bus service became available she transferred to Meadowview, also a two room school, and rode the bus. She usually had the bus drop her off at a cousin's house near the school because school grounds were not safe until a teacher arrived. Some older boys were there only because they had to attend school until they were 16 and sometimes they caused trouble.

*After the bus dropped me off I would walk to school with my cousin, Norma Jean Kilday. Her father, Bart, was my dad's first cousin. Her mother, Leatha, and my mother were especially good friends. We'd wait until time for classes to begin so the teacher would be there. I think he got there earlier but would go down in the woods to smoke before coming to the school.*

Rose was a good student and an eager learner. The school had no library but had a shelf of books that were exchanged periodically. She always took books home to read and then waited for the next batch. High school was in Baileyton and required an early long bus ride in the morning and arriving home late in the evening. Many students dropped out as soon as they were of age. Of her beginning class of about 70 only 20 persisted to graduation.

She continued to be an excellent student and at graduation was the class valedictorian and gave the graduation student speech. Her parents were very proud of her. The school principal encouraged her to continue education at the college level but the family had no money to send her to college. The principal knew of Berea College in Kentucky that had a special mission to serve capable young people from the mountain areas of Appalachia who had limited financial resources. She applied and was accepted, although her father thought she should get a job and her mother didn't want her to go so far away. Rose had only been out of Tennessee once on a short trip to North Carolina. Nevertheless her parents supported her decision. She did get a summer job at the Magnavox plant in Greeneville putting components in radio circuits as they went on the assembly line and she earned a little money for her first year at college. Just before she was to leave for Berea her grandfather Riggs died and she couldn't leave until after his funeral. She missed Freshman Week so arrived late, being driven by a local family whose daughter was already a student and didn't need to be there for Freshman Week. So Rose arrived at college apprehensive, behind in establishing relationships with classmates and already terribly, terribly homesick.

# GENEALOGY: ELVA ROSALBA MOORE

## Pedigree Chart

Jul 17, 2017

**16 William MOORE**
b: 1818
d:

**8 Alexander MOORE**
b: 1836
p:
m: Dec 7, 1856
d: 1900
p:

**17 Mary Ann BRANDON**
b: 1816
d:

**4 James MOORE**
b: May 8, 1867
p:
m: Apr 17, 1892
p:
d: Nov 29, 1945
p: Greene County TN

**18 William DOBBINS**
b: 1802
d:

**9 Nancy DOBBINS**
b: 1835
p:
d: 1903
p:

**19 Charlotte BRANDON**
b: 1798
d:

**2 Edward Syril MOORE**
b: Jan 12, 1893
p: Greene County TN
m: Nov 22, 1924
p: Greene County TN
d: Jul 1961
p: Johnson City TN

**20 John P. KILDAY**
b: 1808
d: 1875

**10 Elijah KILDAY**
b: Jan 13, 1842
p: TN
m: 1858
p:
d: Jun 30, 1894
p:

**21 Jane JOHNSON**
b: 1818
d:

**5 Eliza Jane KILDAY**
b: Jan 29, 1869
p: Greene County TN
d: Jun 14, 1948
p: Greene County TN

**22 Hagan CONKIN\***
b: 1817
d: Feb 9, 1865

**11 Amie R. CONKIN (CONK)**
b: Jun 27, 1838
p:
d: Dec 15, 1896
p:

**23 Barbary MOLTEN**
b: 1817
d:

**1 Elva Rosalba (Rose) MOORE**
b: Jul 5, 1931
p: Greene County TN
m: Sep 7, 1952
p: Berea KY
d:
p:

sp: **William Romig RAMSAY**

**24 William Barron RIGGS**
b: Jun 24, 1814
d: Dec 1886

**12 Samuel M RIGGS**
b: Jul 9, 1855
p:
m: Apr 30, 1874
p:
d: Aug 11, 1914
p: Washington County, TN

**25 Lucretia PEOPLES**
b: Dec 25, 1813
d: Jul 7, 1912

**6 William Garrett (Jennings?) RIGGS**
b: Feb 17, 1886
p:
m:
p:
d: Sep 8, 1948
p:

**26 G FITZJEAROLD**
b:
d:

**13 Matilda Ann FITZJEAROLD**
b: Nov 21, 1855
p:
d: Oct 6, 1920
p:

**27 Sabra**
b:
d:

**3 Willie Lochiel RIGGS**
b: Jan 21, 1906
p:
d: Mar 29, 1952
p: Johnson CityTN

**28 Solomon FLEENOR**
b: 1793
d: 1855

**14 John Q. FLEENOR**
b: Feb 15, 1821
p: Rich Valley, VA
m:
p:
d: 1861
p:

**29 Ruth Elizabeth KAYLOR**
b:
d:

**7 Laura Margaret FLEENOR**
b: May 12, 1879
p: Tennessee
d: Jan 20, 1959
p:

**30**
b:
d:

**15 Sarah Adaline GOBBLE**
b: Aug 25, 1841
p: VA
d:
p:

**31**
b:
d:

Prepared Jul 17, 2017 by:

# CHAPTER 4

# GROWING UP BILL

Six weeks after Rose had been born in Greene County, Tennessee, Bill was born in Bethlehem, Pennsylvania. It was August 19, 1931 and the effects of the great depression were still sorely felt. His parents were told by a doctor that they shouldn't have had this third child. They already had a daughter and son (John and Patricia) and didn't need another mouth to feed. Today they may have been encouraged to have an abortion, but even if that had been an option then, the strong faith and family orientation of John and Gertrude Ramsay would have made such a suggestion inconceivable. So baby Billy was taken home to 48 E. Garrison Street, a small duplex with two rooms downstairs and two upstairs. The walls between the two units in the duplex were so thin that there were no secrets between the Ramsay's and the Gemberlings who lived in the other half. The story is that when one drove a nail in the wall in their kitchen to hang a pot the other kitchen could hang a pot on the other end of the nail. Bill remembers some things about the house and those early years until he was six or seven when they moved out of town in the countryside between Bethlehem and Allentown.

## Memories of Living in Town

*The house must have had a basement because I remember rocking too hard in a rocking chair in front of the cellar stairs door and going over backward and down the stairs head over heels. I remember sitting on someone's lap when I was two while the adults discussed names for the new baby, Richard Morris, who completed the family in February 1934. With Johnny, Billy and Dicky all under five, mother must have had her hands full. Patty was seven by then and helped as she could. We had a little shed in the back of the small yard behind the house and I wanted badly to have a horse we could keep there. I would feed it grass clippings. Needless to say that didn't happen, but we did have a* dog. Schnitzer was a Scotch terrier and a treasured pet. Sometimes mother would send us to the butcher shop to beg a bone for the dog. The butcher, a wise and compassionate man, would be sure to find a bone with some meat on it because he knew that before Schnitzer got it, the bone would serve as the base for soup for the family.

With two bedrooms upstairs Mom and Dad had one and we four children had the other. Patty had her own bed and we boys slept together. This was before queen sized beds were invented. The nightly question was who slept in what position? Dick as a toddler had pulled a pot of boiling water over and scalded himself almost fatally, which for a time caused him bladder problems. If you slept in the middle of the bed you might get wet. On the other hand sleeping on the outside was dangerous because if you happened to let your hand dangle over the edge the wolves that lurked under the bed in the dark were apt to bite it off. Oh, the struggles of childhood!

We had running water, but no hot water heater. We heated water on the stove. Saturday night was bath night and we boys usually had our bath together in a big galvanized wash tub in the middle of the kitchen. I think my resistance to insurance salesmen dates back to those baths. The insurance man came to collect his weekly premiums on Saturday night and always wanted to "see the boys." There we'd be naked in the bathtub with him going on about how we were growing and the water getting cold and us wishing he'd go. More positively I remember the ice truck delivering ice for our ice box and all the others on the street. We'd put a sign in the window turned to the amount we wanted 25/50/75 and the ice man would chip off the right size block, pick it up with his ice tongs and bring it to the house. In the chipping there were always slivers of ice created that were like treasure to us kids. We'd run after the truck and collect ice slivers to suck on. Milk was delivered to the door too and in the winter sometimes a little ice formed at the neck of the bottle before we'd take it in and that was another treat. Better yet was snow ice cream after a good snow which we scooped up before it got dirty. Once in a while we'd hear an airplane and everyone would run out of the house to see this marvel travel across the sky.

*When I first went to Franklin Elementary School, about a block from home, I was excited to be following my older siblings, but then the parting with Mother made the excitement turn to terror and for a couple days I escaped and ran home. Then I learned to love school and was a responsive student. We'd been taught to be polite and respectful and were somewhat shy around grown-ups so we usually presented no problems for the teachers. I did get into trouble in first grade on one occasion. The early grades had been invited to go up to the 6th grade classroom to see a skit they had prepared and we were excited. We were warned not to touch the inkwells which were part of every sixth grader's desk, but restless hands found their way to the ink and soon it was all over hands and anything touched. I was sent out into the hall to sit on the steps for a time of "punishment." I was handling the humiliation, guilt, and emotional trauma pretty well until another teacher came by and said in a shocked voice, "Billy! I never expected to see you here!" Then I lost it — and, as is obvious, still remember it.*

## God's Good Man

Father, John Gates Ramsay, during layoffs from Bethlehem Steel struggled to keep the family fed by selling products door to door and anything else he could do. He became involved in movements to improve the lot of the unemployed and, back at work in the mill he became a leader in the attempts of workers to organize for collective bargaining. Unions at that time were organized around particular crafts or trades such as plumbers, boilermakers, electricians, etc. These trade unions left out many workers and were ill equipped to bargain in the new industrial settings that followed the industrial revolution. The workers at Bethlehem Steel did form a union and John Ramsay was its first president. He was respected and loved by the workers who came from a multitude of ethnic and cultural backgrounds. The family was exposed to all kinds of cultures – Scotch-Irish, Pennsylvania Dutch (German), Italian, Greek, Polish and many others who retained much of their ethnic heritage. Diversity was very real but so was the "melting pot" as all struggled to become fully American and in their common struggle for fair pay, reasonable security for their families and safe working conditions, they learned to get past differences and celebrate their shared humanity.

Other communities with industrial complexes were having similar struggles and a move for "industrial unions" was underway. The Steel Workers Organizing Committee (SWOC) of the American Federation of Labor was formed as was the Committee for Industrial Organization which later became independent of the AFL as the Congress of Industrial Organizations (CIO). Many years later the two unions merged again to become what is known today as the AFL-CIO. In those early years of development John Ramsay played a significant role. He was a delegate to the convention that established the United Steelworkers of America which became one of the large unions within the CIO. He continued his leadership in Bethlehem as well as his involvement in the larger labor movement and it was not without struggle.

*I can remember helping stuff envelopes with notices about the SWOC and sensing the excitement and even fear that went along with the early attempts to organize. There was violence as picket lines were formed and sometimes attacked. Mother was afraid to send us to school for a time because of threats against Dad and the family. Through all this Dad and Mother remained strong in their Christian faith and behavior, active in the Presbyterian Church, and trusted by the workers. Others sometimes became loud, profane, beer drinking, prone to hate, but never Dad. Some years later in a book, To Win These Rights by Lucy Randolph Mason, she called him "God's good man," and that he was. The president of Bethlehem Steel, Eugene Grace, went to the same church we did and things got tense there. I remember the Graces' cushioned pew in the sanctuary. They were held in some awe as royalty might be and undoubtedly were critical to church support. When the struggle between the union and management was especially intense the church elders asked Dad to leave the church to preserve its peace and unity. He asked for time to pray and think about the matter. When he gave them his answer he said, "If this is the church of Eugene Grace I'll leave, but if it is the church of Jesus Christ I'll stay." He stayed and went on to become a church leader as well as a union leader for the rest of his life. We children felt very much a part of the hopes, fears and struggles of the times.*

## Vacations and Trips

The children got to take turns going on trips with Dad when he had to go to other cities on union business and John and Gertrude never failed to provide a family vacation, usually at the beach at Cape May or one of the other coastal resorts. The family often visited Grandpa and Grandma Ramsay at their big house outside of Bethlehem. It was a mansion with three floors, a tower and a sub-cellar underneath the basement where the children were sure they could find buried treasure if allowed to go down there. Most visits were at times when other family members came so there was a lot of interaction with aunts, uncles and a bunch of cousins. Grandma Ramsay had a wonderful pantry where the children would find a bin of white sugar and sliced white bread. At home there was only whole wheat bread and brown sugar. Sneaking a buttered slice of bread sprinkled with white sugar was the best treat one could imagine partly because it was "forbidden fruit." Grandma was very gentle and probably knew what was being done but smiled and kept quiet.

There were visits to Hidden Paradise, the Martin farm near Emmaus occupied by Gertrude's brother Ed and his large family. The children would play with the Martin cousins, help in the garden or with other chores and sleep in the sweet smelling hay mows in the big Pennsylvania barn. On lucky weekends Uncle Clarence would take off from Medical School in Philadelphia and join them and tell wonderful stories after dark in the barn. The children would be bedded in the hay and he would perch on a rafter high above them. Like Eustace Bright in Nathaniel Hawthorne's *A Wonder Book* he left his nephews and nieces heads full of wonder and adventure and, sometimes, fright with tales like *The Big Green Eyes*.

## The Little Bit Club

The Ramsays had many guests in their home, no matter how limited the facilities or pantry and this continues as a family tradition. Daily prayer and devotionals were part of family life and participation in church – Sunday school, choir, children's activities, Christmas programs. The family held "quiet times" and each member had a little notebook to record his or her self examinations, confessions, inspirations and guidance and then there was sharing. Mother had helped the children organize a "Little Bit Club" through which the children and their friends could do their little bit for others. They raked leaves, picked up litter and other little services. Bill remembers on one occasion their little bit turned out to have a wider impact.

*We children were in the habit of pulling our wagons and roller skating, with those old metal skates that had a key to tighten them on our shoes, and the result, as they traveled over the rough sidewalks, was a fair amount of noise above the usual noises of children at play. In one house a ways down the block lived an elderly (we would have said "really old") woman who didn't tolerate the noise well and often would come out and fuss at us. Then one day the woman didn't appear but one of her adult children did and requested consideration in keeping the noise down as their mother was quite ill in bed. Conscious stricken we told Mother who confirmed that the woman was very, very ill and not expected to get better. The Little Bit Club decided to pool pennies we could collect and buy her a flower. We made a nice card wishing her to get better and delivered it with one single rose to her house giving it to one of the care givers. It turned out that the woman had a son in management of Bethlehem Steel and he related this story saying his mother was recovering and the event that started the recovery was the love and care of these children. That story became instrumental in easing negotiations between labor and management going on at that time.*

Father John was a good worker and a wise and humble man who gave no cause for offense, but was a stumbling block to the old order where workers were expected to behave much like slaves and accept the decisions of those who knew better. At one point he was offered a management position at the mill, which would have recognized his leadership qualities, provided higher pay and security and also removed him as a stumbling block. He declined and some of the local press of the time hinted that he must be out of his mind or a communist. His strong and evident church connection gave the lie to the latter suspicion. News media beyond the local area recognized a good David versus Goliath story. *PM* magazine headlined a feature, **"The Man Bethlehem Steel Couldn't Buy!"** Reporters and photographers descended on the Ramsay home and the whole family had pictures in print showing them having one of their "quiet times." Bill remembers sitting under the upright piano and hitting his head when he rose.

Union leaders who were active churchmen, particularly in the major denominations at that time, were rare, although Phillip Murray, President of the CIO was a devout Catholic and a praying man. Churches were just beginning to consider responsibilities for a "social gospel" as well as for individual faith and worship. John Ramsay was "discovered" by progressive church leadership and soon was asked to serve on committees, speak to concerned people and represent a laborer's point of view in community and national councils. He became associated for a time with a group called Moral Re-Armament that had sprung from the Oxford Group in England and promoted peace through understanding. He was asked to go to a peace conference in Geneva, Switzerland and left his family behind as he sailed on the "Normandy" for Europe. A post card sent to Billy from the ship admonished him to "Have a good time, listen to God and help Mother." He was always faithful in sending cards when he traveled so the family felt connected.

*Dad found himself more and more traveling to other mill towns where there was labor strife and trying to bring understanding in the community of the goals and aspirations of workers and their unions. After a time he was employed by his union, the United Steelworkers of America, to work full-time on these matters. I remember going on a trip with him to Pittsburgh and staying with Aunt Adelaide, who was the youngest sister of Dad's father, but not that much older than Dad. That was probably my first train ride, and when Dad was in meetings it was the first time I'd been away from my parents for any length of time. All part of growing up. I didn't like being away from Mother and remember worrying about her dying. We had become acquainted with death when our cousin Jimmy Martin got sick with an ear infection and didn't recover. His sister Betty, who was my age, stayed with us for a time during his illness so we were close to the tragedy. In Sunday school, we had learned about heaven and the end of time and I prayed fervently that the end of time would come before Mother died so I would go with her. I couldn't imagine life without her. Later when I had a broader perspective of life and death I prayed just as fervently that God wouldn't end the earth prematurely on my account.*

*We had our childhood sicknesses but were basically very healthy and most problems were handled with home remedies. A poultice of a slice of potato would draw out infection, lemon in hot water with honey was good for sore throats along with a cold compress around the neck. Once when we had high fevers Mother wrapped our whole hot little bodies in cold wet sheets and then "mummified" us with wool blankets. I still remember the shock of the cold on my fevered skin, the shivering and then the sweating. But the fevers broke. Someone observed that this was effective but you had to have a healthy heart.*

## **Out of Town**

The family moved from Bethlehem to Salisbury Township between Bethlehem and Allentown. It was still close enough to stay in the Bethlehem Presbyterian Church and other activities but the house had more room and outside space for the family. It seemed like a mansion to the children but years later going back to see the house it was a surprise to realize how small it was. The boys were delighted. No more sleeping in the same bed, places to roam and climb trees and pretend to be cowboys or Indians. It was closer to Hidden Paradise with more treasured visits there. Schnitzer had died and a new dog "Scoot" was a constant companion.

The school was at the end of the road down a long hill while the house was at the top of the hill on the highway route 60. Halfway down the hill the trolley tracks crossed the road. Periodically one would hear the clang, clang and rumble of the trolley as it went between Bethlehem and Allentown. The hill was great for sledding in the winter, but dangerous with the tracks crossing it and an intersecting road at the bottom. One winter Billy was run over by a car at the bottom of the hill. He had on an "aviators cap" with goggles that he prized. The driver had hit his brakes but slid into the sled before he got stopped. In despair, he pulled Billy out from under the car and walked him back up the hill to his house. Then he kept saying to Mother "I ran over his head! I ran over his head!" The front of the sled was badly mangled. Mother pulled off the cap expecting the worst but Billy must have instinctively jerked his head aside for there was no damage. Mother quickly immersed him in a tub of hot water, which was one of her tried and true remedies. Except for a little stiffness and soreness no problems developed.

*We were warned about the highway in front of the house and one night a drunk driver coming too fast around the curve left the highway and hit Dad's big Buick head on knocking it over our hedge. We watched as the ambulance got the man out of the car and saw a bottle roll out. They put the man on a stretcher where he died. I felt sick. Later a car hit Scoot and I heard him yelp. I found him mangled and dying on the side of the highway and, crying, held him and put his head in my lap. I called his name and his tail wagged once.*

*Life wasn't all tragedy and we had great times exploring the fields. There was one big apple tree that had branches going all the way to the ground creating a secret space within and it became the castle, fort, hideout or whatever our imaginary games needed. Up a steep bank across the road we threw a rope over a tree branch and by hanging on, or sitting on, a stick pushed through a loop in the rope we could soar high above the ground falling below us. Once the stick broke and down I went knocking the breath out of me. My brothers got me to the house, still not breathing. And Mother picked me up and "threw" me to the floor commanding "BREATHE." We never disobeyed her when she was in that kind of mood so I breathed. I had periodic trouble with my chest for some years and probably had cracked a rib.*

*We boys were always up to something. We were taught to resist peer pressure. Mother had posted a sign in the kitchen that said "Of all excuses this is most forbid. 'I did the thing because the others did!'" So we didn't join the other boys in chewing tobacco or smoking rabbit tobacco or trying a "drink." But we did experiment on our own. We stuffed crumbled dry leaves in a piece of lead pipe with an elbow joint and lit the leaves on fire. When they were smoldering we each took a drag. At first we just got air, but then, when the hot, acrid smoke reached our end of the pipe we burned our throats and doused ourselves with quantities of water from the hose. None of us ever smoked again.*

Mother was very health conscious and cooked well balanced meals. She saw that the children had vitamins and drank plenty of water. Each child had a mason jar on which a sticker would be attached for each pint of water that was drunk. Getting stickers was a big thing. For a while she decided that punishment should be a healthy as well as a justice thing so when the boys disobeyed or did some offense they had to take a spoonful of cod halibut liver oil. Whatever the case the children grew up healthy and well disciplined.

## The World Outside

It was during this period that the growing conflict in Europe and Asia directly reached the United States. Pearl Harbor on the "Day of Infamy," December 7, 1941, affected all of our lives. Bill was a little over 10 and old enough to understand the magnitude of the attack, if not all the implications.

*We were riding in the car when the news crackled over the car radio. I felt scared.*

*I remember Grandpa Ramsay leaning over and cupping his ear next to a radio trying to hear news through the static about distant countries in Europe. Obviously something bad was going on. Mother's sister "Aunt Grace" and her husband Fred Brandauer were held captive by the Japanese until their liberation in 1944, so the war became very real. They had been long time missionaries in China and were in the Philippines en route to a mission field in Indonesia when the Japanese invaded. When the Americans liberated the Philippines Aunt Grace's brother Fred was a physician with the rescuing force and was able to tend them.*

School children were involved in collecting scrap, knitting squares for blankets, participating in air raid drills and keeping up with the news. The Pledge of Allegiance and prayer were already part of the school day but patriotism and prayer were now more poignant. Relatives and friends went off to war in Europe or the Pacific. The children collected aircraft cards and learned to identify different fighter planes. Sugar and other items were rationed so home adjustments had to be made. Each of the Ramsay children saved up and eventually purchased a War Bond. Women went to work in the production plants. Life was changed forever.

*Our neighbor's son had come home from serving in the Air Force and was getting his private pilot's license. He asked me if I'd like to go with him on one of his flights when he had reached the point of taking a passenger and, of course, I said "Yes!" We went to the little airport and up to a very small two-seater prop plane. To my amazement it was made of canvas stretched over a frame and the canvas rippled as the motor started. I sat behind him and belted in. He took off down the runway and the plane lifted just in time to clear the electric lines. I prayed. Then we were aloft and what a wonderful view we had of the countryside. It was a clear day but a little windy and we bounced around a bit. We raced a train and won. Then he decided to show me his tricks. I almost passed out from straining against gravity when he dipped one wing down and made a tight turn, but learned to lean with the plane instead of resisting it. Then he did some other maneuvers and lastly climbed straight up and went into a stall and then a spiral down. More praying! I don't remember when I caught up with my stomach. At last it was time to return to the air strip before the fuel ran out. The wind had picked up and the first two passes didn't go well and he had to climb into the air as the end of the runway approached at too high a speed. We cleared the electric lines again – and again. Then he made it down safely and I staggered out of the seat and to the ground. Later, when I had learned some Latin in school, I understood the story about the man who got back to earth after his first plane ride and when asked if he was glad to be back on "terra firma" he replied. "Yes, and the more the firma the less the terra." I never was fond of roller coasters at the fairs.*

## Schools, Church and Moves

Meanwhile school days passed with successful advancement. Sometimes Mother served as a substitute teacher. Dad was taking more and more trips as the union-management relationships in Bethlehem matured and things settled down. Still on the payroll of the Steelworkers Union but working for the whole CIO now he was more and more involved in various conferences and meetings of church leaders of all denominations at the national level, representing organized labor and also in Moral Rearmament activities. By the end of 1942 changes in family living were happening that would take the family from the Bethlehem area and then from Pennsylvania. This meant new places to get used to, new schools and new friends. It is no wonder the children were dependent on each other, although close family relationships were deliberately fostered whatever the outside influences. In early 1943 Dad needed to help with union struggles with ARMCO Steel and the family moved to Ashland on the Ohio River in Northern Kentucky.

*I was placed in the sixth grade at Condit Elementary but then moved to the seventh grade at Everett Junior High for the rest of the term after some testing and evaluation. I remember the strangeness of the new environment. The accent of the locals was a combination of southern drawl and mountain twang and we had a hard time sometimes understanding. Unfortunately one of my teachers considered my pronunciation of words closer to "proper" English. When one of the students said "orel" for "oil," or "fahr" for "fire" she would ask me to tell them how to say it. What a great way to win friends among classmates! We had come in the middle of the school year and left at the end of the term but in the process had advanced an extra grade. In the short time in Ashland we discovered the wonderful milkshakes at Pure Milk Company and the great skating rink down by the river where, for the first time I asked a girl to be my partner for a couples skating time. She accepted!*

As was the family custom they immediately went to the Presbyterian Church in Ashland and took part. Mother went to a women's gathering where she was pointedly snubbed and isolated. She was tough and used to struggles and never lost her composure. Finally one of the ladies, meaning well, apologized to her and told her they shouldn't hold her responsible for what her husband was. She informed them that she was 100% with her husband and proud of him and then she left. When she got home that is the first time the children had ever seen their mother cry, but she never exhibited bitterness, only sadness.

Starting in Ashland, 1943 was quite a year for the Ramsay family. They left Ashland after the school term and lived for a couple months in a cabin at

Stoughton's Beach near Slippery Rock, Pennsylvania. Dad was gone much of the time. The children loved swimming in and boating on the river. On one occasion the boys got permission to go down stream to the dam and back in their flat bottomed canoe. They packed a lunch and took off. What a wonderful trip gliding downstream, watching the trees, cottages, field and forests pass. Finally the water widened at the lake above the dam and they ate lunch and swam a bit. They thought they'd better start for home in the afternoon so up the lake they went. But after the lake area the river current became stronger and it was all they could do to make any progress against the current. It was a long trip home and they were exhausted when they got there at dusk but had learned something about going with and against the current. At summer's end the family moved to Columbus, Ohio into a house at 113 Frambes Ave, not far from the Indianola Presbyterian Church.

Then in the summer of 1944 the family was off to Mackinac Island, Michigan, high up in Lake Superior. They had been invited to a conference of the MRA at the Grand Hotel and Dad had some program responsibilities. Everyone had chores to do and for the boys it was mostly collecting trash. Everyone ate together and new food experiences were in store for the children, such as spinach soufflé, which was not their favorite. Everyone, children included, was part of a small group for quiet time, sharing and guidance. MRA held up four "absolutes" as the standards for which to strive – absolute honesty, absolute purity, absolute unselfishness and absolute love. The sessions, the speeches and the songs were wonderful. Influential people from around the world were there and many good things sprung from this movement. Sam Shoemaker, for example, took the small group sharing and accountability pattern and adapted it for people trying to recover from a drinking problem helping to set in motion Alcoholics Anonymous.

*We were all inspired with the goals of the four absolutes and the idea that we could change the world by starting with ourselves. We also found that the greater the sin one could confess the greater the attention one received. Our petty "confessions" of teasing each other or getting into spats paled in comparison with drug use, theft and other offenses. Apparently Dad had a similar problem since he didn't have any big sins to confess and some thought he just wasn't being absolutely honest. For the most part it was a high point for us and we made wonderful friends united by a common faith and desire to make a better world. We loved singing with Cecil Broadhurst "Oh I've Got a Wise Old Horsey." Swimming in the Great Lake was fun, although it was pretty cold.*

## City Living

The family went back home to their home in Columbus, Ohio which was a transportation and commercial hub for Dad's work. New geography and new schools again faced Mother and the children. They immediately became involved in the Indianola Presbyterian Church, sang in the choir, attended Sunday school and youth activities. They took confirmation classes and learned the Westminster shorter catechism. Bill still remembers, *"The chief end of man is to glorify God and enjoy Him forever!"* The boys became Boy Scouts and got paper routes to earn some lunch and spending money. All took lessons on musical instruments. Patty was now old enough to care for the boys for a while so Mother could go with Dad on short trips. They were on one such trip over a weekend when disaster struck.

*Sunday morning Patty had roused us from bed in time to eat breakfast and get to Sunday school. My class was in a little room on the third floor and I remember hearing sirens during the class. Coming down and outside I was surrounded by adults assuring me they'd take care of us. Alarmed, I finally understood that our house had caught fire. I escaped and ran the few blocks home. The firemen had the fire under control but the inside was gutted. A neighbor had seen smoke and was afraid that the children were still in bed. Fortunately we had gone to Sunday school. Our little puppy was not so fortunate. The soot in the vents of the gas furnace had ignited and set the surrounding wood on fire which then went right up the stair case in the middle of the house. Friends did indeed take care of us, not only until Mother and Dad got home that day but until we found another place to live. Our clothes smelled like smoke for months.*

The family moved first to temporary quarters on West 7th Avenue, not far from the campus of Ohio State University. After some weeks they bought a house a block away at number 351, and finally settled in to normal living. The boys delivered newspapers in the area on their bicycles and, sometimes in the winter, on sleds. They did especially well selling "extras" to the crowds who came to the Ohio State football games, telling buyers that the paper had all kinds of information about the teams but also was good to use for sitting on the cold benches. They continued to be part of church and Boy Scouts. The church had marvelous music and until their voices changed the boys were enthusiastic sopranos singing in Christmas oratorios, anthems and hymns. They would go a few blocks down King Street to the extensive Ohio State polo grounds bordering the Olentangy River. Sometimes they carried their boat and paddled around the Olentangy exploring the huge storm sewers that emptied into the river. The family had always been acquainted with the public libraries and each child checked out books. The series of books about twins from different lands were favorites and also adventure stories and historical novels. The boys were able to save enough from their paper routes to go to a movie now and then. They loved Abbott and Costello movies which left them laughing and sometimes a Boris Karloff film that left them shaking.

*In 1944 World War II was coming to its end and President Roosevelt was running for a fourth term against Thomas Dewey and I was in my final year at Indianola Junior High. I was taking a Biology class and never seemed to be able to get an A. No matter how good a job I did on a test or paper the grade was always a B. The teacher was a very sturdy woman with short hair and severe dress who told the students that she had always loved to play with bugs and didn't like dolls and "girlie" things. She was a good teacher, but like her dress, severe. I asked her why I couldn't ever get an A and she informed me that I was a little "pesky" just like my brother had been. I didn't know what, if anything, John had done but I was reaping the harvest. During the electoral campaign she had Dewey signs all around her classroom and after class one day a classmate, Johnny Gump, and I stopped to ask her about her support of Dewey. She started on a rant about the evils of Roosevelt, her eyes getting wild, and shouted that Roosevelt had brought about the repeal of prohibition and she wouldn't vote for him if he came down from heaven, whereupon she lost control completely and delivered an uppercut to my jaw that sent me to my knees. Johnny dragged me out before further damage and she must have regained control of her emotions. After that I always made an A. I guess it was worth it.*

That fall Patty graduated from North High School and entered Ohio State University. John was a sophomore and Bill became a freshman leaving Dick behind at Indianola. Back then Latin was required plus another language. Bill and John took French. Also a practical arts class was required and Bill learned printing. All the children continued to do well in school.

While in Columbus, Dad had worked with union and church leaders to form the National Religion and Labor Council to foster understanding between labor and the church. He had become organized labor's liaison with organized religion and got to know Catholic, Jewish and Protestant leaders. He served on many boards and committees and became friends with leaders in business and industry who shared a desire for social justice and economic betterment for all. J. C. Penney called him a modern day prophet. Norman Vincent Peale had him write a piece for Guideposts. He served on the Economic Justice Committee of the National Council of Churches and on the board of Goodwill Industries. He always shared stories of his family in his talks to make a point about getting along and understanding one another, so the children always felt involved. He told of a time when both Johnny and Billy wanted the only piece of cherry pie remaining instead of apple pie which the family was having for dessert. Billy, feeling gracious, and perhaps, righteous, finally said he would forego the cherry pie so John could have it. John then refused saying then Billy would feel good and he would feel bad. Bill doesn't remember who finally ate the disputed piece. Another story was of Dicky who had been asked by a little friend, "Who is boss in your home?" The friend's mother was known for her sharp tongue and bossy ways. Dicky thought a minute and then said, "God is boss in our home!"

## Skyland Farm

The boys were not thrilled with urban life and remembered their times at Hidden Paradise. Mother also loved to garden and to be in tune with nature so, in 1946 when Dad was to be sent to the South to help with the organizing drive there, the decision was made to look for a farm. By this time the boys were teenagers and anxious to use their muscles. They found a small farm near Lithia Springs in Douglas County, Georgia about 20 miles west of Atlanta. They bought it and moved to Georgia, except for Patty who remained in Columbus and continued at Ohio State.

Rural Georgia! Red clay, with an occasional strip of hard white sandy soil. Dirt roads, tall pines, small farms, little towns, and Atlanta, "the Queen City of the South," across the Chattahoochee River. Lithia Springs, now part of greater Atlanta, once had been a resort with its lithia water reputed to have curative powers. It certainly tasted bad enough. Louise Suggs, the champion woman golfer had come from there. When the family moved there it was a rural crossroads on the Bankhead Highway between Atlanta and Birmingham with a feed store. Their farm was about two miles from the crossroads. In the other direction across the highway and the parallel railroad tracks was the Lithia Spring Methodist Church. Dad moved his church membership to a Presbyterian church in Atlanta but that wasn't practical for the family and they joined the Methodist Church. It was a small frame building with a pot bellied stove, outside bathrooms and a wonderfully warm congregation and minister. Douglas County High School was about nine miles west in Douglasville and the boys rode the school bus. They had to walk a mile from their house to the bus stop.

*The driveway to the house was lined with beautiful old crepe myrtle trees leading up to the open space around the house and barn. The house was a rambling white frame structure perched on piles of flat stones and sections of pine logs. I don't think there was a square corner in the house. Chickens had been used to coming in and out freely along with numerous cats. Each room had a piece of floor board removed to allow the cats to come and go when the doors were closed. Mrs. Hensley, from whom we bought the place, said that when her husband had said "scat" the cats could immediately disappear. The house had wonderful porches, in front, around one side and part of the back and outside the kitchen. There were fireplaces in a couple rooms, although the heat was from a butane floor furnace. It had running water from a well with a pump but no bathroom. After the first cold winter using the outhouse by the side of the barn, the installation of a septic system and facilities went to the top of the list. Seeing black widow spiders in the outhouse added urgency to this decision. The barn was a huge old unpainted structure with a wide passage down the middle and stalls or storage rooms on either side, and a full size wasp infested second story with a front access opening through which hay could be tossed from a wagon. Living here was a step back in time for us but we loved it.*

One winter the butane fuel ran out and refills were unavailable so the farmhouse got cold. It was not insulated and drafty and when the Atlanta area experienced an unusually frigid spell the family lived in a central room that had a fireplace. They had taken the old leaky barn roof's split wood shingles off to put on sheet metal, so had plenty wood to burn. During that cold spell without gas they had to put the milk, water and any other liquid in the refrigerator to keep from freezing. Fortunately fuel became available and the cold spell passed before too many days.

The road on which the family lived was not paved and the red clay could get very slippery when wet. It had no name but a county number so the boys and Mother asked if they could name it and were given permission if they would put up the sign. They made a wood sign saying "Skyview Drive" and nailed it to a locust post and installed it at the point that the road connected with the larger road into Lithia Springs. Fifty or more years later the old sign was long gone but the road name stayed the same and is displayed on a new street sign across from the Lithia Springs Post Office where once the children boarded the bus to school.

On a dark night one could see the glow from the lights of Atlanta in the eastern distance. One night in December 1946 the usual glow was supplanted by a brighter orange light that was obviously a huge fire. Turning on the radio confirmed that it was a major conflagration at the luxurious "fireproof" Winecoff Hotel. One hundred nineteen people died in the fire or jumping out of high windows. Many changes in fire prevention and safety were stimulated by that fire and a haunting country song was written memorializing "The Burning of the Winecoff."

The Atlanta area had many attractions, one of which was the great mass of rock rising on the east side called "Stone Mountain." The civil war sculpture carved in its face was incomplete but amazing anyway. The only amenity at the mountain was a vending shack that sold orange drinks. The family was able to drive the jeep to the sloping ascent on the far side and right on up the mountain. It was an impressive view. About ten years later, when Bill, now married to Rose, was back at Lithia Springs living with his parents while in the Army, the top of Stone Mountain was the site of burning crosses set by the Ku Klux Klan in protest of the growing movement for equal rights for black citizens. Now Stone Mountain is a fine resort.

Father John was a very capable builder with stone and cement work and over time he and the boys built a stone underpinning for the house that looked great. They also cleaned out the nearest cow stall and constructed a concrete feeder and stanchion for a milking room. They acquired a gentle Guernsey cow named Daisy and for the first week or so the boys argued about who got to milk her. After that they argued about who had to milk her, but they did, morning and night along with feeding, watering and cleaning. Daisy was easy to milk and a real pet, but the second cow, Blackie, was ornery and liked to put her foot in the bucket and swat whoever was milking with her wet tail clumped with cockleburs. Mother could always out-milk the boys. The milk was strained and bottled. When the cream rose to the top some would be dipped off to make butter which was put into butter molds. Some milk was sold to neighbors but most was consumed and thoroughly enjoyed. In due course chickens, pigs and ducks were added to the farm. Daisy had a calf they named Buttercup who grew into a beautiful orange and white heifer.

*Later when Buttercup was a year old I took her to the fair in Atlanta under a 4H program and won a blue ribbon. I was thrilled to be at the fair and to win a ribbon even though she was the only heifer in her class so had no competition. Years later brother John gave me a letter written to him at college in 1947 by Mother reporting on Buttercup's ribbon. In the same letter she said that we needed to put some of our excess roosters in the freezer because chicken feed costs were getting high and that the neighbor Mrs. Martin, was going to try a winter garden. Almost in passing, between these tidbits of homey news, she mentioned that Daddy had just come home the day before with a friend, Earl*

*Stanley Jones, and another gentleman who were enjoying the farm. That is the way our parents lived – at ease with everyone from the humble neighbors to a famous world missionary leader. We children were beginning to realize that we were part of a special family.*

## Chickens, Chicks and a Mule

*Dad had always loved poultry and back in Pennsylvania had Bantams. On the farm in Georgia in addition to laying hens and a rooster we started to raise fryers. We would get baby chicks and move them from level to level in cages as they grew. We never made pets of them and they were pretty stupid, trampling and pecking each other. There really is a pecking order. When they reached fryer size of three pounds or so we would hang them by their legs on a clothes line so they would drain and not flop around and bruise themselves when we cut off their heads. Then we had to pluck them, draw them, dress them and package them for sale or consumption. To pluck them we dipped them into the big black iron pot boiling over a fire in the back yard. It was not a pleasant smell.*

*Once when Mother and Dad were away and we boys were responsible for our own cooking some girls at school teased us about starving since our Mother was gone. We invited two of them for supper and roasted five fryers – one for each of us – with cider to drink, vegetables, Waldorf salad and an apple pie. John and Dick were the better cooks but we could all manage in the kitchen.*

For a time turkeys were added to the farm menagerie and a big beautiful Tom would puff out his shining green, purple and black feathers and spread out the fan tail and hiss trying to intimidate the boys. It was all bluff. John would imitate him and "swell up," hiss and strut towards him, and of course he was a lot bigger. One of the young turkeys at the gangly pullet stage became best friends with one of the farm kittens. They would roam around together and lie in the sun on the back porch with the turkey's neck stretched over the kitten's soft back.

The boys had many friends and occasionally had dates with girls but soon learned that dating had serious implications at an early age in rural

Georgia. It was not at all unusual for marriages at ages 15 and 16 and some girls felt that if they weren't married by 18 they were "past their prime" as Daisy Mae sings in the musical "Li'l Abner." Dick had a special friendship with a lovely girl who wanted to marry when she was 15 and he, the same age, was willing. Mother and Dad counseled waiting a bit and offered to try to help her attend college, but she was marriage bound and the relationship faded. She was married to someone else soon after.

Mother loved to garden and the family had fresh vegetables and enough to preserve and freeze for winter. There were wild dewberries and wonderful wild muscadine grapes for the picking. Dad had bought a farm jeep that had a three point hitch, double disc plow and harrow which was used to prepare fields for corn and hay. Cultivating had to be done with a hoe or behind a neighbors mule the boys named "Orkin." One of the union leaders always thought they had named the mule "Orchid" and marveled at the inventiveness of the boys to name such a rough creature after a beautiful flower.

*I really liked to work with the mule —to grab the plow handles and, sweating, run a straight furrow taking out weeds between the rows of corn. You had to watch that the mule didn't stray, singing "gee" and "haw" and using the reins, but it was powerful and, for the most part, willing. Sometimes we'd get on its back and we learned why they call mules "razor backs." Orkin did balk once when all three of us boys out in the meadow got on its back at once. It first reared up dumping me off the back end and then headed for the barn at a gallop. At the barn John, seeing that he was going to dash his head on the entrance leaped off grabbing a swinging door. Dick, who was in front, had slid around so he was hanging down in front of the mules chest with his legs scissored around the neck. Fortunately Orkin stopped before running into the wooden bars crossing the passageway half-way through the barn, and Dick was able to drop off. We never tried that again.*

*We would occasionally go "hunting" with our 22/410 over/under Stephens rifle/shotgun and sometimes got a squirrel which we learned to skin and cook, but we never became real hunters. We were allowed to shoot crows that got in the corn patch and bothered other birds. Once I shot at a sparrow out in the field just for target practice with the 22 and I killed it. I was full of remorse and have always felt badly about it and never wanted to shoot anything again without good reason. It was enough to wander through the fields and woods with our beagle, Jitters, and watch the water flow in Still Creek. We suspected it was called that because there may have been a "still" there once.*

## Lessons at School and from Life

The boys quickly adjusted to school but some things were different. Teachers were not well paid but many were very dedicated and well prepared. Math went through Algebra but the school had no teacher for the Algebra 2 level so the students taught themselves with the principal looking in. Chemistry and Physics were only offered every other year. Georgia had just added grade 12 the year Bill graduated and he graduated at 16. Many students didn't persist to graduation but went to work on the farms as soon as allowed. Drivers licenses could be obtained at age 15. The boys were active in school groups as far as possible given the distance between school and home. Bill played football, although he wasn't a great player, was small compared to others weighing under 140 pounds and the uniforms were too big for him so the shin pads were at his ankles. He edited the mimeographed "student newspaper" and helped with the prom put on by the juniors for the seniors. All the boys made good grades and progressed without any difficulty.

*I remember discovering that teachers, and even textbooks, didn't always have the correct facts. Our History teacher was teaching about labor unions and said that John L. Lewis was president of the American Federation of Labor. Having been encouraged to seek and speak the truth, I raised my hand and advised that William Green was president of the AFL, Phillip Murray of the CIO and John Lewis of the United Mine Workers, which had left the AFL some years before. Her response was that John L. Lewis was president of "all the unions." Now how does one answer a question on a test; the way the teacher is going to grade it or the truth?*

Another learning experience was to discover that black students, who were conspicuously absent from the school the boys attended, had their school in an old abandoned fertilizer factory across the railroad tracks. When new school buses were purchased they went to the white schools with the replaced ones going to the black schools. Little opportunity was available to get to know anyone of the black race in social circumstances and the boys noticed some interesting phenomena in that regard.

*We had very good neighbors – salt of the earth – who eked out a living on a small farm. We were a puzzle to them. We worked hard, shared and didn't act high and mighty and yet had experiences and opportunities outside their world. The children and mother were often in our house for one reason or another. The neighbor farmer had a black man who helped him and they were obviously what one would call "buddies." They would go hunting and fishing and work the farm together but when it was mealtime the black man would not go into the house to eat. They brought his food out to him. It was a choice that both of them made – eating together just wasn't done – and everyone would be uncomfortable. We had many visitors to "Skyland Farm" which we had named the place, and some friends were black church, labor and educational leaders and their families from Atlanta who sometimes came to our house. Our neighbor noticed this and asked if those friends were "Filipino." Cultured, well dressed, confident black people were just not part of their experience. They never made any kind of issue about it and probably simply considered us peculiar.*

Dad continued to work with the CIO's Southern organizing drive which found fierce and sometimes violent opposition. Part of the tension was because of the union's acceptance of black workers as "brothers." On one trip to a mill town in South Georgia the union representatives and supporters were attacked by a gang of "goons" as they were passing out leaflets about a meeting. Dad told the others not to fight back, knowing that violence was not the answer and that the incident would be blamed on the workers. They complied and avoided a serious fight but several were struck by the attackers. Dad suffered a bruise and cut on his cheek. They called the sheriff and were advised to leave town and offered safe passage to the county line. Several doctors turned down requests for treatment but finally one agreed to treat the injuries and even offered to examine their fists so he could testify, if need be, that they had not been used. Of course there was no interest by local authorities in law enforcement. When Dad came home with his injured cheek and a bloody shirt the boys were ready to go do battle, but wiser heads prevailed.

In addition to many visitors, sometimes extended family members came to the farm for visits and, sometimes, extended stays. Dad's sister Wilhelmina or "Aunt Billie" was there for quite a while when she needed a place to be. She was one of the younger sisters and a beautiful and artistically talented young woman. She had experienced serious problems with the birth of her second child and a husband who left her and she developed schizophrenia. As is often the case with this condition she was involved with secretive intelligence operations and communicated "on line" with others. She would interpret news articles as having hidden meaning, such as an article on red clover being used as a cover crop really indicating a red (communist) incursion. She would hurry inside if an airplane flew over for fear they were tracking her and was very apprehensive if the lights blinked. She would talk with her contacts with a clever look in her eyes and her mouth moving and often would laugh and pass her hand in front of her face. Other than that she helped around the house, made intelligent conversation, tatted or crocheted and was quite delightful. We boys tried to discuss her "on line" adventures with her and figure out what it was all about but made no headway in changing or understanding her. At one point John decided, "If you can't lick them, join them," and he began to have his own private conversations, moving his lips, laughing and passing his hand in front of his face. He did a good job of mirroring her. She noticed and went to Mother and said, "Gertrude, I think something is the matter with John!" John returned to normal.

The Lithia Springs Methodist Church was a warm, friendly and worshipful place and the family was quickly involved and made many enduring friendships. The Youth Group was active in study, service and doing things together. The boys sang in the youth choir, went on retreats, and put on plays. On one occasion in 1946 or 1947 the church was invited to send a youth representative to a national Youth Convention in Cleveland, Ohio. Bill was selected to go and the whole group sold cards and conducted other fund raisers to make it possible.

*I was excited but awed by the generous support of the church and all my friends and when the time came boarded a train in Atlanta headed north. Other youth from the area were also on the train and new friendships were quickly made. The housing in Cleveland was in a former bomber manufacturing plant with rows of army cots. The sessions were held in a convention center. The theme was "Christ Above All," and the speakers and music were transforming. It was like a wonderful dream and we left ready to live our faith and change the world. On the trip home we sat in the train cars continuing the fellowship and sharing we enjoyed at the conference. The "Yankee" youth wanted to hear the Southerners talk, enchanted by the "Southern drawl." We obliged them with exaggerated accents – even those of us who really didn't have one. I still love the soft tones of southern speech that takes the hard edges off of "r" and "i". There were students of various races and regions interacting but no consciousness of the differences. When the train crossed the Ohio River a conductor came through the cars requiring all the black people to move to a separate car further back. He was carrying out the law of the states into which we were passing and it made a profound impact on us. I knew the good people of our church and community were part of this culture of separation and realized the evil into which the system had trapped us. Could it be changed without harm to good people – white and black?*

John graduated and went off to college at Berea College in Kentucky. Dad had been on a panel at the college representing workers' perspectives in Christian faith, and had been impressed with the school's emphasis on equality, faith and work. In his high school senior year Bill got a job doing bookkeeping and paying bills for the school snack bar under the direction of the bookkeeping teacher who was a stunning redhead. She asked him to stay after graduation to help finish up the books for the snack bar and paid him $3.00 per hour. He thought he'd arrived at a high level of professional achievement. The minimum wage was 40 cents. Two girls were valedictorian and salutatorian. Bill was third and all three had to give graduation speeches.

Patty was about to finish at Ohio State University and John was a student at Berea College so now it was Bill's turn. He applied to Berea. Berea had an income test which was easily met and Bill's school record and tests qualified him, but he was turned down because the family lived outside of the Berea mountain territory and they had already taken one Ramsay. Georgia had a scholarship program for qualified students that would enable him to go to the Georgia Institute of Technology so Bill applied and was accepted. He was thinking of Industrial Engineering. A telegram arrived from Berea, delayed by having been delivered to the wrong address, saying that an admitted student had dropped out and there was an opening if he could get there by the next day. A phone call was made and the next day Bill was on the train headed for Berea.

*I found out later that John was distraught. He thought he'd finally escaped his tormenting little brother, and I didn't blame him. I was bad about teasing. But he was gracious and by the end of the first term we were the best of friends, lived in the same dorm and worked together at the dairy. I'm afraid we boys didn't fully appreciate the sacrifice sending us to college entailed. It wasn't just the cost of living at college (Berea charged no tuition but students had to pay board, room and fees) which was difficult enough, but the loss of manpower on the farm. How would Mother manage with Dad gone much of the time? Fortunately an elderly neighbor and capable gentleman was available to help and did the milking, animal care and other farm chores for many years. I not only had a child's limited understanding of parental sacrifices but, at age 17, had no idea of the adventures awaiting me in this new place.*

# GENEALOGY: WILLIAM ROMIG RAMSAY

## Pedigree Chart

Jul 17, 2017

Chart no. _____
No. 1 on this chart is the same as no. _____ on chart no. _____

**16 William RAMSAY**
b: Mar 26, 1819
d: Apr 16, 1885

**8 Morris RAMSAY**
b: Jun 4, 1848
p: Fordell, Fife, Scotland
m: Mar 15, 1870
p: by Rev. F. F. Boyd in PA
d: Dec 29, 1892
p: Morewood, PA

**17 Elizabeth SHARP**
b: Dec 25, 1819
d: Aug 13, 1889

**4 William RAMSAY**
b: Nov 23, 1870
p: Shafton, PA
m: Dec 17, 1891
p: Mt. Pleasant, PA
d: Apr 13, 1943
p: Easton, PA

**18 Jacob HELMAN**
b: Dec 3, 1807
d: 1870

**9 Sadie Maria(h) GREER**
b: Jan 2, 1853
p: near Larimer, PA
d: Jul 12, 1927
p: Mt. Pleasant, PA

**19 Maria LONG**
b: 1809
d: Jan 1853

**2 John Gates RAMSAY**
b: Jun 13, 1902
p: Howe, Indian Territory (now Oklahoma)
m: Nov 25, 1926
p: Bethlehem PA
d: Feb 26, 1991
p: Berea KY

**20 John Daniel THOMPSON**
b: 1815
d: June 25, 1890 (1896?)

**10 Joseph Byers THOMPSON**
b: Sep 11, 1845
p:
m: Jan 2, 1871
p:
d: Jan 1, 1881
p:

**21 Mary J. PHILLIPS**
b: 1816
d: 1880

**5 Jessie THOMPSON**
b: Oct 25, 1872
p: Greene County, PA
d: 26 Dec 1944 (1943?)
p: Bethlehem PA

**22 Elias ALEXANDER**
b: Jun 2, 1824
d: Feb 27, 1905

**11 Sarah Jane FLENNIKEN**
b: Jan 2, 1849
p: Carmichaels, PA
d: Jun 5, 1919
p: McKeesport, PA

**23 Mary Ann KERR**
b: Mar 12, 1825
d: Dec 31, 1899

**1 William Romig RAMSAY**
b: Aug 19, 1931
p: Bethlehem PA
m: Sep 7, 1952
p: Berea KY
d:
p:

**24 Johann Gottlieb MARTIN**
b: Feb 9, 1790
d: May 3, 1849

**12 Christian August MARTIN**
b: Jan 23, 1837
p:
m: Sep 20, 1864
p: Bluefields, Nicaragua
d: Dec 14, 1909
p:

**25 Johanna Frederika ZOBISCH**
b: Apr 4, 1799
d: Sep 9, 1842

sp: **Elva Rosalba (Rose) MOORE**

**6 Johannes Theopholis MARTIN**
b: Apr 14, 1869
p:
m: Dec 8, 1898
p:
d: Jan 20, 1933
p:

**26**
b:
d:

**13 Hanna Lydia RENKEWITZ**
b: Nov 5, 1838
p:
d: Nov 20, 1905
p:

**27**
b:
d:

**3 Gertrude Eleanor MARTIN**
b: Dec 28, 1904
p: Bluefield, Nicaragua
d: Sep 23, 1984
p: Berea KY

**28 Samuel ROMIG**
b: 1801
d: 1882

**14 Benjamin ROMIG**
b: Mar 7, 1834
p: Tuscarawas County, Ohio
m: 1866
p:
d: 1903
p:

**29 Elizabeth MINNICH**
b: 1807
d: 1906

**7 Elizabeth Beatrice ROMIG**
b: Feb 27, 1875
p:
d: Feb 9, 1930
p:

**30 Frederick WOLLE**
b: 1814
d: 1844

**15 Maria Elizabeth WOLLE**
b: 1837
p:
d: 1906
p:

**31 Caroline HELWIG**
b: 1815
d: 1854

Prepared Jul 17, 2017 by:

1

# BILL AND ROSE RAMSAY TIME LINE

## CHILDHOOD AND YOUTH: 1931 - 1948

| YEARS | FAMILY AND RELATED EVENTS | WORLD EVENTS |
|---|---|---|
| 1931 | Elva Rosalba born July 5 in Greene County, TN. First child of Eddie and Lochiel Moore William Romig born Aug 19 in PA Third child of John and Gertrude Ramsay | President: Herbert Hoover 2300 banks closed, Star Spangled Banner becomes National Anthem New Cars cost $490 Bread $.08 loaf |
| 1933 | Richard Morris born to John and Gertrude | President: Franklin Roosevelt New Deal introduced Prohibition repealed Hitler takes control in Germany |
| 1934 | Kenneth Harold born to Eddie and Lochiel | Bread costs 10 cents a loaf^ |
| 1935 | Rose grows up on small farm Tobacco is cash crop. No electricity. No indoor plumbing. | Social Security introduced Average new home is $3.900 |
| 1936 | Bill grows up in small duplex Bethlehem Father steel worker, at times unemployed Economic tensions and labor strife | King George V dies, George VI becomes king of England |
| 1937 | Rose attends two room schools at Union Temple and Meadowview | Japan invades China |
| 1938 | Moores continue as members of church at Oak Dale, TN | Amelia Earhart lost in Pacific Germany annexes Austria Minimum wage at .25/hr |
| 1939 | Bill attends Franklin Elementary in Bethlehem, then Salisbury Township, PA Presbyterian Church | Germany invades Poland "Gone with the Wind" premiers New car costs $800 |
| 1940 | John G. Ramsay has become leader in Steelworkers Union | Nazis invade France, Denmark Winston Churchill becomes British PM Air Battle of Britain begins |

| 1941 | Wayne born to Moore family<br>Bill's Aunt Grace and Uncle Fred<br>captured by Japanese in Philippines | Japan bombs Pearl Harbor<br>US declares war on Axis powers<br>Hamburger is 20 cents a pound |
|---|---|---|
| 1942 | Ramsay's move to Ashland, KY<br><br>Then near Slippery Rock, PA for summer | Manhattan project begins in<br>Oak Ridge<br>War in Pacific; battle of Midway |
| 1943 | Ramsay's to Columbus, OH<br>Indianola Jr High & North High<br>Bill's grandfather William Ramsay dies | Battle of Stalingrad<br>German retreat<br>Roosevelt, Churchill, Stalin meet |
| 1944 | Rose starts Baileyton High School<br>Rose writes family history for school<br>Bill's grandmother Jesse Ramsay dies | D-Day invasion in Normandy<br>First operational computer |
| 1945 | Rose's grandfather, James Moore, dies<br>Ramsay's move to Lithia Springs, GA,<br>Skyland Farm with cows, chickens, pigs, etc. | Germany defeated in Europe<br>Hitler & Mussolini perish<br>Roosevelt dies:<br>Truman president<br>Atomic Bombs dropped on Hiroshima,<br>Japan surrenders |
| 1946 | Bill attends Douglas County High School | Truman doctrine implemented |
| 1947 | Bill's brother John graduates from high<br>School and goes to Berea College | India and Pakistan independence<br>First practical transistor used |
| 1948 | Bill and Rose graduate from high schools<br>Rose's Grandmother Eliza Kilday Moore dies<br>Rose's Grandfather William Riggs dies<br>Bill and Rose enroll in Berea College<br>Rose works at candy kitchen<br>Bill works at Foundation School library<br>Rose and Bill join Berea Players but don't<br>know each other. Bill joins Country Dancers | United Nations establishes Israel<br>Marshall Plan instituted<br>Gandhi assassinated<br>Minimum wage is 40 cents/hour |

READY TO GO TO COLLEGE

BORN ON JULY 5. 1931 ELVA ROSALBA (ROSE) WAS TREASURED BY HER MOTHER, LOCHIEL, HER GRANDMOTHERS, ELIZA MOORE AND LAURA RIGGS AND HER BROTHERS. KENNETH AND WAYNE. SHE PLAYED THE PIANO FOR CHURCH AND OTHER OCCASIONS (SEEN HERE WITH MAUDE HAYES). SHE WAS JUST 17 YEARS OLD WHEN SHE WENT TO BEREA COLLEGE, KY .

1. MOTHER GERTRUDE WITH PATTY, JOHNNY, AND BILLY IN CHAIR.

2. BILLY HUNTING EASTER EGGS

3 UNCLE CLARENCE WASHES BILLY'S FACE AT PUMP AT HIDDEN PARADISE

4 BILLY AND JOHNNY IN KNICKERS

5 BILL IS READY TO GO TO COLLEGE, 1948

6. BILL INTRODUCES NEPHEW DAVID TO MARIGOLD AT SKYLAND FARM

# REFLECTIONS 3

## <u>REAL RICHES AND SELF ESTEEM</u>

Looking back at our childhood we realize how blessed we were. We started out in families, one urban and one rural, that were considered "poor" even then, and now would fall well below the poverty line. But we were rich in the things that mattered. We were provided shelter and clothes. We were nurtured with healthy food. We were taught restraint and how to behave, with discipline when needed. We were read to and listened to as we learned to read, sung to and then sung with as we learned the songs. We were introduced to moral laws and given a picture of the joy of a virtuous life as contrasted to the sorrow that comes with wrong living. We learned that we had contributions to make and were expected to make them, even though we may have resisted sometimes. We felt protected and valuable. Most of all we were surrounded by love. We were part of a close immediate family, and an extended family of aunts, uncles, cousins and grandparents. We were part of a community and of a church where people cared about and helped each other. Our identity as children was tied to our families and our community. Not everyone has that privilege as the following story tells.

*A couple had gone to the Smokies for a vacation and were enjoying being together at a restaurant. They noticed an elderly man visiting other tables and talking to the guests and, as they feared, he came to their table and asked if he could sit down. They courteously assented and he asked where they came from and they engaged in a little small talk. Then he said he had a story to tell them. Without waiting for a response he told them that there was a boy who had grown up in the mountains nearby, and for whatever reason had no father but was cared for by his single, working mother. He was very aware that his friends had fathers, but he had none and it made him feel lost. His mother always took him to church and he tried to avoid talking to people because those who didn't know would ask who his father was. He would scoot out of church as soon as the service was over to prevent being caught in that situation. One Sunday a new preacher was there and the boy got caught behind some people who were blocking the aisle. Before he could get out of the church the minister had reached the door and was shaking hands. When he began to hurry past the minister stopped him and asked the inevitable, "And whose little boy are you?" Everyone around grew immediately quiet and the minister, sensing that he had opened up a touchy topic, quickly knelt down and taking the little boy's face in his hands peered at him closely and said, "I can see it now. You are Gods child." The boy went on for the first time feeling that he had an identity and mattered to someone. The old man then said, "I was that boy and that moment changed my life" Then he got up and left. After he had gone, the couple asked the waitress who he was. She told them that most everyone knew him. He had once been the governor of Tennessee.*

Not everyone is as fortunate as we were to have families and a heritage that gave us identity, but we can all share in the confidence that ultimately our identities are as children of a loving God, who has hopes for us and expectations of us.

Children still need the basic "riches" that we were given much more than material possessions. Love and training and nurturing and faith and hope can be provided whatever the economic circumstance. It is more difficult where there is poverty and perhaps equally more difficult where there is too much in the way of material goods. It is more difficult today in America where communities are dispersed, families are fractured and churches are not part of the lives of many. But it can and must still be accomplished. It presents parents with some hard questions. How can you keep family close? How do you create community in the modern world? What can you do together with your children to share with and contribute to others?

One hears considerable talk about "self-esteem" and too often this means just making a person feel good about themselves. That can be pretty superficial. Real self-esteem is a product of knowing one is valued as a member of a family and community and a child of a loving God, and knowing that one is making a contribution. Sometimes visitors to Berea College, looking at its required student work program, would ask me, as Dean of Labor, how we motivate students. We used pay incentives, recognition through awards and we established negative consequences if work was not performed, These were all important. But the motivation much more important than any of these other transient incentives was "expectation," When a person is given a task that is real, provided the resources and direction needed, and expected to perform it well, the underlying messages are: "You are important." "I believe in you." "I depend on you." "I have expectations of you." This is part of the genius of Berea and the other work colleges. Students are not just consumers, but contributors. That is affirming and empowering. It builds self-esteem and it builds community. The opposite approach of caring without expectation fosters a sense of entitlement which says, "You are not really needed." That is not affirming or empowering, nor does it build real, lasting self-esteem.

In our families we were given tasks and expected to make contributions. On the farm Rose was part of the working team necessary to have food, clothing and other basic necessities of living. Bill and his brothers and sister were given chores and responsibilities as well. They carried newspapers to earn school lunch money and hired out to do odd jobs when they lived in town and when they moved to Skyland Farm they helped Dad repair the house, build walls and fences. They were the muscle and sweat under Mother's capable direction to grow produce and take care of animals. This developed skills and fostered a sense of confidence in one's abilities. Self-esteem was never an issue.

Every family has opportunities to share responsibilities, share work and play, care for each other and reach out to those outside the family. Family time together was built into life in earlier times and now may require more intentional choices. Will we have meals together? Will we read, share, play games and travel together or each go our separate ways, seeking self-expression and meaning somewhere else? Will we teach our values to our children or leave it up to a coach, peer pressure, media images or some other person or influence? Will Mom be more than a means of food, laundry and transportation? Will Dad, if there at all, be more than a source of allowance, fix-it man, and authority figure on occasion? It depends on our choices.

# REFLECTIONS 4

## THE MAGIC OF BOOKS AND READING

I, Rose, have always loved to help children, and even adults, learn to read. Whatever method is used there is that moment when it seems to come together and a light dawns in the eyes as a new world of possibilities opens up. Children instinctively want to read and are generally quick to learn. What a difference it makes if they acquire the skill early and then embark on the adventures of reading starting at a very young age. I was a prime example.

We had books in our little two room home. This was not typical of the homes in our rural area of East Tennessee. Mama left high school as a teenager before finishing and got a job working at the Kingsport Press. She was fascinated by books and whenever a copy of a new book was to be thrown away because of some blemish she would save it from the trash bin and take it home. Some were not very good books, but some were treasures. Her little bookcase with glass paneled doors covered by wood filigree was a treasured piece of furniture in our sparsely furnished home. We were proud of our books.

My Dad loved to read aloud. I remember, before we had electricity, that after farm work was done and supper completed in the evening, we would gather in the living room, which was also the bedroom of my grandparents and where I slept with Mammaw Eliza Moore. Daddy would sit in a chair near the wood burning stove with a kerosene lamp hanging above his chair and read. He especially loved the Zane Grey books. *Desert Gold* was a favorite. Mammaw and Papaw would sit in their chairs and listen. Mama would be in her chair with her hands busy over some darning or other sewing project. I would stand behind Daddy and watch his finger follow under the words he was reading. Before long I knew the words and could read, too, so by the time I started school I was reading easily.

This early start in reading led to achievement in school, advancement and discovery of all kinds of people and places through the books the school provided. A traveling library would come periodically and replenish the little shelf of books at the school. I read them all and couldn't wait for the next delivery. So, while I never got out of East Tennessee until a teen church camp in North Carolina and then entering Berea College in Kentucky at age 17, I traveled the world in my mind through books. I also had images of fairies, princesses, cowboys, secret places and adventures which became the fuel for all kinds of imaginary games. Cinderella, Sleeping Beauty, The Mysterious Rider, The Prince and the Pauper, Daniel in the Lion's Den, and other wonderful stories of the struggle of good versus evil, of beauty and love triumphing over ugliness and cruelty, all became the plots of what we called "play-like." I played with my brother Ken, usually in a ravine down from the house, which could be a castle, hideout, or fairy domain. Ken loved "play-like," and would take whatever role I assigned him.

As I grew and finished high school, went to college, got married, taught literacy, traveled, raised children and enjoyed grandchildren and great grandchildren, these early experiences with books proved to be of inestimable value. How important it was (and how blessed I was) to have a mother who loved and acquired books, a father who loved to read, an early start in reading and a loving family that allowed my excursions into fantasy worlds along with the realities of life and work on a small farm. What families provide for their children in the very early years is so important.

# REFLECTIONS 5

## SIREN SONGS

Somewhere in our upbringing we both developed a resistance to doing things because "everyone else" did. We were suspicious of appeals to our appetites or "status" or sense of entitlement. Perhaps it was mother Ramsay's little verse posted in the kitchen saying, *"Of all excuses this is most forbid; I did the thing because the others did!"* Once when we were living in Druid Hills in Atlanta, which had been a very prestigious area, we got a letter advertising something that they knew we wanted because of where we lived and therefore who we were. Rose's reaction was to say that it made her feel like she should put on her shoes. We didn't like the swooning over some singer or movie star or "just having to see" some show or have some record because it was the "in thing." I still resist this kind of appeal and when an e-mail message includes the phrase "must see" I delete it immediately. This attitude may have helped us avoid some of the temptations that promise momentary pleasure but lead to destruction – the siren songs of the world.

In mythology the sirens were creatures who enticed sailors by their songs promising bliss, on to the rocks that destroyed their vessels and their lives. When Ulysses, sailing home from Troy, as told in Homer's *Odyssey*, was to pass by the sirens he wanted to hear their song without imperiling himself and his crew so he had his men plug up their ears and tie him to the mast with instructions not to release him no matter how much he demanded until they were safely past the peril. The songs nearly drove him mad, but he survived. In another story of Greek mythology Jason and the Argonauts were passing the sirens, but one of the companions on the *Argo* was Orpheus whose music was so beautiful that no one could resist it. So he played a more beautiful music than the siren song and they all passed safely. That seems to us a wonderful lesson in resisting temptation.

Listen to a more beautiful music provided by virtue and pure love and the promises of God and the siren songs will not seem so alluring.

What are some of the siren songs of our culture? Gambling with its promise of fortune is one and has ruined many good people. Pornography with its bait of sexual fantasies leads to obsession, dissatisfaction and often criminal behavior. Drugs, with their allure of instantaneous good feelings and escape from pain and demands, lead to addiction and enslavement that destroys health, relationships and life. Gorging oneself on unhealthy or just too much food leads to poor health, the discomforts of obesity, dependency and other difficulties. In our lifetimes the two most prevalent siren songs have been sung about smoking and alcohol.

Cigarettes are now considered undesirable since the health effects on both the smoker and those around have been demonstrated, publicized and understood. Even so some people continue to succumb to its temptation. It never had any appeal to me after my experience as a boy with crushed leaves in a lead pipe and a scorched throat. Rose was used to her father's smoking cigarettes he rolled by himself but it wasn't considered proper for a lady and snuff had no appeal. After a trial at college smoking held no continuing appeal for her and didn't become part of her life. The shift in opinion about smoking has been a somewhat surprising and hopeful change in our lifetime. It seems that it is possible for a culture to shift its attitudes for the better. That has not happened with alcohol, except, perhaps, for drunk driving, which now enjoys lower tolerance and stricter penalties.

We decided at the outset of our marriage that alcohol would not be part of our lives or offered in our home. We have many friends who have not taken such a position and it has not interfered with our friendships, but we feel our choice is the better one. I had seen the results of alcohol at union picnics and other gatherings in my early years and still remember vividly the bottle rolling out of the car that crashed in front of our house and killed the driver. Alcohol was not part of Rose's home and certainly was unacceptable to her Baptist church. Those who used alcohol were pitied or considered undesirable companions and friends. It is often a factor in poverty, car wrecks, abuse and family break ups. As adults we have seen its effect on good friends who at parties might become maudlin, weepy, too loud and boisterous, profane and provocative. Others managed to retain their self-respect and character. But, we asked ourselves, why do it and run the risk? Why contribute to the problems of those who are negatively influenced? Of our six married children's spouses, four came from families that had been negatively affected by alcohol. We wanted no part of it.

Its absence has in no way limited our hospitality, enjoyment of good times or good friendships – in whatever culture we found ourselves. At open house at our home we had our special punch that everyone enjoyed. When we were away from home and were offered an alcoholic drink, we simply courteously declined. I had a friend who abstained for the same reasons we do but got tired of people wanting to know his reasons so he simply whispered to them, "I'm an alcoholic" and they were sympathetic, asking no more questions.

What is our advice? Pray for strength. Pray for others who suffer the problems of shipwreck on the Isle of Sirens. Make a better punch! Listen to a more beautiful music!

# PART THREE

*College Years and Marriage*

# CHAPTER 5

# BEREA COLLEGE, BEREA, KENTUCKY

The college years for most young men and women are a time of significant change and growth and it was no different for Bill and Rose. They had reached their levels of basic physical growth and had been given by their families, churches and schools the mental, intellectual, emotional and spiritual foundations on which to build their lives. Now, for the first time, away from immediate family and home community, they began to find their way into the adult world of choices and independent responsibilities - to search for identity, meaning and purpose. The Danish bishop philosopher Grundtvig observed that one couldn't really educate a person until he or she began to question what life was about. Much more is involved in real education than taking academic classes and acquiring knowledge and this was certainly true at Berea College which provided a smorgasbord of learning and growing opportunities in a relatively safe environment.

Berea, founded by Rev. John G. Fee, as a Christian community dedicated to not just equality but "brotherhood," in the nonsexist meaning of the word, had given birth to a nondenominational church and educational programs at all levels including the college. Fee was opposed to anything that separated God's children one from the other. The major issue of the day that separated people was slavery and Fee was strongly abolitionist, but he also pioneered in co-education, rejection of denominationalism and distinctions between the "haves" and "have-nots." "God hath made of one blood all the peoples of the earth" was his scriptural reference and is the motto of the college.

Teachers at the college were dedicated to service. Most lived on or near the campus and some in the residence halls and they invited students to get to know them outside the classroom. All students had to work, not just for financial reasons, but as part of the educational philosophy and to promote the commitment to equality where everyone shared in the work that needed doing. Labor supervisors were part of the General Faculty with educational as well as work responsibilities and were another important set of people to whom students related. There was a real sense of community. Bill and Rose didn't know all this at the time but it was into this environment that they arrived in the fall of 1948 along with other students, mostly from the mountains of Southern Appalachia and all of limited economic resources.

## Bill Gets Started

The summer between graduation from high school and going to college was spent on the farm. Not turning 17 until mid-August most jobs were closed to him so he worked on the farm. He had little cash to take with him to Berea. With the many moves his family had made and having a brother already at Berea, fitting in to this new place was not difficult, although the level of expectations for reading, studying, homework and being surrounded by able fellow students required some adjustments.

*I remember arriving by train in the early morning hours and being met by student volunteer greeters who helped put our luggage on a wagon and pulled it to campus. I was assigned a room in Williams Building, where my brother John also lived. My roommate was a slightly older student named Fred Nickels. Everyone was friendly and I soon got to know classmates and find my way around the campus. For student labor I was assigned to the Foundation School (the college's high school) Library as Janitor under the supervision of Ms. Marion Cox who was demanding but very fair and supportive. My work schedule was just after supper so I was not able to participate in clubs and activities that met during those hours. The library had big leather couches and chairs as well as stacks of books. In putting wax on the couches and chairs and removing the cushions to clean I sometimes found a nickel or dime which was like a bonanza since my pay was 10 cents an hour applied to board and room. The greater benefit was access to books. After I finished my cleaning, I would often settle in to read and I probably read more that semester than in my whole life before. I remember particularly the biography of Madam Marie Curie. I also had my homework reading to do.*

*I had joined the college Country Dancers, to which John already belonged, and thoroughly enjoyed the dancing and fellowship, but had a hard time because of my labor hours. So for the second semester I changed my labor to the Dairy, which involved getting up at 4:00 AM. No clubs met at that hour. John and I would bring in the Holstein cows from the field, feed them, and milk the ones on whom the milking machines couldn't be used. The milking machines were run by upper class students. We had to clean the milking barn and quickly learned never to walk behind a cow with scours. Each of us workers was allowed only one half pint of milk to drink and by breakfast we were starved.*

Freshmen, along with high school students ate in the "commons" in the basement of Kentucky Hall and upper class students ate in the dining room in Fairchild Hall. Students were served on partitioned aluminum trays - a practice started when the college hosted a Navy program during the war years. Food was dished out by "old" ladies who judged how much each should have. This judgment couldn't be entrusted to other students. Another lady checked trays at the place where they were deposited to be sure the diner had eaten properly. Meals were on a schedule so food offerings were predictable.

*We lived for dinner on Wednesday when there were hamburger steaks or meat loaf and mashed potatoes and for Sunday's noon meal which was usually pork loin and good veggies. Fridays and Saturdays were bad because it was hash in some form of anything left over from the week, or "cheese dreams." Sunday evening was a sack supper which was referred to by students in terms that were not complimentary. It was nothing like being at home with unlimited milk, homemade bread and Mother's cooking. There was no such thing as fast food and we had no funds anyway to supplement our food supply except once in a while when we'd buy a quart of milk and cinnamon buns or on rare occasion a hamburger from Little Mamas or The Carleton. We did sometimes get wonderful milkshakes at Porter Moore's or Elkins drug stores.*

## Rose Struggles

Rose didn't let her summer work at the Magnavox plant in Greeneville divert her from her college plans. Arriving at Berea she found the new environment overwhelming, having little experience with new places. She had been delayed because of her grandfather's death and missed the new student orientation programs.

*Here I was, far from home, with no friends. I missed my family. Everything was strange. Helen Hartman, a girl from my area was already a student at Berea and her family drove me to Berea when they took her. Helen checked on me and encouraged me. I was sent to James Hall and assigned a roommate named Fran Janney from Virginia. She had already made friends and I felt outside the circle. I almost went back home, but the requirements of getting caught up with orientation, starting classes and being assigned labor moved me forward and before long I didn't feel as homesick and isolated.*

That fall Rose wrote home regularly and got letters from her mother. She even got to go home for a weekend with a fellow student whose family lived in the area and on one occasion her mother got a ride to Berea to see her and meet her roommate and new friends. This helped ease the pain of separation from her family.

*My family could provide no support for board and room. In a letter Mama told me that they had sold the annual tobacco harvest for $225.00. This was their main cash income for the whole year. She had bought a new winter hat for $1.00. She sent me a one dollar bill with a letter. Since I couldn't pay for books and incidentals I was a "half day student" and worked 24 hours each week during regular terms and then full-time for part of the summer to cover all my expenses. I was "paid" by credits against my costs at $.10 an hour during the regular terms and $.40 per hour in the summer. Since my work load was heavier, I was required to take fewer classes. Half day students usually attended college five years. I worked in the Candy Kitchen, which was part of the College Bakery. I decorated tea sugars learning to use a tube to squeeze colored icing on to the little tea sugar cube making petite flower designs. When the tea sugar was dropped into a cup of hot tea the flower would float to the top of the cup.*

*We packed the decorated sugar cubes into little boxes which were very popular as gifts. Some local ladies were my co-workers and were expert at making intricate designs. They also befriended me and I was invited to their homes. Modina Baker and Frances Abney became especially close. It was great to have someone to talk to about common things and not just academic studies. I'm afraid I caused some problem for them because I talked as I worked, which was frowned upon by our rather severe supervisor, Mrs. Jones. She thought one couldn't talk and work at the same time. Our friendships lasted even though I moved on to other labor assignments and four years later when my mother died and I was planning my wedding they took me shopping and then did the serving at the reception. Twenty years later in 1972, when we were back in Berea, our children surprised us with a 20th anniversary celebration at the Tab and these two friends were there again. Modina wrote in a memory piece that she always admired Rose because she could work and talk at the same time.*

## **Choices**

Bill had thought to major in Mathematics and Rose was thinking of Chemistry, but of course they had no idea of all the options available. They took aptitude and placement tests. Bill was high in Math and English and very low in Art. For his advisor he was assigned to Lester Pross, a young professor in the Art Department. Rose was assigned to an English professor. All freshmen had to take one survey course in the sciences and one in the arts and humanities. They had to take courses in Western Civilization and English Composition. Later courses in Speech, Language, Mathematics and Psychology were required along with individual choices.

New worlds of knowledge, adventure and opportunities were opened up. Rose loved the survey course section on Geology with Professor and Mrs. Burroughs. She would stay after class and ask questions and they eagerly answered. Dr. Burroughs asked where she was from and would she like to know what was under her home area. He told her about the geology of East Tennessee. She always retained an interest in and a sense of wonder of the earth and its make-up. Bill had a wonderful history teacher, Elizabeth Peck, who made history come alive. He did very poorly on his first tests in the history class, not being used to the amount of reading required or the expectations of understanding significant points, but in the end did well in the course. The Arts survey course section on music was especially enriching with an introduction to symphonies and great music. The performance of the Louisville Philharmonic in the college chapel was a new experience never forgotten. Rose remembers being frustrated with a boy who was walking from the performance with her and wouldn't stop talking. She just wanted to revel in the memory of the music. Later with some experience with classes and opportunities and self-examination Rose majored in Elementary Education and Bill in History and Political Science.

One or two convocations were required each week and many excellent performances and speakers were scheduled. In addition every Sunday a required chapel service was held with many special speakers, musicians and leaders. The gathering of all students and staff together for worship was inspiring and fostered a sense of fellowship, community and unity, even though the students often complained about "requirements." In addition to college worship over the years Bill and Rose individually attended Union Church on campus, or the Baptist or Methodist church in town, a short walk from campus. For a period Bill worked with a Christian outreach group helping with Sunday School at a little Baptist Church out on Blue Lick Road and later was involved in the Methodist Youth Fellowship.

In their first year Rose and Bill independently joined the dramatics club, Berea Players, and had small parts in one act plays which were offered each week, chosen and directed by students. The plays were done at the "Tab" (Tabernacle) – a large rambling and interesting old frame building that had served many purposes over the years. This is where the two first met, although at that time they were each just one of many new friends. Bill remembers playing the villain in a spoof entitled *The Great Western Melodrama*. Rose helped Marie Haines, the student costume mistress. She and Bill also worked back stage. They enjoyed the wonderful major productions, with experienced students, like Hilda Seay, in the cast directed by Dr. Earl Blank, the faculty member in charge. *Hedda Gabler* and *Night Must Fall* were performed that year. The Berea Players and the Tab were to become important to their experiences as students and their lives.

Students were not given much time off and most did not go home except at Christmas because of time and financial constraints. Bill with his brother John did go to their sister's wedding in Cincinnati on December 18, 1948. It was a great family occasion as Patty married Earl Todt with the officiating pastor being Rev. Leon Sanborne in whose home Patty had lived while at Ohio State. Later Rev. Sanborne was to come to Berea to be pastor at Union Church and he officiated at the wedding of Rose and Bill.

There was a short spring break which was nothing like the occasion it later became at colleges nationwide. Bill's best friend, Jim Fish, had invited Bill to go home with him to West Virginia for a few days in April. They would hitch hike there and back. This was before interstates and hitch hiking was not uncommon then. The weather was balmy when they left so they took no heavy coats and hit the road. By the time they had reached Ashland at the West Virginia border the weather had turned cold and it began to snow. Along the Kanawha River near Charleston they thought they would freeze, but they continued to get rides and finally, near Gauley Bridge, WV they were picked up by a friend of Jim's and taken to his home near Summerville. It was cold and there was ice everywhere but Mrs. Fish mothered them and fed them well and they had a good time with Jim's brother Willie and friends before they had to head back to Kentucky. The weather had turned warm and they got good rides until they were between Charleston and Huntington when they were picked up by a cadaverous looking man in an old coupe.

*I slid in next to the driver and Jim sat next to the door with our little bags behind us. We made small talk for several miles and the driver shifted gears to go up a hill and then let his hand come down to rest on my leg. Not wanting to think the worst, I imagined that he was in the habit of resting his hand on the seat beside him. But the next time it happened he began to massage. Jim and I were immediately alert to our situation. The man began to talk of girls he knew in Ashland who would be glad to meet us and "entertain" us. We kept assuring him that we were not interested and didn't do such things. Finally he made his pitch saying that he could give as much "fun" as any girl. We exchanged meaningful glances, as we declined his suggestions, and understood each other. I would reach the ignition key and turn off the motor and Jim would open the door ready to escape when the car slowed enough.*

Fortunately their host lost his temper and pulled over with an oath and the boys grabbed their bags and bailed out. He drove off and they walked a mile up the road before catching another ride, fearful that he might come back with a companion. Safely back in Berea they soon put the experience behind them, a little more worldly wise.

By the time the first year ended Berea had become familiar and even special. There was no question about coming back. Rose worked at the Candy Kitchen and in the Treasurer's Office for part of the summer before going home. Bill went back to the farm, unable to find a summer job, and there was always work at home.

## The Sophomore Year

Having learned how things were done in classes, work and social life both Rose and Bill easily resumed their Berea experience in the fall of 1949. Rose remembers the beginning of the sophomore year. Berea had become familiar she felt very much a part of it.

*In the dramatics area Dr. Blank had left after many years and a new director, Bert Pollack took his place. He was very talented and especially eager to give us younger students a chance to experience acting. Early in our sophomore year, we tried out for parts in the fall major, Arsenic and Old Lace. I played "Aunt Martha" and Bill was "Dr. Einstein." He walked around bent over for the rest of the term. It was great fun as well as a learning experience. All of us in the cast and crew became close friends and we became known by the faculty, staff and students as "the Tab crowd." We acted in or worked backstage on several of the weekly plays. Bill began to become the main lighting technician and I became involved in costumes. We helped with the Foundation School (college high school) production of I Remember Mama - another great experience, where we got to know some of the faculty children and others in the high school. For the spring major Mr. Pollack chose a few of the older students with more experience to produce The Glass Menagerie. It was absolutely wonderful. I've seen it since on film in several versions and none come close to that college performance.*

During the sophomore year, Rose continued working at the candy kitchen and had a second job in the kitchen at food service. Bill worked at the college press running a job press and helping to print the town newspaper, *The Citizen.* He learned about printing and publishing from the editor and supervisor, Albert Schumacher, and also had the opportunity to help a classmate, Corban Goble, with reporting and writing stories for the town paper and for the student newspaper of which Corban was editor. The student newspaper was called the *Wallpaper* because during the war years paper was scarce and a few copies were simply posted on walls. It has since reclaimed its original name *The Pinnacle.*

Both continued to make progress in academic studies with good records. Most classes were excellent, although sometimes students didn't agree with the professors. Some teachers in the Religion department were full of skepticism and not as secure in their faith as students. Others were very encouraging and enlightening. Dr. Ira Martin was especially helpful to Rose and Fran in deepening their faith and understanding. Sociology was a new experience for many students and they learned to take some pronouncements with a grain of salt, as Bill recalls.

*Our sociology professor was talking about aggressive behavior and dealing with it in children. He said that every child had a certain amount of "free floating aggression" and it was important to let it be expressed. If your child kicks you in the shins, he is just doing what is natural and should be understood. Well, most of us had learned to control our "free floating aggression" by the discipline of parents who in no way let us kick their shins and we had no intention of raising kids to think they had a right to do this or that it would go unpunished. If you love the child you teach it self-control. Common sense and home wisdom wasn't disturbed by this teaching.*

After meeting her work requirements, Rose went home in the summer of 1950. Bill stayed in Berea. Through a student friend he had become acquainted with the friend's uncle, Melvin Eplee who owned Eplee's Motel just beyond the Berea Theater. Mr. Eplee offered to give Bill and his younger brother Dick,who would be entering Berea in the fall, a room in the basement of his house in exchange for some evening and night duty at the motel. Bill had a summer labor position at the college press so he stayed and worked, with breaks before and after to go home.

## Junior Year: The First Kiss

Returning as Juniors in the fall of 1950 Bill and Rose were now "old timers" at the Tab. Since the drama department had changed its director each year, the students were more experienced in the way things worked there than the teacher. Charles Randolph Trumbo was the new drama director. Under the labor program, Bill and Rose were able to provide assistance to the director and take major responsibility for the Berea Players and the weekly one-act plays that were a major source of entertainment on campus, as Rose recalls.

*We both had jobs at the Tab and Bill was the technical assistant to Mr. Trumbo and in charge of backstage work for all of the plays. I was the costume mistress and did costumes for all the plays. We had lots of fine old costumes and dozens of pairs of shoes. We were very busy with our work, the plays and our classes. In the spring of our junior year, I took a play production class and as a special project, directed two three-act plays with two 8th grade classes. We performed one play at the city school and the other at the Tab. Bill helped with set and lights for both. Most of our friends were involved in the plays or the work of the Tab and we had great times together. Our major productions were Jane Eyre in the fall and Male Animal in the spring. I was in both plays and Bill did great special effects with lights for the fire in Jane Eyre.*

Mr. Trumbo had rather affected mannerisms and had a petite wife he called "Dearie" who really called the shots. He was quite willing to let the students do most of the work and called Bill, "Little Man," expecting him to be at his beck and call. He told the students "dramatically" about parts he had played. Once, he said, he was on stage playing a royal figure and the attendants were to put a ring on his finger. Instead they slipped on the eye of a "greasy old ham bone." He assured the students that he never broke character. It seems he never got the message either.

Bill had moved to a room in the Tab and he and his roommate took care of the building as well as working on plays. The old building was a haven for all sorts of critters – lots of bats, rats and mice, an occasional possum and even an owl. One unexpected guest gave them a fright.

*Our bedroom had a bathroom next to it that was just at the end of the stage, under which critters could live and hide. One night we heard a noise and turning on the light saw a large rat in the doorway between the bedroom and the bathroom. I remembered seeing a steel trap in the prop room behind the costume room so we found it. We always had some rather hard cheese in our Sunday sack suppers so we baited the trap with it and placed it in the bathroom. In the middle of the night we heard a snap and found a big rat dead in the trap. Congratulating ourselves we set it again the next night and again heard a snap. Pulling the bathroom door open we were staggered to see a skunk caught by its paw. What to do? It hadn't released an odor but if it did all our clothes would be ruined, not to mention disabling our residence and the building for a time. The skunk backed into a hole that went under the stage but couldn't get the trap through. Using a large cardboard poster as a shield we cautiously crept up to the trap and with a broomstick pressed down on the spring to release the jaws. It worked and the skunk disappeared without ever spraying the premises. We didn't set the trap again.*

Dorm rules were quite different in those days. Freshmen girls were to be in their dorms at 7:30 PM and room lights had to be out at 11. So studying was done before then and students got a good night's sleep! Upper class girls had to be in the dorm at 9:30 PM. There was a paper form on the table by the door of the dorm and girls were expected to sign in by 6 PM and to sign out if they left, stating where they would be. Girls did not go to boys' dorms, but the guys could visit until 9:30 in girl's dorm parlors. Rose had a new roommate.

*Fran Janney did not return to Berea in the fall of 1950, so I was assigned a new roommate, Doris Graybeal, a beautiful dark-haired girl from Jonesboro, not far from my home in Tennessee. Doris began college with our class, but dropped out for one year and then returned. She was a music major and a fine pianist, later becoming a concert pianist and music professor. Doris and I lived in Elizabeth Rogers dorm on 2ⁿᵈ floor and soon became best friends. ER was located near the music hall, which was very convenient for Doris. I had a second job at music hall, working in the music listening room a couple of evenings each week. Doris got involved in helping with the plays and became part of our close-knit Tab group.*

*Often I would work at the Tab in the evenings and a group of us would leave about 8:30 and go to the "Hangout" recreation room in one of the college buildings. It was a large room, with a snack bar, several tables and a couple of ping pong tables, a small dance area, and a juke box. We ate, danced, and talked until 9:25, then dashed to the dorm. Of course, the guys went to their rooms, also. I guess the theory was that if the girls were "locked up" the guys would study. The campus was not much fun if there were no girls around!*

Bill continued to be a member of Country Dancers and occasionally was involved in a performance trip. The group practiced every Friday evening. In the spring, the college sponsored the Mountain Folk Festival and folk dance groups from many mountain high schools came for three days of dancing and singing. Rose always came to the final show on Saturday. It was truly beautiful, with a couple hundred young people in a big circle, squares or long-way sets, gracefully dancing in colorful costumes and holding flowering branches of May. The music was wonderful and the singing of the May Day Carol made the coming of spring real. Bill and John had been helping with the faculty folk dance every week, partly because there was a shortage of men dancers and partly to help teach. They got to know faculty members and their spouses in this social setting. Rose's work with the young people and children in dramatics had made her acquainted with faculty families outside the faculty-student relationship, so both of them felt very much a part of the community. Dean Kenneth and Verna Thompson, Lester and Mary Lou Pross, the college physician, Dr. J. Bates Henderson, his wife and their daughter Becky, John and Dorothy Chrisman and many others became more than just teachers or officials but friends. When Bill and Rose returned almost twenty years later it was like coming home.

Students didn't leave campus for entertainment, but they had plenty to do. They enjoyed the Saturday night dances. A folk dance was held at Dodge Gym, the Country Dancer building, and the swing dance was at Woods-Penniman, the women's gym. There were movies on Saturday nights, free to students. Opportunities were provided for concerts and recitals at the music building. Students did not have cars and didn't expect to. Cars were not plentiful in those days. The Tab gang had wonderful times together and Bill and Rose began to "discover" each other as Rose recalls.

*I had a somewhat steady boyfriend in the fall of 1950, but found I preferred the company of my Tab friends, especially the technical assistant! By Christmas, Bill and I were special friends, but very much part of our group. The Tab was a spooky old building, especially after dark, and sometimes I had to work in the costume room in the evenings. One dark night Doris and I were in the back of the costume room going through some items when the lights went out. Bill and his roommate, Fred Cornwall, had crept into the room behind the front counter and turned off the lights. Then Fred threw a shirt that had been on the counter in the air and it opened up and floated down as if a ghost had jumped off the balcony. Naturally Doris and I screamed. That scared the boys to death. They turned on the lights and said they were sorry but it took a long time to forgive them for the prank and we took full advantage of their sense of guilt.*

Bill was especially remorseful because on another occasion he had wrapped Rose in the stage curtain and she had fainted. She began calling him "obnoxious" but it was obvious that they were noticing each other in new ways. Bill remembers their first kiss.

*Rose and Doris were in the Tab office and I came in. No one else was around at the time. The girls had put on really heavy ruby red lipstick, which, of course, caused me to comment on it. Then they dared me to kiss them knowing I'd get smeared with lipstick. I knew it was a set up but couldn't refuse a dare and wasn't sure I wanted to miss the opportunity. That is not the last time it happened.*

## Adventures

The romance was making progress and before the end of the term talk of a future together was getting more serious. Rose's mother came up with a family from home for the performance of *The Male Animal*, the Spring play in which both Rose and Bill acted. She met Bill for the first time. She thought he was awfully young. The term ended with the couple pretty well committed to each other and planning their schedules together for the next year. Rose stayed on at the college for the first part of the summer.

*I worked at the college in the office of Guidance and Testing with Dean Charles Shutt during June and July and went home for the month of August. My mother was not at all well during the summer and I didn't like leaving her to go back to school in September. During the summer Bill and I wrote to each other almost every day. He and his brothers had taken summer jobs in the Merchant Marines working on oil tankers.*

Summer jobs were necessary for Berea students, as well as many others, to earn enough to pay for another year of college. Through associates in the National Maritime Union, Bill's father had heard that men were needed in the Merchant Marines because so many young men had been drafted in the Korean War. John and Bill had received college deferments and Dick was not yet required to register. Being in the Merchant Marines simply meant being employed on a private cargo ship or tanker. Papers had to be obtained from the US Coast Guard and the union made the ship assignments. The boys went to Charleston, SC and took the required tests, got shots, were issued "z" papers and then waited for the union to assign them. John was assigned first on a tramp tanker that went from Charleston to Texas and then California. He had a miserable time. The chief steward sold alcohol and drugs. There were fights and a very unsafe environment. He left ship in California and took a bus home. Dick fared much better being assigned to a more respectable tanker to work in the officers' mess. It was a good experience. A maritime strike delayed Bill's assignment so he went home to wait. Finally, on July 2, 1951 he reported to a tanker of Pan- American Oil, the SS Pan Maine, leaving from Savannah, Georgia.

*The ship was in dry dock getting repairs and being repainted. I reported to the purser. I told him I'd never been on a big boat before and he informed me that it was not a boat but a ship. He signed me up as an "ordinary seaman" and told me to put my gear in the assigned cabin and report to the first mate. I asked some men where the first mate was and they pointed him out. He was most unwelcoming but I told him the purser had said to report to him. He said I was to swab the deck in the passageways, clean the head and "sugie" the bulkhead every morning. I knew the head was the bathroom, a swab was a mop and the deck in the passageways was the floor in the corridors but had no clue about "sugie." He asked. "Don't you know what that means?" and when I shook my head he said, "Well, find out!" I discovered that sugie is a strong soap to wash down the walls (bulkheads).*

*The first couple days I was feeling sick. It seemed strange to be seasick in dry dock. I think it was the change in water. I was able to do my chores and help with the work of moving stores and chipping old paint off the metal deck plates. We used miniature hand-sized jackhammers which on the metal deck made a horrendous noise. My hands were vibrated vigorously and my finger joints ached. The food was plentiful and good, although the men constantly complained. The coffee was thin and bitter but one had to drink it to keep going. I've never liked coffee since.*

*Finally the ship was ready to sail and we went down the Savannah River and out to the ocean. This could only be done when the tide was up because of a sandbar at the river's mouth. I soon got used to the gentle rolling of the ship. We were headed to Texas City to fill our tanks, which basically comprised the whole ship, with high octane gasoline to bring to the east coast. The tanks were mostly dry with a lot of rust on the bulkheads which it was our job to scrape off before we got to Texas. I had no gloves or face mask to protect from the rust dust and none were provided. I'm sure OSHA would not allow it now. By the time we had clamored up the bulkheads and scraped our way to the bottom of the tank, the rust dust was so thick we could hardly see, much less breathe. We shoveled the rust into buckets which were hoisted up through hatches to the main deck and emptied over the side. Later, when I had come home after that first voyage, I got sick and was found to have a form of hepatitis caused by the rust dust in my lungs. Fortunately no permanent damage was done to my health.*

*My fellow sailors were from all over the world and often called names representing their nationality such as Polack or Limey. The common language was pretty much four letter words which all seemed to know well and use regularly. I observed that I didn't really learn any new words but did hear some creative new combinations. Of course I was called "Kid." I had a black roommate who was large, well built and strong. I also found that he was well read and very intelligent. We discussed history, astronomy, philosophy and world affairs. He could not understand racial prejudice since he was aware that he was superior to others in his intellect and knowledge as well as physical prowess. On the other hand he thought women were inferior to men and put on earth for their pleasure and he had girls in many ports. He reminded me of King Dick in Lydia Bailey, a historical novel by Kenneth Roberts.*

*Most of the men were congenial and helpful to the "kid" and I learned to deflect the "propositions" that came my way and to be on friendly terms with my shipmates. One stocky, conceited fellow, however, was determined that I was fair game for his fantasies, which extended to anything that might serve his desires, be it female, male, human or animal. He came in to our cabin and began pawing at me as I lay on my top bunk. I grabbed his wrist and spoke to him in the "common language," and his face showed surprise when he felt my milking hand grip. Then my big cabin mate growled, "Let the kid alone," and that was the end of that.*

*I was to stand watch every night from 8:00PM until midnight. The first hour I was in a cabin at mid-ship on call if anything was needed. Then for the next two hours I stood outside in the prow watching for any light or shape that might indicate something ahead of our course. If I saw something I was to ring the bell at hand to alert the wheelhouse and they would respond with their bell. One bell meant ahead and on the right, two bells the left and three bells straight ahead. Of course I was determined to see any hazard. It wasn't easy because the white caps on the waves sometimes looked like a light that might indicate a boat in our path. Unfortunately I was on watch when we passed off the coast of Miami and there were lights everywhere. I was frantically ringing the bell until the wheelhouse sent word that I should forget it. They knew where we were and didn't need my eyes in that area. Later, as we crossed the Gulf of Mexico, far from land I was on watch one cloudy night and spied a light a good distance straight ahead. Straining my eyes to be sure it wasn't just a whitecap, I rang the bell three times. The bridge answered which meant they had seen it too. I was congratulating myself when the clouds parted and I could see it was the tip of the moon I had seen. No one ever said anything about it.*

*My Berea background served me well on one occasion. I found a scrap of wood from some shelving project in the storeroom and with my pocket knife whittled a dowel like rod about a foot long and 1/2 inch thick. Then I whittled a propeller and fastened it to the rod with a small nail through a hole I'd made in the center of the propeller. I notched the rod on one side and had a crude "whimmydiddle," as it was called in the Berea craft shop. It worked like a charm. When I rubbed a pencil across the notches and held my thumb against the side of the rod the propeller would twirl. As if that were not magic enough, if I, unnoticed, switched the pressure from my thumb on one side to a finger on the other side the propeller would stop and then twirl in the opposite direction at my command. It was fascinating to my shipmates.*

*We went through a wild storm one night when I was on watch with lightning, wind and driven rain. We wore only shorts most of the time since it was hot. The ship was rolling heavily with the waves and in the prow I felt it most severely. I did lose my dinner over the side and then crouched down behind an iron post used for tying ropes to when docking, because the wind driven rain was like bullets and it had become very cold. Thankfully someone came from the midships and told me to come inside. Another time during the day I saw a storm in the distance which had formed a waterspout - a tornado at sea that sucks up the water in a solid column. One feels vulnerable to the powers of nature at sea and I sang a lot of hymns and prayed while on watch. Most of the time the water was a pale greenish blue and sometimes we saw flying fish skimming above the waves. The weather was usually beautiful and the horizon was unobstructed to where the earth's curvature could be seen.*

Having grown up in a union family, Bill was alert to the interactions of the ship's management and labor. Management was represented by the captain, whom one rarely saw, and first, second and third mates who gave orders, and the bos'n who was the working supervisor. The crew, in spite of cultural differences, was strongly union. Whenever told to do any extra work the crew would threaten a grievance. Being an eager college student with the Berea work ethic, Bill offered no such threat. The mates took full advantage of him and had him doing all sorts of jobs no one wanted to do. He realized that both sides were self-seeking and only willing to work together because they needed each other – a precarious balance. He had plenty of time to think and he thought of the future. Never much of a letter writer before, the separation from Rose prompted him to change. He always had letters to send when he got to port. Parting did make the heart grow fonder.

Finally arriving at Texas City it was unbearably hot and the oil docks smelled like burnt broccoli. Mosquitos abounded and were viciously hungry for blood. The crew all received their pay in cash and took off for the bars and brothels. Not being so inclined Bill not only did his watch but covered for others for which they paid him in cash. The problem was the second night some who had already spent or lost all their money in carousing and gambling wanted to "borrow" from him. They knew he had his cash and were unmoved by his protests that he was saving for college. He resisted and determined as soon as he could he would go to a post office and send a mail order. This didn't happen until docking at Tampa since he didn't get to town on his first visit to Texas City.

The ship was being filled with gasoline to transport to the east coast. The night the ship left Bill thinks he was the only sober person on board. The tanker almost ran into a barge and the only response was to exchange loud curses. Had the gasoline filled tanker collided it probably would have exploded. The same danger occurred while going east across the Gulf of Mexico.

*I was standing watch again on a stormy night and there was lightning all around. Since all is open space the lightening was almost like an electrical umbrella which forked down to the sea on every side. As the storm closed in lightning came closer and finally a bolt entered the ocean right next to the ship.*

*I heard it sizzle as it hit the water. What if it had hit the ship? There would have been no one left to describe the fireworks.*

Much later when recounting his sea adventures to his children and then grandchildren, Bill told of a tanker which had been struck by lightning and caught fire and burned but was never consumed. The crew all became skeletons. The fiery ship with its skeleton crew chased other tankers to set them on fire on stormy nights. The account goes on to describe how one night Bill, on watch, saw a ship in the distance ahead that appeared to be on fire. They sailed ahead hoping to give help only to find it was the ghost ship which then pursued them through the night, trying to get close enough to board and spread its fire to its victim. Just as the grappling hooks thrown by the skeletons were catching the rails and pulling the ships together the storm broke and morning came. The sun rose, spreading its red-gold light over the surface of the ocean and the fiery ship vanished in the glow. Bill has a piece of burnt rope which was cut off a grappling hook as Bill and the crew chopped at the ropes to prevent being boarded by the skeletons. *The Fiery Ship and the Skeleton Crew* has become family lore and every so often one of the children or grandchildren asks to see the burnt rope which is kept in an envelope with his "z" papers in a small sea chest.

The tanker pumped some of its gasoline into tanks at Tampa and then the rest at Jacksonville, where Bill's assignment ended. He hitch hiked home with only one bad experience and after a bout with hepatitis and some rest, boarded another ship, the SS Pan Georgia, that went from Savannah to Texas City and then all the way up the eastern seaboard to Portland, Maine. He was a "wiper" on this voyage, which is the lowest form of life in the engine room and the title pretty well describes the work.

*"Hot" is the word that best defines the work as a wiper. The big furnaces that heat the steam to drive the ship were nearby so the temperature rarely was below 120 degrees and sometimes higher. Constant cleaning, moving things around, watching dials and sometimes turning valves kept me busy but I had regular hours and didn't stand watch. One of my fellow wipers was also new to ships and had almost no schooling. He asked me, in his black southern accent, if we would see any sea girls. I said, "You mean sea gulls?" "No," he said "She*

*fish!" and it hit me that he meant mermaids. I hated to burst his balloon, but explained and we had many interesting conversations. He had a bottle of "Black Draft" cough medicine which he kept in his pocket and its alcohol content seemed to sustain him.*

*Not having to stand watch, this time when we arrived at Texas City I was able to go ashore. I went by one of the taxis that hovered around the docks waiting for fares. The helpful young driver showed me the post office, the movie theater and the bus station. He gave me his dispatcher's number and said to call from the bus station and ask for him when I was ready to return to ship. I felt relieved when I had sent most of my cash home at the post office. It was late afternoon and terribly hot with no breeze, so I went to the air conditioned theater and sat through a poor movie twice just to keep cool and relax. It was after dark when I got to the bus station ready to go back to the ship. I got a bite to eat and called the taxi company and was informed that my driver was on another call but would come get me within an hour. I was in no hurry so that suited me and I sat in one of the booths at the bus station with a soda. In a nearby booth was an attractive young woman, made up somewhat heavily and looking just a bit disheveled. I assumed she was what was politely called "a woman of the night." After a while I went outside to wait for my ride. The woman came out and called from the bushes bordering the building, "Hey, sailor." "Who? Me?" I squeaked. "Come over here," she said. "Why don't you come out here," I replied. She came over and asked if she could stand by me. She said if the police drove by and saw her by me they wouldn't pick her up and that she didn't usually work this area. I saw no harm in that and warned her that I was waiting for a taxi to go back to ship. A car pulled up in front of us and a slick looking man rolled down the window and invited the woman to go with him. Apparently she knew him and the response from her pretty red lips turned the air blue. Then the guy offered to take me back to the ship and I said that if the lady didn't want to go with him I didn't either. He had his turn at blue air before he sped off. My taxi came and on the way back to ship I expressed concern for the woman. The driver said he knew who she was and he would go back to get her and take her to her home. I offered to pay the fare but he declined. I hope he did take her home.*

Back across the Gulf of Mexico, around the Florida Keys and then out further in the ocean beyond the sight of land for five days the ship sailed north to the rocky coast of Maine. Disembarking at Portland, Bill took a bus home, stopping to visit his aunt Lydia, his mother's sister, and her family in Boston for a few days. Finally home, some rest and back to school and Rose. What a summer!

## An Eventful Year

So much happened in the year beginning September, 1951 that it is hard to set it all down in good order. The fall term was very busy with advanced classes. Work responsibilities were heavy with new faculty leadership at the Tab. Rose's mother's health continued to decline. Bill had become editor of the *Wallpaper* and Rose often helped him get it ready for printing and distribution. Having worked at the college press Bill knew how to run the large cylinder press needed to print the paper so when needed could do everything form writing and editing to setting headlines in cold type and running the press. The linotype (hot type) for the body of articles was done by full time professionals who put out the town newspaper. Those were busy times. Bill remembers getting involved in policy on race relations.

Berea, arising from an abolitionist base, had at one time served primarily black students. It must be kept in mind that it was not just a college but was a community and church and had educational programs at all levels. By 1900 it had grown in its service to the Appalachian region and while it still had a mixture of students, it was predominately white. On the border between what had been "free" territory and "slave" parts of the state Berea had always been a problem for Kentucky. In 1904 a state representative, Carl Day, was horrified at the mingling of races that was occurring at Berea. It was not just education but social interactions. He introduced legislation to prohibit educating whites and blacks in the same institution and was successful in getting the "Day Law" passed. Berea appealed to the courts and lost at the state level and eventually, in 1908 lost at the Supreme Court under the separate but equal doctrine established by the court in 1896 (Plessy versus Ferguson). Berea established Lincoln Institute near Louisville for black students and the Berea campus became un-integrated for almost 50 years. The tides of equality began to change and in 1950 the Day Law was amended so Berea could once again admit black students although it wasn't until the Supreme Court ruling in 1954 (Brown vs Board of Education) that the separate but equal doctrine was finally overturned as not meeting the requirements of the 14th Amendment of the Constitution. Berea had admitted several black students, mostly international. One of the international students, Obuchukwu Obi, from Nigeria was on Bill's staff at the *Wallpaper*. Bill remembers the times.

*No significant problems occurred in the student body. People in the surrounding area were not sympathetic but were used to Berea being different. Then I discovered that Berea's own Boone Tavern would not serve black people. As editor, I visited President Hutchins who advised me that they were doing the best they could. That didn't satisfy me at the time, but I imagine he was right. I published a report and wrote an editorial calling for Berea to live up to its motto and commitment. The policy was necessarily modified to allow black guests of the college to eat at Boone Tavern if accompanied by a college officer, but a traveling black family or person was not welcome at Boone Tavern. I don't know when that changed but it was clear that it would change. Later in a note from President Hutchins to me he was very gracious in saying, "I have felt that the Wallpaper during the past semester has been a good and a helpful publication. You and your associates raised the tone and the level decidedly." I also spent a lot of time getting advertising from Berea and Richmond merchants and paid off a deficit, leaving the paper in sound financial condition.*

Bill had taken courses in American history, English history, Latin American history, Russian history and Far Eastern history in addition to required courses. He had taken three years of French and learned to read and write fairly well, but never conquered French pronunciation. He was taking courses in Political Science and became well acquainted with Dr. Louis Smith, Dean of the College, who sometimes taught in that department. Dean Smith was a wise and helpful mentor, as well as a scholar and gifted administrator. His dark eyes always had a twinkle behind them. Once he walked with a new student to a beginning assembly and after he had found out where the student was from, the student asked him what he did at the college. Dean Smith said he was sort of a custodian. Imagine the student's surprise when he saw the "custodian" mount the stage and, as Dean of the college, welcome the new students. Alongside Dean Smith, Bill helped with a mock Republican convention in which General Dwight Eisenhower won the nomination over Earl Warren and Harold Stassen. Rose was taking mostly education courses. She hoped to finish all course work by the end of the 1951-52 year and do practice teaching the next fall to complete her degree.

At the Tab the weekly one-act plays continued. The fall major was *Good Housekeeping*. Mrs. Louise Scrivner, a long-time English teacher in the Foundation School, was the new dramatics director and was loved by the students. They called her "Mama Scrivner." Bill was her assistant director for *Good Housekeeping*. Rose did the costumes. Both Bill and Rose were very busy and had the additional concerns about what was ahead. Mother Lochiel's health was failing and Rose felt she should go home. Bill was thinking about graduate school and the draft. They were both just 20 years old but it seemed they had to grow up. They still had fun with their friends but were certainly more serious than in the carefree year before. Early in the fall their relationship was going through a cooling off period. Rose was afraid Bill was losing interest. Bill remembers his feelings at the time.

*It was obvious that we were approaching a decision point. The prospect of marriage with all the unknowns ahead was scary. To marry was not a frivolous thing but a commitment for life. Were we ready for that? But the prospect of a future without Rose convinced me that I wanted to move ahead with her, whatever the obstacles. Then we began to talk seriously about our future together.*

Rose remembers that the cooling off period was over.

*I had been pretty upset with Bill and had even written to my mother that the relationship may not go anywhere. But now we began to think and talk seriously about our future. We planned to take a couple of classes together in the spring term. One of the classes was "Marriage and the Family," taught in the Sociology Department. I had planned to finish up my education courses and be able to do practice teaching the next fall. Then I'd have a teaching certificate so I could work no matter what situation Bill was in. We were talking about future plans in the Wallpaper office one evening and I reminded Bill that he hadn't asked me to marry him yet. He remedied that problem on his knees right then and I agreed. Now we could plan in earnest.*

## <u>Facing the Future</u>

*News from home was not good. Mama was in the hospital for several days in November. Bill's father had some work to do in Florida and the whole family was going there for Christmas. They invited me to go along but I knew I couldn't. When I got home I realized I would need to leave college after finals and stay home to take care of Mama. She had been diagnosed with myasthenia gravis, an autoimmune disease which affects the sensory nerves. She tired easily, did not have good muscle control and had difficulty speaking at times.*

Bill wrote to Rose from Florida wishing she could have gone with them. In a letter from Rose to Bill written on Christmas Eve 1951, she reported, "Mother seems to be getting along fine, however, without her medicine she is almost helpless, (and) she can't eat. A few days ago she started seeing double... The doctor said her eye muscles were so weak that they couldn't work together or focus on anything." Some days were better and Rose hoped to be able to come back to Berea but was beginning to accept that she couldn't stay away from home with her mother so ill.

*In January I went back to Berea, took my semester finals and returned home. Bill took the Marriage and Family class alone and I learned some of the content from his letters. We wrote to each other every day. We did not have a telephone so there were no phone calls. I was very busy at home, learning to cook and manage the house and caring for Mama. I had always helped with chores, but had not done these things by myself. I could always ask Mama for directions and Daddy and the boys were very helpful.*

Mother Lochiel continued to have some good days and then some that were very difficult. The doctors had given the family a syringe and needles with medication to use in case of emergency. In mid-February she had a bad spell and the oral medicine didn't work. She couldn't talk, eat, get up or function at all so Rose had to administer a shot. She wasn't sure she could do it but her father was in worse shape so she did it and the response was good. A few days later she wrote to Bill that her mother was almost normal and was moving around doing things, talking and laughing. But that didn't last and she became less and less responsive to her medication. So it was a roller coaster life at the Moore home with happy times and hard times, but clear that Rose needed to remain there to care for her mother, father and two brothers. She kept up with her Berea life vicariously through letters from Bill, Doris and other friends, always with the hope of being able to return.

Dean Louis Smith had suggested Bill apply for a graduate fellowship with the Southern Regional Training Program in Public Administration and he wrote supporting letters. This program, organized after World War II, required an internship and then graduate courses at the Universities of Alabama, Tennessee and Kentucky, all in one year! The program was motivated by a desire to develop professional administrators for public service to replace the old spoils system that still plagued much of the South. The stipend was $100 a month for a year. Bill's application was accepted and he was to report to the University of Alabama for orientation and internship assignment in early June. He now needed to apply to the draft board for an extension of his educational deferment.

*As all other young men, I had registered for the draft and was subject to call for a two year term of service. I had gone for the required physical and mental testing but expected, with my graduate fellowship, to be allowed to go on to graduate school. I was also struggling with the whole idea of going to war to kill other young men whom I didn't know. The Korean War was underway and didn't have the same negative popular reaction that the Vietnam War suffered later. Nevertheless there was strong pacifist sentiment at Berea and convocation speakers presented various points of view. My brother, John, requested a pacifist classification which was denied by the rural Georgia draft board. He appealed and the case drug on for many months before it was finally denied. He had to refuse to take the oath of service, was "arrested" and finally, many more months later, was allowed to count work he had done after his graduation as "alternative service." But all this was in the future and unknown at the time.*

*I was torn between my Christian belief that "thou shalt not kill," and my sense of duty to my country. I admired the men who had fought in World War II and had the greatest respect for them, but was it right for me to take up arms against an enemy in Korea? I didn't need to decide right away because my request for educational deferment would take precedence and until that was resolved nothing else needed to be done. But I came to the decision that, when the time came, I would ask for a noncombatant classification where I could serve in some other way than carrying a gun. Of course, most assignments in the service are of this nature, but one had to declare oneself in advance.*

## Drama In Real Life

The spring term was different with Rose at home and Bill on the last stretch before graduation. They each wrote to the other almost every day. Rose would tell of her family, Mother Lochiel's condition and respond to Bill's reports on his doings, friends and the activities of campus, in addition to exchanges of endearments and wishes that they could be together. They were sorry to be apart but agreed it was the right thing to do. Rose did get to come to Berea for visits in late February, 1952 and again the third week in March.

*One weekend in March, neighbors who had a daughter at Berea College invited me to go up to Berea with them. I didn't like leaving Mama, but she seemed a little better and I really enjoyed seeing Bill and having a couple days in the dorm and at the Tab. When I returned home Mama seemed to be better but then took a turn for the worse. She continued to weaken and had to spend most of her days in bed. When she tired, her speech became blurred and she had difficulty swallowing. I gave her shots when she got really bad but they didn't continue to help. Finally she had to be taken to the hospital. They tried a new medication but were unable to help her and on March 29, 1952, she died. I called Bill from my aunt's house and he, Doris and another friend, Margaret Smith, came down by train and bus to be with me, Daddy and the boys for a couple days. Bill took some time to spend with Wayne, who was just 9 years old and feeling so lost. They weren't able to stay for the funeral, which was beautiful, but sad.*

106

*Our home seemed empty and lonely during the next weeks. The neighbors were wonderful. I was glad to have been home and had time with Mama and it was good to stay home and have time with my Dad and brothers. I was able to do special things with Wayne, who had a birthday in April. Wayne was a good student and did well at school and I helped him with his homework. We kept busy with house and garden – spring is planting time. Ken graduated from High School in mid-May and I served as his big sister through all the events. I was inspired by the baccalaureate speaker to live a life of service. I also had to serve as chaperone for Ken and his friend and their dates for a movie. Ken was noticing, Betty, one of the Smith girls across the road. Bill and I continued to write letters and make plans. Being absolutely committed to each other, by now we were really ready to be married, but knew we had to wait for the proper time.*

The fall major production, *Berkley Square* was scheduled for the first weekend in May and Rose was determined to go. Bill was director of the play, but not long before production one of the cast members had to drop out due to academic problems and Bill ended up filling in and Mama Scrivner took over as director. The show must go on! Bill's brother, Dick, played the major male role. Bill still had to do much of the set building and preparation with help from Dick, Norman Aich and others. Rose came to Berea on the bus and then Maude and Bill Hays along with Kenneth came up and she went home with them. The play had a good production and response. The time together was enough to cause Rose and Bill to begin to talk about a September wedding. It also increased their desire to be together, however uncertain the future. In Rose's letter of May 5, 1952, she said *"Together we can do anything!"* Bill's letter to her dated the same day observed, *"Perhaps you and I can help change this old world for the better!"*

Bill was not completely happy with the Marriage and Family class and they agreed it was just as well Rose didn't have to take it. Most of the readings talked of marriage as a sociological institution and dwelt on its potential problems. The young couple thought of marriage as a sacrament. They were anticipating life together with love, commitment, optimism and a sense of God's purpose for their lives. They would take the difficulties in stride together. Bill ended up with a B+ but Rose was sure they would have an A+ marriage – and they did. Rose planned to go to Berea to work in the summer and Bill would be in his internship until the end of August so Rose suggested September 7, 1952 as a wedding date.

*Bill wrote to his folks to tell them we had marriage plans and asked about my coming to his home with the family after graduation. I talked with my Dad. He did not want me to leave home, but understood and was supportive, as were other members of my family. Grandma Riggs said it was better to go ahead given the uncertainty of the times. Even so it was a very hard decision. I felt that I should take Mama's place in the house but wanted to get married. We finally decided that to put off marriage would only make the decision to leave home harder later on. I cried a lot but decided we could help the family better in the long run from our own marriage base.*

*Bill would work during the summer as an intern and then go on to Tuscaloosa, Alabama to begin classes at the University of Alabama. We would be married in September and I would either finish my course work at Berea or go with him to the University of Alabama and perhaps take my final education classes there. I hoped to finish my Elementary Education degree.*

*I went to Berea for Bill's graduation in late May 1952. Afterward we went home with his parents to Skyland farm in Lithia Springs, Georgia. It was a lovely place in the country; peaceful and quiet with lots of shrubs and flowers. Bill's parents and brothers, John and Dick, were there. They all made me feel very welcome. One evening we talked with Bill's parents about our plans and explained that we did not plan to buy an engagement ring, since we had very limited funds. Bill's romantic dad felt an engagement ring was important. Next day he took us shopping! We bought a set, not fancy but very pretty. That evening in the living room at the Lithia Springs farm home Bill put the ring on my finger. Now we had to get ready for a wedding.*

# CHAPTER 6

# MARRIAGE

In early June, 1952, Rose left Bill's home in Lithia Springs, Georgia and went to Berea to begin her summer work with Dean Charles Shutt, who was in charge of guidance, testing and counseling and for whom Rose had worked the previous summer and fall. He had agreed to let her work as a labor only student in the hope that she could resume her college course in the fall. Later in the summer, when a September wedding date had been set, Dean Shutt offered to provide the wedding reception, planning it with classmates, Gwen Lanier, Doris Graybeal and Margaret Smith. Modina Baker and Frances Abney from the candy kitchen helped Rose prepare for the wedding and served at the reception. "Pap" Adams at the college press helped get the invitations ready. Reverend Sanborne consulted on planning the ceremony. Two dorm friends helped make the wedding dress. Rose was so grateful for these generous friends who represented the Berea spirit that went well beyond just offering classes.

## Long Distance Romance

*I don't know what I would have done if it were not for my Berea friends. Bill was not here but did get to Berea on some weekends. To save money I had decided to make my wedding dress. I was staying in Fairchild Hall and two of the girls there offered to help. Modina and Frances took me shopping for material and other things. Lola Aaron, Betty McSween and some other dorm girls helped me make the wedding gown using dorm sewing machines. On one of Bill's visits we went to the florist shop and John Bill Allen, the local florist, helped us arrange for bouquets and decorations. We reserved Danforth Chapel for September 7 and talked to Reverend Sanborne about the ceremony. Bill and I decided, as former "Berea Players", we should memorize our vows instead of repeating them after the minister. Doris was to be my maid of honor. Bill's brother, John, was best man. Good friends from the Tab gang, Gwen Lanier and Norman Aich agreed to sing. My brothers and Bill's brother, Dick, served as ushers. Daddy was not at all sure he could be there or could walk me safely down the aisle. It was an emotional time for him. Someone heard him say that he had lost a wife and now was losing a daughter in the same year. Dean Shutt kindly offered to perform the father's role in his name. It is all a little blurry as I look back and it was like being in a dream at the time.*

Bill had gone to Tuscaloosa, Alabama, for a week of orientation at the University of Alabama's department of political science. The fellowship program officials had no problem with his planned marriage and he scouted housing options, college classes and job possibilities for Rose for the fall. He met his fellow students who were from Harvard and other prestigious schools. The fellows were interviewed by representatives from the agencies offering internships. Bill was much impressed with Paul Elza, Manager of Administration for the Oak Ridge Institute of Nuclear Studies, (ORINS) and he was delighted to be assigned to ORINS for his summer internship in Oak Ridge, Tennessee – not too far from Berea or Rose's home near Greeneville.

Bill went home to Lithia Springs for the weekend after orientation and had a meeting with his rural draft board in Douglasville on the following Monday. They were not sympathetic and declined to extend his educational deferment. They thought that four years of college were more than enough. This was not unexpected and an appeal was sent to the state board. A favorable decision was expected at that level. Then Bill left for Oak Ridge to begin his internship at ORINS on Tuesday.

*Oak Ridge was still in a transition stage from being a secret wartime facility to a more normal community. Security was still important with the uranium production plants in operation, but not at the level needed in wartime. The government owned everything, but was allowing the development of the usual commerce and social life of regular towns. I lived in a government dormitory, Charleston Hall. Most of the residents were workers at the production plants or Oak Ridge National Laboratory. The room was small and the building was terribly hot. I ate a lot of peanut butter sandwiches that summer.*

Bill's work at Oak Ridge went well. The Oak Ridge Institute of Nuclear Studies (ORINS) was a nonprofit corporation of Southern universities formed after World War II to provide a bridge between education and the nation's atomic energy program as it turned to the peaceful applications of nuclear energy in medicine, agriculture, industry, and power production. ORINS operated a hospital doing clinical research on nuclear medicine, special training programs in the uses of radioisotopes, graduate fellowships, research opportunities at national laboratories and the Museum of Atomic Energy and related outreach programs to schools and communities. Bill was assigned to work with the Manager of Administration, Paul Elza, and his staff on administrative matters. He visited and made reports on all divisions but his major project was to write a purchasing manual for the whole organization. Dr. William Pollard, a physicist, and later also an Episcopal priest, was the director and a wonderful leader. Bill learned about the inner workings of an organization by participating in matters of personnel, finance, facilities management and other administrative services necessary to run a public service organization. It was a very rich experience with talented and dedicated people. He made many new friends both at work and in the town and met several former Berea students.

*In addition to friends at ORINS and Berea connected friends, I met some new friends from the dormitories. One of these was Jay Reynolds who was planning to rent a house so his wife Joan, expecting their first child, could join him. Jay was an engineer working on the ORACLE (Oak Ridge Automatic Computer and Logical Engine). It was a huge computer covering an entire city block that could process data at great speeds using binary technology. University and other research scientists could schedule its use to process data in a matter of minutes or hours that would take forever or be impossible using traditional calculators. This was before the days of solid state so all the components were vacuum tubes and other devices that took up a lot of space and generated a lot of heat. Jay helped keep the machine running. Now a handheld device by our grandchildren has more memory and computing power than the ORACLE, but at that time it was a marvel. Almost three years later when Rose and I needed a temporary place to stay in the area Jay and Joan took us in.*

Rose and Bill both made budgets trying to save $200 by the end of summer. Rose was making $.50 per hour and would get a raise later in the summer to $.55. Bill had his stipend of $100 per month less withholdings. They had the wedding costs covered in their plans and included $75 for their honeymoon. By using a flat cake and miniature "wedding cake" to go with it they budgeted $14 for cakes. Friends and relatives loaned Rose a long slip, veil and other items. Flowers and bouquets were kept simple with the help of John Bill Allen. For the fall, housing at the University of Alabama would cost about $30 per month. Rose thought housing costs were reasonable and in a letter of June 13, 1952 suggested that Bill's stipend could pay the rent and leave about $45 for food. She planned to get a job and make her contribution. "I'll earn about $25 per week and we'll live in style!" They continued to converse daily through letters in which they shared their increasing desire to be married, their thoughts and dreams, along with practical planning. On the recommendation of Marie Haines who had been Rose's predecessor in the Tab costume room, they planned a, honeymoon at Fontana Village in North Carolina. They also made plans for their lives thereafter.

*I sent Rose a 'radioactive dime' from the Museum of Atomic Energy. I told her about my work and she told me about the many tests she had to give to upcoming freshmen. She learned to use a scoring machine and how to operate a mimeograph. She was also practicing typing. We planned for me to come to Berea over July 4-5. I had an extra day off and the 5th was her 21st birthday. A new friend and former Berea student, Tom Little, would come with me and drive his car. We arranged for him to "double date" with Peg (Margaret Smith) while we were there.*

*I had been advised by men in Charleston Hall that marriage was restricting and I would get tired of my wife. Rose, meanwhile, was told of the problems of marriage from the women's perspective by other girls. We both agreed that that was not what marriage was meant to be and wouldn't be true of ours. She said she felt sorry for those who didn't experience the kind of love, commitment and trust we had which made you a better person. I observed in a letter that she was "my pal, my cohort, my sweetheart, and almost my wife."*

Bill and Tom spent a couple days in Berea over the fourth of July. Then on the next weekend Bill hitch hiked to Chattanooga so he could join his parents at a union gathering at the Mt Lookout Hotel, which later became Covenant College.

*I saved bus fare by catching rides but then had to take a taxi to get to Lookout Mountain in time for the banquet that Dad and Mother had asked me to attend. It cost $4.50 but Dad reimbursed me. The desk clerk gave me a room key when I checked in and I dashed up to the room and set my little suitcase on the bed, noticing that the room had signs of occupancy, but assumed it was adjoining my parents' room. I washed my face and rushed down to the banquet. We sat across from a union official from Texas, his wife and daughter, who was about my age. When she went to her room she found my suitcase and her father opened it to find men's clothes. The clerk's mistake was soon straightened out but everyone at the convention soon heard about it, with all kinds of embellishments, and both the girl and I, along with our parents, took a lot of ribbing. Some people thought it was a very romantic beginning for two young people, but I was already committed and we survived the ordeal in good spirits.*

The commitment and devotion each had for each other and their views on the seriousness of marriage is reflected in their letters repeatedly. In a letter dated July 9, 1952 Bill wrote:

*"I love you, Rose, and realize more and more all the time how much you mean to me. My love for you is much deeper than romance. I depend on my love for you and your love for me. It is one of the best securities I feel I have. I feel what you feel. I experience what you experience. I wish I could express my feeling for you better, but I can't and that is part of the feeling – something beyond verbal expression. All I can say is I love you and I am yours forever."*

In her letter of July 15 to Bill, Rose reported that her brother Ken had purchased a new watch which she felt was more expensive than he could afford and reflected on the upbringing and training of children.

*"Oh, sweetheart, what a responsibility it is to raise children and make them independent, capable of thinking for themselves, and give them the right start in life. I'm glad we both realize that. And we must not only teach the right*

*things we must practice them. Darling, let's be parents like your parents. Let's work to help ourselves and each other grow into people worthy of being parents. We can't do it alone, honey, so we must put our faith in God and completely rely on Him to guide us."*

## Hedda Goes To A Wedding

Bill had completed reservations for the honeymoon at Fontana but they had not finished exploring ways to get there. Rose didn't want anyone to drive them and they were seeking possible loans of a car from family. Finally the problem was solved.

*Realizing we needed transportation not just for the honeymoon, but for use in Oak Ridge, trips between Oak Ridge and Berea and Rose's home, and for our life after the wedding, I bought a car. A friend of brother John's at Warren Wilson College had a 1939 Plymouth coupe that was serviceable, cute and inexpensive, so I purchased it. It was green and had only one seat and an enormous trunk behind. I felt like I'd reached adulthood to have my own car. I drove it to Berea on the first weekend of August. Rose and I named it "Hedda" after the play Hedda Gabler.*

*The car made it possible for me to join Rose in mid-August at home in Lithia Springs where Mother and Dad had planned two showers for Rose. I had to go back to Oak Ridge but Rose stayed on until the end of the week and then Dad arranged for her to fly to Knoxville on Friday and I picked her up and we drove together to her home in Greene County. I went back to Oak Ridge after the weekend and then returned to pick up Rose the next weekend to travel to Berea for the final week before the wedding. The Sanbornes had graciously offered to house Rose and then both of us when I returned the next week, having completed my internship at ORINS.*

In the middle of all this moving about getting ready for the wedding, Bill was notified that his appeal requesting an educational deferment from the draft had been denied. So he requested noncombatant classification. This also was denied by the local board after Bill had appeared before them to make his case on the basis of conscience. The policies of the Methodist

Church did not require conscientious objection to serving in the military but affirmed and supported it as a legitimate choice. He appealed the decision and at the next level was granted the classification 1A0. This is what headed him to the Medical Corps when he was called for duty, which turned out to be October 8, 1952 – one month and a day after the wedding date. Rose and Bill had more adjustments to make.

The summer had come to a close. Rose had finished her work. Bill finished his internship. He reported his impending military service to the officials of his graduate fellowship, realizing that they would not be able to go to the University of Alabama as planned. They cancelled his enrollment and graciously indicated that he should notify them when he was close to the end of his service and he could likely complete his fellowship after that. Decisions on the future would have to wait. A wedding was the immediate priority as Bill remembers.

*Reverend Sanborne or "Sandy" and his wife Marion had offered us a place to stay for the days before the wedding. They also hosted the rehearsal dinner. Having known them from the time of Patty's wedding in 1948 and then during their residence in Berea at the Union Church parsonage on Prospect Street, we were well acquainted with the family. Their children, Kathy, David, Elizabeth and Nancy were like younger cousins. Marion kept us fed and helped with last minute details. Mother and Dad, John and Dick, Patty and Earl all arrived. Where everybody stayed is lost to our memories but we were surrounded by family and friends. The wedding was scheduled for 2:00 PM. Organ music, played by a classmate and local girl, Anita Purkey, started the ceremony. My part, as with most grooms, was not complicated. I entered from a side door to the front of the chapel with the minister and John. Then we waited.*

Rose's part was, of course, more complicated.

*Strangely I wasn't nervous. I was in the rest room next to the chapel in Draper Building. It was used as the dressing room for weddings. Doris was with me and Modina was helping me with my gown, etc. I wondered if all my family was there and someone told me they were. Friends from home, Maude and*

*Bill Hayes, had driven Daddy and the boys up from Tennessee. Bart and Letha Kilday with my cousin Norma Jean also came from home. I wished Mama could have been here. The chapel was full of friends from the faculty, staff and classmates who were still around in addition to our families. When everything was ready Doris and I moved to the back of the chapel with our bouquets. Doris, looking beautiful, walked down the aisle first as the music played. Then it was my turn. On Dean Shutt's arm I processed. I could see Bill waiting for me in the front. Dean Shutt presented me "in the name of her father," and then we were standing before the minister together. The songs sung by Gwen Lanier and Norman Aich were lovely, we remembered our lines without faltering, the minister said the beautiful words of the marriage ceremony with scriptures and prayer, we exchanged rings and finally were pronounced man and wife.*

One can't help but wonder if, in addition to the assembled friends and families, there was not an unseen congregation present at this worshipful celebration – a "cloud of witnesses," including Mother Lochiel, Fleeners, Romigs, Moores, Kildays, Ramsays, Riggs, Martins and Thompsons. From their eternal perspective they would see not only a culmination of their earthly lives in this marriage but the promise of generations to come.

The reception was in the Fireside Room right next to the chapel with Dean Shutt as host and Modina and Frances serving. Everyone was full of good wishes and the couple felt very much supported. As the reception came to an end Bill and Rose prepared to leave in Hedda for Fontana Village, North Carolina where they had reservations for their honeymoon. They had already packed and just had to change clothes. Meanwhile the brothers and classmates led by Patty's husband, Earl, were decorating the car. Earl remembered four years before when Bill had been instrumental in doing the same thing at their wedding.

*Poor Hedda had writing on fenders, windows and doors with white shoe polish or something expressing the usual messages about newlyweds. And there were tin cans tied to the rear. When we finally said our goodbyes and got in the car I turned the ignition key. Instead of a starter sound there was a whistle and a loud bang and smoke belched from under the hood. One look at Earl's face was all that was needed to know it was a prank. It took a while to get the smoke cleared away and get the car started. Then the caravan began. They followed us all through town blowing horns and shouting. Trying to escape I turned up a side street only to find it was a dead end. A woman hanging clothes in her yard threw up her hands in amazement as the whole line of cars jammed up behind. I got turned around and made it back down the street. The others caught up before long and followed us half way to Mt. Vernon. At one point someone with a more powerful car pulled around us and got in front and then slowed to a crawl. When they gave up and turned back to Berea it was getting late and we had a long way to go but now it was just us two.*

They arrived at Fontana well after dark, pretty tired after the events of the day and the long drive. Their little cabin had a kitchenette, bedroom and bath. It was a precious home for those days. They made most meals at the cabin eating out a few times. Marie Haines was working there and they got to visit her. They took hikes, they boated and enjoyed the time alone with each other. Their new life together had begun. A new marriage was born!

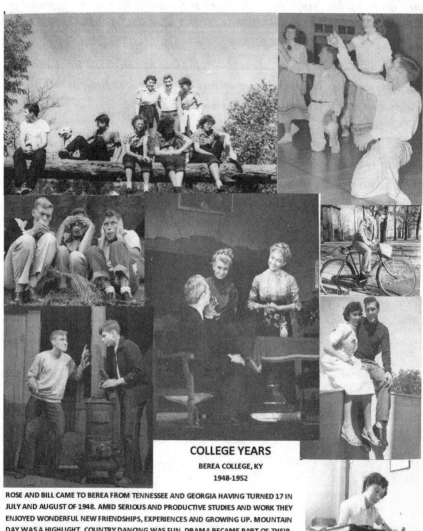

## COLLEGE YEARS
### BEREA COLLEGE, KY
### 1948-1952

ROSE AND BILL CAME TO BEREA FROM TENNESSEE AND GEORGIA HAVING TURNED 17 IN JULY AND AUGUST OF 1948. AMID SERIOUS AND PRODUCTIVE STUDIES AND WORK THEY ENJOYED WONDERFUL NEW FRIENDSHIPS, EXPERIENCES AND GROWING UP. MOUNTAIN DAY WAS A HIGHLIGHT. COUNTRY DANCING WAS FUN. DRAMA BECAME PART OF THEIR LIVES. ROSE WAS MARTHA IN *ARSENIC AND OLD* LACE AND BILL PLAYED AN OLD SHIPS STEWARD WITH HIS BROTHER DICK AS CABIN BOY IN A ONE ACT PLAY. THEY HAD TIME FOR COURTING AND FALLING IN LOVE. ROSE HELPED BILL AT THE *WALLPAPER* OFFICE WHERE BILL FINALLY PROPOSED AND PLANS WERE MADE FOR A FUTURE TOGETHER.

118

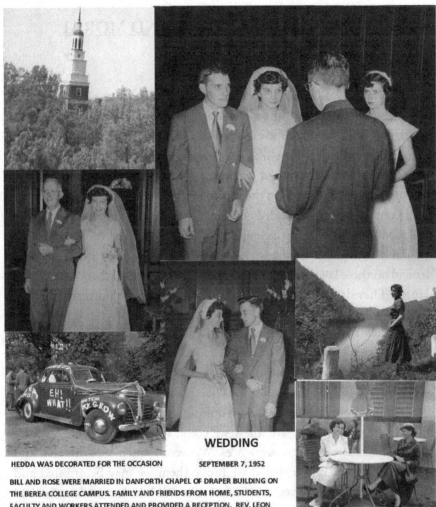

## WEDDING

**HEDDA WAS DECORATED FOR THE OCCASION**

**SEPTEMBER 7, 1952**

BILL AND ROSE WERE MARRIED IN DANFORTH CHAPEL OF DRAPER BUILDING ON THE BEREA COLLEGE CAMPUS. FAMILY AND FRIENDS FROM HOME, STUDENTS, FACULTY AND WORKERS ATTENDED AND PROVIDED A RECEPTION. REV. LEON SANBORNE OFFICIATED. DEAN CHARLES SHUTT, ROSE'S STYDENT LABOR SUPERVISOR, ESCORTED HER DOWN THE AISLE AND PRESENTED HER IN THE NAME OF HER FATHER. WHO WAS AFRAID HE COULDN'T MAKE IT DOWN THE AISLE. ROSE'S BROTHERS WERE THERE WITH A COUSIN AND FRIENDS. BILL'S PARENTS AND SISTER'S FAMILY WERE PRESENT, HIS BROTHER JOHN WAS BEST MAN AND DICK WAS AN USHER WITH ROSE'S BROTHER KEN. ROSE'S ROOMMATE DORIS GRAYBEAL WAS MAID OF HONOR. OTHER STUDENT FRIENDS SANG AND PLAYED THE ORGAN.

BILL AND ROSE HAD A HONEYMOON AT FONTANA LAKE VILLAGE, NC. THEN MOTHER AND DAD RAMSAY TOOK THEM ON A TRIP TO WASHINGTON AND NEW YORK. ROSE AND MOTHER RAMSAY BECAME VERY CLOSE.

# REFLECTIONS 6

## LAWS: NATURAL, CIVIL AND MORAL

As we grew and studied and experienced life as young adults we were aware that one had to deal with the question of rules and laws and customs. By what standards would we live our lives and make our choices. We had learned basic physical laws like the law of gravity when we jumped off a garage roof holding a raised umbrella, expecting to float down like we later saw Mary Poppins do in the movie of that name. We knew fire could burn you and water in a sealed container, unless a pressure cooker, would explode when heated past the boiling point. And we had been taught other natural laws of physics, chemistry, astronomy and mathematics. You could depend on these laws and if you ignored them or violated them you were in danger. These laws, established by the Creator, hold our universe together.

We also learned to conform to behavior expected in different settings. We didn't shout "Praise the Lord!" in a Quaker meeting nor did we panic when someone did just that in a Pentecostal church. We were respectful of others and obeyed rules set by our parents and schools and college. We were taught about righteousness and unrighteousness, beauty and ugliness, honesty and dishonesty. We knew we could disobey and, when we did, learned that there were consequences. We were acquainted with civil and criminal laws and knew that if we broke them we may be arrested and face penalties. We observed that violating moral laws was as dangerous as violating natural laws. We questioned what happens if civil laws or customs conflicted with moral laws? What is the source of authority for laws?

When editor of the student newspaper, I wrote a piece on expediency and morality arguing that ultimately morality was the only really expedient thing. Conduct and choices that were not in accordance with moral laws eventually lead to destruction. I was a young idealistic student and specifically had in mind equal treatment of people of other races. I have learned with passing years that my thesis was a bit simplistic, but I still believe that in the end moral choices lead to good and wrong choices lead to problems, whatever the immediate consequences may be. We have seen a lot of suffering because of bad choices and seen a lot of joy in the wake of good choices.

Besides dealing with questions of right and wrong in race relations, young men of my generation had to deal with the issue of the draft and the competing values of serving one's country and taking up arms against other human beings. At a level closer to daily life we constantly were confronted with rules with which we may not agree, with peer pressure to "go along with the crowd," with unfairness, with temptations to cheat and all the other perils of navigating the river of life. Over time we have made some observations.

First is the recognition that there is a Creator who has established rules for his creation. Some of these rules are discovered as natural laws. Knowing what they are man has been able to construct airplanes that fly, boats that sail the ocean, generating plants that give us electricity, build automobiles and highways, put a man on the moon and on and on. All these things are based on discoveries of laws already in place. We didn't make them but simply discovered them.

We have no doubt that God established moral laws as well which man continues to try to discover and understand. Civilization is based on consideration of these laws and some of them have been expressed in human "rules" and been accepted generally as essential for any society to survive and flourish. Murder is unacceptable. Not telling the truth makes justice and effective communications impossible. Stealing undermines security and stability. Unfaithfulness destroys dependable relationships. Every society seems to recognize these truths. The experience and inspiration of the Israelites over centuries gave us the Ten Commandments recorded in the Bible. The teachings and life of Jesus, also recorded in the Bible, gave deeper insight into what is expected of mankind. It is to love our Creator God and each other. How simple and yet how complex and profound.

Our second basic observation is that mankind was given freedom of choice from the very beginning and each person can and must still choose how to live. The "original sin" was when the first man and woman listened to the tempter and decided they could decide for themselves what is good and evil rather than seeking to follow God's laws. That continues to be the basic struggle of mankind. Through all history attempts have been made to construct the perfect society by man-made laws. They have all failed miserably with many tragic casualties. In our lifetime we have seen Hitler, Stalin, Mao and others delude people and then force them into submission in the name of a better society. Yet we continue to seek the perfect set of laws, programs, institutions, movements, etc. without reference to God's laws. The foundation of America had many economic, political and social reasons, but was unique in acknowledging its source of legitimacy and authority as greater than man himself.

Why does mankind continue down the path of trying to make its own rules rather than discovering the universal rules of God? One of the reasons is that some believe that we are all born "good" and it is our society that corrupts us. They don't believe in a devil or in original sin and mankind is only "fallen" because we haven't quite got it right yet. And, of course, since they don't believe in sin they don't need a "savior" and refuse to accept Christ as more than a good man and wise teacher. How anyone who has raised children, or looked at themselves honestly, comes to the conclusion that we are innately good is beyond us. We are capable of great good and we are called to strive for the good, but we also have the seeds of evil in us. Which master will we serve? We are free to choose.

Another misguided assumption is that we "are just made that way" and are not responsible for our actions, or we excuse the action of others, because it is the fault of someone else or of society in general, or because of our genetics or circumstances. We want to be free to make choices but if they are bad ones and we suffer consequences, or are about to, we want to blame someone or something else. This recognizes that we are capable of doing wrong but excuses us as having no choice. As our son Billy said when caught in a rule violation, "Somebody big shouldn't have let me do it!" Or, even worse, we want to change the rules so what we do is not considered bad at all. As noted psychiatrist Dr. Karl Menninger asked in the title of one of his books, "Whatever Became of Sin?" How can we deal with our faults if we refuse to see them as faults? We must have a standard against which we measure right and wrong and our behavior. These standards are found in God's laws, not in our own attempts to define what is right and wrong. Relativism leads to "might makes right" and chaos.

Getting back to our questions of authority and the relationship of legality and morality, we firmly believe that ultimate authority belongs to God. His moral laws are foundational. Civil and criminal laws, ideally, should reflect His moral laws, but they sometimes do not. How many years passed before laws supporting slavery were declared wrong? It took a civil war and sacrifice of lives before the laws and custom were corrected. Even then the civil rights struggle continued into our era where we had segregation laws which we finally, as a nation, admitted were wrong. Some, like Martin Luther King, Jr., who believed in a moral law having precedence over civil law, were willing to openly violate the unrighteous laws and willingly submit themselves to penalties in order to demonstrate their belief – and they prevailed.

As our society becomes more secular and removed from acknowledging God and universal moral laws we see a growing attitude that what is legal is moral. Unethical, immoral behavior is excused because "it's not illegal!" We should live to a higher standard. In a wonderful passage from Anthony Trollope's book *The Duke's Children,* the duke writes to his son, who is off at college and has reported that he is behaving and not in trouble with the law:

*"Do you recognize no duty but what the laws impose on you? Should you be disposed to eat and drink in bestial excess, because the laws would not hinder you? Should you lie and sleep all the day, the law would say nothing! Should you neglect every duty which your position imposes on you, the law could not interfere! To such a one as you the law can be no guide. You should so live as not to come near to the law, - or to have the law come near to you. From all evil against which the law bars you, you should be barred, at an infinite distance, by honour, by conscience, and nobility. Does the law require patriotism,*

*philanthropy, self-abnegation, public service, purity of purpose, devotion to*
*the needs of others who have been placed in the world below you? The law is a*
*great thing, - because men are poor and weak and bad. And it is great, because*
*where it exists in its strength no tyrant can be above it. But between you and*
*me there should be no mention of law as the guide of conduct. Speak to me of*
*honour, of duty, and of nobility; and tell me what they require of you".*

Will you be satisfied with simply being legal or will you strive for a higher
standard? Will you recognize your capacities for both good and evil and
seek to express the good and restrain the evil? Will you admit that you
have faults and sometimes fail? Will you accept the grace and sacrifice of
a loving God as you seek to do His will, loving Him and your fellow men?

# REFLECTIONS 7

## CRITICAL THINKING

We have noticed that decisions are often made by people, whether policy makers, judges, scientists or just individuals, based primarily on feelings, preconceptions, political positions, opinions, peer pressure or other such influences rather than on careful weighing of evidence, facts and application of logic. Nor are many decisions made after seeking inspiration through prayer or study of the wisdom of history as expressed in scripture or writings of thinkers and scholars. Once made the subjective decision is rationalized by selecting facts, writings, and reasons to support it and make it appear logical. It doesn't mean the decisions so made are wrong, but that they were not made by "critical thinking." Rationalization after the fact is the reverse of so called scientific reasoning where conclusions supposedly follow facts and evidence. Children are very good at using this reverse kind of reasoning to get what they want. A whole culture can do it as well. Years of justification of slavery and then segregation serve as an example of our human ability to rationalize our desires and preconceptions. To complicate matters many cases are complex, with incomplete information and competing evidence and absence of clarity. Yet decisions and choices must be made. No choice is **a** choice itself.

In school we were urged to become "critical thinkers." In working with student interns, we encouraged them to think critically. But what does this mean? First let us look at what it does not mean. It does not mean criticizing. It does not mean just pointing out what is perceived as the mistakes of others. It does not mean simply discrediting others or history or historical figures by finding that there are some flaws in recorded accounts. It does not mean "demythologizing." Yet we have noted among some scholars and teachers and many media types that they love to criticize, to find sensation, to discover scandal, to tear down reputations or beliefs, all in the name of "scholarship" or "news," without really seeking the full truth and without offering insight. Making it even more difficult is the growing notion that truth is trumped by feelings and depends on what one wants rather than what is real. Once in a graduate school accounting class the teacher ridiculed a student for a wrong answer and he responded, "That's a matter of opinion." Everyone laughed. I'm not sure they would today.

We want to be critical thinkers, fair and honest and wise, but we all have "world views," as the late Chuck Colson defined our basic set of beliefs, so we all have biases. As critical thinkers we should try to be objective, to listen and examine evidence, to avoid jumping to conclusions or be influenced by peer pressure or worry about what others will think. But we can't completely set aside our basic beliefs so it is best to admit them and be willing to examine how they bear on our thinking. If we don't believe some things are true and some untrue, some things right and some things wrong, some things beautiful and some ugly, we have no rudders to guide our thinking and must just flounder about or head in a direction which leads nowhere or to destruction. We pray for wisdom with humility rather than knowledge with conceit, for honesty with love rather than cleverness with malice and for being able to make judgments about behavior without being judgmental in terms of people's souls.

# REFLECTIONS 8

## PACIFISM

One of the difficult issues to reflect upon is that of the use of force, even in the pursuit of justice or protection of self or others. Self-defense is a right generally accepted in legal and moral systems. The use of force to protect others is often considered heroism. The control by force, if necessary, of those who are a threat to society is an accepted role of law enforcement, the penal system and governments. What are the constraints on the use of force, by individuals, by law enforcement, by governments? Who determines how much force is appropriate? Is killing another person ever justified? Is there such a thing as a "just war?" These questions are not new and have been pondered by philosophers, theologians and other thinkers for centuries.

It is different when a young man is confronted with the question personally. In a physical confrontation calling for a reaction using force, the response is somewhat automatic. When called to put oneself in the position of using deadly force it is another matter. Young men of my generation faced this call during the Korean conflict as others have at other times of war. It is a question those who feel called to law enforcement or security positions must face. On the one hand we know that taking the life of another is wrong. "Thou shalt not kill." Clearly murder is a sin and a crime. On the other hand taking responsibility for the protection and safety of others is right and sometimes that calls for the use of lethal force. How does one reconcile the two, sometimes conflicting, principles?

When called to register for the draft a response is required by the law. In America the law provides for individual conscientious objection to military service on the basis of religious faith. Some religious groups, like the Quakers, call for such a stand. Others like the Seventh Day Adventist allow military service but support noncombatant status. Mainline churches generally set forth no requirement but support individual decisions to serve or not to serve. As a college student I was temporarily relieved of military service by an educational deferment, but knew the time would come when I would have to declare myself on this issue.

Berea in the early 1950's included many of the Quaker persuasion who advocated pacifism. Convocations were presented about the issue describing the choices. Some speakers pointed to the evils of war and others proclaimed the responsibilities of citizenship. It was just a few years since the end of World War II and almost everyone considered the men who had fought in that conflict to be heroes who had responded to their country's call to a "just war." Was the Korean War a just war? Who decides and on what basis? Should an individual take a position at variance with his country's leadership? Does the admonition to "love your enemies" apply to nations, or make exception for those rightfully responsible for the safety and protection of others, using force if necessary? When is force necessary?

The Catholic Church over the centuries has articulated the concept of "just war" very carefully and their principles made a lot of sense to me. Their position starts with a call on all authorities for the avoidance of war if at all possible but goes on to state that it is sometimes necessary to use force to achieve justice and protect those for whom the legitimate authorities have responsibility. It recognizes that individuals may renounce all violence, but those responsible for justice and protection of others may not do so if required as a last resort after all nonviolent efforts have failed.

"Just War" standards require that acts of war, to be just, must not inflict evil for its own sake, must be done with proper intentions for justice and to restrain evil, and must be appropriate to the circumstances, not imprudent or rash. The threat of the aggressor must be real with serious effects and all other means of dealing with it must have been ineffective. The success of armed resistance must be possible. The harm done should be less than the evil to be resisted. In addition there are considerations of the type and extent of force to be used, the avoidance of harm to innocents in the process, and humane treatment of all. Decisions must always rest with the legitimate authority. In America the civil authorities and not the military make the decisions to go to war or not.

Assuming the war is just and decisions have been made by proper authorities, the personal question remains. What is right for me in response to a call to fight for my country? I didn't feel I should fail to serve but I didn't feel right about killing young men from another country, who probably, like me, had no personal animosity and would simply be carrying out orders. I was familiar with guns and a good shot but, as an idealistic young man, the idea of deliberately killing another human being was against my beliefs, So, I chose to request a noncombatant role where I could serve by helping save lives instead of taking them. Chances were that I would never have had to go to the front lines with a weapon anyway and might be more likely to be sent to the front as a medic than as a foot soldier. But I had to declare myself. I have great respect for those who did not so choose or for those who felt they couldn't serve in a war in any capacity. Each person must choose for himself or herself.

Going through basic training I had to do all the marches, bivouacs and other exercises, but without a weapon. I watched as the men were issued weapons and acted like they were handed new toys. I winced as they learned to attach a bayonet and thrust it with a yell into a dummy. To most of them it seemed a game and they were being conditioned to act like a team and to win at any cost. I can understand why this is necessary. I heard talk about the accuracy and range of guns tested by soldiers who had been in war zones and engaged in target practice on non-soldiers who were walking below their position on a hill. Not all soldiers are noble, but many are. I learned that most firing of weapons is not to hit a particular target but to spray the field with bullets killing any of the enemy who were advancing. I knew that most killing is impersonal by means of artillery, bombs, grenades and land mines. How many of our troops have been killed or maimed by buried explosive devices, grenade launchers and guided missiles? It sounds horrible and it is. As Civil War General Sherman stated years ago, "War is hell!" Yet some seem to make it necessary as they try to impose their will on others by force. World War II seemed clearly a just war for the allies and an unjust war for the axis powers.

Looking back I still think requesting a noncombatant status was the right decision for me at that time, but having acquired responsibilities for a wife and family, I'm a little less sure what is right for a person to do when faced with evil. If someone threatened those for whom I am responsible and the only way I could remove the threat was through force, and I had the power to use it, I would. I would try to follow the principles of the "just war" theory.

I have little patience with those pacifists who maintain that if we wouldn't fight, the enemy wouldn't either. No, there is evil in the world. Sometimes it must be confronted with force. It can be confronted with good but may require sacrifice. Unless you are willing to give up your life for your beliefs and to allow others to suffer, you are not a true pacifist. I try to be a peacemaker and pray I am never confronted with the need to use violence against another. I would not make a good policeman, but I think I could and should use force, if I was able, if it was required to protect those for who I am responsible. I like to think I could lay down my life for others if that were required, but I would first try to prevent injury to them, by force if necessary, if I had the power.

# PART FOUR

*Moves, Moves and More Moves*

# CHAPTER 7

# ARMY MEDIC

For the next three years Bill and Rose were never in one location for more than a few months at a time, except for one stretch when Rose stayed at the Lithia Springs home while Bill was stationed at the Fort McPherson Third Army Headquarters hospital in Atlanta. But by the time two years passed, the Korean War was ended, military service was over, General Eisenhower had been elected President and Bill's and Rose's family was started with a son, William Edward (Bill E.) born in November, 1953, Another year and the graduate program was completed and they had added a daughter, Laura Elizabeth in December 1954. During this time the strong support of Mother and Dad Ramsay was always there along with love and help from other family and friends along the way.

Right after their honeymoon Bill was notified to report for induction into the United States Army on October 8, 1952. They had a month of marriage after the wedding before the two were again separated. In one of her letters while Bill was getting situated in the Army, Rose observed that "We seem to spend more time writing each other letters than being together." But before Bill's entering military service they had a whole month together.

*A honeymoon is never long enough but after our time at Fontana, Rose and I were able to continue to be together for the rest of September and the first week of October. We wouldn't be going to the University of Alabama in the fall and had a little time before reporting for military duty. We went to Warren Wilson College where John was teaching and Mother and Dad were visiting as they began a trip to Washington and New York. They invited us to go with them and we gladly and gratefully accepted the offer, so we travelled north, leaving Hedda with John. Rose had only been out of Tennessee to its bordering states of*

*North Carolina, Georgia and Kentucky so it was a new experience for her. We visited the capitol and Supreme Court buildings in Washington and in New York went up to the observation floor of the Empire State Building and saw the other sights of the city. We enjoyed the trip immensely. It was like a second honeymoon, and Rose was bonding with Mother in a special way. Then we came back to Warren Wilson, Mother and Dad went home to Skyland Farm and Rose and I drove Hedda to visit Rose's family in East Tennessee before returning to Georgia. Then I prepared to report for duty.*

Rose vividly remembers the day of parting on October 8, 1952.

*Mother and I drove Bill to Douglasville where he and a group of other inductees gathered to start the process of becoming enlisted men. We went back home where I cried and cried. Mother tried to console me and showed me pictures of Bill as a baby. I cried even more and told her I wished I were pregnant. I poured out my feelings in a letter that afternoon, but it was never sent because, after induction, the men were told to go home and report back the next day for transportation to Fort Jackson, South Carolina. What a wonderful surprise to have one more chance to be together. Somehow it made the parting the next day less painful. Bill arrived at Fort Jackson on October 9 and wrote to me almost daily telling me what was happening. I wrote a letter to him every day although he had no address yet and I didn't get to send my letters until two weeks later on October 22. We did manage a couple phone calls during that time.*

At Fort Jackson, Bill and the other men were issued uniforms and other gear, tested, examined, given shots, and received basic orientation to army life. Private William Romig Ramsay's identification number is US53131430 and he had to memorize it right away. He did well on basic tests and was given the test for potential officers, which he also passed. He scored especially well on the "codes" test and was considered for the Signal Corps but his IAO classification and interest in being a care giver directed his assignment to the US Army Medical Corps. On October 17 he was sent to Camp Pickett near Blackstone, Virginia to begin basic training – first eight weeks of infantry training and then eight weeks of basic medic training. A number of his new companions were Seventh

Day Adventists whose church called for noncombat service but most of the men were not noncombatants. Many of the men who entered training with him had not completed high school, much less had any advanced education, and Bill always felt sorry for them because all the opportunities for further training or "good" assignments went to those, like himself, who had already received the advantages of good education. For example, all the guys could drive but a written drivers test was given and most failed it. For a college graduate it was simple. So Bill became a driver and followed the troops driving an ambulance on some marches instead of having always to walk. Some of the less educated men went to Korea immediately after completion of basic training and were wounded or killed. After his service was over and it became financially possible, Bill always supported wounded veterans charities in memory of these fellow soldiers.

Meanwhile on the home front Rose was more and more becoming part of the family. She became fond of Dr. Witherspoon Dodge (Doc), a minister and leader in social issues who worked with father John Ramsay on the National Religion and Labor Council. Doc was staying at Skyland Farm. He wrote a book of his experiences as an itinerant minister in the South titled, *Southern Rebel In Reverse.* The presidential election was approaching and Rose, along with the family, was staunchly for Adlai Stevenson. Her letters include quotes form Stevenson and his supporters emphasizing the desire for world peace. The fear of nuclear war with Russia was on everyone's minds.

Rose received her final check from her summer work at Berea and wrote that she had deposited it in the bank, bringing their balance to $70.48. She wrote, "I feel much more secure!" Some of their funds had to go to repairs for Hedda, but later a small Army dependent's allocation (about $50 per month} began to arrive and that helped.

## Separation, Travel and Training

Dad, Mother, Doc and Rose traveled together on CIO and Religion and Labor Council business to Columbus, Ohio, where they stayed with Patty and Earl Todt. Rose loved playing with the two children, David who was between two and three. Susan was just beginning to say words, but could express herself eloquently with grunts and her large soft brown eyes. Aunt Rose became a favorite of little Susan. Later when she pretended to be Aunt Rose, David told her she couldn't be because her feet weren't big enough. Rose's letters began to make more and more references to having a family. With the Todts she saw many of the natural and historic sites in Ohio, including, Ash Cave and Indian mounds. Ever since her introduction to classical and semi-classical music at Berea she continued to enjoy it and listen to it when she could, which she did at the Todts. Dad Ramsay liked to play canasta and Rose enjoyed watching and listening to the banter during games.

*On the trip back to Georgia Dad had some business in Greeneville, Tennessee, regarding reported Communist activity of concern to the union and the community. I was able to go home and stay overnight. I fixed a special meal for Daddy, Ken and Wayne and visited Maude and Bill Hayes. I advised my family that I was planning to go on a trip west with Mother and Dad Ramsay. They would have liked me to stay with them and, again, I was torn between conflicting responsibilities and opportunities. When we got back to Lithia Springs, I had a letter from Bill giving me his Camp Pickett address and I could send all the letters I'd written every day since he went away.*

*Before we left on the trip west, which was planned to end at the CIO convention in California in mid-November, Dad arranged some meetings in Virginia and said they would "take Rose to see Bill." I was thrilled. Bill was able to get a weekend pass and together we went with Mother and Dad to Virginia Beach. I saw the ocean for the first time. I also saw Bill in uniform for the first time and I thought he was cute! We talked about my moving to Virginia and getting a job in Petersburg or Richmond so we could be together at least some weekends. Otherwise it would be Christmas before we would see each other and it looked like Bill would only have one day off then.*

Rose had written in her letter to Bill of October 30, 1952.

*"I miss you so. Five weeks until I can see you — five years — five centuries — five lifetimes! We're married and we love each other. It is only natural and right*

136

*that we want to live together have our own home, have our family, build and plan for the future. But because of selfishness, greed, pride and lack of Christian feelings, there are armies, heartaches, separation and loneliness...."*

Bill was getting into basic training and doing well. He was in much better physical condition than many of the other men and had no trouble with daily calisthenics, drills, chores and marches, although he got tired. He met a classmate, David Auxier, who was in the next company and met the brother of another classmate, Sherrill Bastian, who was finishing training and scheduled to go to Korea or Japan. He made friends with Roger Lilly from Ohio and they remained friends throughout the years. The cultures represented in the barracks were quite interesting ranging from the illiterate to the highly educated, the rural and the urban, Yankee and Rebel, all racial types and differing tastes in food, entertainment and music. One Southern country guy played loud country music on his radio trying to drown out the opera being played by an Ivy League graduate across the aisle. Some gambled while a few played bridge. Most didn't think very deeply about policies, philosophy or war. Bill wrote on October 31:

*"They issued 'weapons' (guns and knives) last night. I'm glad I don't have to carry any. It is a terrible sight to see these men so happy to get a rifle. They are just like children with new toys. Most of them never realize the cold facts of war and killing.... It is pitiful."*

Rose, with Mom and Dad Ramsay, embarked on their trip west. Rose's letters, mostly written in the back seat of the car, are full of descriptions of the countryside. She reveled in the changing landscapes from hills, across the Mississippi to plains and deserts in Texas and New Mexico. Blue skies and limitless horizons, gorgeous sunsets, dark mesas, lush irrigated fields, cowboys on horses and cattle, the Grand Canyon, starlit heavens over the vast land, all enthralled her and made her feel the presence and grandeur of God. It also made her want desperately to share the experience with Bill and increased her loneliness. She was also depressed by the outcome of the presidential election and felt that the less fortunate people would suffer and the country faced a greater risk of world war. She expressed her feelings about both her wonder at God's creation and her loneliness and discouragement but assured Bill that she was really not depressed because they loved each other and looked forward to a future together. She gave details of their travels including a frightening incident on the way to Santa Fe.

*"I almost got gassed! We had adjoining rooms and each room had a gas heater. I kept mine on pretty late, sitting up writing and had the door between our rooms closed. I couldn't raise my window. I turned the heater off when I went to bed and woke up early with a headache but went back to sleep. Later Daddy and Mother got up and Daddy came in to light my heater. About an hour later Mother came to wake me and said the gas smelled bad. I hadn't smelled anything, but I had a cold. My head still ached but I hopped out of bed and got into my housecoat and went in to take a bath. I was starting to brush my teeth when I began to get deathly sick and my head started to whirl. I knew I must get to Mother and Daddy's room. I dropped my toothbrush and got to their room and grabbed the foot of their bed. I remember saying, "I'm sick!" and Daddy catching me. Then I blacked out. The next thing I remember was Mother's voice saying, "Take a deep breath! Take a deep breath!" They had turned off the gas and opened up the door and windows. The cold air snapped me out of it and I lay on their bed and gradually recovered, but my headache didn't go away until noon".*

The morning after this incident, as they were traveling in New Mexico they heard that Phillip Murray, President of the CIO, had died on November 9, 1952. Phil Murray was Dad Ramsay's leader, fellow Christian and close friend. He, also, had been a steelworker. The western trip had to be put on hold and when details were secured, Dad Ramsay drove Mother and Rose to Phoenix so he could catch a plane there to go to Mr. Murray's funeral in Pittsburg. Mother and Rose stayed and were able to visit many sights in the area and do some shopping. They were like two school girls on a holiday. Rose particularly enjoyed watching an old Indian do sand painting.

The CIO convention in California was cancelled and Dad came back to Phoenix to begin the drive back home to Georgia. They visited more wonderful parks, including White Sands and Carlsbad Caverns in New Mexico and the Alamo in Texas. Rose fell in love with San Antonio and wrote Bill that she hoped he'd get assigned to army medical school there so they could both enjoy this beautiful and exciting city - a wish that came true just a few months later. Rose marveled at the different landscapes, cultures, and people she saw coming across the country. She wrote on November 21, 1952:

*"I am writing this in the car. We are heading home now – will get home tomorrow around noon. I am trying to listen to Mother as I write this. She is reading to us all about Louisiana. We spent the night in New Orleans and are now driving out on a neck of land between two lakes. It is simply beautiful. Honey, it's amazing the difference in cultures, atmosphere, everything, in different sections of our country. I don't see how any one group can call only their type "true Americans." The thing that makes America such a great and wonderful (place) is the fact that she is made up of so many cultures and nationalities"*

Bill was in the middle of infantry training and, since he was not involved in weapons training, he was often working in the office typing reports or in the storeroom building shelves or sorting materials. Most of the men were learning to use the bayonet and throw grenades. Bill also continued to drive the ambulance on marches and other vehicles on various errands. At one time, he drove one of the big troop transport trucks to take the company to a mock battle area and bivouacked with the troops in tents and went on maneuvers. The weather was very cold. Even though the guns were firing blanks as the troops crawled under fences and across rugged ground, one guy got shot by a blank cartridge plug in the chest and had to be taken to the hospital.

The travelers arrived home on November 22 and had arranged for a call from Bill on the next day. Rose remembers counting the days until they could see each other again.

## Camp Follower

*I was determined to find a place to be and get a job close to Camp Pickett so we could be together on weekends. Bill had written that he could almost* *always get a weekend pass. The men would often be told that there would be no passes but then, when the time came, they were granted, especially if you hadn't messed up during the week. I had considered going to Martinsville, VA, to be with my former Berea roommate Fran Janney but decided to look at Richmond instead. In late November, 1952, I took a bus to Petersburg where I had made a reservation at a hotel. Bill got a 24 hour pass for the weekend and was able to join me. What a wonderful reunion. We had so much to share. On the following Monday I took a bus to Richmond, about 30 miles north, to start looking for a job and place to stay. On the bus I met a girl who said she worked at a photo lab and offered to introduce me for an interview. She took me to Galeski's Photo Studio and the owner gave me tests like the ones I had administered to students, so they were a snap. He hired me right away. Dad had suggested getting a room at the YWCA, which I did. One of Bill's companions, Bill Ross from Massachusetts, had a wife, Lorraine, who also had come to find a place near the base. Lorraine and I roomed together at the YWCA and she got a job in an insurance office. She was a wonderful companion and friend and her husband, Bill, had a car so he and my Bill could come together to Richmond on weekends. We would get rooms at the King Carter Hotel for $6.00 and be together from Saturday, when the guys arrived until Sunday evening when they had to return to base. My work was boring – checking and sorting photographs, putting them in little albums and pricing them. It paid little but kept us fed and the rent paid. My fellow workers, mostly women, tended to complain a lot and had feuds and used curse words, but we got along. The boss appreciated the fact that I didn't do those things.*

The two Bills were able to get passes almost every weekend and the couples wrote to each other between weekends. Rose got to attend a reception in Richmond honoring Lucy Randolph Mason and talked with Lucy, who was a union leader and close friend of Mother and Dad Ramsay. She had sent Rose and Bill a wedding gift. The weeks passed and infantry basic was completed before Christmas.

*It was a relief to finish the strenuous activities of infantry training and begin to learn the specific skills needed by a medic – treating different wounds and trauma, various bandages and slings, basic medicines and emergency procedures. We still had marches and drills but not as much. For our first*

*Christmas together, Rose and I found a small tree branch and put it in a vase in the hotel room and hung a few decorations on it. We had bought a few presents for family, trying to stay within a $2.00 limit for a present, and Rose had sent them to the family in Tennessee and to Georgia for distribution. Now our attention was on the end of basic training and the next assignment. We had interviews on base and it was clear that those who could learn quickly would be sent for training as technicians in areas of critical need. Ultimately I was fortunate to be assigned to go to the Medical Field Service Training facility at Fort Sam Houston in San Antonio, Texas, for training as an X-Ray technician.*

Time seemed to pass more quickly after Christmas with Bill finishing his time at Camp Pickett and Rose continuing to work in Richmond. She enjoyed her companionship with Lorraine and looked forward to Bill's visits on weekends. Mother and Dad Ramsay drove Hedda, with some difficulties, up on their way to the rescheduled CIO convention in Atlantic City, so Bill and Rose now had a car. Having transportation they started to visit historic and scenic sites in the area. They became acquainted with the James River Plantations and Colonial Williamsburg, and never lost their love of that area.

Roger Lily was to go to Fort Sam Houston also, but Bill Ross was assigned elsewhere so there was a sorrowful parting with Bill and Lorraine when it came time to leave Camp Pickett and Richmond. A short leave was provided before reporting to Fort Sam so Bill and Rose drove Hedda to Tennessee for time with Rose's Dad and brothers. They had to stop periodically to add water to Hedda's steaming radiator. Then they drove back to Skyland Farm. What a relief to have the basic phase of military service behind them and to be able to look forward to having a place in San Antonio together.

## San Antonio

*We weren't sure Hedda was up to a trip to Texas and took her to our friendly mechanic to check her out. He fixed the radiator and made some needed adjustments and told us she would get us to Texas, but please don't try to bring her back. Hedda served us well in San Antonio and we did bring her back.*

*Having just come back from her western trip a couple months earlier, Rose was eager to show me the features of the land we crossed and to return to San Antonio together. What a beautiful, colorful, music filled city with its historic sites, its Mexican restaurants, especially Casa Rio where Rose had dined on her earlier trip, and its river running through town. We soon learned that the river walk was off limits and dangerous after dark. Since those days it has been developed and made safe. The Mexican influence added a special flavor to the city and we were surprised to learn that it was originally a settlement of German immigrants.*

*I reported to Brooks Army Medical Center at Fort Sam Houston and was given orders for starting my training. We had to complete in four months what normally took two years in a vocational/technical school. Of course this was our sole assignment and if we failed we were threatened with being sent to Korea. We studied hard. The instructors were very good and the facilities excellent. The students were all capable as well.*

Bill and Rose quickly found an apartment in the home of a family named Daum. It became their first "home," Bill could be home almost every night and weekends, and with Hedda they could explore the city. Just as they were getting settled, they experienced an unsettling incident reminding them that they were now in a big city.

*We had gone to a drug store with another couple, after a movie, to pick up supplies and just as we stepped out on the sidewalk we heard a shot and saw a man across the street stagger out of an alley and fall on the grass between the sidewalk and the street. Bill and his friend, named, Bill Bull, quickly crossed the street and knelt down by the man, very much the newly trained medics. We wives followed in time to hear the man say, "I've been shot!" The two of us called an ambulance and the police and got blankets from a nearby motel. The guys loosened the man's collar, felt his pulse and did a brief examination which showed a small hole in his abdomen, with no exit wound. He said his name was Rocky. With the blankets they made him as comfortable as possible waiting for the police and ambulance. A small crowd had gathered including a small blond girl who stood twisting her purse in her hands.*

*When the police arrived they took charge and asked a lot of questions and the ambulance came to take charge of Rocky. A policeman turned to the girl and asked her who she was and she replied, "I'm Frankie, and I shot him!" whereupon she reached in her purse and pulled out a small revolver which she handed to the policeman. We almost fainted. We spent the next several hours at the police station answering questions, signing forms and hearing Frankie's sordid story of a love triangle. We heard later that the bullet had lodged against Rocky's spine and that he would recover. What an introduction to city life in Texas. We felt like we were in the middle of a soap opera.*

Bill and Rose's little home became a refuge for many classmates and other soldier friends who were in training classes, like Roger Lily who was being trained as psychiatric technician. They became especially close friends with another soldier and his wife, Don and Jackie Lelong and often went on picnics, took trips around the area and went to events together. Rose was a gracious hostess as well as a working girl.

*I immediately applied for advertised positions and got a job at the big department store downtown, named Wolfe and Marx, in the credit office. I met some nice co-workers, including a Spanish-American girl named Marie who became a close friend. The Daums also became good friends as did the next door neighbor who later got me a better job in an insurance office with shorter hours. Finally we had an almost normal life with our own home, friends, work to do and time for enjoying life together. Bill was doing well in school and we both learned all the bones of the body.*

*By late April I was very glad to be working part-time. I was tired and not feeling well. A visit to the base OB confirmed our hopes – a baby was on the way! Our friends and neighbors shared our excitement. I went out and bought a maternity dress, which was really not needed at that stage. Our baby was due in early December and who knew where we would be by then.*

The weeks went swiftly by and Bill completed his course, getting to shake hands with the general, as head of his class. He had to report back to Fort Jackson in South Carolina to get his next assignment. They almost hated to see their time in San Antonio come to an end, but they missed the green hills and mountains of home, and with Rose expecting a child, going home was such a blessing.

*Rose had talked with the doctor and he said she would be all right to travel if she sat comfortably, moved around enough and lay flat every couple hours. I had arranged for a soldier friend, John Woolheater, to drive with us, thinking to share driving and costs. We'd be a little crowded in the coupe, but would stop often. A couple days before we departed John broke his finger and had it in a cast so he couldn't drive at all. We stopped often so Rose could lie on a blanket at the side of the road. I don't know what people in passing cars thought. Sometimes she would travel facing backward and kneeling on the seat. (No seatbelts in those days.) It was not the most comfortable trip and we were tired by the end of it, but coming home to Skyland Farm and Mother and Dad made it all worthwhile.*

*I reported to Fort Jackson and my initial next assignment was to Fort Bragg, North Carolina, but a fellow soldier from California who was assigned to Fort McPherson in Atlanta suggested we switch and the assigning officers agreed so I would be stationed only 20 miles from home. We had a good rest at Skyland Farm before I started work at the base hospital of Third Army Headquarters at Fort McPherson.*

## Home Base and a Baby

Rose settled in to the house at Skyland Farm, grateful to be with Mother as she moved towards childbirth. She helped with the farm and house chores and in the garden. They did some canning and freezing of produce. Mother and Dad traveled a good bit, but had Mr. Lipsy to help look after the animals and chores. Dad's widowed sister Katheryn, had come to stay for a time and added an interesting and sometimes frustrating element to home life. She seemed to imagine herself as a "grand lady" and didn't do much, which was quite a contrast to Mother who was at home in elegant company but was "down to earth" and loved to work. Bill was able to be home most nights and sometimes was on call in case of emergencies at the hospital requiring radiological services.

*I worked with two civilian technicians and another enlisted man under the supervision of a noncommissioned officer who often came to work a little bleary eyed and said, "I'll take the darkroom today." We took all kinds of x-rays, performed radiology tests such as Intravenous Pyelograms, barium gastro intestinal examinations, and fluoroscopic procedures with a radiologist. We developed and dried the films and provided them to the radiologist or ordering physician. Our patients were soldiers from the base, dependents and civilian workers. Occasionally there were emergencies. I remember one poor man who had tried to use a chain saw to cut a log across his lap. The saw had gone through the log and down to the bone above his knee and we had to determine the extent of bone damage before surgery. We were well trained and had good equipment and a good working group. We soon got to know the doctors and nurses and other hospital personnel. We soldiers had minimum requirements for drills and inspections so could almost imagine we were out of the army – but not quite. In due course I was promoted to Private First Class and then Corporal.*

Skyland Farm was always a place of hospitality and became a place of retreat for fellow workers at the hospital as well as visiting family members and friends from time to time. Bill and Rose enjoyed the little Lithia Springs Methodist Church and its warm friendly people. Bill was home enough to help with chores and he and Rose plowed and planted a big garden in the spring of 1954. But before that the family had grown by one small baby boy.

*All went well with my pregnancy. I developed a special yearning for the French pastries I had always liked, and Bill provided them as often as he could. I was in touch with Bill's sister, Patty, in Columbus, Ohio, who sent me material on "natural childbirth." In my Tennessee community it was only recently that babies were not born at home, as I was, so I expected childbirth to be "natural." I was naïve. I read Dr. Grantly Dick Read's book on childbirth and practiced the exercises and breathing techniques he recommended.*

*I was due in December but by November it looked like I might be early. Bill was well known in the hospital by this time and I became acquainted with the very personable and competent army doctors, who had no experience with or interest in "natural childbirth." Dr. Wilson delivered our baby, and Dr. Hall, took care of him after birth. On November 14, 1953, Bill was home and a fellow x-ray technician, Marty Zanotti was visiting. Mother and Dad were away. Just after midnight, my water broke and we knew it was time to go to the hospital. Marty drove us all in Aunt Katheryn's big old Packard. Labor was a new experience for me and I found that it is well named. The nurses gave me a spinal and scopolamine and with me out of it our baby was born on the 15th, weighing over 6 pounds and healthy. It took me several days with terrible headaches to get over the spinal. I thought there must be a better way to bring a baby into the world. We named our first son William Edward after his father and my father and affectionately called him Billy (Bill E). When I got home, Mother was there and I was so glad to share this new adventure with her. She was so kind and helpful. She and Billy developed a very special bond which lasted all her life.*

Billy was tucked in a new crib that Mother and Dad had provided, with a pretty blue blanket. Life was stable and good. Pleasant days passed swiftly. Skyland Farm had a wonderful 1953 Christmas with a fragrant Georgia Pine, its long needles decorated in the living room and stockings hung at the fireplace. Marty gave Billy a teddy bear, which he loved. His crib, blanket and teddy became his security over the next years as the family moved. Winter passed and then a lush Georgia spring with garden planted followed by a hot summer with the beautiful crepe myrtle blooming along the driveway.

*We had Billy baptized at the little Lithia Springs Methodist Church in May. By April, we knew another baby was on the way. We were happy. We wanted several children and wanted them close in age. Patty, who was also expecting in December, her third child, planned to have "natural childbirth." She belonged to a support group in Columbus. She sent me more material so I became aware of centers also in Milwaukee and New York that were starting to look at childbirth from a mother's perspective. I got news from home that Ken had married Betty Smith from a neighbor's family. Ken was 19 and Betty 16. In June, Bill's brother John married Winona Lotz. We went to Berea for the wedding and stopped to see Daddy, Wayne, Kenneth and Betty on the trip.*

*They were all getting along well. Wayne came back with us to Lithia Springs for a week and then we took him home.*

The Korean War ended in July. Bill was now approaching the end of his military service and had been advised by the graduate program that he could begin in September at the University of Alabama. He would take an earned leave from Fort McPherson in September to begin graduate work and then return for the first week in October to muster out of the Army at the end of his two years. He and Rose had been blessed in their first two years of marriage with good assignments, new friends and experiences, the beginning of their family and the satisfaction that they had completed their duties well.

*Only one hurdle arose in the final months of service. Mother and Dad were going off on another trip and they suggested they leave their 8 millimeter movie camera with us so we could continue to record Billy's growth. He was a happy active baby doing something new almost every day. I'd never used the camera but I stopped at the PX on base to get some film and asked for 8 mm movie film. The woman clerk asked if I wanted reel or cartridge. I didn't even know there were two kinds and had no clue so I was confused and said I'd have to check. She got all excited and asked me more questions about the camera which I couldn't answer. It turned out that a camera had been stolen from the PX and she was convinced I was the thief. I didn't know this at the time but found out when I was called to the base military police office, read my rights and accused of stealing the camera. I explained the circumstances and offered to go home and get our camera for them to examine. They weren't interested and weren't about to accept my story since they said I was their only suspect. The matter drug on for several days while I tried to clear my name, fearing it might interfere with my discharge. I was lamenting the problem with one of the hospital volunteers I had become friends with and she was horrified. It turned out that her father was the base Provost Marshall. She talked to "daddy" and very quickly the accusation against me was withdrawn. Thank goodness I wasn't a new arrival with no reputation or friends. Except for that incident, my time at Fort Mac had been a very fine experience.*

# CHAPTER 8

# THE SOUTHERN REGIONAL TRAINING PROGRAM IN PUBLIC ADMINISTRATION

After two years of military service Bill and Rose were ready to resume their plans for graduate study. Now they had a baby boy and were expecting again in December so Rose was no longer exploring immediate options for completing her degree and teaching certificate. She loved being a mother and looked forward to raising a large family of happy children with a strong faith. She was also committed to helping Bill complete the graduate program and then find their places to work and serve in the world. While in Georgia, they had finally traded Hedda for a more recent and spacious Pontiac and they took off for Tuscaloosa, Alabama in September, 1954.

## Alabama

Bill joined five other "fellows" at the University of Alabama to begin graduate studies in public administration. It turned out that, due to military service interruptions, two of the others were also Berea graduates – Fontain Banks and Bob Cornett. The other three were Dana Brammer from Mississippi, Herb Wilkins from California, and Harris Behrman from Kentucky.

*I had known Fontaine Banks at Berea where he was a year or two ahead of me. He was elected president of student government in my sophomore or junior year and was intensely political. He was not a great scholar but a very hard worker and ambitious. His aspiration was to one day be governor of Kentucky. He was a good and loyal friend and became a figure in Kentucky politics, never becoming governor himself but working for a number of Kentucky governors in various capacities.*

*Bob Cornett was also a year ahead of me at Berea and was a basketball star. He was held in affection by all and had a wonderful sense of humor, a healthy dose of common sense and a way of putting things in perspective. He and his wife, Jean, with their two sons, acted as host and hostess for most of the group's meals together. Bob went on to become budget director for the Commonwealth of Kentucky and then executive for the Council of State Governments. He and Jean developed bluegrass music festivals and camps in Kentucky and Florida. In his later years, Bob has been an advocate for community based education and arm chair philosopher.*

*Dana Brammer was an excellent student, but constantly feared he would fail. After each test he would be in misery for fear of messing up, but he always did well. He and his wife, Jean, had the warmth and politeness that one often finds in southerners. He went back to Mississippi to work in state government there.*

*Herb Wilkins was charming and always helpful, as well as being a good student. Coming from California he was more experienced in the wider culture than the rest of us, but was humble and never overbearing. He became a treasured companion to Rose and myself and often helped us out.*

*Harris Behrman was the most scholarly of the group and had no problem with the theory and methods courses that sometimes gave the rest of us trouble. He had a keen mind, but it tended to get into the clouds rather than deal with the realities of earth. He went on to become a lawyer.*

They were a very compatible group, working together and supporting each other. Rose was quickly friends with the two Jeans. All enjoyed shopping for bargains at the Jitney Jungle and weekly meals together, usually, with the very gracious and capable Jean Cornett hosting them in their student housing.

Bill, Bob and Herb often studied together at Bill and Rose's apartment, sometimes dividing the enormous amount of reading required and then sharing the important parts with each other. The courses were hard and demanding but, even with the amount of work, some of the professors were so good that it was a pleasure to study with their guidance. York Wilburn, on loan to Alabama from Indiana University, taught a Constitutional Law class that was fascinating. Rose was a stay-at-home mom, made possible by the fellowship stipend and GI educational benefits Bill received.

*We had found a second floor apartment in an old house with another family downstairs. It took a lot of cleaning, but we had plenty space and a decent kitchen. It was sparsely furnished and our own furniture consisted of Billy's crib, high chair and stroller. He had become very attached to his bottle, blanket, and teddy bear. I would walk around the neighborhood pushing the stroller under the large shade trees and met other young mothers or nannies. I noticed that there were alleys behind the houses on the streets and smaller houses on the alleys where the black people lived and mostly worked as maids or nannies for the white folks. I got to know some of them. It was great to be able to be with our son, shop for groceries and prepare meals in our own place. Sometimes though, I missed fruit from the orchard, produce from the garden, fresh milk real butter and country eggs. However humble our circumstances, I liked to entertain the other students and friends and help Bill study. We had to get used to the pervasive odor off the Warrior River below the house caused by a paper mill up stream, and to the rattles and whistles of trains through the night from the tracks along the river. It was extremely hot when we first arrived and we sweltered but then as autumn came it cooled off. I noticed the heat, especially since I was getting heavier each week.*

Alabama used a semester system which ended in January, but because Tennessee was on a three term system, the fellows had to complete the semester's work at Alabama by Christmas and report to Tennessee early in January. It was what students call a grind but moved right along with all progressing well. At Thanksgiving, Mother came to stay for a while to be support for Rose and enjoy Billy. She stayed into December, hoping the new baby would arrive. That didn't happen and she had to return home. The guys were making bets on the date of birth. Christmas vacation arrived and all the other fellows left and still no baby. Finally on December 23 the doctors at Druid City Hospital induced labor and the baby was born –8 pounds 2 ounces and healthy. Bob Cornett won the bet with the closest date.

*I was worn out. First from the waiting and then from the induced labor, which was no fun, and then gas given at the end which made me quite sick. All our friends were gone and Bill had to take care of me, Bill E. and the marvelous, beautiful baby girl. We named her Laura Elizabeth for two great grandmothers, Laura Fleenor Riggs and Elizabeth Romig Martin. We took her home from the hospital on Christmas day and staggered through a week before we had to move on to Knoxville. Bill had arranged for a rental house in Knoxville but was notified at the last minute that the owners had decided not to rent so we were without a place to go. Friends in Oak Ridge, Jay and Joan Reynolds, offered to take us in while we looked for housing. On the last day of December 1954, Bill took me to the airport in Birmingham and I boarded with two babies, one only a week old, for the trip to Tennessee. Between a helpful stewardess, a kind seatmate and a bottle, blanket and teddy bear, we made it and were met at the Knoxville airport by Mother and Dad and taken to the warm home of the Reynolds in Oak Ridge.*

Bill, meanwhile, with all their belongings in the trunk and back seat of the Pontiac set off to drive to Oak Ridge on New Year's Eve. It was cold and snowing. In the wee hours of the night, he crossed the floating White Wing bridge that marked the entrance to the Oak Ridge reserve and found his way to the Reynolds home, a little numb, but so glad to be there safely with his little family and good friends.

## Tennessee

*We had a few days before the term started at the University of Tennessee and the time was spent finding a place to live. Student housing was not available but we found an older home on Magnolia Avenue that had a three room apartment on the second floor with its own kitchen and a shared bath with another apartment occupied by on older couple. The younger couple who owned the house lived on the first floor with their little baby. The apartment had no separate entrance and the rooms were not all connected but it had enough space so we moved in. Billy had his crib, blanket and teddy. Baby Laura had to be put to bed in the collapsible carrier we had for the car. We had no idea what adventures awaited us in that place. I got started with classes and we settled in. Mother had come to help out for a few days which provided welcomed relief for Rose.*

*The term went well with some more marvelous teachers, especially the head of the Political Science Department, Lee Greene, who was a stickler for good composition and grammar. We had to take an advanced accounting course that was designed for engineers and gave some of the fellows trouble. The professor told us at the beginning of the class the number who would fail and then he set about to make that happen. With my bookkeeping from High School and my experience with accounting of the student newspaper at Berea, I had no problem, but it was a sad course.*

After a few days in the apartment they discovered that the house was infested with rats – not little mice, but wharf rats. The landlord provided a big rat trap.

*Mother was still with us, thank goodness! We had seen a big rat in the kitchen. Having rats running around with babies lying helpless was not acceptable. We set a rat trap under the sink in the kitchen and soon found a dead rat in it. So Mother and I set it again. Jean Brammer was visiting and the guys had all gone to a Tennessee versus Vanderbilt basketball game. We heard the trap go off and we went into the kitchen. The trap had killed one rat and hit another which was running around the floor dazed. I grabbed a broom and pinned it to the floor and yelled, "Kill it!" Mother grabbed a butcher knife from the counter and stabbed the rat, while Jean leaned against the wall and screamed. The guys, returning from the game, opened the front door just in time to hear the screams and bolted up the stairs to see me still holding the broom on the rat, Mother with a bloody knife and Jean screaming with her hands in front of her face. It took a while to get everything sorted out and cleaned up and our nerves calmed. I don't remember who won the game, but Mother and I had defeated the rat.*

Rose and Bill talked about finding another place, but didn't do anything right away, Mother left again and life moved on, with special attention to noises in the night. The housing was not the best and Rose was busy with feedings, diapers and other facets of motherhood, as well as preparing meals for herself and Bill and continuing to be a place where the other fellows could come for fellowship and respite from studies. Washing diapers was a daily chore.

*I didn't have a washer and dryer, of course. I had to wash Billy's diapers by hand in Tuscaloosa although occasionally we used a laundromat. (Now we live in an era when nobody washes diapers. They are disposable.) In Knoxville I had to wash a couple dozen a day. When you took a soiled diaper off you first rinsed it in the toilet and then put it in a lidded pail of soapy water. When the pail was full or I needed diapers, I rinsed them out in the bathtub until they were basically clean. Then I put them in a big pan of soapy water and boiled them on the stove. Then back to the bathtub again for a final rinsing. By this time they were quite clean and white. If I hung them outside on the upstairs porch they would quickly collect soot belched out from chimneys of all the coal burning stoves in the area, so I hung them inside. It took longer to dry inside and cluttered the apartment, but had to be done every day.*

One day, after they had been there for about three weeks, Bill was feeling sick and stayed home to rest and study. They heard someone groaning as if in distress downstairs and Rose called down to ask if anything was wrong. The young man said his wife had twisted her ankle, but was all right. Later they heard thumping as if someone was locked in a closet. Then they heard the unmistakable low scream and heaving of a woman in distress.

*Hearing the fear and agony in the scream jolted us and Rose put the babies down and headed downstairs with me following. The door to their living room was ajar and Rose pushed it open. We saw our landlord standing in his undershorts looking wild, with his wife lying on the floor beneath him holding the baby in her arms. He had obviously just knocked her down. He was about twice my size. I told him to move away from her or I would call the police. He said it was none of my business and I said I was making it my business. Rose was looking for a weapon she could use if he attacked me. As with most abusers who are cowards, he backed down and hastily put on clothes and left the house. The commotion had brought the woman with whom we shared the second floor to see what was happening. She said she heard the groans and it wasn't the first time but she didn't want to interfere and she excused her husband for not coming down because, "He doesn't have his teeth in." We never did figure that one out. We helped the battered wife and baby get settled and decided to look for other housing that night. I called Dana and Jean Brammer and they came right over. Jean stayed with Rose and Dana and I went out to follow ads for housing. Later as we came home we saw through the window, the couple making up. She had told us she considered leaving him, but didn't have the courage, and it was clear she wouldn't leave this time either.*

Bill and Rose found another apartment further away, in Fountain City and stayed there for the remainder of their time in Tennessee. They were not satisfied to leave the wife abuse matter without some follow up so Bill, accompanied by Herb, went to see the man. He said he was not a drinker or on drugs and had no head injuries or anything else that might account for his behavior. He said, "I guess that's just the way I'm made!" We talked to him about the inadequacy of that excuse and urged him to never repeat wife beating and to get help if he couldn't control himself. Wouldn't it be convenient if we could excuse all our misconduct by saying, "That's just the way I'm made?"

The new apartment was two very small rooms, but the surroundings were pleasant, with a yard where Rose could get outside with the children and the air was clean. An older couple with teenagers owned the house and lived in the main part of it. They wanted to be like grandparents. They owned a "mom and pop store" and sometimes shared produce, which was past its prime, with us. As time went on the only problem was the rent.

*The rent was reasonable but after a time we didn't have the funds to pay because the Veterans Administration had cut off my payments when we left Alabama. The VA had a rule that if you left a school you weren't eligible for payments for a period of time. I explained, with help from university officials, that we had not left the graduate program but were required to attend all three cooperating universities in one year. I expected payments to resume right away and assured our landlords that they would be paid. We used up what savings we had, we borrowed from our friends to tide us over but still no response* from the VA. *Our landlords said they understood but began acting very cool, locking their doors, which they hadn't done before, and we were aware that they didn't trust us. Finally I asked Dad to help us out and, of course, he did immediately and the problems disappeared. We didn't receive any VA payments the whole time we were in Tennessee and really lived day to day as best we could. I remember one time we were down to 15 cents and used that to buy a crossword puzzle book to work together.*

Other than the payment problem we had a pleasant time in Fountain City. Rose didn't have a car and wasn't a driver in any case, so she was pretty much house and yard bound and it was winter and often rainy. But she enjoyed the children and the family was all together, even if it was close quarters.

*I did have one real scare. I was hanging a diaper in the yard. There was no coal soot here. The wind was blowing and it blew the door closed. I had left Laura in her bassinet and Billy playing on the floor. Laura was just two months old and Billy a little over a year. He was walking now and he liked to see the baby. He would go to the bassinet and try to peek over, which meant he might turn it over. I could no longer see them with the door closed and it had latched so I couldn't get in.*

*I found a window that was not too far off the ground. I took the screen off and found that it was unlocked. I had to push a table aside that was under the window but managed to get through it. The babies were fine. I was careful about propping the door open after that. When I look back on it, I think about how hard it was. If you don't think it's hard it at the time, it's not hard.*

The three month term at Tennessee quickly came to an end and it was time to move again, this time to the University of Kentucky in Lexington only about 40 miles north of Berea. And it was spring!

## Kentucky

The trip to Kentucky was well planned but memorable for all that went wrong. Herb Wilkins was going with Bill and Rose and the babies. They all went to Rose's home in Greene County, about 50 miles from Knoxville

155

and spent a day there. Herb was then to drive Rose's Dad's truck with luggage and belongings to Berea, where they had arranged to stay with the Sanbornes and the Stricklers, who were neighbors. Bill and Rose and babies would follow in their car. They left after supper and drove at night so Billy and Laura would sleep in the back seat of the Pontiac and they wouldn't have to stop for meals. The road was twisty, winding its way over Cumberland Gap as it passed from Tennessee into Kentucky.

*It was beginning to rain and the forecast was for real storms and possible flooding. Herb was in front of us and we could see his tail lights, but visibility was poor as the rain increased. We hadn't gone too many miles when I felt a tire blow out and pulled over on the shoulder. Herb, unaware of our plight drove on. The babies were asleep and I knew how to change a tire. It meant unloading the trunk in the rain to get to the spare tire, taking the wheel with the flat off and putting the spare on and then stowing everything back in the trunk, but it didn't take too long and we were on our way again. By the time we crossed into Kentucky, crossing Cumberland Gap like the pioneers of many years ago, the rain was coming in torrents and the radio was reporting flooding in Pineville and Barbourville through which we had to travel. Water was over the roads in places. Near Barbourville, about midnight, another tire went flat. OH NO! I trudged under an umbrella in the driving rain to the only house we saw some ways up the road and knocked on the door. A woman with a frightened voice hollered, "Go away!" and in spite of my entreaties refused to open the door. I gave the bad news to Rose back at the car. Time to pray!*

*A truck pulled in behind us with two guys in the cab. They were out looking for a friend who was on the road somewhere and they thought he may have encountered trouble in the storm. They quickly grasped our plight. They said there was an all-night service station in Corbin that might have a tire and could help us. We jacked up the car and took off the flat tire and put it in the back of the truck. Then we all, Rose and babies included, crowded into the cab of the truck and went to Corbin. While Rose changed diapers and made the little ones comfortable on a table in an all-night diner next to to the station, I explored tire possibilities with the service station guys and our benefactors. They had a compatible used tire but wouldn't take a check so I had to agree leave what cash I had, my camera and watch, to get the tire changed. One of the station attendants took me back to the Pontiac and we mounted the wheel and drove back to Corbin. It was raining the whole time but slacking off a little. Finally back on the road, we got to Berea as the rain stopped and dawn began to show on the horizon. Poor Herb had arrived hours earlier, his pants wet from holes in the truck's floorboard, cold and not knowing where to go. We found him in the cab of the truck parked in front of Boone Tavern Hotel. He had gone into the hotel, but in his wet and unkempt condition was viewed suspiciously and he went back to the truck. We finally got everyone settled. Thank God for Good Samaritans on the road and friends in Berea. Herb and I went back to Corbin a week later to retrieve my watch and camera.*

At the University of Kentucky, Bill and Rose were able to get married student housing. What a luxury to live in their own house with a small yard. It was just a little war-time flat top prefab structure but seemed spacious after the cramped quarters they were used to. Spring was beautiful with the redbud trees in full bloom, the crab apples blossomed and then the dogwoods. The VA finally got the GI benefits straightened out and they got all their back payments at once and could pay back their loans from family and friends and have enough to feel secure.

*Billy and Laura were growing and thriving. While Bill was in classes, I could take the children for walks in the fresh spring air. I arranged to take care of a baby for another graduate couple nearby and earned a little extra income. We had trips to Berea and had friends visit us. The end of the program was in sight and Bill had been offered and accepted a position at the Oak Ridge Institute of Nuclear studies when he finished in June 1955. My brother Ken and his young wife, Betty, and Daddy and Wayne were doing well. God had seen us through and life was good.*

As at the other schools, Bill and the other fellows had excellent teachers for the most part. At Kentucky the course in public finance with James Martin was especially appreciated. The fellows were by now able to read volumes and write long papers and had learned how to respond to different types of professors.

*We had one professor who was fascinated by minute details. He knew the names of legislators' wives, their hobbies and obscure facts about public figures, past and present. We would store away some obscure fact and then on an essay test, no matter what the question, work that little tidbit into the answer. It would always get a special note of praise written on the graded test paper. We did learn a lot about the intricacies of the legislative process in his course.*

Just before the end of the semester when the students were struggling to get their final papers written and cram for exams, the residents of the student housing project in which Bill and Rose lived were notified that they would need to move to another area, which would be provided, so the flat tops could be razed and a new modern student housing tower could be built. The students objected and appealed. They asked that the plans be delayed for a couple weeks. They were turned down and told to move.

*We had been happy and settled in our little flat top and it seemed wrong to make us move just before school was out. Another move seemed more than I could bear, especially now with two little children. I cried! Mother and Dad came and took Billy with them to their home in Washington. Bill, Laura and I moved to another pre fab unit not far away. It never felt like home. To accentuate the distaste of this move, they didn't begin clearing the old flat tops until long after we were gone. That bitter lesson in the evils of bureaucracy was not lost on students of public administration. But all in all the three months in Kentucky had been a good time.*

The SRTP fellows all completed their work well and all looked forward to regular jobs and a more stable life. The fellows with their wives had become close friends and they would miss their comradeship, picnics, gatherings, and shared experiences. But it was time to move on.

Bill's folks had sold Skyland Farm and moved to Macomb Street in the Cleveland Park area of Washington, DC. They already had Billy with them so Bill, Rose and Laura went there, stopping in Columbus, Ohio, first, for a visit with Patty and Earl Todt. Patty and Rose talked about childbirth education. Their third child, Billy Lynn, had been born a week after Laura and Patty was enthusiastic about her experience with natural childbirth. David and Susan adored their new baby brother.

*We went on to Washington, glad to see Billy and Mother and Dad. On June 12, 1955, Laura was baptized by Reverend Elson at the National Presbyterian Church where Bill's dad was an elder. Billy was fascinated by the stained glass windows and proclaimed with wonder in his high piping voice for all to hear, "There's the baby Jesus."*

*Bill went back to Oak Ridge to get started with his job and find housing for us.*

*The children and I had a great time in Washington. Laura liked all the attention and activity and Billy was always happy around his grandma. The Washington Zoo was only a few blocks away and Mother and I put the kids in strollers and walked there several times. Billy especially liked the hippopotamus and the way he opened his huge mouth. He referred to it as hippo-mo-u-th. But soon we heard from Bill that he had found a place to stay and it was time to go. Mother and Dad took us to Oak Ridge. We were ready for this final move in a year of moves.*

# BILL AND ROSE RAMSAY TIME LINE

## COLLEGE, MARRIAGE ARMY AND GRADUATE SCHOOL: 1949 - 1955

| YEARS | FAMILY AND RELATED EVENTS | WORLD EVENTS |
|---|---|---|
| 1949 | Bill works with John at college dairy | NATO established |
| | Rose continues at candy kitchen | Berlin blockade ends |
| | Both get roles in Arsenic and Old Lace; | Germany partitioned |
| | Rose is Martha; Bill is Dr. Einstein | Mao, communists rule China |
| | Rose chooses Elementary Education | USSR tests atomic bomb |
| | Bill chooses History and Political Science | Cold War dominates world |
| 1950 | Bill and Rose both work at Tab (dramatics bldg.) | Korean War begins |
| | Rose does costumes, Bill lights and other backstage | Average yearly wage $3,210 |
| | Both appear in plays and progress in studies | Gas costs 12 cents per gallon |
| 1951 | Bill works summer in Merchant Marine; Rose in Berea | Occupation of Japan ended |
| | Rose and Bill date and by late fall are engaged | Bread costs 12 cents a loaf |
| | Rose's mother, Lochiel, is ill; Rose goes home | |
| 1952 | Lochiel dies March 29; Rose at home, Bill graduates, | Britain's King George VI dies |
| | starts internship in Oak Ridge. Bill and Rose marry | Elizabeth II becomes Queen |
| | in Berea on September 7. Bill drafted into US Army | |
| | October 8. Rose travels west with Mother and Dad | Polio vaccine successful |
| | Bill at Camp Picket, VA for medical corps training | |
| | Rose moves to Richmond, VA | |
| 1953 | Bill sent to Fort Sam Huston for x-ray training | Dwight Eisenhower President |
| | They move to San Antonio, Rose gets jobs | Joseph Stalin dies |
| | Bill assigned to Ft McPherson Hospital in Atlanta | Elvis Presley becomes known |
| | They move to Skyland Farm at Lithia Springs | |
| | Bill E. born 0n November 15 | |
| 1954 | Bills completes military service and begins graduate | Korean War ends |
| | program at U of Alabama. They move to Tuscaloosa | Brown vs Board of Ed decision |
| | Laura born two days before Christmas in Alabama | ends segregation in public schools |
| 1955 | They move to Knoxville for winter term at U of | Khrushchev is Russian leader |
| | Tennessee, then to Lexington for final term at U of | Minimum wage is 75 cents/hour |
| | Kentucky, Position accepted at Oak Ridge Institute | |
| | of Nuclear Studies (ORINS). Family moves to Oak Ridge | |

BILL WAS TOP IN HIS X-RAY CLASS.

BILL E BORN AT FT MCPHERSON IN ATLANTA

BILL BECAME PVT RAMSAY OF THE ARMY MEDICAL CORPS. ROSE TRAVELED WEST WITH MOTHER AND DAD RAMSAY. SHE ESPECIALLY LIKED SAN ANTONIO.

THE SOUTHERN REGIONAL TRAINING PROGRAM IN PUBLIC ADMINISTRATION COMPLETING TWO YEARS OF ARMY SERVICE BILL JOINED FIVE OTHER "FELLOWS" FOR GRADUATE STUDY AT THE UNIVESITIES OF ALABAMA, TENNESSEE AND KENTUCKY,

THEY MOVED TO TUSCALOOSA, ALABAMA WHERE BILL E WOULD BE A YEAR OLD IN NOV. 1954. ON DECEMBER 23, LAURA ELIZABETH WS BORN AT DRUID CITY HOSPITAL IN TUSCALOOSA. A WEEK LATER THE FAMILY MOVED TO KNOXVILLE, TENNESSEE. IN APRIL 1955 THEY MOVED TO LEXINGTON, KENTUCKY.

# REFLECTIONS 9

## "THERE ARE ALWAYS A FEW"

When I was in basic training at Camp Pickett, Virginia, we had a very smart, capable, black sergeant who stood in front of the ranks every morning and gave the order of the day, impeccably dressed in his uniform. He would also inform us of any problems he'd noticed. These remarks would usually be preceded by the words, "There are always a few!" Then he would go on to cite infractions of rules, poor housekeeping or personal care. There were always a few who messed up and made everybody look bad and, sometimes, suffer. I never forgot his phrase and recognized that in every situation there were indeed "always a few."

Later when I was given responsibility for "personnel" at the Oak Ridge institute of Nuclear Studies, my no-nonsense, plain spoken boss advised me, "Bill, you have to start with the knowledge that 90 percent of the people are no d...d good. In recruiting you are looking for the 10 percent and most of them are gainfully employed." So the "few" had become ninety percent. I kept that bit of wisdom in my mental repertoire.

Much later, when I was responsible for labor and student life at Berea College, one of the areas needing attention was counseling services. We organized a continuum of counseling services beginning with peer counselors in the residence halls to more experienced head residents to professional counselors and finally psychiatric services. The idea was to meet the needs at the earliest possible level but have a referral system that would get the student to the level needed. Most needs could be met by good listening and referral to related services in academic, financial or other areas. Some required more professional help in sorting out home problems and relationship problems. Some needed skills in controlling emotions or seeing beyond an immediate crisis. A very few had mental health problems that required psychiatric care, and very rarely, medications, as in the case of schizophrenia. We arranged with a Berea graduate who was a practicing psychiatrist in the area to come once or twice a week to conduct individual or group sessions for those referred through the system. After a time, I had lunch with him at Boone Tavern to review the program and asked whether or not we were referring students to him who really didn't need to have that level of attention. His response was a definite "No!" and he reported that his professional journals claimed that something like 95 percent of the population would benefit from psychiatric attention to reach their full potential. We weren't about to send essentially all student to a psychiatrist, but I noted in my mental archives that the "few" that had grown to "ninety percent" had now expanded to close to 100 percent. Then it struck me that this was consistent with the Christian insight that we are all sinners in need of salvation. So the psychiatric journal was close to right. We all need help, but from a different source than they might recommend. We are a fallen race and need a savior.

# REFLECTIONS 10

## <u>JUST MADE THAT WAY</u>

We recorded our experience with the wife abuser whose only excuse was, "I guess I'm just made that way!" We reflected that it is not a sufficient reason for his behavior. To give in to impulses or feelings, no matter how strong, when they are harmful to others or to self is not acceptable in a civilized society. We all must learn restraint and we all have choices to make. On what basis will we make those choices? Departing from God's moral laws, man's attempts to determine what is good and evil always fail. This has been true since Adam and Eve were seduced by Satan into tasting the forbidden fruit of the tree of the knowledge of good and evil.

It seems to us that one of the wrong notions that lead to many problems is the idea that we are just the product of our genetics and our society. This leads not only to excusing detrimental behavior, like wife beating or sexual deviancy, and other wrong choices, but to the idea that if we just had the right genetics and society we could solve all problems and live in utopia. How many examples must we see before we accept that those man-centered ideas lead to destruction?

Hitler wanted to create a super race and society by getting rid of undesirables, such as Jews and handicapped children. His means to achieve a super race was to build a war machine that threatened to conquer the world and caused misery, death and devastation. Marx and Lenin had a blueprint for a just society where all were equal and the common people were in control. To get there required bloodshed. There was much bloodshed but communism never reached its utopia. Mao led a revolution in China to overthrow dictatorship and free the people. He ended up substituting a new dictatorship that denies people freedom. Typically, utopians believe they are progressive and seeking the good of all so they justify the "sacrifices" required to achieve their goals by their "noble" ideals. But many people just aren't smart enough to understand so they have to be reeducated, or forced to comply or removed as stumbling blocks for the "greater good."

On the individual level, if we are not committed to God's moral laws, we are like a ship without a rudder driven by the winds of passion, fashion and confusion. If our feelings are in conflict with moral standards it is the standards that are wrong. What is true must give way to what we want to be true. We've all seen the tendency in children to believe things are what they want them to be regardless of the facts. This is especially true when they are caught in some misdeed and don't want to admit to it. We try to teach them to be truthful and honest, knowing that we all make mistakes and must learn to ask and receive forgiveness of others, of God and of ourselves. Repentance and redemption is the road to follow – not denial or rewriting history to suit ourselves.

In this era of focus on "my rights," the ideas of determinism and rejection of moral laws leads to "anything goes." In the jungle of "anything goes" man is free to construct whatever rules he wants and they will change depending on the whims of society, changes of leadership, media fads and self-serving desires. Thus in the arrogance of the modern world, marriage can be redefined, gender can become a matter of choice, an unborn child can be declared not to be a living human being and, accordingly sacrificed. Make no mistake, this is just the beginning of the road to anarchy, instability, decay of civilization, loss of meaning, misery, and destruction. And the road was supposed to lead to a better society of tolerance, diversity, self-realization and happiness. We have lived in a golden age in America. But it won't last if we continue down the road of determinism and a man-centered rejection of God. A person, a nation and a society can't avoid the choice of what god they will serve. Like the ancient Israelites, we are free to choose, but oh, the consequences of the choices we make. Like a computer program, if one won't choose any god, he will go to a "default" god. There is no avoidance of the choice. Will we serve the god Eros feeding our passions, the god Mammon in pursuit of worldly goods, the god Moloch to whom we sacrifice our babies, or some other god? These gods have power and can reward their worshippers temporarily but only the one God can provide eternal rewards.

# PART FIVE

*Oak Ridge Years: 1955 -1967*

# CHAPTER 9

# OAK RIDGE

The "moving years" were over. Bill and Rose had moved 12 times in the first three years of marriage during military service and graduate school and were ready to settle down. They were both just 23 years old and now had two little children. Billy was 19 months old and Laura six months. The only furniture they owned was Billy's crib and high chair. But now they would have a place of their own to call home in Oak Ridge, Tennessee. They would have a steady income from what appeared to them to be a staggering salary of $4356 per year. Bill had a good job at the Oak Ridge Institute of Nuclear Studies as Administrative Assistant in the University Relations Division headed by Dr. Wladmir Wladmirovich Grigorieff. Paul Elza, Manager of Administration, who had chosen Bill as an intern three years before, continued to serve as his mentor.

How to record the Oak Ridge years presents a problem. So much happened with family, at work, in the community and beyond during those years. When they left in 1967 they were quite different – in their mid-thirties with a family of five children, battle hardened in civil rights, experienced in work, contributing citizens, leaders in church and ready for whatever adventures lay ahead. Thinking of these years as a cake with many layers of years, this presentation examines slices or themes that progressed through the layers, not independent of the rest of life or what was going on in the outside world, but giving a picture of particular areas of experience. Family growth, work progression, civil rights, childbirth education, literacy, community changes, and other themes are treated in these slices of life in the Oak Ridge years.

Oak Ridge was the stage set for the next act in the lives of Bill and Rose. It had an interesting history and features that had impact on those living there. Oak Ridge was a different town from others in the country. It had a very short history, dating back to only 1942 when it was created as the Clinton Engineering Works to carry out a secret wartime program called the Manhattan Project. It was a highly secretive project and even after its purpose was dramatically thrust on the world scene with the dropping of the atomic bomb in 1945 the community continued as a security conscious, limited access, military-like enclave. The transitions from "secret" to "open," from US Army control to civilian control, from full employment reaching over 82,000 in 1945 and then reducing to less than half of that in a few years, and from building a bomb to harnessing the "new" atomic energy for peaceful uses is a story of drama and complexity. The transition stretched from 1945 to 1959 when the city of Oak Ridge was incorporated as a self-governing community.

Before the war ended, the federal government already had a plan for converting their operations from wartime research and production to peacetime developments. In 1946, still under Army control, a representative "city council" was appointed to begin to help with the transitions. Paul Elza was on that first council.

*Paul Elza was the most capable manager I've met in over 50 years in administrative work. I was so fortunate to have been chosen by him, first as an intern and then as an employee of ORINS. I remember him telling me about one of his early experiences. In 1945 ORINS had been organized as a corporation of Southern universities under the leadership of Dr. William G. Pollard, as part of the move to peaceful uses of atomic energy and Paul was part of the organization from its earliest days. The newly formed Atomic Energy Commission (AEC) took over responsibility for Oak Ridge, as it passed from military to civilian control, in 1946. AEC contracted with ORINS to provide links between the nation's atomic energy program and higher education, and to operate programs for it. Almost everyone in Oak Ridge, other than construction workers, had come from other parts of the country. Paul was at a reception and a woman asked him the usual question, "Where are you from, Mr. Elza?" Having been born and raised in the area of the old railroad whistle stop, "Elza," which was the site of the Elza gate to the Oak Ridge reservation, Paul replied, "I'm from right here!" The woman immediately called her husband over and remarked, "Look, dear, they've trained one of the natives!"*

The former security gates were opened to the public in 1949 and Oak Ridge began to take on the character of a normal community. It was still totally government owned and operated by agencies and contractors until a year after Bill and Rose moved there in 1955. The population had dwindled to 30,000, or so, and residents were eager to be able to buy their own homes and individualize them, or buy lots and build. Congress passed legislation providing for the sale of homes and lots to citizens beginning in 1956 with first priority given to residents of the homes they were now allowed to purchase. The government gave an option of guaranteed repurchase if federal facilities were closed. Once private ownership of property was established the town began to plan for self-government.

*Having completed a graduate program in public administration, I was very interested in the process of moving Oak Ridge from a federal government operation to a self-governing town. It was a community with many residents of a high educational level, good schools, good employment opportunities and great potential. AEC employed a professional public administration consulting service to prepare a master plan for the town. How should it be organized? What would be its financial needs and budget? What tax system would be appropriate? What were the personnel needs and how could present personnel be moved into the new structure? This was before the days when "transparency" became a buzz word and the consultant followed a path more in keeping with the secret history of the town. Their idea was apparently that the report would be so comprehensive and professional that it would be accepted as a whole without question. No one was privy to its provisions until it was complete and released with some fanfare for all to see. I read it with great interest and found it to be excellent with sound recommendations and compelling reasoning but with no humility or provision for negotiation on particular items.*

*What followed was even more interesting. The report became to be seen as an attempt to impose some outsider's judgment on the local citizens and soon it was politically lethal. Anyone who wanted to get elected to the council or selected for any leadership position had to disassociate from the report. It went to a shelf from which it never reappeared, at least in public. Why? As far as I could tell the opposition started from two main sources and spread from there. First, it provided for a combined police force and fire department, which was a fairly new cost-saving concept considered progressive at the time. Both firemen and policemen objected strenuously and convinced the community that firefighting services and police protection were at jeopardy, not to mention their jobs – and many had served for years and were loved by the town. The second source of trouble was, again, from a cost savings recommendation in the administration of medical services, up to then provided in the government hospital. The report recommended that the anesthesiologist not be employed by the hospital but arranged on a contract basis – an arrangement that has since become the norm. But the local physician in that role was a long-time medical provider, and a beloved woman, who would, under the recommended system, be "unemployed." The whole medical establishment and the community at large were immediately up in arms. The rest of the report was quickly dismissed as suspect. It was a good lesson in the value of involving the subjects of a report in its development. The authors of the report had ignored the social and political environment and people's feelings.*

Oak Ridge was not only young as a community but as an age group. There were almost no retired folk, lots of young couples and children. Residents had roots in other parts of the state and country, bringing the cultures of their backgrounds with them, so there was little established common heritage other than the shared war effort. This allowed opportunity for new ideas. In the scientific community, once released from the single purpose nature of the Manhattan Project and then the all-pervading government programs and facilities, the freedom and diversity gave rise to exciting entrepreneurship. Meanwhile the usual commercial and business services of a community blossomed. New housing developments were added to the old government built homes and the old homes were renovated or replaced. All the prefabricated flat tops were removed and Oak Ridge began to look more and more like the modern city it is today. The Tennessee Valley Authority created Melton Hill Lake by putting a dam on the Clinch River, opening new vistas and recreational opportunities in the Oak Ridge area.

Another way in which Oak Ridge was different when Bill and Rose moved there in 1955 was the separation of the races. The town had been built under the separate but equal doctrine of the Supreme Court and the laws of Tennessee. The Scarborough community was built apart from the rest of the town to house the black population. The streets there were named after black colleges and leaders and they had their own school. Some black workers were well educated and served in scientific or technical jobs, some were clerical workers, but many occupied the lower paying service jobs. Their community may have been built as "equal" at the outset but was anything but equal by 1955. And public services such as restaurants, hotel, dormitory lodging, bowling alleys, barber shops and laundromats were still denied to black residents and visitors. This presented problems until equal public services were achieved in the late 1960s.

Churches were an important feature of Oak Ridge over the years and took on more community responsibility as the town moved away from government control and largess. Most denominations were represented along with nondenominational congregations. When the community voted on the ownership of the hospital, as it left federal control, it became a Methodist hospital rather than a municipal hospital.

These years of transition and growth were exciting giving ample opportunity for the young growing family to participate as homeowners, parents of school children, church members and citizens as well as through employment. The year after their moving to Oak Ridge was a presidential election year, 1956, and they immediately became active in supporting Adlai Stephenson and Estes Kefauver (a beloved Tennessean) who ran against a second term for President Eisenhower. They were full of idealism and optimism about the future.

# CHAPTER 10

# THE FAMILY GROWS

Billy was a toddler and Laura an infant when they moved to Oak Ridge. The family had been used to transient living and now would have to find housing, furniture and basic utensils to start home life on a longer term basis.

*After completion of the graduate program at Kentucky we had gone to Mother and Dad's home in Washington. Rose stayed there with the children while I went to Oak Ridge to start work, find housing and prepare for the family's arrival. Since I had spent my internship in Oak Ridge three years before, I was familiar with both the work setting and the town and had friends in both places. Housing was still all government owned and scarce but I found a two bedroom duplex not far from ORINS. Although it was on busy Illinois Avenue, I could fence in the back yard to create some safe play space and we could start looking for more permanent quarters. Johnny and Margaret Bradford lived in the other end of the duplex and were very kind and helpful. At work a new SRTP intern, Joe Johnson, had just started and I enjoyed getting to know him and helping him get oriented. I scrounged around yard sales and found some basic furniture – bed, chest of drawers and some chairs but no table. With the help of Jay Reynolds and Joe Johnson, I borrowed a truck and picked up the furniture I'd purchased. We were unloading the pick-up truck which had high wood frame sides, when Joe in jumping off the back caught his large class ring on a bolt of the frame and his weight caused the ring to cut his finger and shuck the flesh off the bone. I rushed Joe to the emergency room where they had to remove the bone, amputating his ring finger. Meanwhile Jay had found the finger and was totally unnerved. I dreamed that nightmare for weeks afterward. Joe recovered quickly but his hand with the missing finger was always a reminder of that night. Joe went on to complete his internship and graduate study and later served as president of the University of Tennessee.*

Mother and Dad brought the family to Oak Ridge. Now Rose and Bill could set up housekeeping, eating on a table made of boxes until they could find a real one at a yard sale. They enjoyed their months on Illinois Avenue. Margaret undertook teaching Rose to drive and she got her license. Since Johnny dealt in used cars, they bought a big, luxurious Hudson Hornet from him. Billy and Laura grew. A stray beagle dog wandered in and was adopted and named Phoebe. She had puppies and eventually all, including Phoebe were given away, except for one. He had been stillborn and pushed aside but they were able to revive him and felt a special bond with him. They thought of naming him Lazarus because of his "resurrection" but couldn't imagine calling that name out the door, so they named him Boris for Boris Gudonov, a 16th century Russian tsar of questionable lineage. The pup was obviously a half-breed, looking like a chow rather than a beagle. As he grew, he was very patient with and protective of the children.

After they had been a year in the small duplex, residents of Oak Ridge were being given the opportunity to buy their homes but the duplex where Rose and Bill lived was scheduled to be demolished for road widening. They were able to move into a much larger duplex with three bedrooms on each end in the Woodland area at 142 Manhattan Avenue. The Dentons, in the other end, did not plan to buy the duplex but to exercise their priority on another property, so Bill and Rose purchased the duplex from the government with a mortgage, and began their experience as home owners. When the Dentons moved Bill and Rose added one bedroom from the rental end to their unit and then rented a two bedroom unit for a time. A ledger sheet preserved from January 1958 shows the house value at $8100 with a mortgage of $5700. The family had a little over $500 in the bank and credit union and owed the credit union $1200, probably for an automobile loan. Eventually they took over the whole house and had plenty of room as the family grew. They put up a fence, built stone walls, planted trees and shrubs and made a patio from marble slabs picked up at a nearby quarry. It was a great neighborhood with Brian and Johnnie Waters with their children on one end, the Harvey family below and Bill and Virginia Busby and their children just around the corner. Bill Busby was a fellow worker at ORINS. The house was only a block from the Woodland school where all the children would begin their schooling. But at the beginning, it was only Billy and Laura and they were not yet school age.

## Billy

Billy was a gentle child from birth without a selfish bone in his body, like his grandmothers Lochiel Moore and Gertrude Ramsay. Rose could depend on him to be kind and helpful in caring for his little sister.

*Billy was so sensitive to others that I sometimes worried about him. Once when Laura had repeatedly grabbed his toys, I told him he didn't have to let her. His response was, "It makes her happy!" He learned quickly and was very obedient and understanding beyond his years. Visiting Grandma and Grandpa Ramsay in Washington when he was three he noticed that Grandpa was often away (he traveled on union business) and when he returned from one trip Billy told him, "Grandpa, you can stay here. We'll let you!"*

He was fascinated by the natural world. His teacher noted that he was late for school some mornings and Rose investigated. She always sent him on his way early enough, so she followed him and found him stopping all along the walk to school to observe ants and other bugs. As soon as he could read, he devoured books about science and nature and became a reliable source of all kinds of information. He was also fascinated with tools and how things worked and he had very capable hands. As he grew older, his brothers and sisters depended on him to fix anything that was broken. He was Daddy's helper too and he understood reasons for behavior.

*When Billy was quite small, he would get down on the floor with me when I was fixing the washer or a drain under a sink and his hands would shake in eagerness to hold the tools. If I laid a screwdriver down beside me and then went to pick it up, it would be gone. He had it and wanted to use it. It wasn't too long before he could.*

*One day he was throwing rocks in a puddle making the water splash and I asked him why he liked to do that. He thought for a moment and said, "Power!" I was amazed.*

*He rarely required any punishment but when he did something he shouldn't he was miserable until he had received punishment, however mild, and then would be happy again. Once when he had erred he moaned, "Somebody big shouldn't have let me do that."*

Billy had a very analytical mind and was curious about things. Sometimes on a test he wouldn't do well, not because he didn't know the answer, but because he wanted to explore all possibilities. For example, once he was given an exercise where an assortment of coins was given and the student was to decide what to buy with his money from a list of priced items. Billy considered all the options instead of quickly allocating his pennies, nickels and dimes. He became a rock collector and learned all about minerals, gems and fossils. Going to Washington was always a highlight experience for him. Grandma Ramsay took the children to the zoo and other museums.

By the time the Oak Ridge years were over, he was a bit small and thin compared to classmates, but strong, ready for high school, a fine student, a clarinet player and he had a healthy mind and body. He had become a Boy Scout and was a great example for his younger brothers.

## Laura

Laura was a force from the beginning. She had sparkling dark eyes full of interest in everything. She was very independent and didn't like anything binding her. As a baby she threw off her blankets and, as soon as she was able, escaped her crib and divested herself of clothes whenever possible – except for hats, which she liked. She never crawled, but scooted on her bottom with one hand propelling and the other ready to grab things or do other mischief. She was sturdy and had tremendous will power. When she decided to walk, she powered herself up on her dimpled legs in the middle of the floor and walked.

*I was used to compliant Billy and thought we had parenting down pat. Laura was a shock. If I told Billy not to touch something because it was hot, he would say, "hot," and not touch. Laura immediately touched to find out what "hot" meant. She was in to everything and often pulled Billy with her. She was also beautiful, great fun and very affectionate. When they had their bath and were ready for bed, we'd often have a romp on our bed. Bill would stand by the bed and they would push him and he would stagger and fall to the floor amid their squeals of laughter. They would have continued all night but finally were tired enough to go to bed. Laura was not a good sleeper and both Bill and I were sleep deprived for a time.*

Laura loved to play outside in the dirt and sometimes looked like a refugee child, except she looked too healthy. She climbed up on a neighbor's wooden trailer on one occasion and sat down on a serious splinter, requiring surgical removal. She climbed to the top of a dresser and ate a whole bottle of baby aspirin and had to have her stomach pumped. She did not travel well and resisted getting in the car.

*On a trip to Washington we stopped around Abingdon. VA, at a tourist home for the night. Billy slept with Rose and Laura with me. She was so excited to be in my bed that she kept giving me big slobbery kisses. I was good and wet before we went to sleep. The tourist home wouldn't take a check and this was before credit cards, so we had to pay in cash. We decided to stop in Radford to cash a check at a bank but the bank wouldn't cash an out-of-town check. Not knowing quite what to do we were driving through town and stopped at a stoplight. A car pulled up next to us and we recognized Dr. Hall, who had been the army pediatrician who took care of Billy while we were at Fort McPherson. He recognized us and we all pulled in to a parking area. After sharing news and memories, we told him of our check cashing difficulties and he told us to follow him to a bank his father owned, where we had no problem getting some cash. He also gave us some medicine to help Laura travel more easily. Instead of calming her it made her drunk and she made the rest of the trip most interesting.*

Later they found out that Laura was strongly left handed and had some vision problems that required glasses. She was thrilled to be able to see what was on billboards and road signs and became a much better traveler. She wanted to do everything Billy did. When he went to preschool, she "debriefed" him as soon as he was home. The preschool was a parents' cooperative and Bill became treasurer. When Laura went, she enjoyed it more than Billy had. She loved arts and craft and music. When Billy was in first grade, Laura immediately learned everything he did. She had a remarkable memory and could turn the pages of a book and "read" it before she knew her letters and words. By the time she got to school herself, she had two younger brothers and had found her place in the family as the family's second mother and first mother's capable helper.

*The hardest child raising years were when Stephen was born. Billy was three and Laura was two and now they outnumbered us. We still had a great time together and with friends but got tired and frazzled. Two years later when John was born, Laura was enough older that she took over major responsibility for the younger two. Billy had always done what she wanted and now she devoted all her energy and will to caring for her family – especially baby John. She continued in that role when Jim was born two years later and the boys readily accepted her authority. She would set up a schoolroom and teach them whatever she had learned at school. If she wanted to play girl things she dressed them as girls and they did what she said. She was physically agile and strong and could best all three younger ones in a wrestling match. Jim once remarked, "My sister, Laura, is 'puhfect!'"*

As might be expected Laura did very well at school. She was in plays, sang, made art and craft items, read everything and had a lot of friends. She was very protective of her brothers and her friends. Once when some other girls were picking on her rather small and frail friend, Ivy Lynn, Laura reported the incident to Rose and said that she, "Sort of threw them down." Whatever she did was done well and with energy. She was a favorite pupil of her piano teacher, Mrs. Epps, and she wanted to be like her. Years later she also teaches piano. By the time the family left Oak Ridge, she was a new teenager and a lovely young woman. Her brothers were getting to be as big as she, but they continued to adore her and look up to her. What a blessing she was and is to the family.

## Stephen

The first of three to be born in Oak Ridge, on July 18, 1956, Stephen Gates Ramsay arrived. His birth was a vindication of Rose's study and work on childbirth education and her exercises and breathing techniques. She had no anesthesia or shots and was ready to get up and dance after delivery. This is the way it should be done. She "roomed in" with her little blond blue-eyed bundle of joy. He was a happy child, quick to smile and laugh. As he grew he liked to run and hide, which made it hard for Rose with two other toddlers to manage. For a while they put a halter on Stephen and had him on a leash when they went shopping. Some people frowned judgmentally and others smiled knowingly. He loved the feeling of fur and buried his face in it if he could. They barely got him stopped in a restaurant before he grabbed and immersed his spaghetti sauce smeared face in a passing woman's fur coat. She never knew how close she came to disaster.

*Stephen could understand when I told him something or when Billy and Laura said things, but he was slow to talk himself. Instead of saying individual words, he began to make sentences of rather guttural gibberish with all the expression of someone telling a story. We felt we should understand him. We began to figure out word combinations. He linked words together. The word "hot" was "hotdog." The word "hat" was "haton." Cow was cowboy, etc. He continued to love words as he got it sorted out, sometimes not understanding them fully. Someone asked him what he wanted to be when he grew up. He answered, "A doxology." Of course he meant a doctor. Once, playing with one of the other children he said, "I'll be the doctor and you be the helicopter." We think he meant "doctor's helper." It was interesting to watch his language skills develop quite differently from the others.*

As a toddler he could be very persuasive. He loved milkshakes and would tell the person he was trying to influence with his bright blue eyes, "I like milkshake. You like milkshake?" He was hard to resist.

*He was so cute that everyone wanted to pat him on the head. This was fine until the dark cloud of a two year old settled over him and then, when someone patted his head, he would rub his own head and say, "Wipe it off!"*

As John and Jim joined the family over the next four years, he became the ringleader of the three younger boys. Rose talked about "Billy, Laura and 'the boys,'" making Billy ask on occasion, "What am I?" As they grew and played together, the boys made up their own language and their made up words often sounded like whatever thing or feeling it represented. For example, "ooolaar" meant lethargic or laid back. Some of the words were to substitute for words they weren't allowed to use and they foolishly thought their parents didn't understand what they were saying. Stephen and John were especially close and could almost read each other's minds. Stephen was ten when they left Oak Ridge and he was the leader of "the boys."

## John

John Robert made his appearance on May 30, 1958, and quickly became the special charge of big sister Laura. His sense of humor was evident very early as Bill remembers.

*I was changing his diaper, using those big safety pins with which you sometimes stuck your finger, and had my tongue protruding from the corner of my mouth, which was a family trait in mother's family. Then I noticed that baby John was mimicking me with his little tongue stuck out and his eyes sparking. He continued to add fun and humor to the family as he grew.*

It became obvious early that John loved numbers and to figure. On trips he would stand behind the driver's seat, before the days of seat belts, and watch the odometer and speedometer and calculate how long it would be before they go a certain number of miles. He was very competitive, always considering the odds and cheering for whatever he chose to win. They used to joke that if John saw two leaves falling he would take bets on which would hit the ground first. He kept score of gas stations by their brand of gas. Rose remembers this trait having impact on his school work.

*The beloved first grade teacher, Grace Smelcer, had taught Billy, Laura and Stephen and they were all avid readers. When John came along she was not surprised at his reading ability. What was new was his desire to read more books than anyone else. She told me she never had a student who read so many books. His name was always first on the list of number of books completed.*

As soon as he was old enough, John knew all the baseball stats. He kept up with the teams he chose and loved all sports. He loved the thrill of competition and adventure and seemed to have no fear.

*I had let the kids go out to the back yard and decided to check on them, presumably playing in the sandbox we had built under the wild cherry tree. The other children were concerned because John had climbed high up in the tree and couldn't get down. He was just little and his legs were not very long. He had on one piece overalls. I thought about calling the fire department but, instead, calmly talked him down, limb by limb. Then I about collapsed as I hugged him in relief. Another time John had become unhappy about something and decided to run away from home. He packed a few treasures in a back pack and went out the door. I watched as he went down the walk to the gate and looked up the sidewalk to the street corner just above our house. Then he turned back and came to the house. I asked him why he had given up his attempt to leave home and he answered, "I'm not allowed to cross the street!"*

John was fun to have around and could always make his mother laugh with his foolish faces, noises and comments. Whenever the boys got into mischief and were about to be reprimanded, the others would push John forward to make mom lose her resolution to scold. It usually worked. Really the only problem with which little John struggled was his temper. If something didn't go right he would go into a rage which didn't last long but was not acceptable. He worked on overcoming it and did.

*We discussed his temper with him and treated it as an evil spirit trying to control him. We suggested that when he felt mad he run to the back door, open it and fling the temper out into the yard. He did this and gradually learned to control his feelings until he became a very even tempered boy.*

John turned nine the month the family moved to Atlanta and was full of fun, responsible and very athletic. He never lost his love of mathematics or of sports.

# Jim

Born on January 25, 1960, Jim only had seven years in Oak Ridge, but they were formative years. He was the baby of the family for ten years but wasn't spoiled. He had an irrepressible spirit and a lot of confidence from the beginning. There was a rough time when he was still an infant. He began bleeding from his intestines. He ran a fever and was weak and the doctors didn't know what was causing the problem. But there was help form a higher source.

*I was really worried and prayed hard for Jim's healing. I was rocking his hot little body in a rocking chair and was calling on God to help when I felt the guidance to turn Jim over to God. I did and dedicated him to the Lord. I felt a sense of peace and comfort, replacing the fears and tension that I had felt for days. This was God's child, entrusted to us for a time. Jim's fever left, the bleeding stopped and the doctors never understood what happened. I knew that Jim would always be guided and cared for in a special way. And he has been.*

Jim was very outgoing and positive. Whatever happened he would bounce back, like the little Japanese ceramic doll someone gave us that had a round weighted bottom and no matter how many times you pushed it over it would stand upright as soon as it was released. He was a good playmate and also related well to adults. Dr. Pollard was a favorite with Jim. He enjoyed our friend Glenn McClanan, who lived with us for a time and had one of the old-style Volkswagens. Jim called them Glenn Cars and they became that to the whole family. He never went through the dark days usually experienced by two year olds.

Jim, John and Stephen for a time couldn't imagine a better job than garbage collector. They would hear the garbage truck and the clang of cans and watch the men roll the cans down the sidewalk to the truck, twirling them on their bottoms and making a grand noise. What could be better?

*Jim had a remarkable friendliness and self-assurance, which attracted attention and comment. Once he wondered aloud, "Why does everybody in the world love me?" Perhaps it was because he loved everybody.*

As his brothers and sister had been Jim was a good student in kindergarten and first grade. Like the others he loved books and stories. Whatever role he was given in a family skit or game he cheerfully played. He tended to be persistent when he wanted something but was a most enjoyable child.

## Three More Children

Rose thought she was through adding children to the family. For the first eight years of marriage she had been pregnant much of the time. Now her youngest, Jim, was ready for school and she was happy with her five wonderful children. She was involved in church, community activities, literacy, childbirth education and found time to help in the schools. True to her Berea experience she often helped with costumes for school plays and events. It was a busy and productive life. Then out of the blue in the summer of 1965 Rose's brother, Kenneth, called and needed help. Betty had left him and their three children. What was he to do? To make a long story short Ken moved to Oak Ridge with Ricky, Kathy and Larry, and for a year they all lived in the same house. That meant eight children between the ages of five and thirteen. The school teachers at Woodland were so helpful and Rose spent a lot of time at the school with two in kindergarten, and one each in grades two through seven. The children had some catching up to do and needed some dental attention. They were unused to the Ramsay family routines and expectations, but everyone did remarkably well under the circumstances. Ken decided to change his employment and, for a while went to barber school. (The rest of that story is told in a subsequent section). When he moved to a place of his own with the children he met a neighbor lady, Glenda Keys and in July 1967, shortly after Bill and Rose had moved to Atlanta, they married. Later Ricky, Kathy and Larry went back to their mother in Greene County.

# CHAPTER 11

# FAMILY LIFE AND FUN

Later sections of this account will follow the slices of the Oak Ridge years covering work and the causes in which Bill and Rose were involved, but they had wonderful family times and couple times during this period as well. They went camping as a family and, sometimes with other families, and at least once just as a couple. Cades Cove in the Smoky Mountains was a favorite place with a hike to Abrams Falls and picking up sourwood honey on the loop as they returned. Fall Creek Falls on the Cumberland Plateau and Deep Creek below Bryson City were memorable trips. Some summers they joined Mother and Dad Ramsay and other parts of the family on the Atlantic shore in Delaware or Maryland. They often took Wayne with them. There were wonderful trips to Washington, DC.

*We had purchased our first new car – a Kombi, which was a Volkswagen bus, and had put in the upholstery ourselves fitting it for family travel and camping. Each child had a place. It had 40 or 50 horsepower and had trouble on hills or if the wind was hitting the flat front. When going to Washington we would stop at Rose's home in Tennessee and have supper and then put the kids to bed in the bus and drive all night. We had some memorable snowy trips but, when the snow stopped, we loved the sight of the moon glistening on the white expanses of the fields along the roads in Virginia. When we arrived in the morning, Mother would take charge of the children and we would go to bed.*

*On another trip we headed west. I had a conference to attend in Denver and we took some vacation time and drove across the plains. The wind was from the west and the bus had a hard time getting up any speed. We had brought along camping gear and every other night camped out. Then we'd stop at a motel the next night and get showers, clean up and be on our way again. The kids got bored driving through Kansas and when we suggested they look at the scenery they said, "We've seen it!" Jim was interested in most everything; Stephen wanted to sleep; John busied himself counting gas stations and calculating time and distance. Laura and Bill read or organized word games. Sometimes we all sang songs. It was a way to organize the noise. Because of the headwind we were late getting to Cimmeron Crossing, Kansas, on the Arkansas River where there is a city park with camping facilities. As we pulled into the park looking for a camp site, a big man with a cowboy hat and guns slung on his hips came up to the car. We noticed his sheriff's badge and wondered if we were in the wrong place. The kids were wide eyed. He welcomed us, took us to a camp site and then brought us some firewood. We slept, some in the bus and some in a tent. I remember waking in the morning to the soothing sound of doves cooing, with everything shrouded in mist rising from the river. What a beautiful spot.*

*In Denver Rose and the children visited friends, Bill and Lil Miller, while I went to my meetings. The Millers took Rose and the children up a mountain past the snow line and they played in the snow. Little Jim almost disappeared in a drift. I had anticipated making good time driving on the way home with a tailwind but the wind shifted and the bus fought it all the way home too. My foot was tired from trying to push the gas pedal harder when it made no difference.*

Bill and Rose joined the Presbyterian Church and over the years taught Sunday School and took other responsibilities. Stephen, John and Jim were all baptized there. Bill was ordained as an Elder. The laying on of hands invoked feelings of awe and humility at the realization of the generations of Christian ordained from St. Peter on through the centuries. They went through turbulent times as the congregation struggled with positions on social issues, the Bible as God's Word, leadership styles and the usual things that divide churches. They had good friends on both sides of most issues but some of the basic beliefs of Christianity were being questioned as a move toward humanism crept in.

*We were dismayed as more attention was given to "demythologizing" the Bible than seeking its wisdom and instruction as the Word of God. We always considered ourselves liberal on social issues, like civil rights, but based it on our commitment to follow Christ, not some humanistic do-goodism. His sacrifice and Good News was for all men. His instruction is to love each other and to serve those less fortunate. Faith, not works, is what matters at the core, and true faith then is manifest in works. We stuck with the church, but were more and more aware of its move toward a different, man-centered gospel than the good news of Christ.*

Bill and Rose continued their family traditions of Bible study and prayer in the home as well as attending church. Christmas and Easter were celebrated from a Christian perspective, although Santa Claus and the Easter Bunny were enjoyed as well. They had always made offerings and supported charities as they could, but now with a steady income they looked seriously at tithing.

In the early Oak Ridge years, they still had to watch pennies carefully but they decided to increase their giving to reach a tithe. They committed to a tithe of gross income because that commitment took precedence over taxes or other deductions before their take-home pay. It took three years to reach this tithe and then it continued ever since. God's promise about "the full tithe" recorded in Malachi 3:10 says, *"Put me to the test.... I will open the windows of heaven for you and pour down for you an overflowing blessing."* The promise has been kept.

In the community they enjoyed the plays of the theater group, but never got involved themselves. They went folk dancing with a group that did a lot of international dances and had a good time with their fellow dancers. They took a ballroom dancing course at the Ethel Howell studio, learning fox trot, waltz and jitterbug and that was fun. At the end of the course they won the "American Award" for best ballroom dancers in the class. Rose remembers.

*We came home one evening from dance class and were not quite ready to stop so we put on a record and danced a little around the living room. The teenage girl from next door who was babysitting was thrilled. She said, "I love to watch old people dance!" We were still in our twenties.*

The problem and expense of baby sitters is a concern of young families. Couples need time to do things together and still be assured their children are safe and cared for.

*As our family grew we met other young couples through school activities, church and other friends who faced the same questions we had about child care. We formed a "baby sitters' club" in the Woodland area. Members were young couples with small children who agreed to sit for each other. The task of scheduling and keeping records of the number of hours each couple sat or used was rotated among members. It worked beautifully. Since we had a number of children and often a baby, I would stay home and Bill would go to sit for the requesting family. He had a great time telling the children stories. Most were not used to having stories told without looking at a book. But it could be done when they were in bed with the lights out so was very effective. When we went out we could be secure, knowing that our children were watched over by a mature, experienced father or mother.*

Rose always had a special interest in teaching reading and sometimes helped in the school. She shared a love of watching children begin to read with the children's first grade teacher, Grace Smelcer. Grace fondly recounted the story of one eager little girl who said to her, "Oh teacher, if I tud only weed!" She also became involved in teaching literacy through a good friend, Ida Coveyou. Under a Job Corp program, Rose taught young people who had managed to get through school without learning to read. She also helped with literacy classes for adults, some of whom had other languages than English as their primary language. Later, she became certified as a literacy teacher using the methods of missionary Frank Laubach in teaching English to a variety of populations. It was always exciting for both teacher and student when one began to be able to read and communicate effectively.

The family often visited John and Winona after they had moved to Celo, NC. They had two sons, Martin and Loren, the ages of Stephen and John, Their home was in view of Mount Mitchell and other peaks of the Black Mountains, with their rushing streams and lush growth of rhododendron and laurel. John was building a dairy there and also taught school in nearby Micaville. After a few years at Celo, John and Winona decided to go to graduate school in Ames, Iowa. Mother and Dad Ramsay and their children's families decided to purchase the house at Celo and make it a family vacation place. It later also became the retirement home of Mother and Dad Ramsay. Celo became a very special place for the whole extended family.

## Celo

Everybody should have their Shangri-La, their magic place of dreams away from the usual business of life. The house at Celo, which Grandma Ramsay named Happiness Hill, was that for Bill and Rose, Billy, Laura, Stephen, John and Jim, as well as numerous aunts, uncles, cousins and friends.

*We had all enjoyed such wonderful times at Celo, hiking, playing in the creeks, inner-tubing in the South Toe River and enjoying the invigorating air of the mountains, along with the fellowship of family and friends that we didn't want to give it up. We all agreed to form a Celo Family Association, buy the property and commit ourselves to vacationing there in summers when school was out. Mother and Dad put up most of the funds, but we all participated. It was a good decision for our family. Oak Ridge was a half day away.*

Beginning in about 1961 Mother spent the summers at Celo and Rose would come and stay with the five children. Bill would come up on weekends. Patty and Earl came as they could and their children - David, Susan, Billy Lynn, and Fred- sometimes spent extended periods. John and Winona, Martin and Loren were there as their schedules allowed and Dick came occasionally. Dad's sister, Billie Richards, stayed there for a time. All brought friends so there was almost always a good sized group. Rose's Dad came with Wayne for a visit the first summer she stayed there and they took him up to the Mount Mitchell tower. It was quite a hike uphill from the parking area and he was breathless but pleased when he got there. Later that summer Wayne called to report that their Dad was ill and hospitalized. Rose went to the veterans' hospital in Johnson City and was able to visit with him. He died in July and Rose was with her brothers for the funeral. She was glad he had been able to be with her and the children at Celo just a little earlier.

*We loved being at Celo. It was great to be away from the pressures of life in Oak Ridge and to work with Mother, making a garden, feeding hungry children, taking excursions to the creek, going up the mountain, enjoying the Hemlocks Park on the river, talking and playing games. Dad Ramsay was still working at first, so was in and out, but later retired and then they both stayed year round. Generally everyone would work in the morning and then have the afternoon for fun and games. Bill would come on weekends and for vacation time and we had wonderful adventures. We visited Linville Gorge and Bill made up stories about the Salamander People who lived in caverns beneath the mountain, tending the fires in the earth and accounting for the mysterious Brown Mountain Lights that were a phenomenon of the area.*

*Once Mother was off on a trip with Dad and I had our five, Martin and Loren and the Todt cousins by myself. Of course I had Laura to help and she was as good as another woman. The boys would take turns inserting themselves into a stack of inner tubes and then let the others tackle them until they rolled down the hill to be stopped by the rock wall half way to the road. I was amazed that no one was hurt. We did have mishaps like a badly cut foot from wading in the river and stings from stepping on a yellow jackets nest. In both these instances, John was the victim.*

Some family activities became traditions on White Oak Creek Road at Celo. For the Fourth of July, Grandpa would dress as Uncle Sam and drive his little tractor and cart in which the Queen (Susan or Laura) was ensconced. When they acquired a pony, Danny Boy, he would join the parade, perhaps ridden by David, the oldest of the grandchildren. Others would march with or without special costumes. Once Bill, dressed up as an old woman of the mountains with a "wig" of moss from the creek, walked on stilts, supported by Earl. Whoever was at Happiness Hill at the time marched in the parade or joined the spectators lining the road.

*Rose and I would write a little play each year based on a fairy tale and have the children, in costumes Rose had put together, perform it for the community.*

*We'd hang a blanket on a line at the porch, which served as a stage, or on a clothes line in the yard, and arrange chairs for spectators. The cast for Goldilocks and the Three Bears, Sleeping Beauty, Cinderella, Aladdin, or whatever we were doing would be expanded to give parts to whatever number of children (and sometimes adults) we had there at that time. Both the children and the spectators loved it and came to expect it every year.*

One year many of the family went to the Martin family reunion at Hidden Paradise, near Old Zionsville, Pennsylvania. They took that year's play, Aladdin, on the road to the reunion, to the delight of all attendees. Grandpa Ramsay played the Sultan, Billy and Stephen were the Genie and Aladdin. Laura was the princess and others played characters to round out the cast. The tradition of family plays continued through the years, now into new generations. At the reunion the children got to know the lively Martin family and understand where Grandma Gertrude got her zest for life.

The men of the family, assisted by the children, had constructed a small A-Frame building on the high bluff overlooking the back yard of Happiness Hill. It had built-in bunks and spending the night in the A-Frame became a special event and rite of passage for the boys in the family. After all there were bears in those woods. When Jim was deemed old enough to have his turn, he was excited but a little scared. Grandpa Ramsay had said he'd sleep there too. Jim asked him if he could kill a bear and Grandpa replied that when the bear opened his mouth he'd reach down his throat, grab his tail and turn him inside out. Jim said, "I'll sleep with you!"

*Jim was also fond of Grandpa for another reason. Dad loved to play cards and we had great games of canasta, which he usually won. He loved ice cream even more and after a game would say. "Who'd like ice cream?" Jim was delighted because Grandpa didn't just give you a small scoop; he'd unwrap a carton or two and cut each person a huge slab with a butcher knife.*

The Weatherford family came for a visit and everyone went up to Mt. Mitchell and a group decided to hike home on the mountain trails. They got lost from the trail and hacked their way through the laurel jungle finally, as the day turned dark, coming out on a road not far from White

Oak Creek Road and Happiness Hill. Those not on the hike had become worried and were searching the roads going up different hollows until they found them looking weary but happy to have had the adventure.

Boris, their dog came to Celo with the family and sometimes stayed with Mother when the family went back to Oak Ridge. During one of these periods he must have eaten poison and died. Mother and Dad buried him and the family grieved. But other dogs came into their lives. First a little female with features of a border collie wandered in to Happiness Hill and attached herself to Rose. Rose named her Cindy and became very fond of her.

*Cindy must have been abused because for a long time she wouldn't go past Bill or any other man when they opened the door for her. She was very sweet and sensitive to me. She loved to retrieve a thrown ball, but had a hard time giving it up for another throw. The kids adored her. She stayed with us for the rest of our Oak Ridge years and many years beyond that before succumbing to cancer. Taking her for a final visit to the vet was very hard for me. Stephen went with me as we said goodbye to our little friend and companion.*

At another time the children found a little puppy half drowned in White Oak Creek and brought him to the house. He was barely alive and very mangy with his eyes clouded. They spooned some food and water in his mouth and made him warm and comfortable in a box with rags. They named him "Moses" because he was rescued from the bulrushes. Jim was especially attached to him and Bill and Rose were worried about his reaction if the little dog died. His eyes were already glazed over and they didn't expect him to last the night. They put the box in the shed and talked with Jim about how sick he was and the likelihood that he wouldn't survive. Jim said, "But I prayed for him and he is going to be all right." The next morning when we looked in the shed, the puppy was playing around. He continued to struggle with mange, which the vets said had such a hold that he'd likely never be rid of it. Eventually they arranged to have him taken to an animal research lab that was interested in his condition and promised to give him a good home. White Oak Creek was the site of many picnics and adventures.

*I was always interested in waterways and knew that White Oak Creek ran into the South Toe River and it flowed into the Toe and then the Nolichucky, which became part of the French Broad and eventually helped form the Tennessee River, which finds its way to the Ohio, which flows into the Mississippi and finally the Gulf of Mexico at New Orleans. Some of us decided to take our old flat bottomed canoe down to the South Toe and boat down river to a bridge that crossed the river in a couple miles. We estimated the time and arranged to be met at the bridge. We never made it. We did get to sit in the boat and float a few times and once capsized it. (I can still see Susan being catapulted out of the prow into the water). Most of the time we had to carry the boat over shoals or slog through shallows deep in silt from the mica mines. Finally as it was getting dusk we abandoned the river and found a road. Leaving the boat to be picked up later we made it home, having an increased appreciation for Lewis and Clark.*

After Dad Ramsay retired and he and Mother stayed at Celo year round, they became very involved in the community. Dad helped organize a Yancey County "tomato co-op" to encourage tomato growing and set up a processing plant to prepare the produce for market. Happiness Hill had a good field of tomatoes and all learned how to care for them and when to pick them. Dad also had some chickens and they acquired three horses, in addition to the pony, Danny Boy. The boys learned to care for the horses, Lady, Sparkle and Merry Legs, and to ride.

*From the first, Mother and Dad had joined the little country Presbyterian Church between Celo and Micaville and served there as they could. I enjoyed dressing the children up on Sunday and going to church. I helped with vacation bible school. The people were so genuine and friendly, although, as usual, there were divisions. In one situation members were choosing sides and a member of one group asked, "Have you talked to John and Gertrude Ramsay?" The reply was, "It won't be any use talking to them. They see good in everybody." Rev. Chapeau, a refugee from Hungary or Czechoslovakia, became the inspiring and faith-filled pastor and a good friend. The church was quite different from our Oak Ridge church. The music and singing was somewhat of a shock but Mother said, "They are making a joyful noise." It was a good experience for our children.*

The times at Celo sound like an idyllic life and to a large extent they were. With plenty to do and without the distractions of "city life," the children got along well with only minor squabbles, which are to be expected. On occasion parental discipline was required but rarely. Once when Grandma Ramsay scolded Jim for some infraction of rules he said, "Grandmas aren't supposed to scold!" It was rare, but both Rose and Grandma had authority and the children knew that there were boundaries. On one trip back to Oak Ridge with all five children, the bickering and complaints verged on outright combat in the rear of the station wagon. Rose tried to settle them but they refused to sing or play games and the level of conflict grew. Rose threatened the children with dire consequences if they didn't stop the quarreling. They didn't stop.

*It was hard enough to negotiate the sharp curves around Hot Springs without the noise of conflict in the back seats. Rose had tried unsuccessfully to get the kids to behave and finally told me to pull over at the side of the road. There was a space right across from a country store and I pulled over. The kids, sensing impending doom, began to repent of their misdeeds but it was too late for Mom. She went around to the back of the station wagon, rolled down the back window and proceeded to pull one child after another out and give each a swat on the behind. Several old men sitting on a bench in front of the store across the road watched incredulously wondering just how many kids were in the car and slapping their legs in laughter as they watched the drama unfold. I'm sure in their retelling the number grew and grew until it was like "the old woman who lived in a shoe and had so many children she didn't know what to do." Later Stephen maintained that he never got his swat. He said he pushed Jim out twice.*

The Celo years changed as families grew and moved. When Mother and Dad moved to Berea in 1978, Happiness Hill was rented to another family and eventually sold. The children continued to return to Celo and take their spouses and their children, as they had families, so they could experience sliding down the mossy rocks at the waterfall into an icy pool at the bottom. First it took your breath away and then your body tingled and then got warm and invigorated. Another generation enjoyed swimming at the Hemlocks and tubing down the South Toe and hiking in the Pisgah

National Forest. The mountains were beautiful and clearly related to the Smokey Mountains with their misty mornings as the vapor lifted from the valleys. Stephen, who always had a way with words, once remarked on such a morning as the sun came up and the clouds rose, "Look, the mountains are taking off their pajamas!" What a beautiful place and what wonderful memories.

# CHAPTER 12

# CHILDBIRTH EDUCATION

Years before Celo and before the three younger boys were born, Rose was busy trying to change the way women experienced childbirth. She had been in communication with Bill's sister, Patty Todt, while Bill was still in the army and graduate school. Patty had sent material and Rose had read it along with the book by English physician, Grantly Dick Read. She gathered material from childbirth education organizations in New York and Milwaukee which gave information on classes to teach exercises, breathing and physical and mental preparation for childbirth. She was determined to avoid the spinal she'd had at Billy's birth and the gas at Laura's when she had her next child. When she was finally settled in Oak Ridge in 1955 she was ready to go to work. She quickly found that the obstetricians were adamantly opposed to any such nonsense. "Why would a woman want to subject herself to the pangs of childbirth without the benefits that medical science provides?" The OBs knew how to deliver babies. The woman was a necessary part of that but they were in control and women liked it that way.

*I did find support from our family doctor, Dr. Marsh, who didn't fully understand but was patient oriented and willing to go along. I also found a nurse, Jean Welshons, and a physical therapist, Mib O'Brian, who were interested. In addition several pregnant mothers were anxious to have the kind of information and help offered. We organized classes and advertised them and began teaching about the process of birth, its stages, breathing techniques to use during contractions, and exercises to prepare for the effort required by labor and delivery. We included husbands or other "coaches" to be able to help in the process. We had good material from the other centers and excellent instruction and inspiration from our nurse and physical therapist. Classes were started at the Presbyterian Church in June 1956, in time for Bill and me to attend in anticipation of our third child due in July. We practiced and prepared. Jean attended me in labor and delivery, along with Dr. Marsh. Of course Bill was excluded since fathers, at that time were thought to carry germs, become faint or get in the way. The nurses at the hospital were not too happy and were very negative about "rooming in," but with Dr. Marsh's help all was accomplished and it was wonderful. Now I could speak with confidence about childbirth education and natural childbirth from personal experience. The difference between my first two deliveries and the third was like night and day.*

By the end of 1956 with the help of Jean Welshons and Mib O'Brian and enthusiastic mothers like Jesse Noritake, Sybil Nestor and Eleanor Pegel, there was a strong active childbirth education group in Oak Ridge. Contact increased between the Oak Ridge group and other groups springing up around the country. Rose was on the phone a lot. Childbirth education was an idea whose time had come.

*Some women who seemed interested at first were really interested in "women's rights" and birth control and the fears of population explosion. We were interested in the wonder of bearing babies and bringing new life into the world as God intended for women. Soon these women were no longer interested in the group.*

In 1947 The Maternity Center Association in New York had hosted a visit by Dr. Grantly Dick Read, who had by then written a second book about natural childbirth, titled, *Childbirth Without Fear*. A natural childbirth association had been established in Milwaukee in 1950, and other groups like the ones in Columbus and now Oak Ridge were organized. Representatives from various groups met at the Maternity Center in 1955 and 1958 and began the formation of a national association. A first board meeting was held in 1961 and they determined to hold a convention in Seattle in 1962. Rose had birthed two more babies with natural childbirth techniques and continued her leadership of the group in Oak Ridge. She was asked to serve on the board of what was named the International Childbirth Education Association (ICEA) and she attended the convention in Seattle.

*I was obviously excited and a little scared. I was just a farm girl and now housewife from Tennessee and not a world traveler. But I now had delivered five children - three by natural childbirth and was passionate about childbirth education. I also had strong backing from Bill and the others in the Oak Ridge group. So I left my family and flew to Seattle. In the excitement of the convention and related meetings I offered Oak Ridge to be one of the sites for four regional conferences to be held in 1963.*

Oak Ridge did host a conference. The others were in Madison, Wisconsin, Washington, DC and San Francisco. It was exciting for the Oak Ridge group to be recognized as one of the strong centers for childbirth education and to host a regional conference. They got busy and did a first class job. What a privilege it was to meet some of the international leaders and have them come to Oak Ridge. Dr. Niles Newton who taught at Northwestern University Medical School and authored several books, including, *The Family Book of Child Care,* came to participate. She was the leading researcher on the emotional aspects of pregnancy and childbirth and also a strong advocate of breast feeding. Bill and Rose hosted an older lady from England who had developed exercises and breathing techniques and written manuals to use in childbirth education classes.

*Miss Mable FitzHugh was so English! Rose and I and the children were charmed by her English accent and her independent spirit. I remember once in the middle of a discussion with a group in our home, Mable informed everyone that she was a bit tired and would take a moment to rejuvenate herself whereupon she plopped down on the floor at full length and "relaxed." In a few minutes she was up again full of vigor. She made you a believer in rest, proper posture, breathing and exercise.*

The Oak Ridge group continued to be a strong chapter of the ICEA, offering classes and encouraging groups in other cities. ICEA grew from its modest beginnings to over 8,000 members. As the movement gained strength, the medical establishment began to change. Leading doctors like Dr. Robert Bradley embraced natural childbirth with an emphasis on the husband's role. Gradually the concepts and techniques found their way into the medical schools and hospitals so that by the time Rose and Bill's children were married and beginning their families childbirth classes, birthing suites, labor coaches, rooming in, family visitation, and even fathers attending birth were accepted as the norm.

# CHAPTER 13

# CIVIL RIGHTS

From the perspective of the history of mankind the civil rights struggle in the United States of America represents a small period of time. In other days and places, civil rights were only for the dominant class. Those not privileged by birth, conquest or social caste were not included. The Judeo/Christian heritage gave rise to the ideas that were represented in the founding of America. They found expression in the Declaration of Independence which held that "… all men are created equal, that they are endowed by their creator with certain inalienable rights…." But racial prejudice was deeply engrained in the culture and the economic system and the struggle in America to live up to its ideal still goes on. The most dramatic manifestation of racial discrimination in the USA was the institution of slavery which wasn't resolved until the Civil War. President Lincoln issued his Emancipation Proclamation in 1863 and the 13th Amendment abolished slavery in 1865. The right to vote for black citizens was not nationally confirmed until the 15th Amendment in 1870. Needless to say these legal actions did not solve all the problems.

In 1896 the Supreme Court established the "separate but equal" doctrine, supported by many black leaders who wanted equality but did not wish to be assimilated into the majority society. As the years passed it was increasingly evident that the doctrine was flawed and became a cover for racial division and discrimination. The struggle for racial equality, and more profoundly for "brotherhood", continued and found expression in all kinds of places in various ways.

In Oak Ridge, Bill's and Rose's years of 1955 to 1967 were years of great change. It was an exciting and challenging time to be involved. "Separate but equal" was still the law of the land and Oak Ridge had been built accordingly. Cracks were showing in the old doctrine, especially in public education with the Supreme Court's 1954 decision in *Brown versus Board of Education*. Schools in Oak Ridge were still segregated and public services were generally discriminatory, even though all property was still owned by the government and many services were offered by government contractors. On the other hand the programs offered in Oak Ridge for graduate fellowships, faculty research, training in the use of radioisotopes, and other opportunities to come to Oak Ridge for education, training and research were open to all, A number of faculty, scientists, technicians and students from primarily black institutions, like Tuskegee Institute and the University of Puerto Rico, came to Oak Ridge. Bill remembers in his first years at ORINS struggling with the tension between open opportunity in the programs on one hand and closed doors in services on the other.

*That first year in Oak Ridge, 1955, the news was full of civil rights situations in other places. Rosa Parks had refused to go to the back of the bus and the whole issue of equal public services was heating up. One of my responsibilities was to help with housing for visiting scientists, faculty and others coming to Oak Ridge under the programs we administered for the Atomic Energy Commission. I quickly found that most housing options were closed to black visitors, including the government owned, contractor operated dormitories and hotel. Two incidents illustrate the problem and difficulties encountered.*

*A visiting scientist had been denied a room at the Alexander Hotel. (There were no other hotels or motels in town at the time.) I remonstrated with the manager to no avail. I pointed out to him that a few weeks earlier he had accepted a black researcher from the University of Puerto Rico. His response was that "He wasn't black; he didn't speak a word of English!" Racial prejudice wasn't rational. A "foreigner" was acceptable but not a black citizen.*

*At another time a young black technician had come for a course in radioisotopes and was refused a room at the dormitories. The contractor who ran the facilities had no policy against black occupancy but was afraid of violence. There had been an incident previously where a shot had been fired into a door when a black person had been admitted. I went to the dorm, in which I had lived as an intern several years before, and met with the residents. I appealed to their sense of humanity and their union brotherhood but to no avail. They were afraid, if they were not prejudiced. The young man didn't want to cause any trouble and said he had other arrangements. When I looked into it, I found he was sleeping in his car and the weather wasn't warm. I consulted with Rose. She remembered an incident before we were married when she was traveling by bus and the bus had stopped in a small town at a café/bus stop and passengers had a chance to use the rest room and get refreshments. Everyone got off except a black girl. Rose asked if she was getting off and she said, "They won't serve me." Rose felt keenly the injustice of this and offered to get her a sandwich. She gratefully accepted and they ate together on the bus. The waitress, when Rose expressed her feelings, was very apologetic but that was the culture enforced by state laws.*

*Naturally we invited the young man to stay with us while he was taking his course. He was a fine young man and became a friend. Our good neighbors raised no objection when they saw a black man coming and going from our house.*

Bill raised questions about the housing policies in town and apparently some of the housing managers spoke to their AEC contacts. When AEC officials asked about this young man who was "causing trouble" the ORINS leadership was supportive of him. By this time, any federal official in authority knew that it was just a matter of time until policies would have to change. By 1957 Martin Luther King's eloquent voice began to be heard on the national scene and in 1960 President Kennedy issued an executive order prohibiting discrimination in federal programs.

*Now some of the government officials who had not been supportive of our efforts for equal treatment were inspecting us to be sure we had equal opportunity posters prominently displayed.*

In 1963 Dr. King gave his "I have a dream" speech to the assembled throngs in Washington, DC. President Kennedy was assassinated that same year. Then in 1964 the Civil Rights Act was signed into law by President Johnson. There were still battles to be fought – Selma didn't happen until 1965. By the time Bill and Rose left Oak Ridge in 1967, equal opportunity and even "affirmative action" was the law of the land. Until then there were several years of struggle in Oak Ridge to achieve equal public accommodations and community acceptance. Rose remembers working with others to find a way to live together with respect and love.

## Community Relations Council

*We joined the Community Relations Council (CRC), which was an unofficial group to promote racial equality and friendship. Bill became chairman of the group. We were aware that the housing and school separation denied our children the opportunity to get to know friends of another race. We set up a family exchange program. Anyone who wished could sign up and the program would facilitate family get-togethers across racial lines. I remember once a little black boy and Stephen, who was about two, were fascinated with each other's hair and rubbed each other's heads. Stephen had very fine blond hair. The black child asked his mother, "Why is his hair so funny?"*

*We became good friends with several black families and our children felt at ease with them. The children had invited one of their friends, a black girl, to visit them at Celo when they were spending time there in the summer. Arrangements were made and Bill was to bring her from Oak Ridge when he came to Celo that weekend. He remembers the feeling of unease on the trip because he knew it they were to stop for bathroom use or refreshment he could run into trouble. There was no incident but it was a reminder of the injustice of discrimination.*

One of their good friends, Sally McCaskill, had a son, John, who was ready to apply for college. They asked Bill to look over his completed application before sending it in. It was a revelation of the difficulties of breaching the gap between cultures. For example in answering the question, "Next of kin? (nearest living relative)" John had put in a name Bill didn't recognize. Bill asked why he hadn't listed his mother with whom he lived and he responded, "That is my uncle and he is the relative that lives closest to us." Years later when Bill and Rose were in Berea and Bill was working at the college one of the little girls who had sat on his lap to hear stories as part of the exchange program attended Berea. Bill and Rose were able to host her proud parents at her graduation.

Bill and Rose often commented that, except for them, the mainline church members were conspicuously absent from groups working on civil rights. Almost all of the white members of the CRC were Jews and Unitarians. Later, of course, it became very popular to be for civil rights, but back then it was not readily accepted by many good church leaders and people.

At one point in the effort to achieve open public services the CRC decided to sponsor a full page ad in the *Oak Ridger* listing all the citizens who would go on record as supporting equal public services. They were successful in getting more than a thousand signatures and filling the page in the newspaper. The experience taught them a valuable lesson about prejudging.

*We had canvassed our neighbors to get their signatures with good success, but had not asked one couple because we were sure they wouldn't sign and didn't want to embarrass them. They were older than we and were very friendly good neighbors, but we knew they were from rural Alabama, not highly educated and had the accent and appearances of the stereotype of what were called "Georgia Crackers." So we didn't approach them. Imagine our surprise when their names appeared in the big ad. Later we had occasion to talk to them about the ad and her response was, "There ain't going to be no difference when we get to heaven!" We learned our lesson.*

Gradually progress was made with eating places, housing and other services. The bowling alleys had posed a problem. By this time Bill was responsible for the "personnel" function (now called human resources) at ORINS. The employee recreation program fell in this area and ORINS had a bowling team. Since the ORINS program was a relatively small operation by itself, the bowling team belonged to one of the large Union Carbide leagues. Carbide ran the production plants and Oak Ridge National Laboratory. One of the young very able technicians in the ORINS Medical Division signed up to join the team, but he was black. The bowling alleys said they wouldn't allow him to play.

*We had a meeting of the team members to discuss the problem and I maintained the position that our activities were open to all employees and insisted that he remain on the team. One of the senior scientific people who imagined himself a good bowler and wasn't known for his tact, argued that the sport was competitive and it wasn't right to penalize the rest of the team by insisting the young man be part of it. The young man, who was present and had a slight stutter, said with some difficulty, "I know how to bowl." The tactless man asked him where he'd bowled. The young man said he'd bowled when he was in Europe in the army. "What was your average?" asked tactless. The young man replied "240", I was second highest in my theatre of operations." Tactless was speechless. His jaw dropped. If he got close to "200," he thought he was doing well.*

ORINS held firm and Union Carbide wasn't willing to evict the ORINS team from the league so top management talked turkey to the bowling alley management. Since their leagues were the main source of income for the alleys, the bowling alleys were integrated. Finally the only two holdouts for equal services were the laundromats and the barber shops. Rose was puzzled by the laundromats.

*It seemed crazy to me that they wouldn't let a black woman do her own laundry but if she came as a maid with her white employer's laundry it was permitted. I don't see how they could monitor it.*

Some advocates of civil rights decided to picket the laundromat and did so. A local Ku Klux Klan unit heard of it and came to cross the picket line and wash their white sheets. There was no violence but the remnants of a culture of separation died hard. The barber shops were the other hold outs. Visited by CRC members the barbers weren't belligerent but afraid. They said they didn't know how to cut a black's hair. No one would break the line. The story of what happened is a joy to tell.

## The Barber Shop

*We were at an impasse with the barbers, who were really nice fellows. A former classmate of ours, who was working on civil rights in Kentucky, sent me an article about some graduate students at a university who wanted a barber on campus and sold advance tickets for haircuts to lure a barber to come. That seemed like a good way for us to proceed. We had all the people who had signed the ad to support equal services as a start for soliciting prepaid haircuts. We developed a voucher and explanatory material and advertised in the paper. It caught the imagination of people and we soon had enough haircuts sold to support a shop for a year even if it didn't get any other customers. With this in hand we advertised for a barber. A couple brothers from New Jersey responded and we soon had an agreement for them to set up shop in Oak Ridge. They leased space by the hardware store and began to set up shop. Everything looked good until the building was burned down one night. The official ruling was spontaneous combustion originating in the hardware store, but it was seen by the barber brothers as a sign that they should go back to New Jersey. They left and we were holding pre-payments for a year's worth of promised haircuts. We prayed.*

*This was just the time that Rose's brother, Ken, called for help when his wife left him and their three children. They came to live with us and in conversation with Ken, who had a job at a factory in Greeneville, I suggested that this was an opportunity to change his employment if he was so inclined. I asked him what he'd like to do. He responded out of the blue that he'd always wanted to be a barber. Bells went off and we asked about his attitude toward opening a shop to cut hair for all. He said he'd have to learn anyway and he had no problem with accepting everyone. He enrolled in barber school in Knoxville while he and the children lived with us and quickly became proficient at cutting all kinds of hair. We did a lot of research on space, equipment, supplies and costs. We let the other barbers know of the plans and they were relieved to have the pressure off of them. Ken was the perfect person – an East Tennessee boy with no axe to grind and a personality, so important to a barber, of getting along with everybody.*

*We leased space near the building that had burned, purchased good equipment, and with help from others made an attractive facility. We took all of our savings, including that of our children who were very much part of the venture, borrowed a little more from the credit union and soon were ready to open "Ken's Barber and Style Shop." The grand opening was covered by publicity as the mayor and one of the black leaders in the community had the first haircuts. It worked beautifully and some of the original voucher holders were still getting their hair cut there more than 40 years later when Ken retired.*

205

The other barber shops soon followed in being open to all, but Ken's became an institution in Oak Ridge, employed several barbers and he was honored for its pioneering success. Bill and his boys were always offered complementary haircuts when in Oak Ridge. Years later, when Bill had retired and was living in South Carolina, he needed a haircut and dropped Rose off at the grocery in a small town to find a barber. He had seen a shop in an older section of town so he went there and parked in front and went in. It didn't look like a usual barber shop with typical chairs and counter with appliances and supplies, but there were chairs lined up and hair on the floor. A young black man entered from the rear and asked if he could be of help. "Do you give haircuts?" Bill asked. The answer gave a sense of "déjà vu." "Yes, but I don't know how to cut no white man's hair!" Surely God has a sense of humor.

When they left Oak Ridge in 1967, the whole civil rights situation had changed there and everywhere, but there still remained much to do to realize the goals of all people living in harmony as children of a loving God.

# Chapter 14

# Hospitality

Bill and Rose both had come from homes where hospitality was a natural part of family life. No matter how limited the accommodations or how sparse the pantry, sharing with others was expected and enjoyed. The Moore home had offered food and lodging to visiting ministers, teachers and others as well as family. The Ramsay home often had visitors from many places and extended family members spending time there. At Celo, with grandpa and grandma Ramsay, when Rose and the children spent summers there, it was rare to be without some guests staying for a time or coming for meals and fellowship. Bill and Rose continued this tradition wherever they were and in the Oak Ridge years had many interesting guests. In addition to the young black man who stayed with them while attending a radioisotope course, the visiting leaders in childbirth education and Rose's brother Ken's family, they often had visits from Mom and Dad Ramsay and other family members. The children especially enjoyed Uncle Dick (Bill's younger brother) who was unmarried and came and went at will in his Volkswagen bus. He told stories of his travels and his experiences among the Otomi Indians in Mexico.

*Glenn McLanan, who lived with us for a while when he was an exhibits manager for ORINS, was another favorite. He had become a family friend after a period in Mexico with Dick just after they graduated from college. He had a green Volkswagen that he left with us when driving an exhibits van and the children, especially Jim, thought the "Glenn Car" was "cool." When Glenn later was getting serious about a Berea graduate named Reba, he brought her by to get our approval. Eventually he completed a law degree and he and Reba returned to his home in Princes Anne County, Virginia to practice law. We often visited them at Virginia Beach where Reba served on the city council and sometimes as vice mayor. In addition to law practice, Glenn became a state senator.*

Another noted visitor who knew the family through Bill's brother John was Richard (Dick) Chase. He was a marvelous story teller and gave Bill and Rose several of his *Jack Tales* books to share with the local schools. Later in the years when Bill worked at Berea College Dick would come to Christmas Country Dance School. He had become somewhat of an eccentric character, but was always a friend. On another occasion the family hosted Myles and Aimee Horton, who were friends of Bill's family. Myles was director of Highlander Folk School which offered courses for those interested in social justice. The courses were often racially mixed and before civil rights was respectable in the South, they presented a problem for the established state leadership. The school had been located in Monteagle, Tennessee, near the Alabama border, but they were "run off" and moved to a location near Knoxville.

*Myles loved to tell his stories and was very entertaining. I remember one story especially. He had been called before a state investigative committee that, like the national Un-American Activities committee of Senator McCarthy, was seeking out communist infiltration. Highlander was suspect. At one point the committee counsel held up a letter written on Highlander stationary and asked Myles who was responsible for the stationary. Myles responded that it was set out for guests and students to use as they desired but he guessed he was the person responsible for the stationary itself, if not what was written on it. The lawyer pointed out that the salutation on the letter was, "Dear Comrade!" He asked Myles if he could think of any group that used such a salutation. Myles thought for a moment and then answered, "Well the Communist Party is reported to use it and the other group I am aware of is the American Legion." Myles, always good humored, continued to promote causes for justice and became a kind of folk hero.*

Family members, Berea friends, exchange program guests, church friends, colleagues from work and community organizations and friends of the children, were often found around the dining table and all made life more interesting. Bill and Rose began having a New Year's open house party at home instead of leaving the children with a sitter and going out to celebrate. They invited others to join and soon the party came to be an expected part of New Year's Eve for family and friends. Rose, assisted by Bill and the children, would make a wonderful array of crackers and cheese, sliced meat, veggies and dips, meatballs, candies and marvelous cookies, including (a family special) cream puffs. Bill learned to make a punch using apple juice, ginger ale and lime sherbet which was very popular and became a tradition. That simple punch is still enjoyed by children and grandchildren as they create their own traditions of hospitality.

*We had open house parties at other times than New Year and often combined friends and family who might not know each other. We had decided that alcohol would not be part of our lives and didn't serve any at our parties, although at Christmas parties elsewhere for ORINS employees and other such social occasions alcohol was often very much a feature. Once Bill's boss came to one of our parties and brought along a bottle of vodka. I gently relieved him of the bottle and told him I'd keep it in the refrigerator for him to take when he left. It didn't occur to me at the time that he might not appreciate my response to his "gift" but we never heard any more about it.*

# CHAPTER 15

# WORKING INITIALLY AND BEYOND

The position of an administrative assistant at ORINS was Bill's first professional job and he was quickly busy with budgets, forms and procedures. He was the person to make physical and fiscal arrangements for conferences and meetings. He designed booklets and other printed materials. He projected costs, made reports, helped with travel arrangements, housing and catering for gatherings. He soon became well acquainted with the initials that went with federal programs – ORINS (Oak Ridge Institute of Nuclear Studies), AEC (Atomic Energy Commission), TVA (Tennessee Valley Authority, ORNL (Oak Ridge National Laboratory), Y12 (the uranium refinement complex including a huge centrifuge), K25 (the sprawling gaseous diffusion plant in Oak Ridge to separate uranium isotopes), NSF (National Science Foundation), DOL (Department of Labor), etc. etc. He processed applications for fellowships for graduate students, research participation for faculty and other programs for review by selection committees. He reviewed the Q-Clearance forms on visitors which had to be submitted to the AEC for acceptance in some programs and to have access to sensitive information and facilities.

*Some meetings and conferences were held in Oak Ridge and a few were arranged in Gatlinburg, Tennessee, where there were more hotels and meeting facilities in a great natural setting. Some of the attendees were eminent scientists like Wernher von Braun, the former German scientist called the "father of rocket science" and Michael DeBakey, renowned heart surgeon. I was just the gofer, setting up for meetings, picking people up at the Knoxville or Johnson City airport and trouble-shooting on conference arrangements where needed. My services were mostly anonymous but sometimes noticed. After one conference I received an honorary PHD (Piled Higher and Deeper) degree with appreciation signed by the president and the chairman of the board of Clemson*

*University. A few Berea science teachers came to Oak Ridge under one of the*
*programs we administered and it was good to see them. Dr. Frank Gailey in*
*biology and Dr. Tom Strickler in physics were two that I remember.*

Nuclear science had been dramatically thrust on the world scene ten years
earlier but science teaching had not yet caught up with its development.
ORINS and others had been addressing the problem in higher education
but not in the high schools. In 1956 a grant from the National Science
Foundation through the AEC was given to ORINS to develop a 'traveling
science demonstration lecture program" to stimulate and support nuclear
science teaching in high schools. This "traveling teacher program" would
identify master teachers in high school science, train them in presenting
nuclear science in exciting ways and send them to high schools throughout
the country to help other science teachers upgrade their science classes.
Seven teachers were selected in the summer of 1956 and trained in Oak
Ridge under the tutelage of Dr. R J. Stephenson on leave from his position
as professor of physics at the College of Wooster. Ford Motor Company
agreed to furnish each teacher with a station wagon. The teachers built
demonstration models of nuclear reactors and other devices to use in the
program. The models were such that they could be replicated by a typical
high school shop. They embarked on their travels in the fall of that year.

*The teachers were not only wonderful teachers but fine people and we enjoyed*
*them immensely. Joe Bowles, an educator from North Carolina had been hired*
*to direct the program. I provided the administrative support. Joe and his wife,*
*Maxine, and daughter, Judy, became very good friends. Rose and I became very*
*close to some of the teachers also. Frank Starr and Eleanor, from Iowa, were*
*at our house when Rose went to the hospital to deliver Stephen and became*
*his god parents. They stood with us at Stephen's baptism at the Presbyterian*
*Church. We kept up with Bill and Lil Miller over many years and visited them*
*at their home in Colorado. It was an exciting group and a pleasure to be part*
*of getting the program up and running. Over 1200 schools had requested a*
*visit the first year. The teachers would visit only about 250 during the year,*
*spending a week at each school.*

In October of 1957, with the cold war still very evident, the United States was shocked by the Russian's launch of "Sputnik" as the first artificial satellite in space. This alert to America underscored the needs for improving science teaching that the traveling teachers program was addressing in a small way. The reaction by President Eisenhower and Congress to Sputnik led to the creation of NASA and the National Defense Education Act. There was a growing interest in science in general and in nuclear science in particular. The American Museum of Atomic Energy, operated by ORINS for AEC, had traveling exhibits to acquaint communities and schools with the basics and potentials of nuclear energy.

## Moving Up

After a couple years in the University Relations Division, Bill was transferred to the central administrative offices to supervise various administrative services for all divisions of ORINS. The Medical Division with its clinical research hospital, the Special Training Division with its numerous courses in isotopes and radiation safety, the Museum Division with its large public exhibits and extension programs, as well as the University Relations Division all had their particular facilities, programs and styles of management. Providing them with mail services, telephone operations, reproduction services and doing budget and procedures analyses and reports involved a number of employees. They required scheduling, direction, training and review.

*I had observed the various styles of management in the different parts of ORINS and came to the conclusion that there was not one right way, but there were ways that were less effective than others. In University Relations, it had been more manipulative. In Medical it was more autocratic and in Special Training more collegial. Dr. Pollard was a great leader who listened intently to whomever was talking to him and responded with sensitivity and wisdom. I remember once reviewing a matter with him while he gave me his undivided attention, his pipe just inches from my nose and his eyes looking directly at me. It made me realize that this great man was really paying attention and I should be careful what I say. Paul Elza, as Manager of Administration and my boss, was a gifted and highly respected administrator who tolerated no nonsense. You*

*learned not to try to cover anything up or give less than your best, but he was*
*unfailingly fair and wise in his judgments. He trusted me and gave me some*
*difficult problems to solve over and above my routine duties.*

Wendell Russell was a colleague with whom Bill worked closely at ORINS.
He and his wife Lois became very good friends to Bill and Rose, who
often visited Wendell, Lois, and their three children, Wendy, Larry and
Randy, at their home in Knoxville. Sometimes they shared anniversary
celebrations and went to events together. Wendell was tall and always
smiling and active – a real "type A" personality. Lois, a teacher at Knoxville
College, was more reserved, but they both were lively and fun. In later years
Wendell was moved to the Exhibits Division as Bill moved up in central
administration. Bill and Wendell had many enjoyable and productive trips
together on ORINS business. A few years after Bill had left Oak Ridge,
Wendell died from a heart attack while in Washington on a business trip
with Paul Elza. They mourned the too early passing of this dear friend
and colleague.

The first time Bill had to hire a new employee as an assistant to himself, he
made the mistake of seeking someone who would be simply an extension
of his time – to do things he could do if he just had the time. It didn't
work out very well and he learned to find people who could do some things
better than he could do even if he had the time. He also learned to be
specific in instruction and decisions. He had come to the conclusion that
one employee was not right for the job and had told him he needed to seek
other employment. There was no need for immediate action and no date
was set for ending the employment. Bill was satisfied that he had handled
the matter in an honest but kind manner. The problem was that the
employee made the mental adjustment that he had time to do better and
he would prove himself to be so valuable that he wouldn't be terminated
after all. That didn't turn out to be the case and when considerable time
had passed and he hadn't left, Bill had to set a date for his termination
under much more difficult circumstances. He didn't make that mistake
the next time.

*We had a black man (I will call Lewis Lanagin) who was the technician in the reproduction room. He ran the addressograph, mimeograph, dittograph and related machines and did a good job. But he had a huge chip on his shoulder and caused a great deal of grief and complaints because of his attitude. I liked him, and we got along well, but he was not able to relate with others even though we tried to help. He had graduated from a small college and had been trained as an embalmer, but had worked in the reproduction room for a number of years. He had a bad home situation – married but no children. Perhaps he felt he was working at a job beneath his capabilities, and that was probably true. If someone called him "Lewis" he took offense as if they had said "boy!" If they addressed him as Mr. Lanagin he assumed they were being sarcastic. He and everybody else were unhappy.*

*Finally I called him to my office and told him I knew he was unhappy and that he was making others unhappy to the point of affecting his and their work. I suggested he find a situation more suitable to his interests and set a date a reasonable distance away for his departure. His response was that "I knew it was coming! Every time the phone has rung for the past three years I thought that I'd be fired." I expressed my sorrow that he had lived under this burden for so long and pointed out that it was confirmation of his need to make a change as well as our need to change the situation. He left not too long afterward. Years later, with all the rules and attitudes about assumed discrimination in employment, I probably would have faced a discrimination complaint, but I knew it was best for ORINS and felt that it was best for him too. The story doesn't end there and has a happy ending.*

*Years later, when I had left Oak Ridge and was working at the Southern Regional Education Board in Atlanta, I had occasion to fly to Knoxville for a meeting. When I returned the rental car to the airport to catch my flight home I parked in the designated area. A uniformed security man, with sidearm and all, came up as I got out of the car and I wondered if I'd parked in the wrong place. Then I recognized Lewis Lanagin. My life flashed before my eyes for a moment, but he beamed at me and called my name. He put his arm around my shoulder and took me to the security office for a cup of coffee. He told me that I had done him the biggest favor of his life by firing him. He finally had to take stock of himself. He found a career in security work and he loved it.*

214

*He looked great in his uniform with his happy face and none of the sneering dark looks he had suffered before. We had a great visit and I thanked God for His providence.*

Bill continued to progress in management and was made Head of Personnel Services. He was in charge of recruitment, employment, administration of position classification and pay scales, fringe benefits and other personnel matters. Paul Elza, never one to mince words, advised him at the outset that "Ninety percent of the people are no d...d good, so you are looking for ten percent, and most of them are already happily employed." Bill especially enjoyed recruiting trips with Wendell Russel of the Museum Division seeking "exhibits managers" to man the traveling exhibits. He met and worked with a lot of interesting people.

*On one occasion I was reviewing a clearance form on a visiting pathologist, Stefan Issarescu, who was going to work in the Medical Division's cancer research hospital on radiation effects and treatments. Looking over the list of his family relations on his wife Ileana's side, I noticed the surnames Hohenzollern, Hanover, Romanov and Habsburg. Having been a history major in college I recognized these as covering most of the royal families of Europe. Ileana, princess of Rumania, was the great granddaughter of Queen Victoria on one side and Tsar Alexander II on another. She had been married to Anton Habsburg, Archduke of Austria. I got to meet her and she was very gracious and charming. She was noted and loved for her relief work in Europe during two world wars. In later years she became a nun and then established an Orthodox monastery in this country becoming "Mother Alexandra."*

Later, Bill was again promoted, becoming Head of Management Services, which included personnel, administrative services, contracts, audits and other administrative units. Under the Manager of Administration he worked closely with the heads of Fiscal Services and Technical Services to provide and coordinate the basic operating systems of the organization. He also was given special management tasks as needs arose. One of these was to arrange for the atomic energy exhibit at the 1964 World's Fair in New York.

## World's Fair

ORINS had been given the responsibility for creating and placing the Atomic Energy Commission's exhibit in the science hall being constructed at the New York World's Fair site. The Exhibits Division designed and constructed a wonderful exhibit with a great deal of hands-on interactive attractions. It was put together in a series of panels creating a room with colorful displays, information and devices on the panels and free standing items within the room. The panels were each made of a size to transport and move around easily and could be locked together as a unit sturdy enough to withstand use by the viewers. Wiring for lights and other electrical devices was installed in each panel with plugs between the panels allowing one circuit to serve the whole unit. Only one source of electricity would be needed through a main connecting cord. Based on years of experience with traveling exhibits the whole thing was well done with forethought to ease of setting up and operation,

*Wendell Russell and I went to New York to arrange for delivery, installation, maintenance and janitorial care of the exhibit. We had estimated that the cost of delivery, installation and care would be about $10,000. The building in which it was to be erected was under the supervision of the National Science Foundation and was not yet complete. We had been advised to meet with the building contractor to explore the placement of our exhibit. A couple vice-presidents of the large construction company in charge of the building took us to lunch. They explained that due to union demands to which the Fair management had agreed, we had to use union teamsters for delivery, union expo workers for moving panels from the trucks to the designated area, union carpenters for putting up the exhibit and union electricians for hooking up the electrical service. Above that we'd need a maintenance contract and a custodial contract. The construction firm had all these services and relationships in place and could take care of it for us for $70,000. Explaining the simplicity of the exhibit's installation made no difference. It was obvious that they were using "union demands" to justify the exorbitant costs. Being well acquainted with unions, I didn't believe this was necessary and we told them we'd consider their offer.*

*We visited a union leader and he assured us that, while the unions wanted their part of the work and wanted to see that good work was done, they were not interested in gouging the exhibitors. It became clear that, rather than negotiating reasonable individual arrangements, the pattern was to pay everybody off and pass the cost to the country, agency or other organization paying for the building or exhibit. We went to see the labor relations counsel for the Fair to assess how rigid were the rules and seek his assistance in reducing the costs. We felt responsible for the use of public funds entrusted to us. I'm sure our little project was a minor blip in his array of concerns. He told us that we were in New York and not in Tennessee and he advised us to pay. The implication that we were backwoods boys out of our league raised our hackles and we decided to explore further options. The theme of the exposition was "Peace through Understanding" but it seemed to us that peace was usually maintained through pay offs.*

*In our various conversations we found that the Teamsters Union had a program to make truck drivers instant union members for a day for a reasonable fee so we could get the panels delivered reasonably with our own driver. We found that expo workers didn't like to work in the wee hours so if we arrived during that time our driver and a companion could unload without objection. We found that we could write contracts for set-up, electrical work and maintenance that were based on pay as you need rather than a fixed price. We talked to some very sleazy agents of cleaning firms, one of whom suggested a bribe for preferential treatment, but we found a responsible firm for cleaning that offered to do the cleaning for a reasonable sum. They said industrial carpet was a better floor cover than the tile we had planned and since they were equipped with state-of-the-art carpet cleaners they would install the carpet at their expense if we agreed to their service.*

*We advised the building construction firm that we had made other arrangements and worked out all the logistics and details. Everything went well and we ended up getting everything taken care of for $7,000. Wendell and I were satisfied, as were ORINS and AEC, but we agreed that we wouldn't want to do that every day. We'd rather be in Tennessee than New York.*

## New Horizons

Opportunities to participate in professional organizations were offered and Bill attended conferences and meetings of the American Society for Public Administration in various cities as well as local meetings in Knoxville. A workshop at Indiana University entitled "Building Support for Program Goals" was especially meaningful, emphasizing the importance of listening to others and involving them before reaching decisions.

Bill was elected to the board of the Council of Southern Mountain Workers, based in Berea and attended conferences in Gatlinburg and other places. He served for a number of years, enjoying his association with the Council's director, Perley Ayers and then his classmate, Loyal Jones. Bill's father had been a member of the Committee on Economic Justice of the National Council of Churches and Bill was selected to serve on that committee for a term, attending interesting meetings in New York.

Bill joined other Oak Ridge residents to explore the idea of starting a college in Oak Ridge. The resources of the laboratories and highly educated personnel, which could be tapped for the college, made it seem like a viable enterprise. The idea caught the imagination of the community and the College of Oak Ridge was incorporated in 1964. Funds were raised and a board of trustees formed. Floyd Culler, a respected engineer, was elected chairman and Bill was secretary of the board. It reached the point of employing a founding president, Sumner Hayward, who was excited about the prospect. Potential sites were considered but finding financial resources was difficult. Shortly after Bill and Rose had left Oak Ridge in 1967 Sumner Hayward resigned to accept leadership of the Great Lakes Colleges Association. Ultimately the college passed on its ideas and resources to other higher education institutions interested in having a presence in Oak Ridge.

Bill and Rose also became involved in a local development organization, the Clinch and Powell River Valley Association (CPRVA), organized under a TVA program for tributary area development. Wendell Russell was president and Bill was chairman of the human resources committee.

At various professional meetings he and colleagues from ORINS, the University of Tennessee, TVA and other agencies discussed professional matters, politics and the exciting moves in the country towards greater equality and the development of communities where all can enjoy productive lives. President Kennedy had called for citizens to be of service to their country and after his assassination in 1963 President Johnson had embarked on the ambitious war on poverty.

The management staff of ORINS, with Dr. Pollard's and the Board's approvals, investigated ways to contribute to the development of the human and natural resources of the area. Drawing on the experience of creating bridges between higher education and the atomic energy program they speculated about doing the same thing in regard to the new initiatives in resource development. With a grant from the Department of Labor ORINS prepared a report called "Manpower for Development" which made a number of suggestions for linking education and community development and using the facilities in Oak Ridge for manpower training. The report called for upgrading vocational training using the high technology of Oak Ridge. It suggested other ways to mobilize the resources of education, industry and government in the area for development, including internships with community service and development agencies involving students and faculty to both contribute and learn.

*Wendell and I, with the help of an engineer, Leo Waters, of Union Carbide put together a proposal for a training program for unemployed or underemployed persons, using the sophisticated facilities of the Y12 plant. ORINS would manage the contracts, provide the coordination and recruit trainees, Carbide would provide the facility and training, and the University of Tennessee would offer the "trade related instruction" in math and English. The major funding agencies would be the Department of Labor and Department of Education. We called it the "Training and Technology" project. The training was to be a hybrid of apprenticeship and institutional training, using actual Y12 production facilities to prepare trainees for jobs in space age level welding, nondestructive testing of materials and industrial glassblowing – all areas where the demand exceeded the supply of trained workers. On a visit to the Undersecretary of Labor, Stanley Rutenberg, he told us it would be a miracle if we could pull off such a program requiring the cooperation of so many departments and organizations, but he encouraged us and supported the project. It was funded and very successful. The program's graduates were highly employable and leapt from unemployment or underemployment into high paying jobs.*

After the first class of graduates was so successful, some Department of Education officials accused the program of "creaming" or taking capable trainees rather than the hard core poor. It was true that the application and selection process tried to offer training to those who had potential for learning, but all were either unemployed or in minimum wage, dead-end jobs, like gas station attendant. As an experiment the program took ten percent of the applications from the bottom of the stack – those who would have been rejected – and added them to the trainee mix. Surrounded by motivated fellow trainees they did as well as the others.

## The Internship Program

The Tennessee Valley Authority had established its "Tributary Area Development" (TAD) program a couple years before President Johnson declared the War on Poverty in his1965 state of the union message. The Clinch and Powell River Valley Association (CPRVA) under this TVA program included Oak Ridge. One of the first tasks of a TAD organization was to determine what was already in place and what needs were not being met. County and city officials, school personnel, industrial leaders and citizens were consulted about possibilities. What manpower needs and opportunities did business and industry have? What training programs were available? What were the problems in the schools? What natural resources were available? What opportunities were there for cultural and recreational activities? What about the area's infrastructure? A lot of work needed to be done just to get to a planning stage. TVA came up with some funds to start an experimental program that would place student interns at the disposal of CPRVA to carry out some of its research. ORINS agreed to administer the programs and the University of Tennessee provided the educational connection. The idea was for student interns to both contribute and to learn.

Four interns were selected from the University of Tennessee and each was given an assignment in a different county in the region. Each intern was provided a committee which was composed of a local sponsor (such as a county executive), a university professor and a technical resource person. The committee was not supervisory and may not even meet, but rather it represented points of access and assistance for the intern. The intern was to use the committee rather than the other way around. It took a while for the students to adjust to this new posture. Their projects had been designed by the agency with help from ORINS. TVA provided the technical assistance person. A professor from the University of Tennessee was selected to help with research resources, quality of reporting and documentation and to assist in setting and assessing learning objectives and outcomes. Whether or not the student received academic credit depended on his situation and the policies of the university. Academic credit and learning were not considered synonymous. Each intern was to prepare a comprehensive report, in good form and properly documented, which was then published by ORINS and given to the agency. For the students it introduced a new discipline of "usefulness" as well as scholarship to their research and reporting. One intern observed, "The way I write this report will determine not only whether I get an 'A' or 'B' but will have an effect on people's lives!"

The first four internships in 1964 were so successful that funds were secured by TVA and ORINS to have more in 1965. One of the first four interns compiled a list of the various federal programs and grants available to Campbell County, Tennessee. He collected information from the various arms of the Departments of Agriculture, Education, Commerce, Labor and other agencies. He did such a thorough job that the report became a "best seller" beyond Campbell County, especially in Washington, and served as the first listing of what became the "yellow pages" of federal programs. It also brought the internship program to the attention of many agencies. It became clear that the program had great potential and would spread beyond TVA and the East Tennessee area. TVA encouraged contact with other agencies to expand the program. By the time the second group of interns' work had been completed, there was support for the following year from the Economic Development Administration, Office of Economic Opportunity and other federal and state agencies.

*I had been given leave from my regular administrative duties to pursue and coordinate the new programs of "resource development" at ORINS, including the internships. As we moved into a much larger scale program covering a wider area more staff was needed. In addition to liaison with supporting agencies, internships needed to be developed with local sponsors and universities needed to be visited to find interested faculty and students. My brother, Dick, suggested I get in touch with a colleague of his who worked with the American Friends Service Committee College Program, getting students involved in service projects. So Bob Sigmon came for an interview and it was clear that he was the man for the job. He caught the vision, but it took some doing to convince him that it was not a moral wrong to accept a decent salary for doing something worthwhile. I think his wife, Marian, was on my side.*

*With Bob's good services we soon had internships set up in several states for the summer of 1966 with economic development and community service agencies, and it looked like the program would quickly expand further. Agencies were eager for the help of motivated, bright students, and outward looking teachers were seeking opportunities to be involved. Sponsorship was growing and local participation in cost-sharing allowed even faster growth.*

Another staff member, Mike Hart from Tennessee, was added. However, because of the rapid growth, problems were developing in the ORINS governance structure. ORINS was changing its name to Oak Ridge Associated Universities (ORAU) and attention was drawn to what its purpose and priorities should be. The ORAU Board of Directors was strongly supportive of the new resource development initiatives but the larger Council had some unease, and even hostility in the case of a few members. The Council, made up entirely of university scientists, had misgivings about getting away from a science focus and into the messy social issues of the day. Although the name changed that year from ORINS to ORAU, it was still a science orientated organization. Leadership on the Board saw an opportunity to strengthen the internship program by moving it to a base with more political involvement, more conducive to public policy matters. Many of the same university presidents on the ORAU board were also involved in the Southern Regional Education Board (SREB) with headquarters in Atlanta and decided that would be a better location for the internship program. The training programs based in the Oak Ridge facilities and other activities directly serving the local area were to stay at ORAU.

*Rose and I were faced with a difficult decision. We were well established in Oak Ridge. Bill had a good job and bright future at ORAU. The children were doing well in school. Ken was established as a barber, lived near us and was planning to marry his neighbor. We had purchased a baby farm and had been clearing it for a future home with some land. Should we leave all this that we had built up over 12 years? Should we move to Atlanta to continue to develop and direct the internship program or remain in Oak Ridge? The internships program represented some insecurity in terms of financing whereas ORAU was stable and my position was well established. We prayed and our guidance was to take the risks and go. Who knew what the future held? The internships were important and exciting and would do best with continuity of leadership. So we began to make preparations at work, in the community, with the children's schooling and activities and at home to bring our Oak Ridge years to a close and start a new adventure.*

# BILL AND ROSE RAMSAY TIME LINE

## OAK RIDGE YEARS: 1956 - 1966

| YEARS | FAMILY AND RELATED EVENTS | WORLD EVENTS |
|---|---|---|
| 1956 | Ramsay family moves to 142 Manhattan Ave<br>Stephen Gates Ramsay born by "natural childbirth."<br>Rose and Bill get involved in childbirth education<br>and civil rights in Oak Ridge. Join Presbyterian<br>Church. Bill helps launch "Traveling Teachers" | Hungarian uprising crushed by Soviets<br>Civil rights struggle continues in USA |
| 1957 | Bill is promoted to ORINS central administration | Russians launch Sputnik |
| 1958 | John Robert Ramsay is born<br>Rose continues leadership in childbirth education | Cassette tapes introduced |
| 1959 | Billy at Woodland School<br>Laura becomes Rose's good helper<br>Laura at pre-school | Cuban revolution<br>Alaska, Hawaii become states<br>War in Viet Nam |
| 1960 | James Moore Ramsay is born<br>Rose involved in literacy programs<br>Continue work on equal public services | World population over 3 billion<br>Gas costs 25 cents a gallon<br>New home average cost is $42,700 |
| 1961 | Stephen starts school at Woodland<br>Bill adds personnel services to ORINS duties<br>Celo becomes special vacation place<br>Rose's father Edward Moore dies | J F Kennedy president<br>Berlin wall constructed<br>First manned space flight<br>Bread costs 22 cents a loaf |
| 1962 | Rose goes to Seattle conference of International<br>Childbirth Education Association (ICEA) | Cuban missile crisis<br>Second Vatican Council |
| 1963 | Oak Ridge hosts ICEA Regional Conference<br>Celo summers continue | Kennedy assassinated; LBJ president<br>M L King "I have a dream" speech |
| 1964 | ORINS begins internship programs<br>Bill and Wendell Russell arrange Atomic Energy<br>Exhibit at World's Fair in New York | Civil Rights Act passed<br>New York World's Fair<br>Beatles first visit to USA |
| 1965 | Kenneth moves in with Rose and Bill<br>with Ricky, Kathy and Larry | Winston Churchill dies<br>Singapore becomes independent |

ORINS begins resource development programs
Including" Training and Technology Project"
Bill becomes coordinator of new programs;
employs Bob Sigmon

1966 Ken's Barber and Style Shop opens,          Several nations gain independence:
     ending segregated haircuts in Oak Ridge      Lesotho, Botswana, Barbados
     Decision is made to move Resource Development
     Internship programs to SREB in Atlanta
     Family plans to move in the spring.
     Ken moves to own house and meets Glenda
     Bill and Bob Sigmon coin the term
     "service-learning"

OAK RIDGE, TN IS WHERE STEPHEN, JOHN AND JIM WERE BORN AND WHERE ALL GREW FROM BABIES TO SCHOOL CHILDREN. LAURA WAS THE SECOND MOTHER. IF SHE WANTED TO PLAY GIRLIE THINGS SHE DRESSSED THE BOYS ACCORDINGLY. JOHN WAS OFTEN INTO ADVENTURES AND LOVED A THRILL. STEPHEN WAS THE LEADER OF "THE BOYS." JIM WAS ALWAYS HAPPY AND AGREEABLE. BILLY WAS THE ELDER MODEL AND THE FIX-IT BROTHER. ALL WERE READERS AND DID WELL IN SCHOOL. THE BEREA YEARS, 1955 UNTIL 1967 WERE FULL OF FAMILY ACTIVITIES, COMMUNITY SERVICE AND WORK. VACATIONS AT THE BEACH AND SUMMERS AT CELO HELPED KEEP THE FAMILY CLOSE AND LINKED TO GRANDPARENTS AND THE WIDER FAMILY.

## CELO

HAPPINESS HILL WITH MT CELO IN THE BACKGROUND HOLDS MANY MEMORIES: THE REFRESHING WATERFALL UP WHITE OAK CREEK; GRANDMA RAMSAY AND HER WONDERFUL FLOWERS , GARDEN AND STICKEY BUNS; HELPING GRANDPA PUT UP A FLAG OR PLAYING CARDS OR EATING ICE CREAM; RIDING THE RAPIDS IN THE SOUTH TOE RIVER AT THE HEMLOCKS PARK; A HIKE TO MOUNT MITCHELL; RIDING DANNY BOY, SOMETIMES IN A PARADE. SEVERAL GENERATIONS GATHERED IN 2005 TO CELEBRATE.

JOHN R, BRIAN,BILL E, REBEKAH, DALE MOODY, ANDREA TODT-MOODY, FRIEND, DANIEL, LOREN, ALEXANDER, JACOB STEPHEN, ? TODT, ? TODT, HANNAH DUGGINS, ADRIENNE, JOHN PAUL, STEPHEN COMPTON, KRISTIN GINER, INGELISE AMBER, JENNIFER ESCOBAR, EILEEN, MICHAEL, JOSEPH, ? TODT, RALPH EDWIN COMPTON
(BILL, ROSE AND OTHER ATTENDEES WERE NOT IN PICTURE)

# REFLECTIONS 11

## PRESSED DOWN AND RUNNING OVER

We grew up in families that supported the church with what little they had to give and shared freely with others as they had the opportunities. Like hospitality, which was part of our lives, sharing provided a peace and sense of well-being. As the poet James Russell Lowell tells us in *The Vision of Sir Launfall:*

> *The holy supper is kept indeed*
> *In whatso we share with another's need.*
> *Not what we give, but what we share,*
> *For the gift without the giver is bare;*
> *Who gives himself, with his alms, feeds three —*
> *Himself, his hungering neighbor and me,*

After my army basic training to become a medic, I noted that those of us who had been blessed with a good education got all the advantages and the guys who had little education got shipped to the front lines in Korea. Some got wounded or killed and I always felt the injustice of the biblical observation that "to those who have, more is given" but it was a fact of life. Once we were settled with a job, we started to give to veterans' organizations, thinking of those fellow basic trainees who were sent directly to the battlefront and not sent for advanced training or good assignments. But with a growing family and very modest income, it took us a while to work up to giving a tithe to church and charity. We did get there and continued throughout our lives. When we wondered if it should be a percentage of our gross or net, we decided not to be like the Pharisees and quibble over rules and just took the tithe off the top before anything else. We never regretted that decision and have been blessed, if not with wealth, with plenty for our needs and even sometimes, "running over" as the Bible promises: *Give and it will be given to you. A good measure, pressed down, shaken together, running over will be put in your lap for the measure you give will be the measure you get back.* (Luke 6:38, NRSV)

Years later I was asked by a former pastor to give a talk on stewardship at his church. I remembered a story that seemed to me to capture the dynamics of giving.

The college administration building, like others, was heated by steam running through radiators. One winter the president's office was cold and the radiator didn't seem to be putting out any heat. Physical plant was called and came to examine the pipes, the radiator and its valves. They found that there was steam in the pipes and decided the valve letting the steam in to the radiator must be defective so they replaced it. The radiator still did not get hot. Someone said to check the valve on the other side of the radiator and they did. They found it was the defective one and replaced it. The radiator worked well after that change. As long as nothing was going out, nothing could come in.

A pool can become stagnant if it has no water running through it. Our lives can become stagnant if we fail to give and share.

# REFLECTIONS 12

## SAVE THE WORLD

Rose calls our years in Oak Ridge our "save the world" years. We were finally settled in our own home, had a small but steady income and were expanding our family. We were full of idealism and enthusiasm, ready to play our part to make the world a better place. So we were real busy with employment, raising five children, church activities, community organizations and national causes. Our primary causes outside home and job were civil rights, childbirth education, literacy, service in church, world peace, political involvement and education. We got so busy that I remember once threatening to give up brushing my teeth. Did we succeed in saving the world? I told our children later that we had fought the war on poverty and lost. Jesus told us that the poor would be with us always, but we thought he must have been wrong. Now we know he was right. He wasn't making a cruel judgment but simply stating a fact. We are a fallen people.

I think it was Winston Churchill who said, "Any man under 30 who is not a liberal has no heart, and any man over 30 who is not conservative has no brains!" We were full of heart during those years, but gaining wisdom from experience. I remember hearing my dad and mother's brother Ed talking once about all that needed doing in the world and Ed told dad to slow down and leave some things for the next generation to deal with. We took up the challenge and have watched as new generations continue to do so. Why are we, generation after generation, not able to "save the world?" We'll talk about that a little later.

We were part of some movements that made a difference and others that seem to have little or no widespread effect over our years of living. Most are a mixed bag. What it usually boils down to is not "Did I make world shaking changes?" but "Was I able to help someone?" Humility is one of the lessons learned.

## Childbirth Education

In childbirth education, the movement of concerned women, like Rose, and supportive husbands, doctors and researchers made significant changes in the way childbirth is perceived and practiced. Until these changes, pregnant women were treated much the same as those who had a sickness or injury. Heavy anesthesia and pain medication, forceps deliveries and other procedures taught in medical schools were practiced by obstetricians to relieve women of the pangs of childbirth. These approaches were gradually supplanted by involving women in the process as participants rather than as patients, giving them knowledge and techniques to help themselves, providing training in preparation for the hard work of childbirth and including family for emotional support. Now there are birthing rooms, rooming in, family visitation and fathers present, all of which happened over a relatively short time thanks to the efforts of those who saw this as a better way. Rose experienced the difference personally after the first two children birthed by the old methods in 1953 and 1954 and culminating in a whole different experience when Jennifer was born "naturally" in 1970 with Bill in attendance.

Childbirth education and the resulting differences were mother, child and family affirming changes. Unfortunately during the same period, the evil of widespread abortion was established, also in the name of affirming women but at the expense of taking the life of the child. The contrast between the excitement of new birth on the one hand and the disposal of an inconvenient pregnancy on the other is clear. Childbirth education celebrates the miracle of birth and recognizes the woman's unique role in bearing and nurturing new life. Abortion on demand attempts to reduce the unborn child to a clump of cells and violates the woman's role in nurturing life in the name of her right to her own body, as if she created herself, and it destroys the only innocent party involved.

## Civil Rights

In civil rights, we also saw successes as society and laws changed to remove barriers to equal treatment regardless of race. In the process we made wonderful friends across the lines of color that once made interracial relationships difficult. It is now so common to see black and white people sitting together, eating together, laughing together, worshipping together, studying together and interacting freely that we almost forget how it used to be. But there is still prejudice in both races. There is still stereotyping. We are still a long way from the true freedom from enmity and division that Reverend Martin Luther King dreamed of achieving. We knew, early in our struggles for equal public services, that those engaged in the movement had different views and reasons for joining the struggle. Some were concerned with rights but not responsibility; getting their share but not considering their contribution. Some were meeting a need of their own to express themselves. I remember a young white man who was very disturbed when it looked as if we might be successful in getting an equal services ordinance passed because we would lose the need to protest and struggle. Our participation was always instructed by our faith and commitment to our oneness under God and the call to love each other. The real struggle still goes on in the hearts of men and women of all races.

## Literacy

In literacy, improvements have been made. Not only did Rose and others in that movement make an immediate difference in individual lives, but attention to greater opportunities for literacy found its way into educational systems. The problem of illiteracy has been reduced. Programs for learning to read and learning English as a second language are found everywhere. In addition to improving a person's quality of life, literacy in a common language is important as a uniting force among people. Some communities have considered establishing bi-lingual systems and we would advocate the learning of other languages, but would want to retain a common language. People separated into language groups find it difficult to communicate effectively. The new illiteracy problem is among us older folks who haven't learned the language of computers and texting.

## Church

Rose had been raised in a Baptist Church and I in the Presbyterian Church. When we lived in Lithia Springs, we were members of the Methodist Church. Coming to Berea in 1970 to work at Berea College, we first joined the Union Church and then moved our membership to the United Methodist. We have held offices in various denominations but do not consider any one denomination as having an exclusive hold on the Church of Jesus Christ. The church, in its universal sense, is the body of Christ, regardless of the labels assigned. At the revival on Edisto Island with all churches participating we felt the sense of this unity in Christ beyond our different styles of worship, rituals and pronouncements. We have a special appreciation of the Catholic Church as the one reaching back to the beginnings of the church, in spite of its errors and flaws which caused the schisms and separations over the centuries. We understand the power and beauty of rituals as found in the Catholic and Episcopal churches and also the quiet devotion of the simple services of the Quakers. We appreciate the free expressions of joy and praise of the Pentecostals, the commitment to discipline of the Presbyterians, the discipleship and accountability of the Methodists, the mission emphasis of Moravians and Baptists, and the many other expressions of faith found in America and around the world. Lutherans, Mennonites, Seventh Day Adventists, Mormons, Jehovah's Witnesses and others are all seeking to find what is true and leads to the Kingdom of God.

We do not accept the idea, however, of all religions, or even all denominations of Christianity, being equally true. All may be equally searching for meaning and for God, and have discovered partial truths, but it is ridiculous to maintain that all are true, if truth means anything. We believe that there is such a thing as truth. All is not relative or, like beauty, just in the eye of the beholder. If there is no truth, there is no basis for conversation, study, science, civilization or righteousness versus evil and all is chaos. But all is not chaos. There is order in the universe and there are moral laws as well as physical laws.

In John 18: 28-38 it is recorded that when Pilate was faced with Jesus, he finds no basis for condemning him other than the cries of the mob and Jewish leaders who wanted him gone. He looks for a reason to release him. That would be the "right" thing to do. Jesus, faced with torture and death on a cross, says, "For this I was born and for this I came into the world, to testify to the truth. Everyone who belongs to the truth listens to my voice." Pilate then asks, "What is truth?" and turns Jesus over to be crucified, washing his hands of the responsibility.

What is truth! Not long before facing Pilate, Jesus had told his disciples that he was going to leave them. Thomas said they didn't know where he was going and asked how they could know the way. Jesus replied, *"I am the way, and the truth and the life, No one comes to the Father except through me."* (John 14:6, NRSV) He didn't set out a ritual or a procedure to follow, an organization to join, a set of words to say, and wasn't limiting his statement to a particular group of followers. He knew he was going to endure the cross as a ransom for **all** humankind, whether or not they were aware of it or understood it, satisfying the requirements of justice for the consequences of sin,. This is true whatever ones denomination, ethnic group, religious affiliation or condition. It is an undeserved gift. It is available to all by the grace of God, whether or not they call themselves Christians.

We are to spread this good news, not to solicit members for our particular group and not to impose any particular ritual. Rituals, creeds, cathedrals, fellowship with others and teachings can help us in our journeys, but are not the central point. Churches who fail to keep Christ as *"the truth, the way and the light,"* have strayed from the gospel. Some try to increase membership, accommodate to the surrounding culture, isolate themselves as the only "right" way, or otherwise divert people from the central commands to love and serve God and each other and thankfully accept the redemption offered by Christ. In our lifetime we have seen such a weakening of churches, but we have also seen many ministries faithful to the basic tenets of worship, ministry and service in the name of Christ, who came that all men might live.

## World Peace

Looking over the time line of our lives we certainly see the prophecy come true that there will be wars and rumors of wars and natural disasters. Our generation had great hopes at the end of World War II that a new era of peace was possible. We supported the United Nations in our naïve hope that nations would work together and find alternatives to fighting. Not to happen, although some good has been accomplished through cooperation. The Korean War, Vietnam War and Gulf Wars came in rapid succession. Wars everywhere on the globe continue, often with people in the same nation fighting each other. Now the War on Terrorism, thrust upon America by the destruction of the Twin Towers in New York and continuing throughout the world, perpetuates the conflict between peoples. ISIS threatens in its attempt to impose a Caliphate by force. Persecution of religious minorities, especially Christians in other countries, is pandemic. Refugees are a result in astounding numbers as nations and relief organizations try desperately to help. We still hope for world peace, but have certainly not achieved it in our generation and don't see it ahead of us in our lifetime. We have to be satisfied with our own attempts to be peacemakers in our own relationships and communities. We continue to sing and pray, "Let there be peace on earth, and let it begin with me."

## Politics

We never quite fit under the labels of Democrat or Republican, liberal or conservative, but we wanted to participate in the political process and recognized the need for differing perspectives and the necessary struggle to find common ground and ways to work together. In general we were liberal in our social views on civil rights, worker's rights, provision for those in need, care for the elderly without family resources, and education and training. On the other hand we were conservative on matters of moral standards. We had found in our college years at Berea College that this stance was shared by many there. But we were uneasy about the tendency which had begun back then and later became epidemic to throw away customs, trash the accumulated wisdom of civilization, expect the government to answer all our needs and pay little respect to history, all in the name of freedom. Some professors and preachers were "demythologizing" scripture. Some "intellectuals" sneered at old rules and behaviors. Critics looked for scandals from the past to tear down historical (or current) leaders. An insatiable media looked for anything that would draw attention.

Negative campaigning began to dominate politics in the 1950's. Civility began to disappear. The media thrived on conflict. Politics became highly divisive with candidates pitting one group against another. We also saw the rise of executive power as opposed to congressional control. Through provisions in government contracts, conditions attached to government funds, executive orders, rules and regulations, the considerations of elected representatives could be bypassed. Meanwhile the courts increasingly became tools of interest groups to override laws passed by legislatures with which they didn't agree. Carefully chosen and crafted cases were brought before selected judges who were known to be willing to substitute their judgment for the enactments of legislatures – state and federal. At the same time, the moral consensus once held by a majority was weakening and people began to consider what was legal rather than what was moral to be central in determining behavior. Lawyers had a field day, while religious leaders became marginalized or joined the crowd to become rationalists for a "new morality." Our generation, not only did not improve politics, but was implicated in its decline. It is clear that political solutions are not going to solve all our problems and, in fact, cause some of the problems.

## Education

Over most of our earlier years, the answer to most problems was thought to be education. If people just knew enough they would make the right choices. This was tried in combatting alcoholism. It was tried with drugs. It was tried with sex. It hasn't worked. I used to give a talk to new students on making wise choices. The choices they would make during their college years would affect their whole lives. Now they were away from home and communities which had offered direction, advice, guidance and sometimes restrictions. Now they would have choices to make – choices of friends, behavior, habits, entertainment. How would they fill their time and with what would they fill their minds. They could do just enough to get by or could embrace new opportunities and do more than was required. They could choose wholesome friendships and habits or just go with the crowd. There was not a course called Truth 101, and even if there were, they would have to make choices before they had completed it. So they would have to make choices among imperfect alternatives and without having all the information needed or being able to understand and consider the various potential consequences. I suggested that until they had arrived at the place of full knowledge, and, more importantly, wisdom, they rely on the wisdom of those who cared about them – their parents, ministers, teachers and friends with more experience. They would still need to make the choices, but need not be without help. I don't know how many times a student in trouble observed, "I should have listened to my mother."

I have spent most of my working life in institutions of higher education and believe that education is a wonderful thing and knowledge is to be sought after, enjoyed and used. But knowledge is not wisdom. As we learn, and in the process find out how much we don't know, we should experience humility, not arrogance and pride in our great knowledge. Thomas Carlyle wrote that the end of education is action and not a thought "though it be the noblest." I observed that the relationship of education and action is a two way street. Not only do we apply what we learn to our work, but we learn from our work, so learning continues. It seemed to me that all learning, unless by divine inspiration, is ultimately from someone's experience and interpretation of that experience. This learning is then passed on in books, scholarly papers and teaching. One of our goals in developing the service-learning idea was to break down the division between classroom and workplace. Our Berea College experience contributed to that idea, although even there, it is an effort to include the workplace as an important part of the educational enterprise.

Another observation is that America's strength in education is, in part, from its great variety of institutions and models. Yet there seems to be constant attempts both within the academy and in government to homogenize education in the name of standards and accountability - both of which have their place. We like the idea of, private and public institutions, charter schools, extension education, terms abroad, internships and experiential education as well as great books and traditional academic studies. Not every institution need do all these things. The tendency of government and accrediting agencies to operate from a more limited model is to be resisted. We certainly found this to be the case in getting recognition for the work colleges. Sometimes the pressures are subtle and unintended. For example, accounting standards for higher education call for categorizing expenses so they can be compared with others and with norms. Berea's student industries fall into the "auxiliary" category and so gradually become to be thought of as auxiliary to the central educational program. Yet they play an important educational role and many students enter their life work through their learning in the industries, not to mention the liberal education lessons received in working.

We found that saving the world through education was not enough. It takes more than greater knowledge or greater skills to build a better world. We all want education for our children, but something else needs to be added to lead them to productive lives of meaning and purpose. Those who are blessed with high intelligence or great talent need to use their abilities for more than material gain, fame, power or self-expression. *"From everyone to whom much has been given, much will be required, and from the one to whom much has been entrusted, even more will be demanded."* (Luke 12:48, NRSV)

## What Is Wrong With Us?

There are those in each generation who try to save the world. Thank God there are, because there is evil in the world and it would overwhelm us if it weren't for those who resist it and try to make life better. But the fact is that we can't do it by ourselves, just by being smarter or working harder. We should be smart and we should work hard, but must do it with humility and the knowledge that we can't do it alone, or even all together, without divine guidance and strength. The struggle between good and evil, beauty and ugliness, sickness and health goes on in spiritual realms beyond our comprehension. We can be instruments for "Thy Kingdom come" and should respond as we are called.

I often observed that I could relate more easily to Moses than to Jesus. Moses was an organizer, a rule giver and enforcer, a negotiator, a judge, a writer and a decision maker. Jesus didn't organize, lead a rebellion or take a position of formal leadership. He taught. He healed. He served. He surrendered comfort and power and ultimately life itself. Yet he made world shaking changes. The commitment to give of oneself unstintingly has been reflected in other saints over the centuries, by the grace of God and we are all the beneficiaries. We do need to organize, plan, care for those given into our care, be responsible citizens, and live righteous lives. But the real changes come in human hearts and not in laws or programs.

One of Mother's favorite words was "surrender," and she was one of the most selfless persons on earth. As some say, "Let go and let God." We all have within us the capacity for good and the capacity for evil and we must choose, praying for guidance and strength. We are called to do what we can, but not to fall into the trap of thinking it all revolves around us. "If we could just get this law passed." "If only we can get the right court decision." "If people would just do as we tell them." I'm not being defeatist but trying to put things in perspective. We are responsible for doing what we can and what we are called to do, but the weight of the whole world is too great for our shoulders. We can just pray for the strength to respond to the needs around us. I especially like a prayer attributed to St Francis of Assisi:

> *Lord, make me an instrument of your peace;*
> *where there is hatred, let me sow love;*
> *where there is injury, pardon:*
> *where there is doubt, faith ;*
> *where there is despair, hope*
> *where there is darkness, light*
> *where there is sadness, joy*

*O divine Master,*
*grant that I may not so much seek to be consoled as to console;*
*to be understood, as to understand;*
*to be loved, as to love;*
*for it is in giving that we receive,*
*it is in pardoning that we are pardoned,*
*and it is in dying that we are born to Eternal Life.*

*Amen.*

Jesus always spoke directly to the person with whom he was confronted. He never responded to stereotypes or classifications but to individuals, be they fishermen, tax collectors, children, an adulterous woman, a Roman centurion, the blind, lame or demon possessed. Too many crusaders have hurt others in their quest for a better world justifying the damage by the nobility of their goals. We were not able to save the world, but we hope we did some good and we hope we did little harm. We are satisfied to leave the rest to others and to God. As preacher/writer Rick Warren says in *The Purpose Driven Life,* "It's not about you!"

# PART SIX

## Atlanta Intermission

# CHAPTER 16

# SERVICE-LEARNNG

Oak Ridge had been "home" for 12 years. The three younger boys had been born there and the family had grown up there. They were established and very busy at work, in church, in the community, in school and with many friends. Ken was on his own and planning remarriage. The barber shop was thriving. The children were all healthy and progressing well at school. It was tempting to keep things as they were and relax a little. What would it mean to uproot and move into the unknown? The decision to move was made with much thought and prayer. Once it was made, it was embraced and the hard work of moving was joined. Bill had to pass on responsibilities at ORAU, preparing to leave dear friends and colleagues, and maintain the momentum of the fledgling internship program as it established a new base. Trips to SREB in Atlanta and to agencies in Washington were necessary. Rose and the children had to plan for new school experiences, new medical providers, organize the accumulated life's belongings, deciding what to take and what to leave or dispose of. The house and the baby farm would have to be sold and a new house found in Atlanta. Meantime daily life must go on.

*We were going to move to Atlanta, Georgia – not far from our old home at Skyland Farm which was long gone and now part of the metropolitan area. Lester Maddox had just been elected governor. He was famous for a few years earlier standing in the doorway of his restaurant, The Pickrick, wielding an axe handle to prevent being "invaded" by "undesirables." No violence actually took place and The Pickrick actually employed a number of blacks, but the axe handle became a symbol of resistance to integration. At a farewell party at ORAU, Paul Elza presented me with my very own axe handle autographed by my friends and colleagues. We never had to use it.*

While the board of SREB had embraced the move of the internship program to Atlanta, the staff leadership had some fears and resistance. SREB had a prestigious reputation for research, policy development, symposia and assisting in legislative support for higher education. It was not an action agency and these interns would be directly involved in all kinds of difficult social issues, like legal services to the poor. Furthermore the program was based on a series of grants from various agencies - temporary funding that was unpredictable. And the young men coming to lead the program were unknown quantities. But adjustments were made, friendships and respect established and the program flourished. SREB was a good base and provided essential support. The internship program was where the term "service-learning" was coined and first began to be used.

*The internship program had exploded in size while we were still in Oak Ridge with support from other agencies than TVA – primarily the new Economic Development Administration (EDA) in the Department of Commerce and the Office of Equal Opportunity (OEO). We felt that we had developed a sound pattern for productive internships now tested by a couple years. I held a meeting in my office in Oak Ridge, before the move to Atlanta, to come up with appropriate terminology for our internships. Wendell Russell and Bob Sigmon were there. We were familiar with cooperative education, field experience, practice teaching and other descriptive phrases for linking classroom learning with actual experience but none seemed to describe our pattern and we sought a phrase that would do so. We considered "work-learning" and "action-learning" and "experiential learning" and finally settled on "service-learning" because it not only suggested a link between experience and classroom but also implied a value dimension. The student was not just to learn but to contribute to meeting a community need. This phrase took hold. The internships at SREB became known as service-learning internships.*

Donald Eberly, the director of the National Service Secretariat, had become a friend of the program and of the family. He was asked to participate in a conference on "service-learning" with others who were doing similar programs in other places without using that phrase, and was to evaluate the SREB program. In his book, *National Service: A Promise to Keep* he records this about his report.

*"It was a superbly designed operation and I said so in my report. About the only flaw I could see was the use of 'service-learning' as a descriptor. If the idea was to gain the currency it deserved, I thought it needed a livelier name."*

Don consulted a friend who was a Greek scholar and came up with the phrase "Diakonia-Paedia," and used that name in his report. He was asked to interpret it and he explained that the word "diakonia" means "community with a service connotation, as in "deacon," – a person who serves the community. "Paedia," he said, had the same root as "pedagogy" or teaching. Thus it meant community service as a teacher, or "service-learning." Others suggested to Don that not everyone had the benefits of his Harvard and MIT education and it would be hard to understand, not to mention pronounce. In his book he observes:

*"I haven't seen a reference to "Diakonia-Paedia" since then, but "service-learning" soon became a fairly common term on the nation's campuses"*

(*National Service: A Promise t Keep*, Donald J. Eberly, John Alden Books, Rochester, NY, 1988. LOC 88-92043. ISBN 0-9605818-3-9.)

*As soon as we got beyond East Tennessee and the TVA area we found many other programs for getting students involved in community service like the Urban Corps and VISTA volunteers. We were able to gather leaders together to share ideas and experience, encourage each other and explore legislative and policy possibilities. Many of the leaders who eventually formed the National Society for Internships and Experiential Education (NSIEE) attended these conferences. The phrase "service-learning" came to be used in a great variety of programs across the country.*

# Chapter 17

# A Home in Atlanta

Bill had gone to SREB several times to get his office established and program arrangements made. He also scouted out possibilities for housing the family. With five children between seven and fourteen, they needed space and a good location for schools. Mother and Dad had come to Oak Ridge to care for the children while Bill and Rose went to look at possible homes. The real estate agent referred by SREB insisted on showing them suburban housing developments. Bill and Rose were interested in being closer in. When the realtor said that SREB liked their people to live in these suburbs, Bill and Rose resisted and suggested that they be treated as mechanics or common workers, to no avail. They looked into housing in new racially integrated developments but found them way beyond their price range, probably because successful black professionals had created a high demand for housing previously denied to them. They visited houses listed for sale in the newspaper and finally found another agent who seemed to respond to their needs and preferences. Rose remembers finding the "dream house,"

*Our new agent, Clara Stromberg, was very much in tune with our needs and wishes and was tireless in exploring possibilities. She knew neighborhoods, schools, traffic patterns and property values. We were concentrating on older sections of Atlanta that had been fine areas some years ago but had declined so prices were lower and yet were areas that showed signs of resurgence. Several places we looked at were possible but none seemed right. We had passed a house with a beautiful big front lawn on Springdale Road in the Druid Hills area that I thought was just the kind we wanted but it wasn't for sale. Later we passed that way again and I saw a for sale sign in the yard. Clara was on it immediately and scheduled a visit. When we went up the long drive through the large lawn, past the blooming azaleas and dogwoods on one side and pecan*

246

*trees on the other and then entered the large brick house with Tudor trim, I knew this was it. It had five bedrooms, four bathrooms and a walk up floored attic. In addition to a wonderful front staircase it had a back stairs to the kitchen area. It had a side door opening under a porte-cochere.*

When the whole family came to look they stayed at a motel on Ponce de Leon Avenue. It was hard to get used to the constant sirens and other noises of the big city. Visiting the Springdale house, the kids were immediately exploring and picking out their rooms. The owners, the Flynns, were a lovely family of elderly siblings whose parents had lived in the house but had passed on. They had hoped to have the lot rezoned to allow apartments. It was a corner lot at Springdale and the Byway on the edge of Druid Hills. The lot behind the house extended up the Byway towards Briarcliff Road which had numerous apartment buildings. The rezoning had been denied, but meanwhile they had not maintained the house and now were ready to sell "as is" at a fair price. Bill remembers seeing the results of the lack of maintenance.

*It was a fine old house on a beautiful lot on a lovely street and not far from main roads to carry one to work or schools. But what I saw immediately was the space where bricks had fallen out above the main entrance and suspicious breaks in the slate roof. Once inside I noted the need for repapering or painting and the rather small kitchen. The bathroom behind the kitchen was horrible and unusable. When we got to the wonderfully spacious attic, the sun was illuminating seven small holes in the roof. It would take a lot of work to fix it up, but it seemed worth it and we had plenty of hands to do the work. Rose saw none of these problems but only the original grandeur of the place and it was love at first sight. We made an offer. Someone else made a higher offer, but the Flynn's liked the idea of our family living there and with Clara's help we arranged to buy it. We got a mortgage approved that would cover the costs of immediate repairs needed. We had no problem selling the baby farm in Oak Ridge, rented the Oak Ridge house for a time and then sold it.*

*Before everything was in place we used sleeping bags and ate out a lot. A favorite restaurant was "The House of Eng," where Jim's favorite was egg drop soup. Once when he was sick that is what he wanted and it seemed to be the remedy he needed. It was spring and there were 17 dogwoods in the yard, pecan trees, lots of azaleas and plenty of grassy space.*

Over time improvements were made to the house and it was a wonderful home for the family and for many guests over the next three years. Bill E., Laura and John each had a small bedroom. Stephen and Jim shared a larger one and Rose and Bill had one. The family repapered the parlor with red and gold wallpaper. Next to the large crown molding it was lovely. The dining room had a long table that could seat twelve or so. The front yard was big enough for the boys' football games. If it hadn't been for the house, the years in Atlanta would have been much more difficult. Big city life was different. The children were in two different schools, and neither was close enough to walk to. They were large and not particularly parent friendly. What a difference from Oak Ridge. With work on the house, Bill's travels, school and activities, five growing children and the pressures of traffic, sometimes Rose felt pretty well stressed. But she loved the house and never quite believed she was really living in her "palace." She was always a gracious hostess in her lovely home even though she didn't have a butler, cook or maid.

*The Flynn's had a caretaker named Jimmy Dean who wished to continue his duties, but with Bill's and my willingness to work and "child labor" we didn't need his services. We did discover evidence of his work under sinks and in various other places, which mostly consisted of ingenious repairs with wire and tape. The phrase "to Jimmy Dean something" came to mean fixing things with duct tape, baling wire, or other material at hand.*

## Schools

Billy entered his freshman year and Laura started 8th grade as a sub-freshman at Druid Hills High School. Rose drove them and the younger boys caught a school bus that stopped in front of the house. Billy was identified as "college bound" and put in advanced classes, but he insisted on taking a shops class where he could thoroughly enjoy working with his hands as well as his head. His favorite teacher was Mrs. Eyles. His special friends were Geof Arapian and Lester Whitter. He did so well in high school that he was chosen to attend the Governor's honors program and sent some weeks in the summer at Mercer College in Macon. He lived in a dormitory and when he entered Berea College a few years later he had the option of dormitory living there but opted to stay at home (Berea then) saying about dorm life, "I've done that!"

Laura had no problem with classes and joined the drill team with her good friend Susan Woods from across the street. They got to wear neat uniforms and became friends with other girls in the group. The three younger boys entered Fernbank, which went through grade 7. It was a privileged school in terms of facilities, equipment and teaching but rather rigid in rules and culture. Parents were not allowed past a line in the front hall without permission and a badge. The food service called the "cafetorium" was run by a dominant woman who offered food as an educational as well as a nutritional experience. Students were expected to eat there and the menu was featured in school literature. There were signs posted promoting it and discouraging other options. One said, *"DON'T BE A DRAG AND BRING A BAG!"* Rose remembers the lunch bag issue.

*Our children liked different lunches and preferred to have their own choices. Stephen loved peanut butter. Baloney was a favorite of others. They all liked fruit and treats, so they took their own lunches. At one point I was called by a school person to see if there was a problem. The assumption was we couldn't afford the cafeteria and they might be able to help. I assured them we were fine and the children just preferred their own lunches. John decided to respond to the disapproval of self-made lunches and convinced his classmates on one day to all bring sack lunches. When the question was asked, "Who brought their lunches today?" and every student raised a hand the poor teacher was dumbfounded. It was a school scandal to the students' delight.*

Stephen attended Fernbank for two years and then graduated to become a sub-freshman at Druid Hills. Under school integration rules, the high school was subjected to "busing" and a group of black students from a less privileged area were brought to Druid Hills. There were no racial problems but certainly a cultural conflict. At one point Stephen had his lunch money extorted from him at knife point in the rest room. He just made sure he didn't have to go. Jim was the one to suffer most that first year in Fernbank, although overall he also did well.

*Jim was a happy child and, as most children in the early grades, automatically wanted to love his teacher. Unfortunately his teacher was well past the age when she should have retired. She had taught the principal of the school when he was a child and he was still in awe of her. Jim reported that she told them "God will strike you dead, if you tell a lie!" Her account of Noah's Ark, which she taught as "history and not religion" focused on the folks clawing at the ark's sides as they drowned because they had been evil. Jim observed that "Even when she smiles she is frowning." She seemed to have a special dislike for boys. On one occasion Jim didn't understand some instruction and she was impatiently telling him what to do when he said he understood before she had finished her explanation. She back handed him across the face and he duly reported this to us. We knew we couldn't let this go so we went to the school and talked to the principal. He was quite upset but fearful to confront her so he said he would go take her class and would send her to talk to us. We did talk to her and, of course, she denied having struck Jim but we could tell she had and she knew we knew. God didn't strike her dead for telling a lie, but she was able to control herself and Jim had no more problems. From the principal's comments it was obvious that he thought I worked for the school accrediting agency which he confused with the Southern Regional Education Board. We didn't try to correct his misconception. Jim continued to fret over the incident until we suggested he draw a picture of his teacher that expressed his feelings. He did so and that seemed to relieve him so he could return to his natural happy state.*

## Church and Community

Bill and Rose and the children joined the Presbyterian Church on Ponce de Leon Avenue and found wonderful worship, fellowship and instruction there. The children went to Sunday school and the parents became part of the Clarion Class where close friendships were developed. The church had a strong outreach, especially to a large Hispanic population. The underlying message was the love commanded by Christ and the gospel rather than patronizing humanism. The youth minister provided an active program including showing of old classic movies that were both entertaining and wholesome. The church sponsored a Boy Scout troop in which Billy could participate and Bill helped as a volunteer. Rose found others interested in literacy and volunteered to work with Atlanta Literacy Action program. With the program director, Mary Hammond, she went to churches and schools cooperating in the program in many parts of the city. It was estimated that there were 250,000 people in Atlanta that needed these services. In 1969, she was certified as a Laubach "senior teacher" and "teacher trainer." She overcame her reluctance to driving in traffic and managed to negotiate the difficult street system of Atlanta, even picking Bill up at the airport on occasion. Billy and Laura learned to drive during their Atlanta years. Billy undertook a paper route, mostly delivering to apartments on Briarcliff Avenue. Delivering papers was not too hard but collection was sometimes a hassle.

Druid Hills had beautiful homes and trees and shrubs and flowers, and also an agreeable mixture of older folks and younger families living in the grand old houses. The Glenns across the street were a very friendly family. The father, John, worked at home as an actuary. The Woods next door to them became good friends. Susan Woods and Laura became best friends. The father, Jimmy Woods, worked with one of the organizations seeking to bring social justice and equal opportunity to the city and region. Next to them lived a pediatrician and his wife, who did modeling, and a precocious little boy named Ian. Further up the street lived the McKinney's with whom Rose became very close. An elderly couple named Lantz lived just two doors up in a large house and became like an older aunt and uncle. They had been missionaries and he still taught some at the International Theological Center.

*We liked our neighbors and had good friends in church but we missed the small town atmosphere we had enjoyed in Oak Ridge. The children were not as free to go home or to activities with friends and I had to do a lot more driving. Once I had to go to a party to "rescue" Laura and Susan when the parents had left and some boys came in with liquor. Most women worked outside the home and sometimes I felt a bit isolated in my big beautiful house. Bill was gone a lot and there were always things that needed attention. On the other hand, we had abundant company between visiting family, friends and foreign exchange students. Hospitality continued to be a significant feature of our home.*

Bill and Rose had signed up to be host family for international students, mostly connected to the International Theological Center, Morehouse, Clark, Spelman and Morris Brown colleges. Edith Johan from India became like an adopted daughter and later married and became an American citizen. Her friend Olive Das also was a frequent visitor. An Indian man named Manick Samuel joined the group. He was studying to become a minister. He also was a fortune teller of sorts and predicted that Rose would have another child, which was not contemplated at the time but turned out to be true. Daniel Mkwinawzi, a tall, soft spoken Zulu was another foster student. Phillip Akpan from Nigeria became very close to the family. His wife and children were uprooted during the Biafran civil war and he didn't hear from them for a long time. They had lived in a cave and fed on mushrooms until they could go home. Later the wife, Martha, came to be with Philip in Atlanta.

*We loved Philip, but he was sometimes a nuisance and when he called at about 2:00 am one morning I mentally sighed. He said Martha was having severe pains in her abdomen and he was desperate. I told him to call a taxi or an ambulance and get her to Grady Hospital emergency room. I'd meet him there. Still groaning inwardly, I got dressed and drove to Grady, which was the huge general hospital in downtown Atlanta. The emergency room was crowded with people in chairs and on the floor, many of them in bad shape with sickness, pains or wounds. It was like a scene from Bedlam and the medical personnel were stretched very thin. I spotted Philip and Martha in a corner and went over as Philip was coming towards me. She had not yet been seen and was in pain. Finally when her turn came they determined that she had severe gastroenteritis, which I knew from my army medic days meant inflammation or infection in the intestines. They gave her medication and released her. We took her to our house and Rose put her to bed. She remained there several days under Rose's care and finally was well enough to go back with Philip to their apartment. When we had first arrived home with Martha, Philip told Rose, "I was in despair and then when Bill came through the door at the hospital, I saw God!" I know he didn't see me, still resisting the call to help, but God could use even my reluctant soul. Later Martha died of cancer and we always wondered if she had been misdiagnosed in that frantic emergency room.*

The regular host family students were not the only international guests. On one occasion Rose got a call asking if we could take a Japanese boy who attended Mercer College in Macon, Georgia and needed a place to stay over Thanksgiving holidays. Takashi Yamashita came to stay for a while. He was about 17, the first child and only son in his family and had been very pampered and spoiled. He was very polite and couldn't understand that Rose did all the cooking, cleaning and other housework herself. He observed that American women are very busy. For several days he slept late and came downstairs about 11:00 saying he was ready for breakfast. Rose cured him of that habit and he kept asking "Is custom? Is custom?" He tried very hard to fit in and even wrote to his mother for a recipe for special rice pancakes and made them for us. Unfortunately his cooking oil was not hot enough and was soaked up in the pancake so they were inedible.

*We became fond of Takashi and appreciated his trying so hard to fit in and be helpful. For Thanksgiving dinner I prepared the usual turkey, dressing, cranberry sauce, etc. for a big crowd. In addition to our family of seven, Mother and Dad Ramsay were joining us. Brother Dick with a friend from Australia would also be there, along with Takashi. With 12 happily eating around the table, mother was telling an interesting story of their travels in her animated vivacious way. Takashi was unused to having women carry on conversation in mixed company and suddenly blurted out in amazement, "Old woman velly intellesting!" There was stunned silence and then everyone enjoyed a good laugh.*

Another memorable meal was when the family had a Russian visitor. A Quaker group was hosting a peace conference in Atlanta and expected international guests. Bill and Rose were asked to be host to a Russian gentleman and his interpreter. Yuri was a teacher of scientific communism at the University of Moscow and a very courteous and interesting guest. It was obvious that he felt he had to be careful what he said about communist Russia. Before our evening meal on the day they arrived he presented Rose and Bill with a small jar of black caviar. Knowing the reaction the children would have to eating tiny raw fish eggs Bill decided to warn them.

*I explained that caviar was a special treat to Yuri and his sharing it was important to him so we should each have a taste and appreciate his gift. Jim, who had taken a special liking to Yuri, as Yuri had to him, was anxious to please. When we were all around the table with crackers on which to put the caviar I asked, "Who would like some caviar?" Jim immediately responded enthusiastically, "I want some, I'll have two!"*

Bill had to travel a great deal to universities, Washington agencies, development districts and conferences. For each group of interns, regional conferences were scheduled where the interns would share their experiences and articulate what they had learned. Where possible the family would go along or one of the children would accompany him on trips. One of the conferences was arranged in Charleston, South Carolina and the family went and vacationed at the Isle of Palms. That became a very special place where they returned many times. Celo continued to be the summer vacation choice with grandma and grandpa now retired there full time. Even on vacation hospitality often intruded.

*Eleanor Pegel, a Catholic friend and neighbor from Oak Ridge, called to tell me about a young girl who was in a bad family situation and needed a place to be away from home for a time. Could we help out? Having some reservations about introducing a 15 year old girl into our family, I agreed to try to help. Bill picked Mary up at the Atlanta airport, even more concerned when he saw the long hair "fall" and heavy pancake make-up adorning the teen. We were getting ready to go on vacation to the Isle of Palms and would have to take Mary with us. Not surprisingly she communicated best with Jim, who was still under 10, but very outgoing and at ease with everyone. On our way to South Carolina, I found that Mary had an envelope full of pills she was taking. They were apparently some kind of anti-depressant and she had been given enough to last for an extended period. I confiscated the pills and assured her that she would have them as needed. Our time with Mary was sometimes strained and awkward but she seemed to adjust enough to get along and I think the time on vacation and later back in Atlanta was helpful to her. It sure made us appreciate our own children more. She went back to Oak Ridge and we heard from her occasionally, the last time while she was a college student at the University of Tennessee.*

Bill met many kindred spirits in his visits to agencies, colleges and universities. Many became friends of the family and visited the house in Druid Hills. They came to know and enjoy Dean B.R Brazeale from Clark College and his family. They exchanged Christmas cards with Dr. Martin Luther and Coretta Scott King and had scheduled a visit from that family, but something intervened.

# CHAPTER 18

# SERVICE-LEARNING EXPANDS

At SREB, Bill, Bob and Mike were very busy and on the road a good deal. Staff members of other projects and administrative personnel were supportive and helpful, although the upper management continued to be apprehensive for a time. They were provided good office space, first at SREB headquarters at the edge of the Georgia Tech campus and later a very nice suite in an upper floor of a bank building on North Peachtree. Especially encouraging were Dr. Harold McPheeters, leader of a project to improve mental health care education, Helen Belcher, a nurse heading a program to foster excellent nursing education and Bill O'Connell in general management. From time to time the internship program had to supplement staff with temporary help. Besides Donald Eberly these additions included Ed Angus and Rich Ungerer who made important contributions. At universities and colleges and other student service programs another gallery of personalities became involved, not to mention the students from schools across the South. Mike Goldstein of the Urban Corps, Jane Kendall of NSIEE, Tim Stanton and others took leadership roles in the movement.

*I spent considerable time in Washington finding sponsors and visiting agencies to arrange funding. We found that local sponsors were quite willing to share costs so we could double the program without increasing the cost to the sponsoring organization. That meant more visits to local development organizations to arrange projects and visits to universities to find students and faculty in essentially all southern states from Texas to Maryland. As the program's reputation spread we were asked to help get similar programs going in the western states, mid-west and northeast and were glad to assist other regional organizations.*

*I enjoyed my share of visits to universities and colleges and to local communities. I got a good response from students at a prestigious law school in Virginia and architectural students in Tennessee in spite of warnings by faculty that we might find no interest. I remember working out an internship in a small very rural community on the eastern shore of Maryland where one man was mail carrier, policeman and trash collector, using a bicycle as his vehicle for all these jobs.*

The internships were organized as "projects" rather than "positions." The intern was given a manageable piece of work for the assigned organization that could be completed or advanced within the period of the internship. Most organizations had no positions open but none was ever found that didn't have a list of projects that needed doing if they just had the time or personnel. At the end each intern wrote a comprehensive report for the organization recording the project and making recommendations where appropriate. The report had to be well documented and written to high academic standards as well as being useful. Reports were published by SREB, with the intern's name. Soon the program had a library of very interesting reports covering all kinds of community development topics. A plan for developing a landfill for a rural community, a town renovation project, a survey of manpower available for industrial development, a plan for an emergency response system in a town, provision of legal services to the poor, the efficient cutting of sorghum and production of molasses, low income housing and many other examples were represented, in the reports always with a focus on the specific local situation.

*After I had left SREB and was at Berea College, I was asked by Don Eberly to write a chapter for a book to be edited by Michael Sherraden and Don entitled National Service: Social, Military and Economic Impacts. (Copyright 1982 Pergaman Press Inc.) I wrote a chapter on the potential impacts of national service on education. Although our internships were short term, I was convinced of the value of youth service whatever the length. I included statistics showing the comparative costs of different activities of young adults. At that time, a year of national service would cost an estimated $6600. A year's employment at minimum wage would be $6968. A year at college cost $8900. Juvenile incarceration cost $18000 and military service cost $21000. Giving* *young people an opportunity to contribute in community service seemed a real bargain and that is not counting the enormous social benefits.*

A few years after Bill went to work at Berea College he received a note from SREB that they were cleaning out files and would be glad to send him the library of intern reports. He did receive them, organized them and catalogued them on cards and stored them at his office. When he retired from Berea in 1994 he had them moved to the Library archives where they sat for another 20 years. Later they were taken to Elon College for their service earning archives.

*After three years at SREB, it was obvious that the idea of service-learning had a life of its own now; the internships were expanding and other organizations and institutions were getting interested in having their own programs. The states of North Carolina and Georgia wanted to set up statewide programs. Some universities were establishing service-learning centers. Many individual arrangements were being made between community agencies and schools. I remember when the head of the Atlanta metropolitan economic opportunity agency got a call from a local seminary saying they would like all their students at a certain level to have a community service experience. Could he use some? He asked, "How many students are there?" and was told it would be about 70. He responded, "I'll take them all!"*

*I felt that the task I had been given when leaving Oak Ridge had been accomplished and I should be looking for the next challenge. I began looking at opportunities and was seriously considering one in Washington with the Department of Labor when, out of the blue, came a call from Willis Weatherford, president of Berea College, asking if I'd like to come and talk to them about a position as Dean of Labor. I said I would like to talk. The result was a move to Berea in the fall of 1970.*

# CHAPTER 19

# JENNIFER ROSE

By the summer of 1969, Rose knew that she was expecting another child. This was a surprise but the whole family was delighted. She found an OB, Dr. Nutter, in Mableton, a little town on the west side of the metropolitan area, who was connected to Holy Family Hospital that encouraged natural childbirth. Bill had hurt his left knee changing a tire on a snowy trip in South Carolina. The knee was weak from an old injury received playing high school football. He was on crutches when time came for the baby to be delivered, but he was allowed to be there for the birth.

*It was great to have Bill with me when I went to the hospital and started the labor process. The training and practice paid off and I felt a sense of pleasure knowing that the struggles in childbirth education had resulted in changes that made this experience possible. Bill coached and encouraged me. He said he could understand why doctors wanted to "deliver" the baby, because it was hard not to try to help the mother by hurrying things along and yet the training made it clear that the process had to go through its stages and took some time. When he saw the baby enter the world she was grayish blue for an instant and then she took her first breath and turned a beautiful healthy pink. She was a lovely baby girl and we were thrilled. We named her Jennifer Rose. Two days later, on Valentine's Day, 1970 we took her home. Stephen held her. Laura was excited to have a sister. When she was in her crib at home, the boys would sit and just watch her breathe.*

So when the family moved to Berea in the fall of that year there were six children, including baby Jennifer, and Rose's faithful dog, Cindy, with three puppies. Some of the faculty wags suggested that Rose, and not Bill, should be Dean of Labor. It was hard leaving the beautiful house on Springdale Road but the family was ready for a new phase of life. The Atlanta intermission was over.

# BILL AND ROSE RAMSAY TIME LINE

## ATLANTA YEARS: 1967 - 1970

| YEARS | FAMILY AND RELATED EVENTS | WORLD EVENTS |
|-------|---------------------------|--------------|
| 1967 | Family moves to 1020 Springdale Road in Druid Hills area of Atlanta<br>Bill & Bob Sigmon begin work at SREB<br>Internships greatly expand through south<br>Billy and Laura attend North Druid Hills High<br>Younger boys attend Fernbank Elementary<br>Family joins Ponce de Leon Presbyterian Church | Nigerian Civil War |
| 1968 | Rose gets involved in literacy program<br>Family becomes host family for international<br>Students from Nigeria and India<br>Service- Learning spreads across country | Assassination of MLK and<br>Robert Kennedy<br>Tet offensive in Vietnam<br>Minimum wage is $1.60 per hour |
| 1969 | Constant improvements of house<br>Hosting of foreign students, guests, etc,<br>Bill traveling to Washington and colleges<br>Family travels when possible. Celo continues | Nixon elected president<br>Moon landing<br>Eisenhower dies<br>Woodstock festival |
| 1970 | Jennifer Rose is born; Bill is present<br>Internships expanding and decentralizing<br>Billy beginning to think of college<br>Bill accepts position at Berea College<br>Family moves to Berea in October<br>Housed in Oakwood Cottage temporarily<br>Children begin Berea Community Schools | Kent State U killings<br>Nasser dies; Sadat leads Egypt<br>Gas costs 36 cents a gallon<br>Bread is 25 cents a loaf<br>Hamburger is 70 cents a pound<br>New cars average $3,450 |

**ATLANTA YEARS: 1967-70**
BILL TRAVELED A GREAT DEAL VISITING UNIVERSITIES AND AGENCIES. ROSE LOVED THEIR BIG HOUSE, ITS BEAUTI-FUL YARD AND LOTS OF COMPANY

**JENNIFER ROSE**

ON FEBRUARY 12, 1970 JENNIFER ROSE SANG HER FIRST SONG AND CHARMED EVERYONE. BILL WAS ON CRUTCHES BUT IN ATTENDANCE AT BIRTH FOR THE FIRST TIME. THE BOYS JUST WATCHED THEIR NEW BABY AND LAURA (left), AT 15, WAS THRILLED TO FINALLY HAVE A SISTER. THE FAMILY WAS NOW COMPLETE.

# REFLECTIONS 13

## <u>WORK AND VOCATION</u>

We like to work. There is something satisfying about accomplishing a task whether by the sweat of the brow or by the application of the mind or both. Plowing a straight furrow, weeding a flower bed, finishing a complicated tax form, teaching a child to read or preparing a family meal can all give a sense of well-being. And working along with others can be a special blessing as the added values of sharing and relationships should make work even more enjoyable. It often takes more than one and working together to accomplish a task.

We know that some work is tedious, disagreeable and difficult. We know that many people hate their work. Work that is repetitive and useless can be exhausting, frustrating and debilitating - like the task given to Sisyphus to roll a boulder up a hill just to see it roll down over and over for eternity as punishment by the gods for his avarice and cruelty. But productive work should not be approached as punishment even though it was because of his sin that Adam was banished from Eden and made to live by the sweat of his brow. Even before their banishment he and Eve were to tend the garden, but it was then a joy. If work is undertaken as "tending" it is transformed from a curse to a blessing. We like to think of work as "service." We appreciate the work (service) of others that makes our lives better – the electric company linemen that keep the power coming into our homes, the farmers or migrant workers who are essential to our having food, the coal miners who produce fuel for the power plants that light our cities, the steelworkers who make the girders that allow us to cross rivers safely on strong bridges, the doctors and nurses, the ministers, the artists and musicians who enrich our lives, and countless others who make their contributions.

As Dean of Labor at Berea College, I pondered the reasons for work, the values of work and the dimensions of work. I explored the different meanings of the words work, job, labor, service, career and vocation. **"Work"** generally means a purposeful exertion of energy. **"Labor"** developed from "labere" which means tottering under a heavy load or fatigue and hardship. One reference on the word **"job"** said it has roots in the task of gathering camel dung by the lowest caste in India and referred to the camel dung itself. Sometimes students and others could relate to that concept of their jobs. **'Service"** suggests doing something of value for others. It adds a value dimension to work. **"Career"** is used to denote a profession or line of work or series of jobs in a particular field of endeavor. The Latin work "carrus" from which career evolved meant a wheeled vehicle and developed to denote a racetrack. This may be the origin of the concept of the "rat race." Vocation adds a dimension of a commitment of oneself to a life work and implies a calling or sense of purpose serving a higher power. It all gets pretty confusing and I can't claim to have sorted it out. I have noted some thoughts, stories and observations of others.

Work is essential for living. If our heart stops "working", we die. If someone doesn't work, no one eats. Gandhi asserted, "He who eats but works not eats stolen food." Most people have to work to "earn a living." The question is not whether or not work is necessary but who works, how they work, what work they do. What we do and how we do it makes a world of difference to ourselves and to others. For example, serving food is a daily task which may be performed in a great variety of settings and ways. It can be done by a mother in a family as an expression of love and caring. It can be done as a volunteer at a soup kitchen as a service to those in need. It can be done grudgingly by a waitress who hates her job and is just waiting for a chance to do something else or by a waitress who loves her job and enjoys making things just right for her diners. Food can be thrust at prisoners out of a sense of duty to keep them alive. What a difference the context and attitudes involved in serving food can make to the enjoyment of food, not to mention the digestion. And it makes a difference in the life of the one serving.

At its best work, meaning performance of a task, should
    meet a real need
    provide a fair return to the worker
    be a means of expression by the worker
    bring a sense of satisfaction as it accomplishes its purpose
    contribute to the growth of skills and knowledge of the worker
    give the worker a sense of dignity and well-being,
    be appreciated as a contribution to community.

The Shakers, a religious sect who were extremely creative and industrious, saw work as a form of worship. How could it represent anything less than ones best if it is ultimately done for God? The Scottish philosopher and poet, Thomas Carlyle (1795-1881) observed:

> *"... there is a perennial nobleness, and even a sacredness, in Work.... There is always hope in a man that actually and earnestly works; in idleness alone is there perpetual despair.*
>
> *Blessed is he who has found his work; let him ask no other blessedness. He has a work, a life purpose,,,, as a free flowing channel, dug and torn by noble force through the sour mud swamp of one's existence, like an ever deepening river there, it runs and flows – draining off the sour festering water... making, instead of pestilential swamp, a green fruitful meadow with its clear flowing stream.*
>
> *Labour is Life: from the inmost heart of the worker rises his god-given Force... breathed into him by Almighty God."*

That sounds pretty idealistic and inserts the idea of a calling or life –work beyond just the performance of a task or job. We have noticed that people who have found their calling, whatever it is, are happier. We worked on civil rights issues with a somewhat older Jewish couple in Oak Ridge. The husband was a physicist and the wife had a passion for teaching literacy, sometimes for pay, but mostly as a volunteer. Rose shared that interest and together they taught children, youth and adults, who had been bypassed by the educational system, how to read. They were successful and it made them happy. We have other friends who have been very successful in careers and material success who are miserable. They haven't found a calling beyond successful careers, trading their labor for money and position, and that is not enough to find meaning and fulfillment. I remember an illustration of that from the comic strip "Doonesbury" some years ago.

> *Aristocratic New England Congresswoman Lacy is walking through the halls beneath the capitol and sees a new janitor. She made it a point to know the names of the janitors and introduced herself saying, "I haven't seen you here before. What is your name?" He replies, "My name is Fred and I've only been here a week." Congresswoman Lacy says, "Excuse me, Fred, but you don't look like a janitor." He explains, "Until a week ago I was a highly paid lawyer. I graduated at the top of my class at Yale fourteen years ago and got a good job with a prestigious law firm in New York. For fourteen years I worked on an anti-trust case that just went to court and was declared moot! So I quit. This is the first socially useful work I've ever done. God it feels good!"*

Some random examples of attitudes towards work give an idea of the spectrum of possibilities for work having or not having meaning beyond a paycheck or basic necessity.

In Oak Ridge, I interviewed a man for a position in the technical services area requiring refrigeration-service training and experience. His application showed that he had adequate training and experience and we discussed that and the conditions of the job. Then I asked him what he liked about his line of work. He smiled and got excited as he described the thrill he got when he had finished working on a refrigeration unit and he turned on the power and he could see and feel the frost begin to form on the coils. He loved his work. He was hired.

I talked to an army sergeant who said he hated the army and his work. I asked him why he didn't get out and do something he liked. He said he only had twelve more years until retirement so he couldn't afford to leave. I was sad that he would choose to condemn himself to twelve years of misery in the prime of his life - suffering so he could retire.

At Berea a freshman student came in to complain about his student labor assignment in Food Service. He wanted to be a photographer and had some talent in that area. He went on and on about how demeaning it was to have to work in the kitchen. I advised him that the record he earned at that beginning job would be very important to anyone considering him for a job more to his liking. Furthermore I suggested to him that the nonstudent men and women with whom he worked devoted their working lives to seeing that students were well fed and took pride in their work. To call it demeaning was not very kind to them. He was a bright young man and thought about this. Some of the regular workers were helpful and good to him. He regretted his attitude and finished out that term well, earned a good record and the next year was hired in the public relations department, where he did very well as a photographer.

A student feeling a job is beneath him reminds me of a humorous story that would not be true of Berea graduates. A young graduate had been offered a job in an accounting office and reported for work as arranged. The supervisor was a bit at a loss, having forgotten the new employee was coming in that day. He said it would take a while to get together some work for him to do but meanwhile he could sweep out the office. The young man drew himself up and said, "Sir, I'm a college graduate." The supervisor replied, "I'm sorry, I forgot. Here, I'll show you how."

Whatever task you undertake, whether it is your first choice or not, do it well. Find satisfaction in a job well done. Your vocation should transcend your immediate job. Sometimes a calling is completely separate from a "job." A wonderful little novel, *The Dean's Watch* by English author Elizabeth Goudge includes the story of an elderly woman who was admired and loved by all in her family and community and couldn't quite understand why? In my own words I have summarized the part of the story about the beloved woman in the story.

*Miss Mary Montague came from a family blessed with good looks and good connections. They were not royalty but associated with the upper classes. As a young girl she had been pushed by a brother and fallen down a flight of stair, sustaining injury to her back which left her slightly stooped. As she grew, she entertained youthful dreams of someday marrying a great explorer or ambassador and going to exotic places and taking her place among interesting and exciting people. When her older sister was planning her wedding Mary was excited about being a bridesmaid, but she was not asked to be in the wedding party at all. She knew it was because she was misshapen. She took stock of herself and her dream world and asked herself what she was supposed to do with her life.*

*The family always went to church and that seemed to be the extent of their religious commitment, but now Mary began to try to find out what a Christian was supposed to do. The answers in the liturgy, lessons and scriptures seemed clear. Christians are to express love for others. They are to love unconditionally. What did she love unconditionally? She loved her cat and had once saved her from a dog even though she got scratched in the process. Beginning with the cat she began to try to love those around her. She got to know and love the servants. She loved the children born to her brothers and sisters as they came along. She was the one who stayed home and took care of her parents when they were aging and needed care. She cared for neighbors and friends, never asking any return, As time went on the nieces and nephews loved to visit Aunt Mary and sought her advice and shared confidences with her. Others did the same and knew she could be depended upon for care and trusted with secrets. She became the object of love and admiration and never understood why. She had found her calling and pursued it unreservedly, and she was happy*

One can't help but think of Mother Teresa.

My jobs have been varied but, looking back, my vocation seems to have been helping others achieve good things. During college I found I was better at directing and producing plays than I was at acting. I could see that the stage was set, the props and costumes were provided, the lines were learned and presented effectively and an audience assembled so those in the drama could play their part. That has been the kind of role I have played in various positions, in volunteer activities church and in family. Rose has been a homemaker in the finest sense of the word and underlying that has been a call to nurture others and to strive for a better community and world, which she has done by raising and tending a family, in church activities, through childbirth education, teaching literacy, working for civil rights and, more fundamentally, promoting mutual love and caring among all kinds of people.

Whether in a paying job, at home, as a community volunteer or just in everyday life, do your best at the tasks you are given and seek to know what are your callings or vocations and follow them with joy. Jobs are stations along the way. Callings or vocations are life's work which may sometimes not involve a "job" at all. Do whatever it is you do for the glory of God and you will find your reward. (Read Colossians 3:23-24)

# REFLECTIONS 14

## MOVEMENTS AND INSTITUTIONS

We have been involved in movements, organizations and institutions all of our lives. I grew up in a family that worked hard to create better conditions for workers through organized labor. Dad and Mother Ramsay were part of the Oxford Movement, or Moral Re-Armament (MRA), and a great variety of church, labor and charity organizations, all striving for a better life. As a young wife and mother, Rose was an important contributor to the development and spread of childbirth education, and she served as a literacy teacher. We were active in civil rights. I served on the boards of the Council of the Southern Mountains and Pine Mountain Settlement School. We were part of Berea College as students, alumni and staff. I worked at Oak Ridge Associated Universities and the Southern Regional Education Board. I studied public administration which touched on how movements, institutions and agencies come into being and change over time. We were officers in churches and held positions in professional organizations. So we have had opportunity to watch movements and organizations develop and change. Reflecting on our experience and observations we see some patterns.

Typically new movements, organizations and institutions begin with an inspired person or inspired people who see a need and get others to join in trying to meet the need. Whether it is organizing a union, starting a church, establishing a college, launching a business or beginning a community or professional organization the pattern seems to be the same. One or a few dedicated persons commit themselves to achieve idealistic goals and often do so with great sacrifice involving risk of comfort, security and even life. But they are willing to give all for their dream. Others join and they become successful.

Time passes and the movement or organization grows. It acquires a "donor base" or clientele that must be cultivated. It now has a constituency which has expectations. It may accumulate property, profits and endowment. Nonprofits acquire purchase exemption from taxes. Contributions are officially qualified for tax deductions and that status must be protected. It becomes incorporated for protection against any lawsuit. It no longer depends primarily for direction and decisions on a founder with a mission, but on a board of trustees who elect the officers who oversee the affairs. Trustees and officers are expected to be prudent. Risk, which was a factor in the organization's beginning, is now something to be carefully avoided. Over time preservation of the organization may become more important than its mission. After all, unless the organization is strong, how can its mission continue? Insurance, audits, data bases, and employees to manage the various aspects of the organization become important. For nonprofits, a professional vice president for development is hired and arranges fund raising, often with outside agencies, and all public relations and publications are put under his control. This results in communications with supporters always having a fund-raising slant. It works and the organization thrives. If it is a private business and has a record of profits it may be bought out by a new owner more interested in profits than the service or products originally central to the business. Whatever type of organization it may have lost some of its initial fervor and sense of purpose. It reminds one of the message in the book of Revelation to the church in Ephesus.

> *I also know that you are enduring patiently... and that you have not grown weary. But I have this against you, that you have abandoned the love you had at first.* (Revelation 2:2, NRSV)

I am not suggesting that growth, prudence and wise management is bad. I have been a party to helping it happen most of my professional life. But how does an organization keep its focus on its mission encumbered by the weight of success? Perhaps it can't. Sometimes organizations need to cease to exist. I think of the group that fought hard to change laws and attitudes in regard to using tobacco. The effort was successful and I don't hear any more from them. Others have simply changed their mission to some other need, like Ester Seals, that will be worthwhile and attract support. Some develop new initiatives when old ones are no longer relevant, like Pine Mountain Settlement School undertaking leadership in environmental education when a residential school was no longer needed. Some gradually shift their emphasis to appeal to a greater donor base, as Habitat for Humanity, which began with an emphasis on a Christian imperative to help those in need and now doesn't mention its faith origins. The facts are that success carries with it new challenges.

Lincoln Steffens, an investigative reporter of a century ago suggested in his autobiography that the best way to ruin a good movement or organization is to give it money. Obviously the problem is not new.

I once observed at a time of financial crisis that it was probably a good thing, because it makes one examine what is really important. How can one avoid the shackles that come with success? I can't answer that, but think that being aware of the dangers is the first important step. Are leaders spending more time on "development", "bottom line" and "investments" than direct services? Are trustees or officers selected for their passion for the mission or for their expertise in managing funds? Is the organization still true to the underlying moral base or need that gave rise to its existence? Has it become more concerned with its "standing" and image in the media than knowing it is doing what it was created to do whatever others might think? Is everyone too comfortable? These are hard questions to answer. Leadership with vision and courage, not just good management or success financially or reputation, important as those are, is critical.

# PART SEVEN

*Berea, 1970-1995*

# CHAPTER 20

# LIFE IN BEREA

Coming back to Berea was like coming home. But now they were a family of eight, Bill had a position of responsibility and there were many differences from the Berea Bill and Rose had left eighteen years earlier. The country was still reeling from the turmoil of the sixties and racial tensions reached even to Berea, but it still felt welcoming and safe. It was wonderful to find familiar faces on the faculty and staff and also exciting to meet new friends. Willis Weatherford had been President for three years and was determined to strengthen the Berea Student Labor Program as a central part of the Berea education and experience. The dean of labor would be a member of the administrative committee along with the president, academic dean and vice presidents for finance, business and development. New federal and state laws were changing the landscape of student financial aid. Getting moved, settled in and started on the job presented many challenges.

Bill still had responsibilities at SREB for transfer of leadership of the internship program. He and Billy came to Berea early in September to be there for the beginning of the new academic year, scout out housing, get introduced and oriented, start Billy in his last year of high school, which included several college classes, and finalize arrangements for the move in October.

*I was pleased that my office would be in Lincoln Hall, where the labor office had been for decades. It looked much the same with the long counter dividing the work area from those coming in for information or services. The college had a housing policy that allowed new staff to rent college housing for up to five years while they got settled in the community, if they stayed. Our family was to be housed in Dixie House which had once been the home economics practice house for the Foundation School (high school). It had been converted to a residence and was occupied by Dudley and Ginger Howe and their family. Dudley was director of physical plant and was building a home in town, but it wasn't completed. Carl Warming who was vice president for business offered to put us in Oakwood Cottage until Dixie House was available in the spring. Two single women college workers, Grace Butgereit and Edith Gott, were living in the cottage and would move to other single housing. Oakwood, a small two story frame house was about 1/3 the size of our house in Atlanta, but we could manage temporarily. It was on the campus drive to Talcott Hall and very convenient to campus buildings, hospital and schools. Dixie House was just beyond it at the end of Talcott Hall and had plenty space.*

Rose, meanwhile was busy packing and organizing for the move. Mother and Dad Ramsay had come to help with the move and by October 1970 all was ready.

*I hated to leave my dream house in Druid Hills and the friends and neighbors there, but was excited about going to Berea. I felt that it was truly the Lord's leading and the right thing to do. It was a little scary and humbling to see the moving van loaded and driven away with all our earthly belongings in one truck. It would arrive the next evening after we had reached Berea. We spent a night on the way to Berea in Knoxville with Wendell and Lois Russell. They had a cat named Liza Jane and when she saw Cindy and her three puppies she decided to settle at once whose place this was. She went to Cindy and swatted her and then to each of the yelping puppies and stalked off, having settled the matter. We went on the next day to Berea. When I saw Oakwood Cottage, I knew the truck was bigger than it was and not everything was going to fit. I was right and stacks of boxes stayed on the porch or in the basement the whole time we lived there. Unfortunately a few of the sturdy boxes we had accumulated to pack books, which didn't need to be unpacked immediately, were originally for whisky so for our time in Oakwood Cottage our porch advertised Jack Daniels, Old Turkey and such.*

*We got settled in and everyone had a place to sleep. The kitchen was tiny (and we had just finished remodeling the one in Atlanta) but we could manage. In fact that first winter we hosted several family members during Christmas Country Dance School held the week between Christmas and New Year. Bill's brother John had been a leader in the school since his college days. He was the director of the John C. Campbell Folk School in North Carolina. He and Winona, her mother Mrs. Lotz, and Martin and Loren stayed with us. Also and Patty and Earl came that year as well, with Bill Todt. We put all the boys in the basement on cots and managed to fit everyone else in somewhere. We planned a big meal and invited the McLain family and Loyal and Nan Jones and their two girls, Susan and Carol, to join our crowd. Loyal was the director of the new Appalachian Center. He and Nan were classmates from the early 50's. We had a lovely meal at our little house. Everyone took off their shoes as they arrived and there was a pile of 17 pairs of shoes in the entrance hall.*

It was wonderful to be in the midst of old and new friends and wholesome families. Former president Francis Hutchins and his physician wife, Louise, became enjoyable friends rather than the somewhat aloof and formidable personages of Bill's and Rose's student days. Louis Smith, always a friend and benefactor, became a favorite with the children, with his dry wit and pocket full of candy treats. Family friendships with other Bereans were quickly formed.

## The Weatherford Family

The Weatherford family was very special to us. Willis was a tall distinguished gentleman with clear blue eyes and white hair, looking the part of a college president. Anne was also tall and gracious, with soft brown eyes and Southern accent. They were both equally capable with their minds and their hands, and equally at home in distinguished, elegant company and with those who work with their hands and have not had the benefits of higher education. They loved gardening, tending horses, and working and serving in home, community and church. Bill has a fond memory of Anne that demonstrates her loving and confident but humble character.

*Years after Willis and Anne had retired to their beloved home in the Blue Ridge Mountains of North Carolina, and after Willis's death, Anne had come to Berea as a distinguished guest for a literary occasion. She called and asked if we could drive her to see Golda Bailey, who had been her housekeeper at the president's house for many years. Mrs. Bailey lived in the country east of Berea in the Red Lick area, not far from our home at Pilot Knob. We drove her to the Bailey home and entered the small, neat living room. I can still picture Anne and Golda sitting side by side on the couch, holding hands like loving sisters, chatting away about their families and shared memories.*

There were five Weatherford children. Edie, Julia, Will and the twins, Susan and Alice, became like cousins to the Ramsay children. They shared adventures together in school at Berea, and hiking and visiting at Celo or Blue Ridge. Edie went with Laura on a trip to Samoa with Grandma and Grandpa Ramsay, attending a Christian Endeavor conference, and a few years later was maid of honor at her wedding.

## The McLain Family

At the same time Bill and Rose returned to Berea, Raymond and Betty McLain and their children came, like a gift from the Muses, to add a dimension of Appalachian music to Berea's offerings. Known as "Bun," Raymond had been director of Hindman Settlement School, where Bill's brother Dick had served on the staff of the school for a time so the families were acquainted. Now they became close friends. Bun, a talented musician, had organized "The McLain Family Band." Bun played the guitar. Their son Raymond played banjo and fiddle. Alice, the elder daughter, played mandolin or guitar with her little sister Ruthie usually playing the double bass. All of them sang. Their specialty was Bluegrass. They were talented musicians and performers, delighting their audiences, They composed and arranged music, songs and dance and regularly played for folk dances and other occasions at Berea and elsewhere. Young Raymond, with a happy face and a body that expressed music, was a virtuoso on banjo and fiddle, but could play any instrument. Alice, a younger version of her lovely mother, most often played back-up and sang in a sweet but strong voice. Ruthie bounced, standing on a chair so she could reach the neck of the double bass that was much bigger than she was, as she plucked and thumped the strings, She also had a commanding voice. All of them interacted with each other as they played and sang, charming their listeners.

Betty and Bun were like a sister and brother to Bill and Rose. Raymond, Alice and Ruth were like part of the family and two younger children, Nancy Ann and Michael were added to the mix. Bun and Betty are now gone, but the children, grown with families of their own, continue to make musical contributions. They often perform together. Alice became a teacher as well as a musician. She married Al White who is also an accomplished musician and music leader, continuing an Appalachian musical tradition at Berea College. They are always willing to share their musical talents with joy and a becoming humility. Alice is a favorite teacher of Eleanor Sartor, one of Bill's and Rose's great grandchildren, so the relationships go on into new generations.

## The Early Years

The children were like birds out of the cage. They could walk everywhere. They could ride bikes or walk to Berea Community School, which had just opened the year before. It was constructed in three circles to be an "open school" with no interior walls between classrooms. What a difference from the prison-like atmosphere of the big city schools. It took some getting used to and teachers arranged bookshelves and other furnishings to create some division between classes. The children thrived in this atmosphere and had some excellent teachers.

*Living on campus, the children were quickly friends with many college people of all ages. Laura remarked, "Everywhere I go somebody knows me!" What comforting words those were for a mother of six, just come from the big city. I took Jennifer walks on the beautiful campus paths accompanied by faithful little dog Cindy. That first fall the barberry bushes seemed especially brilliant red and I thought of a phrase from a poem quoted in a play we had done in our student days, "October's bright blue weather!" What a blessing it was to be in Berea.*

The children soon became part of a gang of faculty and town children who went to school together. They played a free ranging soccer kind of game they called "gooch ball" with the only boundary being the part of campus they were on. In the winter they went sledding on alumni hill or in the cemetery and ice skated, when it was cold enough for the ponds to be frozen. Most of the teens belonged to a folk dance group then led by Martin Ambrose. The five Weatherford children, the three Levey boys, Margie Drake, the Gaileys, John and Louis Henderson, Laura and Kenneth Menifee, the Prosses, Stricklers, Chrismans and others became like a huge extended family. What a change from the Atlanta experience. Jennifer quickly became the campus baby and grew up surrounded by caring and interesting people.

It didn't take long for Bill to feel at home in the labor office. Wilson Evans, who had been dean of labor for a number of years, was still there, but now handling the burgeoning financial aid needs and opportunities. He reported to Bill and was very helpful as a colleague in connecting with the past. When Wilson had moved into the financial aid area a couple years before, Douglas Massey, who had been director of alumni affairs, had been appointed by president Weatherford as dean of labor. Shortly after his appointment he was tragically killed in a car wreck and Jim Bobbitt, director of institutional research, had been acting dean since then. So the labor program had been maintained but its leadership unsettled for several years. Bill determined to make no quick changes for the first year while he learned the ropes. He had been provided an able assistant in Hazel Wehrle, who had been employed in the accounting office and knew records and payroll procedures well. And, appropriately for that office, they had a very talented group of students working in it.

*I decided to review the work records of students in all departments and deal with any who were behind in their hours, finding out what the problems were and figuring out solutions. When my student workers gave me the list it contained over 300 names. It clearly wasn't just a matter of a few students with problems but a systemic problem involving supervision, follow-up and consequences. I also found that most of the janitorial positions were held by seniors. Having been a student janitor in my early student days, I knew that these students, being smart, had figured out the easiest way to meet the "labor requirement." They could get their area cleaned in an hour or less and get two hours credit. Where was the supervision? Many students performed very well and used the labor program to gain skills and make a contribution, but the perception that student labor was a "requirement" to be met in the least demanding way needed to be changed. The labor program was a financial and practical necessity but was much more. It provided "opportunities" to be embraced as part of the educational program and for personal growth and development.*

This attitude of student work being simply a financial necessity was reinforced by the pay structure. Students were all paid almost the same no matter what their job with small increments for longevity in the job. So to remain a janitor for four years was rewarded more than advancing to positions of greater skill and responsibility. In addition the advent of federal college work-study funds, for which some of the most-needy students qualified, to help with books and supplies had been handled by adding the work-study funds to the student's pay resulting in some students earning more than others for the same job. Federal rules were not completely clear but required that federal funds used be reported to the students and couldn't substitute for funds already in place. The financial aid budget, in spite of the new largesse of federal grants, which were mostly unavailable to Berea students because of Berea's no-tuition policy, was over $300,000 in the red. Clearly some changes needed to be made in Berea policies and procedures at several levels. This was a good challenge for one trained in public administration.

*The more I learned about how things worked the more I realized that basic changes needed to be made without losing sight of the goals and ideals of Berea. In addition to my commitment to the values of student work, my knowledge of the federal establishment from the years with the internship programs and my personnel administration experience in Oak Ridge were going to be very helpful. I thought that president Weatherford had been clever to know of my background and how it could be put to use. We had served on the board of the Council of Southern Mountain Workers together but didn't know each other well. It turned out that he had no idea of what I had been doing but had called me because Dean Louis Smith had suggested it based on his experience with me as a student and his helping me receive my graduate fellowship. Louis Smith played a significant role in my life at critical times. I felt that the Lord had led me to Berea at this time both for our family and for Berea's need to address issues of the labor and financial aid programs.*

Other threads were weaving that would help. The federal financial aid programs were growing and offering major assistance for the kind of students Berea chose to serve, if Berea could develop a way to help students claim them. In addition a chance encounter by a member of the Berea development staff, Harry Kalas, on an airplane flight with a representative of the Educational Foundation of America resulted in a three year grant to enable the labor program to examine itself and share its experience with others. So Bill was able to employ additional staff and be in touch with other colleges with similar interests. Wilson Evans would be retiring and Bill hired John Heneisen, who was well versed in financial aid, a creative administrator and a kindred spirit. Bill and John set about to restructure the "no-tuition" system as a basic step to access federal student aid, solve financial problems and provide the financial means to overhaul the labor program. The expertise, support and assistance of Leigh Jones, Vice President for Finance, was critical as well as encouragement from President Weatherford, other members of the administrative committee and ultimately the board of trustees.

*Because Berea charged no tuition to its students it was often referred to as "low cost education." While that was true for the student, it was not an accurate phrase. It cost Berea as much to educate its students as other liberal arts colleges. Faculty members were paid competitive salaries and other workers were compensated at rates comparable to other institutions. There were differences because of the labor program, Berea's healthy endowment and policies to promote "simple living" and avoid a culture of high cost, but the main difference between Berea and other colleges was that Berea collected no tuition.*

Because Berea charged students no tuition the only costs against which they could claim financial aid were board, room and fees, which were minimal. Berea students, the very kind of low income students for which the new financial aid programs were designed to help, could receive only a small amount of aid. A comparable student attending Centre College or Transylvania would receive maximum aid. Berea's not charging tuition was denying its students and the college needed financial support from the new programs.

*We decided to institute a different approach that declared the real cost of education at Berea as the starting point and then shared with students the funding sources for meeting that cost. Students would be guaranteed that the costs normally covered by tuition would be met by resources other than their own, since by admission policy they didn't have the means to pay. Under this approach, with the total cost of education being declared, federal and state financial aid available to the student could be claimed to help meet the cost. The college would provide a "tuition scholarship" from the endowment to meet whatever costs were not met by other nonfamily sources. In addition for those who needed additional help with costs of board and room, books supplies and living expenses other financial aid would be available. Students would still have "no tuition" from their own resources, but their eligibility for federal aid could now be factored into the equation. This made possible an enormous new source of support since all but international students at Berea qualified for federal and state aid.*

How to reflect all of this in new "term bills," financial aid applications and reports and college accounting was a task. In addition, the labor program contributions had to be incorporated in the system. How much were students paid directly? What value should be placed on the labor program's contributions to meeting the costs of education? Could a new payment system be implemented that would encourage better use of the labor program by students and college departments? What are student workers anyway? Are they employees or students? Are their payments wages or financial aid grants? What about minimum wage laws? Years earlier a special provision had been inserted in the national tax laws by Congressman Carl Perkins of Kentucky that declared that payments to students in a work program required of all students as part of the educational program were not to be considered wages for tax purposes. Congressman Perkins was chairman of the powerful house ways and means committee of Congress and had close ties with Alice Lloyd College and knowledge of Berea. So payments to students during regular terms were not taxable as wages.

*When Rose and I were students twenty years earlier no cash payment was made to student workers. It was all an accounting record and we received a voucher telling us how much we had "earned" at ten to fifteen cents per hour to apply to board and room and fees. If we had enough of a balance and needed daily living funds we could request a payment from the accounting office, but this was pretty rare. Now we wanted to revise the pay structure in a way that emphasized the financial value of student work, provided incentive and recognition for advancement in skills and responsibility and gave students enough pocket money to meet daily needs and learn money management. We recognized that what was paid to students did not reflect an accurate measure of value. Some students in early assignments were a net loss while experienced students in technical areas were worth a lot more than they were paid in cash. We ended up making two major adjustments.*

*First we established four (later five) grades of positions running from beginning to journeyman and on to leadership. Pay scales increased with each level and each grade had progressive pay steps that recognized service, experience advancing skills and assumption of responsibilities. It was not unlike a classification and pay system of an employer the students would encounter when they entered the outside world of work. Working with labor departments, positions were placed on the scale giving flexibility for moving students through the department's progressions of skill and responsibility. The amounts of pay were substantially increased so the cash value of student work to the student was more significant and the incentives to advance were greater. The funds to accomplish this were provided by the new access to federal financial aid.*

*Second we established a "labor grant" as part of the package designed for each student to meet the cost of education. This grant, which was the same for every student, would record that the labor program as a whole made a significant contribution to the operations of the college, helping pay the student's term bill. The amount of the grant was calculated so that, when added to the payments made to a student who worked the maximum hours at the minimum pay on the scale, would substantially exceed the current minimum wage. Thus it could be said with confidence that the student was compensated well for work.*

With all the approvals and changes in records and procedures, the new system was implemented and worked well. One thing about colleges is that the student population turns over almost completely every four years so changes quickly become established. Students responded well to the higher pay, new incentives and greater understanding of the roles of endowment, federal aid, labor program, other financial aid and their family resources in financing their education. Few seniors now secured janitor jobs but aspired to positions of responsibility and leadership. The system was designed so that each student was expected to at least reach a journeyman level position by the senior year. The new structure in place, attention was moved to identifying and articulating the educational and developmental values realized as students moved through the program. Meanwhile contact with other colleges and special conferences and meetings on student work and higher education made it an exciting time to be at Berea.

Meanwhile on the home front the first winter passed and the children became well established in school and community. Billy would be graduating from high school. Laura would be finishing her junior year. Stephen was completing his first year in high school. John and Jim were in seventh and fifth grades. Jennifer was at home and learning all kinds of "acts" to put on for her brothers and sister and their friends. She could "look concerned" on command. The family attended Union Church, which was founded by John G. Fee as a central part of his utopian community where there was to be no divisions because of race, sectarianism, or economic condition. Reverend Harley Patterson was pastor. He had been in Oak Ridge and later in Athens, Georgia, so we knew him slightly, but he and Frances became very close friends. Jennifer and Harley Patterson were especially fond of each other and when she could walk well enough she would toddle up the church aisle to greet him and he'd pick her up. She promptly removed any pens he had in his shirt pocket. Bill E. continued in scouts in a troop at Union Church and achieved his Eagle Scout rank and also earned the God and Country Award. The church had some tensions and later became divided resulting in the Pattersons leaving. The children began to attend the Methodist youth programs and Bill and Rose followed them to the Berea United Methodist Church with Clyde David Burberry as pastor.

In the spring, the move from Oakwood Cottage to Dixie House was to take place. The additional room would be most welcome and Dixie House sat on a pretty piece of campus with a back yard and plenty of space around it. After the Howes had vacated the house, the very helpful workers in physical plant repainted rooms, consulting Rose on the paint, and performed whatever maintenance and repair was needed. It was to be the family home for the next four years so it is the first home Jennifer really remembered and she always loved it.

*It was quite a sight to see all of our furniture and goods carried from Oakwood just half a block across lawns and walks to Dixie House. We had lots of help, but not from Bill. A week earlier he had suffered another incident with his "trick knee," and it had swelled up as it had just before Jennifer's birth. The doctors said he had a piece of torn cartilage that was interfering with the joint and needed to be trimmed off. This was done and since it was before the days of laparoscopic surgery it took a painful while to heal. We put him to a bed, borrowed from the college, in a downstairs room at Dixie House so he could observe the move. In the process he got the flu and had some miserable days half doped with pain medication. He remembers listening to a Burl Ives record playing in the room across the hall some of Jennifer's favorite songs like "Angus McFergus McTavish Dundee" over and over. But we got moved and settled in to a very pleasant and convenient home. It had five bedrooms upstairs and large kitchen, dining room, parlor and family room downstairs. Soon we had lots of comings and goings of the children's friends and fellow students.*

The children found wonderful fellowship and recreation in the teenage folk dance group and when Martin Ambrose wanted to "retire" Bill and Rose took over leadership of the group. Rose also quickly became involved in hosting international students and she organized a very lively host family program offering a "local family" to all international students. The international student advisor was delighted and host families were recruited through the churches. Time moved swiftly. Billy was joined by

Nell Nestor, a girl from Oak Ridge to go to his senior prom, graduated and entered Berea College in 1971. Laura enjoyed her senior high school year, was a member of the homecoming court, graduated and joined Billy as a college student in the fall of 1972. The three "boys" were getting involved in sports. John played basketball and all three played soccer, which was just beginning to be seen as a major sport. They were in school plays and other activities and were all excellent students. The high school put on the play, *Arsenic and Old Lace*, in which Bill and Rose had acted as college students, and Laura played the sister, Martha, which was the same role as Rose did twenty years earlier. Pictures of Rose as Martha and of Laura as Martha looked like the same person.

## Dramas

President Weatherford had decided to reopen the outdoor drama "Wilderness Road" and for the next five or six summers the play was offered at Indian Fort Theater. Almost twenty years earlier the president's father, Willis D. Weatherford, Sr. had led the effort to establish the drama for the Berea Centennial in 1955. Paul Greene, a North Carolina playwright and creator of several other outdoor dramas, was commissioned to write the play. It told the story of the Civil War struggle in Kentucky, where families were split in their loyalties to the Union and the Confederacy. Berea was right on the line between the slave and free areas and had been founded by an abolitionist preacher who dreamed of a community where all were welcome and treated each other as children of one God. Berea's founding was not the central theme but it figured into the play as young John Freeman struggled to find his way between conflicting pressures, wanting only peace and justice.

*We really enjoyed the drama and all the people coming to see it in the summers. In its previous season in the 1950's my brother John participated in it, helping with the dances among other roles. Many of our friends and the children's classmates were involved and in the summer of 1975 Stephen played the part of a Union soldier carrying a flag up a hill and getting shot. I think he had two lines. One of the most poignant scenes was the two armies camped on two hills across from each other singing and then both praying for victory to the same God. All of our children knew all the lines by heart and our dinner table conversations for several years were peppered with quotes from the show.*

Bill and Rose had graduated in 1952 before the outdoor drama started and almost all their dramatics experiences were in the old Tabernacle or Tab, housing the theater.

*September 7, 1972 was our 20th wedding anniversary. I got Rose a bouquet of roses and we were happy to be back at the site of our wedding with our wonderful children. On some excuse the children told us we had to go to the Tab, where we'd spent so much time as students, to meet somebody. When we got there it was a surprise anniversary party. Many of our former teachers and friends who had attended our wedding were there. Billy had grabbed the bouquet of roses and carried them by bicycle from Dixie House to the Tab before we arrived. It was a wonderful occasion and full of memories of plays, courting and studies and friends and celebration of God's blessings.*

The Tab party was especially poignant because not long after, the venerable building burned to the ground. One still hot summer night something ignited inside the building and by the time the flames burst through the roof it was mostly consumed. The wonderful collection of costumes and props and scenery were gone. Bill remembers the night.

*I remember waking up having fallen or been propelled out of bed with the feeling that there had been an explosion. Our bedroom faced away from the main campus and I looked out the windows and then went through the house looking out windows in all directions. I saw nothing out of place so I got back in bed. A few minutes later the boys came running in from their rooms at the campus side of the house and said they saw a fire over on the main campus with flames rising above the buildings bordering Main Street. I looked and saw the flames from what I feared was one of the dormitories. I threw on some clothes and ran over while someone called the fire department. It was the Tab making an appropriately dramatic ending to its long history. When the fire trucks arrived, it was too late to save anything. Since there was no wind other buildings had not caught fire but windows were broken from the heat, trees withered and walls scorched. With fire hoses gushing water the firemen were able to cause the walls to fall inward and soon nothing was left but ashes and smoke. Billy had thought to bring my camera and I got some dramatic pictures. Later Anne Weatherford gave me one of the old square nails that had been found at the site of the old structure. It was strange to watch the room that had been my living quarters twenty some years before and the place where Rose and I had met and grew to love each other disappear before my eyes. Whatever spirit woke me that night knew what the Tab had meant to us. It was like losing a dear friend.*

# CHAPTER 21

# THE DANISH CONNECTION

The high school age dance group was doing well and had several opportunities to perform for others. They participated in the Berea Mountain Folk Festival and were christened by Rose and Bill "The Berea Festival Dancers." Performing at a centennial ball at a country club in Old Washington at Maysville, Kentucky, on the Ohio River was an experience for the young dancers as some guests got carried away by the revelry. Later the group danced on stage at the Louisville Center for the Arts for an occasion hosted by the Kentucky governor. At another time, in Lexington, they demonstrated Appalachian dance and helped welcome a sister city group from France. Performing as well as dancing for fun lent an element of excitement and pride to the group and everyone tried hard to know the steps and figures, watch their posture and look neat and smiling. Then the opportunity came to take a group to Denmark. Ethel Capps, director of the Berea College Country Dancers, Bill's brother John and others had been in communication with the Danish Dance and Gymnastics Association and had exchanged visits of leaders. They decided to start a teenage exchange program to stimulate interest in traditional dance in both countries. Bill and Rose were asked to lead the first group in the exchange in the summer of 1973. Rose was excited but thoughtful, knowing there would be preparations to put in place.

*I wasn't sure I was ready to leave Jennifer, who was only three, and be responsible for a group of teens in a foreign land. I hardly knew where Denmark was. But what an opportunity for the young people and for us! Laura was 18 and like a second mother to Jennifer. Grandma Ramsay was delighted to offer her services and look after the family. Stephen was to be part of the group as was nephew Martin. Two other boys, Richard and John, and a girl, Liz, from the Berea group would be joined by Connie and Steve from Somerset, Kentucky, Linda*

*from Brasstown, North Carolina, Greta from Homeplace, Kentucky, Wilma
from Peterstown, West Virginia and Kim from Herndon, Virginia for a total
of 12 dancers. We had no musician but purchased a very nice tape player with
speakers and set about to record the music we would need. This was not to be
a professional performing tour but an exchange program with the dance being
something we could share. So we prepared to go to Denmark.*

At the spring festival the dancers who were to make the trip to Denmark,
got together and went through dances that would be their repertoire. Plans
were made, air tickets purchased and arrangements for transportation to
Dulles airport near Washington. Dorothy and John Chrisman would drive
along with us in our station wagon. We were to stay overnight in Herndon
with dance leader Barbara Harding and her friend Mary Burger. They had
arranged for the group to perform at a park in the area. Everybody was
excited and a little scared. The first plane was to go from Dulles to London
and then another plane to Copenhagen where Danish hosts would meet
the group. As often happens, plans don't always go smoothly.

*Our good hosts in Herndon got us to the airport and we checked in and boarded
the plane. There was plenty of space so seating was no problem. Looking at
the faces of the teens you could tell this was their first airplane flight and they
were wide-eyed. We waited on the plane for a long time and then the pilot
announced that we were going to New York instead of London, to pick up a
load of passengers who were stranded there due to a problem with their plane.
So shortly we ended up at the airport in New York City. They told us to get
off the plane but we couldn't leave the part of the terminal we were in since
we were already cleared for international travel. The group was pretty tense
and other travelers were not happy either. I asked the stewardess if we could
plug in our tape player and do a dance. She was delighted for a chance to have
a diversion while everyone waited so we got ready to dance. A few of the group
tried to hide but we had enough for a set and we danced in the airport to the
applause of the other passengers and the easing of tensions of everybody. As soon
as we finished a man rushed up to us and said, "You must be from Berea!"
Berea's reputation had preceded us.*

The plane was finally re-boarded but much more crowded and in due course the group arrived in London. The airport was a madhouse of confusion and, of course, the connecting flight had long since gone to Copenhagen. The teens stretched out on suitcases trying to catch some sleep under Rose's watchful eyes while Bill navigated the airline counters to arrange an alternate flight. Finally all was arranged and the group boarded a SAS flight to Copenhagen. At the last minute it was discovered that Kim, the youngest, was not there. She had gone to the rest room and came running up the ramp just in time. With the strong coffee served and the jitters from a confusing trip there was not much sleep on the flight which arrived in the wee hours of the morning Danish time.

*The Danes, of course, had no idea of what had happened to us when we didn't arrive as scheduled. All the host families had gone home and they had posted a person to watch for us for the five hours we were late. When we arrived our crowd was easily identified and it was communicated to us that we would all go downtown to the Danish group's headquarters building to figure out how to disperse us to our hosts. The only problem was that our luggage had not made the flight but would probably arrive on a later flight. By this time we were zombies. We left Steve, the eldest of the group, with a Dane at the airport to retrieve the luggage when it arrived. After much discussion in Danish at the headquarters the teens began to be delivered to their hosts. The Danes spoke very little English and we spoke no Danish. Bill and I had no idea who was doing what and felt that we had lost control of the our charges, but the Danes took good care of us, the luggage did come and we were finally safely in Copenhagen.*

The group had a wonderful time with their host families, visiting castles, seeing the little mermaid and dancing for and with the Danes. The food was different, especially the heavy rye bread and the wonderful cheeses. The sweet rolls and desserts were sublime. They loved visiting Danish bakeries and quickly recognized the sign that looked like a pretzel. They saw the crown jewels, the changing of the guard at the royal palace, Hamlet's castle looking across to Sweden, beautiful fields of golden grain and green leaves of sugar beets. They were hosted in Copenhagen, at Aarhus and Fuglse Center and the youth schools at Haubro and Morse.

The following year Julius Bidstrup and a group from his school at Haubro came to America as the first Danish visit under the youth exchange so friendships made were continued and expanded. Bill and Martin went to Christiansfeld in southern Jutland where Bill's mother had once lived. Her uncle Frederick Martin was buried in the Moravian cemetery there. They tried to pick up a little of the Danish language but had little success with the pronunciation – but did learn to say "tak" for "thank you" and to sing some Danish songs and to say "skoal" with glasses raised in a toast.

*We were having a party at a club house on one of the fjords, where the main entrée was eels, and I was sitting next to a Danish lady who smiled and nodded, as I did, as we passed plates of goodies. Finally I took my courage in hand and remembering some words from the Danish-English dictionary I'd been studying asked her in Danish (I thought) how many children she had? She looked at me curiously and responded in English, "Three weeks." I'll never know what I asked her and we went back to nodding and smiling. But we did learn to communicate and most of the young Danes spoke English quite well having learned from the early grades in school.*

The tour came to an end too quickly and the trip home was uneventful but full of new memories and determination to go again as soon as possible. Many subsequent groups of young people came from and went to Denmark over the next years and many Danes stayed at the Ramsay house. Much later nephew Bill Todt and son Jim spent extended time in Denmark and learned the language. Nephew Loren married a Danish girl he met at the Ramsay home and lives in Denmark. Jennifer Rose spent a term in Denmark, became fluent in Danish and did annual singing tours there for years after she finished college. The connections and friendships have lasted now for more than forty years. Forty-four years later, in 2017 Jennifer, now grown and a dance leader and singer, at the Danes request, sang the national anthems of both Denmark and America at the Danes' annual celebration of American Independence Day at Rebild in Denmark.

# CHAPTER 22

# COMMUNITY AND COLLEGE

With activities in church and community and college the family was busy and the children growing quickly. The boys delivered newspapers to earn a little extra money. John and his good friend Kelly Ambrose were mainstays on the high school basketball team and the family attended games. Rose was on the phone about host families for international students and arranging housing for various visiting groups in addition to Danes. Billy had found a hobby and his student labor in making rock jewelry. Laura was an attractive and active coed. She played on the girls' field hockey team and pursued her piano playing at the music building. In her freshman Man and the Arts class they put on the musical "Brigadoon" and she shared the leading female role singing with a young tenor named Ralph Compton. Ralph wasn't the only boy noticing Laura and soon Rose was often found at the kitchen table talking to young men who followed Laura around.

*Laura had grown up with a bunch of brothers who thought she was wonderful and did her bidding. She thought of boys as brothers and didn't quite understand the attention she was getting. Once she asked, "Why are they following me around?" In time she figured it out.*

Many students, besides Laura's admirers, sought out the warmth and love they found in Rose's kitchen. With her rural East Tennessee background she was a kindred spirit to many of the girls and able to give advice and encouragement. Stephen graduated from high school in 1974 and entered college in the fall. Some of his girl-friends joined the regular visitors to Rose's kitchen and kept coming after any special interest in Stephen was past. Along with cooking, cleaning, phoning, walking Cindy with Jennifer,and "mothering" students, Rose did a little quilting. Grandpa Ramsay had given her a quilting frame apparatus that allowed one to work on one small portion of the quilt at a time. Rose's mother, Lochiel, was a quilter and had left a lot of partially finished quilt covers. Jennifer would often play under the frame while Rose sewed above her.

*Why is it that one has unwanted expletives lurking in one's mind just ready to be involuntarily expressed at moments of distress? One of these escaped my lips while sewing a quilt when I stuck my finger with the needle. Why is it that a child upon hearing such a word immediately apprehends it and wants to use it? As soon as I'd inadvertently, but quietly, expressed myself I heard Jennifer, playing underneath the quilt frame, chanting the word. I had taught my baby her first curse word! I wished that teaching her more appropriate things were that easy.*

Shortly after their arrival at Berea, Bill and Rose decided to look for some land so when the Atlanta house sold they would have some real estate. They would be renting college housing for several years. They found 130 acre piece of land on Clear Creek near Disputanta, about 9 miles south of Berea in Rockcastle County. It was $100 per acre, which they thought was reasonable, so Bill went to the bank to get a loan until the Atlanta house sold.

*I met with the bank president, Morris Todd, and told him I needed $10,000 for a short term loan and didn't want to mortgage the land. He asked me some questions about our reasons for the purchase, our plans and my position at the college. Then he looked at me and said, "Young man, I'm going to loan you the money." This was before the days of over-regulation and bureaucratic barriers to decision making. So we took the children's and our credit union savings for the down payment and bought the property from the Hammond heirs. About 30 acres were below Hammond Fork Road with a nice bottom land and Clear Creek running through. The rest, above the road, was forested mountainside.*

The family enjoyed the property, finding geodes in the creek and exploring the mountain. Soon they were planting a corn crop in the bottom and loving fresh corn and then frozen corn in the winter. With brother John as a partner, they decided to grow sorghum cane and make molasses. They bought a small old mill and tractor engine from which by means of a long wide belt they could turn a car wheel mounted on the mill. Then the cane was fed through the rollers, squeezing out the juice into a big flat pan mounted on stones over a fire.

*Growing sorghum is a labor intensive business. Preparing the ground and planting the seeds was no great problem and sorghum grows well in any soil and weather conditions. It was harder keeping the weeds down and suckering the canes so the main stalks grew fat. Then, in the fall when it was ready, a crew had to cut off the tops, strip off the leaves and cut the canes to carry to the mill. Fortunately we had teen age sons and their energetic friends. Visiting Danish groups sometimes helped with the final stages and enjoyed the cook off.*

*We didn't have an evaporator so boiled a whole panful of the green juice, keeping a fire going below it, until 80 or 90 percent had boiled off and only the sweet molasses was left. All the time you had to skim off the green scum which has a somewhat weedy and bitter taste. It took hours, but at the end it was worth the effort. It was fun to enjoy fresh molasses, share it with friends and sell some as well.*

The family was well known at school, at the college and in town so Bill was sought out by Bob Johnstone to run for school board. Bob was head of the college's Agriculture Department and a member of the school board whose term was expiring. With Bob's help, Bill was elected for a four year term and had productive years, serving as chairman for the last year, and being able to hand son Jim his diploma.

*Running for school board was my first experience at putting myself before the voters and I found all kinds of reasons for support. One man said he'd promised Bob Johnstone to vote for me but he was glad when he met me that I didn't have a beard. A woman called me the morning of election day and asked in her Kentucky mountain accent, "Air you the one who's a'runnin' for school board?" I acknowledged that I was and she asked, "Is it your son who delivers the newspaper?" I answered again in the affirmative. She concluded, "There is so many a'runnin' and I didn't know nary of them but now I know you and I'll vote for you!" I thanked her, glad to have another informed voter on my side.*

*Serving on the school board was a pleasure, but sometimes involved hard work and sticky issues. The former superintendent had advocated closing the school in favor of establishing a county high school in Berea. Those of us elected represented the position of most citizens that wanted to keep a community school. Eventually the county did build a high school and junior high in Berea but the Berea Community Schools continued. Under a new superintendent, Bill Bennett, the school flourished. New programs and buildings were added. School busses were added making it easier for families not in walking distance. School spirit was high. At one point, the board members were asked to play a benefit basketball game against a team of women athletes called the "Redheads." Kenneth Conn, Randy Osborne and Farrel Richardson became teammates as well as fellow board members and friends.*

Superintendent Bennett had added much to the school but ended up having to leave, after Bill's term was over, being unjustly accused of mishandling funds. In an end-of-year financial report he wanted to show some funds promised by local industries as receivables, which would produce a financial picture in the black. The board questioned the appropriateness of this since the funds had not yet been received but agreed to put the question to the state auditor and abide by the auditor's decision. The auditor saw no problem with the proposal so it was done that way. Some disgruntled school personnel and some parents who supported them publicly claimed that funds had been mishandled. The local newspaper, eager for a story ran headlines that implied embezzlement and called for an investigation. In due course the charges were proved false but this didn't rate a headline or even front page coverage and the damage was done.

*I talked to the editor of the paper and he was somewhat apologetic but seemed to take the position that that was how the news media operated. He had made a final report but by that time it was not front page news. I'm afraid he was correct about the way the press operated and continues to operate even though it is not right. A good man and dedicated public servant's reputation was destroyed because of a few peoples' ill will and the media's hunger for sensation.*

At the college the labor program was flourishing, financial aid was in good condition and Bill worked with the other members of the administrative committee in successfully navigating the waters of racial tensions and other college issues. Bill had employed Charly Schindler under the Educational Foundation of America grant and they worked on understanding and communicating the various dimensions of the student work experience. The most useful symbol they developed was a hexagon with each of six sides representing a dimension of the student work program but all part of the whole. One side was "manpower," recognizing that real work was being done. The second was "financial," to reflect the economic benefits to student and institution. Third was "student development," which included both personal growth and career development. Fourth was "community," which indicated a democratic sharing of meeting the needs of the community. Fifth was "education and training," covering both the specific job related learning, like weaving or tutoring, and general education goals of a liberal education like self-knowledge and problem-solving. The sixth side was labeled "spiritual," suggesting that one works for higher purposes than just getting paid, learning, doing ones part or meeting obligations. The hexagon could rest on any of these sides and the importance of the sides will vary over time. For example financial considerations are of immediate importance to a student but the lessons learned will last long after the money is gone. Materials were developed reflecting these observations and shared with students, faculty and labor supervisors and with others at conferences and visits to other institutions.

*We had set up student labor positions in progressions from beginning to leadership and supported this with the pay grades and rates. Now we began to articulate and promote the idea of progressing through the program in a meaningful way, much as one would advance from algebra through trigonometry to calculus in mathematics. What were the lessons to be learned at the different stages and how did advanced learning build on earlier learning? Learning to get to work on time, follow instructions, work with others, and other basic lessons were important in beginning jobs and prepared one to take on more skill and responsibility. Learning about one's strengths and weaknesses, preferences and talents could be accomplished in early jobs. Beginning to take responsibility without direct supervision and instruction built on these foundations and would hopefully lead to being self-motivated, exercising initiative and problem solving. Beyond that taking responsibility for training and supervising others could follow and finally some workers would progress to providing leadership for programs and projects and determining their direction. All this was possible in the labor program. In four short years, working part time, a student could progress from being a janitor to being a building manager or from being a potter's apprentice to being a ceramics artisan, or a teacher's assistant to supervisor of a chemistry lab. We began to talk of "the labor curriculum" as a set of choices for students parallel to the academic curriculum. Some students chose to relate their labor to their academic choices and others to broaden their experiences into unrelated areas.*

## Traditions

John and Winona had moved to Berea with their two sons, Martin and Loren. John first worked with the admissions office and then took over the role of director of recreation extension which included leadership of the Berea College Country Dancers. He also continued to coordinate the annual Christmas Country Dance School between Christmas and New Year's Day. Bill served as treasurer of the school and the whole family enjoyed this annual celebration and learning experience with dancers and leaders from all over the country. The school ended New Year's Eve with a gathering of the 200 plus or minus participants sharing stories and singing and then dancing. Family groups were asked to share something special. Rose remembers that first Christmas in Berea as a family.

*The Christmas we were back in Berea, 1970, Patty and Earl and their four children were here for Christmas School and, of course John was involved along with Winona and their boys. Adding these to the eight of us we had a significant family presence. We decided to sing a couple of the traditional Moravian songs our families had learned from Grandma Gertrude Ramsay and sung with her brothers and sisters at Hidden Paradise in Pennsylvania. It was a fitting introduction of family and heritage but two other families —the Richey family and the McLain family - also shared singing and to say that we were outclassed is a gross understatement. So the next year we started writing skits and presenting them and a tradition was started that lasted many years.*

299

The first skit created the "Little People" where two persons' heads and shoulders were put through a gap in a sheet with the arms pretending to be legs in trousers with shoes on the hands. They looked like midgets with big heads. The dialog was light and silly but entertaining and relevant to the happenings of the week. The first "little people" were Bill Todt dressed as "Rosalil" and Bill acting as "Constant Billy" – both names of dances. Various little people appeared in subsequent years. The next year a more comprehensive skit was created. Bill remembers.

*In "Devils Dream" two contrary views of dancing were presented – one that dancing was a depraved, evil and sinful activity and the other that it was a way of expressing joy and celebration of life and creation. After this preamble St Peter and the devil went down the list of Christmas School participants to decide which ones belonged to heaven and which to the other place. The skit had a Greek chorus that chanted everyone's names in verse. As can be imagined the devil did very well that day as the foibles of people were disclosed.*

The skits were written to include all family members who were in Berea and everyone else who was staying at the house for that week. This became part of the tradition and if you stayed with Bill and Rose during Christmas School that was the price you had to pay. Subsequent skits introduced "dancebots" created by crossing ones arms over the head and then putting a pillowcase with a painted face over the arms, head and shoulders. A jacket around the waist provided arms that swung as the "dancebot" danced. Since "dancebots" could be any gender they were very convenient in balancing out couples for a dance. Like the little people they appeared several times over the years. Another skit portrayed "dances of organized labor" with the chorus always including a strike, picket line and walk-out. The government workers union got tied up in red tape. One year a rapper sword dance was presented as if it were a competitive sport, with cheerleaders, referees with whistles, sportscaster and instant replays. What fun the family and friends had during these wonderful years.

In the labor program traditions were also being carried on and begun. An annual labor day (which for Berea was in the spring) had long been observed. Classes were called off, labor departments walked in costume in a parade led by the president and dean of labor and a special convocation was held. There were awards, displays of products and services and contests. Some of the old traditions, like milking cows, and sawing logs with a crosscut saw were no longer relevant, although on one labor day milking and log sawing contests were held to the amusement of all, and perhaps, to the torment of the poor cow. A young girl from a farm background won the milking contest while some students claimed they thought you milked by pumping the tail.

*In the early 1970's student dress was expressing the culture of "nonconformity" to standards of dress. In the name of nonconformity students were quick to conform to the latest fashions or lack thereof. Louise Gibson, who was director of audio visual services, a Berea graduate and an excellent labor supervisor, suggested we have a special awards banquet for all students and supervisors who received awards and honors for reaching goals of their departments, exceptional contributions and other achievements. She thought that it would not only relieve the labor convocation of the rather lengthy awards process but make a social event for the awards for which students could dress up. We tried it with careful attention to decorations, fancy invitations, menus and programs. Students seemed to enjoy an excuse to dress up and it was a huge success. It quickly became a labor day tradition.*

Another loved tradition of Berea College is Mountain Day. Usually in October, classes are dismissed and almost everyone heads for the mountains east of Berea – an area called the pinnacles because of the towering rock formations. Geologists say the peaks are roughly the same height because the land was once at the bottom of a large inland sea and the hills were formed by a gradual rising of the land and erosion of the soil and rocks as the water receded. The top of the pinnacles do resemble underwater reefs and pebbles and sometimes shells found at the top validate the claim that it was once under the sea. Most hikers walked about two miles from the campus to the base of Indian Fort Mountain and then hiked to the top of Indian Fort or to East Pinnacle or West Pinnacle. At the base of the mountain is a theater area where Berea has produced during two different seasons the drama "Wilderness Road." Lunch was served and various activities provided. Bill, having enjoyed Mountain Day in his college years, often led a group up the trails. Rose and the children frequently went along with him, or as they became part of student groups like Country Dancers, they hiked with their friends. Sometimes they went early enough to see the sun rise from East Pinnacle or even spent the night before on the mountain.

Another highlight event at the college for a couple summers was a performance by the Cincinnati Symphony outdoors on the campus. The McLain family had formed a bluegrass band some years before and were noted for their talent, musicality and liveliness. A symphony had been arranged to incorporate their music and performance with the orchestra and to include some folk dances. Ethel Capps, then director of the country dancers, choreographed the dances to fit the symphony. It was a delicious offering of music and dance.

During the early Berea years, while grandma and grandpa Ramsay were still at Celo, they visited frequently and included their grandchildren in trips they took. Laura, with Edie Weatherford, accompanied them to Samoa for a Christian Endeavor conference, Stephen and Martin went with them to Mexico where they were hosted by Uncle Dick.

# CHAPTER 23

# CHANGES AND THE BIG HOUSE

Bill and Rose knew that eventually they would have to leave Dixie House.

Shortly after arriving in Berea they had purchased 130 acres of mountainside and bottom land in the Clear Creek region of Rockcastle County about nine curvy miles south of Berea but did not want to build that far away from the campus. No housing they looked at was big enough for their large family. They finally purchased an older four bedroom house on Center Street and felt they could fix it up and make it suitable. They wanted to stay at Dixie House as long as possible so they rented out the Center Street house after they had fixed it up, first to an elderly single woman and later to John and Winona. After that they rented it to the Bains who eventually bought it. So Bill and Rose and family never lived there.

*We had noticed a big three story house at 415 Estill Street next to Van Winkle Grove in an area where a number of faculty lived within walking distance of the campus. It looked big enough and sat back nicely from the road, although it didn't look to be in the best state of repair. We had heard that it might be for sale so Bill and I talked about it and I called Mr. McKinney, who lived there with his wife, a daughter and her husband. He was not interested in selling. As time came close to our moving deadline the McKinney house did come up for sale and we quickly made an appointment to look at it. Mr. and Mrs. McKinney had both died. Cecil and Pauline Pullins, the McKinneys' daughter and son in law, had decided to move out. We were enchanted with the place although it would need a lot of work. Our boys were all grown and full of energy so we had lots of manpower.*

The house had been built about 1918 on the foundations of an older Van Winkle house, which reportedly went back to Civil War times. The

McKinneys had been farmers in Estill County and when oil was discovered on their property they built the Big House, as it came to be called, so their 10 children could be close to the schools. After oil and money ran out and the children grown, they had divided rooms into apartments, without separate entrances. They were careful to avoid damaging the beautiful oak columns in the main hall downstairs when they made partitions. Bill and Rose could visualize the removal of partitions, the refinishing of floors, the improvement of the kitchen and the fixing up of bedrooms and baths for very spacious and comfortable living.

*The third floor of the house had three bedrooms plus a small utility room. The second floor had two sections with three bedrooms in each and sunrooms on either end plus one bathroom. That totaled nine bedrooms and one bath on the upper floors. First floor in the back of the house had another bath, a kitchen, breakfast room, utility room and a study, which had been used by the Pullins as a bedroom. The front part of downstairs had a wonderful hall flanked by spacious dining room, parlor and living room plus a sun room, and a foyer opening to a wide front porch. The basement had seven unfinished rooms and showed signs of water flowing freely through. The children immediately picked out their rooms before we had decided to buy the house but it was a foregone conclusion that this was the place for us. We did buy it and then got to work.*

*Before we moved in, we took out partitions and dismantled the apartment sinks. We refinished the kitchen with modern appliances and counter tops. We sanded and varnished the hardwood floors in the front rooms, put carpet in the back hall and linoleum in the kitchen. After we moved in, we continued to work. We cleaned, scraped, painted and wallpapered all over the house. The work never ended as long as we lived there. In fact it was continued after our 19 years by Laura and Ralph who bought the place and are still there 22 years later. They had the house put on the county historic register. What memories hover around in that wonderful house.*

Some things required professional attention. Eventually reroofing was required, windows replaced and siding put on the outside. Bathrooms were added on the third floor and in the master bedroom. Rose remembers the windows in the first year especially.

*As soon as we had decided to buy the house, everyone in town seemed to know and we had all kinds of comments. A number of people had lived in one of the apartments at one time or another. One of our friends said to me, "Rose, do you realize that house has 100 windows?" I didn't believe it so Stephen and I went to count and my friend was right. Someone else asked how I was going to clean all those windows and I replied that I guessed I'd learn to like dirty windows. Bill got a glazier to give us an estimate on repairing and replacing broken panes and storm windows, of which there were a great variety. He found 40 that needed replacement of panes.*

On the second floor, the interior doors to the hall and the bedrooms were paneled with glass panes which had been varnished over for privacy. Eventually replacement thermal windows were installed, varnish was removed and curtains installed where needed, and a few windows were removed in remodeling areas, but the house retains its reputation as the 100 window house. The water problems in the basement were addressed from inside and out and insulation was added to the third floor storage rooms. Franklin type fireplaces and chimneys in living room and dining room were repaired to be used but chimneys to other rooms were closed off. The old gas fired furnace, boiler and hot water radiator system was maintained and, once the house was encased in insulation and siding, it was tight and comfortable. A large overhead exhaust fan was installed in the third floor hall ceiling and window air conditioners were added to den and kitchen downstairs. Once, when repairing a leak in the roof, John jumped from the upper roof to the lower one above the den and porch. Bill was working at his desk when, suddenly, along with a shower of debris, John's legs appeared from the ceiling.

*It sounds like all we did was work on the house, and it did keep us busy, but we also had wonderful family times, gatherings of friends, hosting of many guests and parties. The front of the downstairs with its oak columns between the hall, the dining room, two parlors and entrance foyer was lovely. It especially lent itself to the reds and greens of Christmas decorations with candles on the mantles above the fireplaces, As the grandchildren came along, they loved grandma Rose's and grandpa Bill's Big House. It was truly a family home and place of hospitality.*

The year 1975 was a year of change not only by the move to 415 Estill Street, but in other ways with the children and work. Bill E. (as we now called him) graduated from college with a fine record. He had discovered his life partner in fellow student and country dancer Anne Marshall Hylton and they were married in November. Jennifer, now five years old, started school at the end of summer. Laura was now a college senior and becoming attached to classmate Ralph Compton. Nephew Martin and one of Rose's "adopted" girls, Charlie Harrison, were married in August. Rose continued to make phone calls to find hosts for international students and arrange housing for visiting groups in addition to hosting all kinds of students and others at the Big House, and the traffic to Rose's kitchen continued to flow.

The college made the decision to combine the labor and student life programs. Bill was asked to become Dean of Labor and Student Life and later, with trustee action, the title "Vice President" was added. He now had under his supervision, in addition to the labor and financial aid programs, the residence halls, health service, student activities, counseling, disciplinary matters and other student services.

*The "student life" profession seemed to me to be dominated by faddism. "Values Clarification," was popular suggesting that "it doesn't matter what values you have as long as you know what they are" – which is nonsense. "You can't be both policeman and counselor!" More nonsense! Parents play both roles all the time. Discipline is part of real caring as well as essential for community well-being. We instituted reforms in residence halls and in the counseling and disciplinary systems.*

*In the aftermath of the anti-authoritarianism of the 60's, procedures had become cumbersome with "safeguards." These could be important in complicated cases, but for the most part a student having committed a violation, like being under the influence of alcohol, petty theft, falsification of information, or other nonviolent infractions, just wanted to deal with the matter, accept the consequences and get on with his or her life. We provided that a student could choose to have a dean of their choice hear and judge the case rather than convening courts involving larger numbers and encumbered by more formal procedures. The student could always appeal the decision. Most matters came to be dealt with in this simpler way.*

*A few students who got in trouble learned to work the system, playing one area against another. They couldn't get their homework done because of their student labor or vice-versa or their unacceptable behavior in a residence hall was because of academic pressures or issues at home. They were good at finding a sympathetic ear and when that resource began to question them, they would move on to another sympathetic ear. We established a "probation committee" so that any student who was placed on probation in more than one area – academic, labor or social – would be subject to a committee with representatives of each of these areas to work out a plan together to overcome the difficulties. Thus everyone responsible for the student – academic adviser, labor supervisor and residence hall leader – would be able to help the student and hold him or her accountable. There weren't many students who got in such situations but the system helped those who did and avoided tension among the different parts of the college.*

*Most of the student life staff members were happy with the changes but there were some tensions. Two senior staff members were always at odds and each sought my support for her position against the other. I finally told them both, together, that I was not going to play that game and if they didn't learn to work together and resolve their differences I would have to let both of them go. They learned to get along, or at least stopped bothering me with their rivalry, and they did good work.*

Bill, Laura, Stephen, and later, John and Jim were excellent students, active and well-liked by their classmates and teachers. Having their father as a dean didn't bother them; in fact they sometimes referred to him as "dean dad." Bill E. had moved very quickly into his Berea student role. Laura had always wanted to go to Berea to college. The other boys looked at other options but Berea offered what they wanted plus they had the comforts of home. When Jennifer's time came, much later, she followed in her siblings footsteps without question.

*We credited Laura for bringing us to Berea. She had always maintained that she wanted to go to Berea College. As she progressed in high school in Atlanta, and I warned her that Berea only accepted a few students from out of the Appalachian territory and only students from low income situations. We weren't high income but we were higher than Berea's cut off. She wouldn't look anywhere else although we suggested Agnes Scott and other small liberal arts schools. She kept insisting she was going to attend Berea and said she was sure because she'd prayed about it. When the call came to Bill, unsolicited, from President Weatherford, it was an answer to Laura's prayer and we were all glad.*

Patty and Earl's son, Bill Todt, had spent a year at a folk school in Denmark and then came to Berea to live with us and eventually attend and complete Berea College. He and Bill E. were both tall and lean and would take care of any leftovers from meals without gaining any weight. The horses from Celo - Lady, Sparkle and Merrilegs – had been brought to Berea and had several pastures before settling in at the college's old turkey barn and surrounding grounds in cooperation with the Weatherford family. Lady was a mature, dependable mare and Merrilegs was a frisky but gentle filly. Sparkle had a bit of mischief in him and may take a rider under a low branch or too close to a tree trunk. John kept him under control and all the boys enjoyed rides.

During the boys' later high school and college years, the sport of soccer was becoming as popular in America, as it had been in other countries. Stephen, John, Loren and Jim all played on the college team. In fact while still in high school, John and Jim played on a soccer club team that Stephen coached. They won a regional trophy and Stephen was ecstatic. Under the coaching of Bob Pearson of the college Physical Education department, the boys played well and made lasting friends, many of them from other countries. The Musser brothers, Paul and Scot, were especially close. Paul had lived with Bill and Rose when he first started college. His parents, Harvey and Doris Ann, had been in college while Bill and Rose were still students and Harvey's sister, Mary, had been a classmate. The boys, including older brother, H. A. and sister, Beth, had grown up in Brazil where the parents were missionaries. At soccer games during those years Rose and Doris were the chief cheerleaders. Unfortunately in a soccer scrimmage Stephen was kicked in the leg and had both lower leg bones broken. After painful setting and casting, Rose worked with his professors to keep up his classwork, and when he was able to get out drove and wheeled him to his classes in the science building to complete his pre-med program. John was the team goalie and Rose was afraid that he would be injured, but he was not. John helped Eileen and other college girls organize a soccer team and had to learn that coaching girls was not the same as coaching boys.

## Graduations, Marriages, Births and More

More changes came rapidly to the family in the next few years. Laura graduated in 1976 and married Ralph Compton. Like her brother Bill, she was married in Danforth Chapel on campus. Her reception was at the big house on Estill Street with the front yard decorated with Japanese lanterns hung from the beautiful elm trees that had not yet succumbed to the elm disease. A canopy shaded the musicians, Lewis and Donna Lamb, who fiddled and strummed for background music and for dancing on the lawn. Ralph had been accepted at the University of Virginia medical school so they were soon off to his home state. Also in 1976, John graduated from Berea Community School and entered Berea College. The next year saw the birth of Mark Harrison to Martin and Charlie Ramsay, introducing the next generation to the Berea families. The following year welcomed the addition of Bill and Rose's first grandchild. Elizabeth Anne was born to Laura and Ralph. Regular trips to Charlottesville, Virginia became imperative. In 1978 Stephen graduated from Berea College and entered medical school at the University of Kentucky. Jim graduated from high school and started his college career at Berea College. In 1979 John married Eileen Ambrose in the orchard behind the president's house. Luke Jacob was born to Martin and Charlie and Amber Rose was born to Bill and Anne. Rose helped care for her through some difficult times for Anne.

*Becoming a grandmother was a special experience and I loved it. I had gone to Virginia to be with Laura during the birth of Elizabeth and felt I had to hold her and be part of her growing up from the first days. Ralph was busy with medical school. Laura was choir director at a church in Orange and provided child care for a family with both parents working. When we visited little Elizabeth would squeal when she saw me and come running for a hug. A grandchild's hug is without price. Elizabeth was an alert and responsive child and quickly learned scores of hymns as she accompanied Laura. She was such a joy and I had to see her regularly. She developed a hearty voice and sang her songs with fervor. She liked to sing "Kentucky Babe," and would belt out "… silvery moon is shinin' in the heavens up above, bob-o-link is pinin' for his yittle yady yove. You are mighty yucky, babe of ole Kentucky." We were almost sorry when she learned to pronounce her l's.*

*Then when Amber arrived the next year she also captured my heart. Bill E. and Anne had come back to Berea from Florida where Bill E. had been in graduate school at the University of Florida. Anne had some health problems and for a time I kept baby Amber. What a jewel she was with her wide eyes, star-like little hands and sweet nature. When Anne was well enough to care for her, I had a hard time giving her up. As other grandchildren came along each one was special. We were so happy that our children married spouses who embraced family relationships. We had wonderful adventures with grandchildren over many years. Being a grandparent is truly a blessing.*

In 1980 brother John's son Loren married Inge-Lise Mathiesen in Denmark. Inge-Lise and her good friend, Annelise Matsen, had lived with Bill and Rose for a year as part of the Danish exchange connection and Loren had become attached to her. Annelise taught Jim enough Danish to prepare him for a college term in Denmark and Jim said his throat got sore trying to master Danish pronunciation. Stephen also married that year, to Robin Osborne. Her parents, Sandy and Al, became close friends, and traveling companions of Bill and Rose in later years. John and Winona had separated the year before and John had purchased a house on Estill Street a little closer to campus than the Big House. Mother and Dad Ramsay had decided the time had come to leave Celo and be closer to family so they moved in with John. It was great to have them in Berea. As long as Mother and Dad Ramsay were at Celo the extended family and many friends had continued to enjoy its special beauty and opportunities for fellowship and re-creation. Now the Celo house was rented but the property was retained for several years and family members continued to make visits to the area. It became a kind of ritual for new families as they were formed to have a Celo experience. The childhood years of Bill and Rose's children, except for Jennifer, were fast coming to a close. Jennifer woefully observed, "All my brothers and sister are leaving me!"

The years seemed to go by too swiftly. Rose's little dog, Cindy, had developed cancerous tumors and, after months of treatment, the vet recommended putting her to sleep because she was suffering. It was very hard for Rose and Stephen stayed with her and Cindy through the ordeal. The family had other dogs, usually strays the children brought home and cared for until the owners or a new home could be found. On one occasion a large dog was hit by a car on the road in front of the house and they saw it limp off behind the Lewis's house across the street. They found it lying in the back yard and put it on a blanket and hauled it home to nurse until they found the owner. A little blue heeler they named Bonnie Blue was adopted and loved, but no pet ever replaced Rose's beloved Cindy. The Big House was active with family coming and going, meals for friends and teammates, annual open houses at Christmas time and wonderful guests. Bill remembers one particular series of guests.

*Over one short period our guests happened to include accomplished pianists from around the world. Dick had brought a friend, Isaac, a concert pianist from Mexico. Brother John introduced us to Banechek, a world renowned musician from Czechoslovakia. We had a girl from East Germany who brought us a piece of the Berlin Wall and was an expert pianist, as well as a mathematician. Inge-Lise, from Denmark who was with us at the time was also an accomplished pianist. What a wonderful musical interlude we had over those few weeks. Laura had always provided us with piano music and the piano was in tune, if not a fine instrument. It also served us well at the annual Christmas open house. Rolf Hovey, chair of the music department, would organize guests into a choir to sing carols and he or Laura would play for us. Later, after Rolf Hovey's death, John Courter, a wonderful musician and carillon expert, who had been Laura's organ teacher, took over the provision of music for these occasions.*

# Professional Activities

Bill continued a consulting relationship with Oak Ridge Associated Universities in regard to manpower programs for ten years after coming to Berea. He also maintained a consulting relationship with the National Center for Service Learning and did some writing for *Synergist* magazine on internships and a review of a national report. He wrote a piece on internship supervision for *New Directions for Higher Education* edited by John Duley in 1976. He was active in getting a national organization started concerned with student employment.

*Frank Adams of Southern Illinois University with colleagues at the University of Illinois had written a book on work and the college student. He felt that Berea was a model of making the most of student work and came to visit me not long after my return to Berea. He was an inspiration and I joined the Midwestern Association of Student Employment Administrators (MASEA), attended conferences and for a term served as president. In 1975, Frank and others organized the First Annual Conference on Work and the College Student at Southern Illinois University. Wilson Evans and I went and each presented papers which were included in the conference proceedings and published as a book by Southern Illinois University Press in 1976. At the conference a group began to work on forming a national association which a couple years later became the National Student Employment Association (NSEA). Meanwhile regional associations were formed in the South, West and New England, comparable to the Midwestern association.*

The second year's conference was held at North Texas State University. Bill attended and continued to work with others on the plans for a national organization and it became a reality the next year. In the early 1980's there was talk of reinstituting the military draft and, along with that, discussion of other national service alternatives to military service. Bill's good friend Don Eberly and a colleague, Michael Sherradin, had been commissioned by Pergamon Press to edit a book on national service, examining its potential impact on the nation. They asked Bill to contribute a chapter on the impacts of national service on education. It was published in 1982 in the book titled, *National Service: Social, Economic and Military Impacts.*

312

Bill also continued his membership in the American Society for Public Administration and the National Society for Internships and Experiential Education. After assuming responsibilities for student life at Berea he also joined the National Association of Student Personnel Administrators, but never played an active role. His primary interest was in the relationship between work or service and learning and he continued to write and speak on the subject.

## Births and Death

The five years from 1981 through 1986 saw an explosion of grandchildren and many other changes in life and work. The Big House was being emptied of the Ramsay children as they married and moved on, but it was filled with a variety of students and others who needed temporary housing, usually in the summers.

*Catherine Lois was born to Laura and Ralph in 1981. Ralph had finished medical school and went to Clarksburg, WV for his residency in family practice. Catherine was a beautiful blond child with a lot of spunk. The same year William Joel was born to Bill and Anne who were living in a house they had built at the property on Clear Creek. The house had been built from lumber retrieved from the old college nursing building and Dodge gym, both of which Bill E. had dismantled, with help from cousin Bill Todt, a classmate named Bill Eirich, other friends and members of the family.*

In 1981 Bill's parents, John G. and Gertrude M. Ramsay had been chosen to receive the "Mother Jones Award" for their early work in Pennsylvania to improve the lot of working men and women. Hosted by the Pennsylvania Labor History Society in Bethlehem, John Ramsay gave his last public talk at the occasion. He was already losing memory and some mental ability but did a fine job and the family was proud of him and of mother Gertrude. Bill and Rose drove them to the event and Bill's cousin Grace Price also attended.

*The next year Melissa Rose was born to Laura and Ralph, Benjamin Gates to Stephen and Robin, and Brian Cooney to John and Eileen. Stephen had finished his pediatrics courses at University of Kentucky and was in his residency in Akron, OH. John was in graduate school in mathematics at the University of Wisconsin. We had a lot of traveling to do that year as we welcomed these beautiful babies into the family and into our hearts.*

Early that year brother Dick had called from San Antonio to announce that he and Susana Espinoza had gotten married. Susana was a teacher with Dick in Mexico. The next year Charlie and Martin added a third son, John Paul, and asked Bill and Rose to be his godparents. Then in 1984 two more grandchildren were added. Andrew Albert was born to Robin and Stephen and Colleen Aiden was born to Eileen and John. Jim had graduated from Berea in 1982 and spent a term at the University of Utah in higher mathematics, before deciding that was not what he wanted, came back to Berea and got a management a job in Danville. He prepared to go to Asbury Seminary, having been called to missions work. He found and fell in love with Shawn, a kindred spirit in who was a Berea student and country dancer. They were married so another lovely daughter-in-law was added to the family. 1984 was also the year that Willis Weatherford retired as president of Berea College and John Stephenson was appointed to that position. With the Weatherfords leaving and all the children but Jennifer finished with college and married, it felt like the end of an era. Then mother Gertrude suffered heart failure.

*Mother was a worker. She loved to be busy, usually doing things for others. She and Dad volunteered at the hospital. They attended the senior citizens center. Mother was Dad's anchor as he lost his mental sharpness. I had taken over much of their banking, bill paying and other necessary business, but Mother was the one who made the decisions and managed the house. She had a garden and tended flowers and shrubs, sharing her love of growing things with her neighbors, Wilson and Ellen Evans. She tilled the garden with a mattock, saying that a traditional hoe just didn't have enough heft to it. We thought she was indestructible. But when she had trouble getting up the stairs, she confessed she often felt weak and finally got weak enough to see the doctor. She had an enlarged heart and was having heart failure. After a brief hospital stay, we moved her and Dad to the Big House and she seemed to be recovering. Her sister Lydia came to be with her and the two of them chatted like school girls as they remembered childhood adventures and quoted poetry to each other. After about a week we all went out to eat and she enjoyed the meal and the outing, but the next day was very weak again. Rose brought her a glass of water and she sat up and sipped. Then she fell backward on the bed with Rose's arm around her and stopped breathing. Rose called and I performed CPR while Rose called 911 and the doctor. When both arrived they put her on a stretcher and carried her downstairs and outside to the ambulance and on to the hospital. Dad, who had been sleeping in the adjoining room, came out just in time to see them take her away. We never saw her again.*

Both of Bill's parents had given their bodies to research at the University of Kentucky medical school. When Gertrude was taken to the hospital they were unable to revive her and took her to the operating room to try opening her chest for direct intervention, but all to no avail. Because of her condition no family was able to see her and her body was sent to the medical school. The family was grief stricken by her death and not being able to pay last respects. Her life's mate, John, never did understand. He said "They took her away." Afterwards he often said, "I need to go home," and the family came to realize that he didn't mean a physical house, but wherever she was. In due course her ashes were returned to the family and interred in the Berea cemetery. Dad Ramsay continued to live with Bill and Rose and to attend the senior citizens center, but he never felt "at home." Rose remembers those busy days:

*Life goes on. In 1985 Daniel Bowles was added to Bill E. and Anne's family. He was a dark haired, dark eyed happy child. Jim and Shawn had their first child with the birth of Rebekah Adair. She was blond and blue eyed and alert from the beginning. So now we had eleven grandchildren and it was obvious there would be more. The Big House began to be a children's palace. Once great grandpa John, sitting in the living room, a little bewildered by the teeming small ones, said, "Are there mothers around here somewhere?" They were probably in the kitchen talking with me.*

In 1986 brother John married Risse Layne McDuffie, a widow who had been a classmate and a country dancer. They moved to her log house on Adams Street and John rented out the house on Estill Street that he had shared with his parents. No family babies were born that year. But the next year Robin and Stephen added Michael Aaron, and Charlie and Martin added Joseph Earl. Technically great nephews, Charlie and Martin's boys were like grandchildren and joined in family activities. Having breakfast at Dixie Kitchen with Charlie and her boys became a favorite tradition for Rose.

After John and Stephen had moved out, their rooms on second floor were rented to girls in the summer and occasionally a longer term renter like a graduate student attending Eastern Kentucky University. Rose made it clear that she was not renting apartments, but rooms in her house, and she expected conduct consistent with family rules and patterns. Most of the girls were looking for a home away from home and became very much part of the family. A good number were international students. Also housing for visiting Danes and other groups was frequently provided. For a time physical fitness teachers coming for training in Body Recall, developed by Dorothy Chrisman of the Berea faculty, occupied rooms during their training.

*I came home from a trip one day and Rose wasn't home. I carried my suitcases upstairs and was confronted by three physical fitness type women in the upstairs hall. They looked at me suspiciously and asked, "Who are you?" I replied somewhat defensively, "I live here!" Fortunately they let me pass. After Jim left we also rented the three bedrooms on the third floor and converted the sunroom in the back of the second floor into a kitchen for the renters to use. Before that they had shared the kitchen downstairs and the house would be filled with the wonderful aromas of curry and other spices as students from Thailand, India or Africa made their traditional dishes, as well as the down- home smells of mountain cooking from the Appalachian students.*

## Jennifer Goes to St Mark's

As Jennifer had approached junior high school at the Berea Community Schools, Bill and Rose were not happy with her situation. Every day she had issues about what to wear so she would fit in with the social crowd and the studies were not what they should be. So we moved her to the St Mark

Catholic School in Richmond. Dress code was prescribed, the principal, Sister Elaine Marie was very capable and she had a wonderful teacher in Sister Dianne. She flourished there and formed healthy friendships. For a time she put rubber bands on her teeth so she would look like her teacher who was wearing braces. With the encouragement of the principal, who was looking for wholesome recreation, we introduced folk dancing and soon had a group who loved to dance. Their favorite dance was "Weaving," which is rather complicated and difficult but they did it well, and sometimes performed for others. Jennifer became a teacher and leader, learning to take responsibility. Instead of being a sub-freshman at Berea she was an eighth grade senior at St Mark's. Those were good years.

*One Halloween we decided to have a party for Jennifer's class at the Big House. We had noticed that "party" for teens too often meant hiring a disk jockey to play loud music and parents making themselves scarce. Sometimes this led to unhappy circumstances as older boys might come with alcohol and no one was in charge. So we organized a first class party that the kids would never forget. As they arrived they were divided into groups of three or four each. While one group was being led away the rest stayed with Rose in the dining room where she was setting up refreshments. One by one groups were escorted to a drape darkened room on the third floor where Grandma Gertrude, in Gypsy fortune telling clothes, consulted a green crystal ball in and told fortunes. Jim, as Igor the humpback dwarf, led another selected group out the utility room door and down the creaky, dark back steps to the basement. Behind a gross mask, I was Roach, who would show them the mad scientist's laboratory. We had created an eerie laboratory in the basement where the mad scientist was experimenting with transplanting body parts. There were containers of various organs, brains and bones around. A dummy with a skull face was laid out on one of the freezers getting a transfusion from a bug spray canister. Jennifer was laid out under a sheet on the other freezer and at the appropriate time sat up and screamed, which caused everyone to scream. Martin, the mad scientist, was sawing off the hand of Michaela Pierce, one of Jennifer's friends. (A stuffed glove over a piece of wood.) As the group exited the "lab" they had to go through a dimly lit labyrinth created by panels of old doors. They groped through hanging spiders and worms and webs while a record of wolves howling was playing. Then as they passed through the labyrinth we had rigged up a stuffed wolf hanging on a rope that lunged at them from out of the dark of the furnace room sending them screaming up the stairs with the mad scientist chasing them.*

*The next group was prepared for its tour by hearing the screams of the previous group. As tours were completed, one at a time everyone went above the garage for "airplane rides." Standing on a board and blindfolded with hands on the head of a person in front gets you set for the ride. Two helpers slightly raise the board and move it gently back and forth as the person in front begins to stoop down. It feels just as if you are rising and when told to jump before you hit the ceiling, what you think is a jump of several feet is only about two inches and you collapse on the mat underneath to the joy of everyone who had just done the same thing and are watching. One little girl, involuntarily, let out an expletive when she hit the mat and ripped off the blindfold to see to her classmates laughing to her great embarrassment. Then all went to the safety of the dining and living rooms for refreshments and to relive their experiences and feelings as they talked and talked. That was a party!*

Graduating from St Mark's in 1985, Jennifer returned to the Berea Community School and did very well in classes and social activities. For a time she was the "Berea Pirate" mascot at ball games. A music teacher, Norma Vanover, who worked with schools in the neighboring Garrard County and wanted to use dance in some of her musical productions, had sought help from brother John. The result was that young Jennifer became her choreographer. For several years Rose drove Jennifer to Lancaster regularly while Norma and Jennifer worked with students to put together a version of the Nutcracker Suite as their annual Christmas program at the school. High school years sped by and Jennifer finished her course early, graduating in December 1987. Bill had been elected president of the National Student Employment Association and took a part-year sabbatical to give full time to that task in 1988. Jennifer was to be his assistant before entering Berea College in the fall.

# CHAPTER 24

# YEARS OF TRANSITION

About a year before president Weatherford retired he had asked Bill to take over responsibility for the student industries, including Boone Tavern Hotel. Bill had agreed with the understanding that there would be no quick fix for financial problems and the support of the whole administrative committee would be needed. Bill, of course, recognized the value of the student industries to the labor and development programs and to the image of the college. Boone Tavern had struggled since the long term manager and extraordinary chef, Richard Hougen, had left. Following the centennial year, 1976, business had declined as interstate 75 now was completed past Berea, tourist traffic patterns changed and many other eating options were becoming available. Boone Tavern did almost no advertising or marketing. It seemed wise to promote Berea, including Boone Tavern as a destination, rather than just a stop on the way to somewhere else. This would take coordination of all the industries and the program offerings of the college. Visiting Berea and Boone Tavern could be more than just a night's lodging or a good meal.

*The director of campus activities, Mim Pride, was doing a wonderful job in her area and had some of the best managerial skills I had seen in my career. I moved her to be manager of Boone Tavern and she immediately took steps to control food costs, improve service, with upgraded student labor, and offer first rate hospitality. With the help of my secretary, Faye Burton, and Cecilia Wierwillie, wife of the basketball coach, we organized a hosting program using retired faculty and staff to greet and socialize with guests. The hosting was very popular with guests and with the retirees. Mim gave students major responsibilities, allowing some advanced students to become hotel managers. Working at Boone Tavern had always been considered a less desirable labor assignment, but now became sought after. Some students who had taken management responsibilities graduated and immediately were employed by major hotels in responsible positions.*

In the craft industries, new leadership was acquired as positions became open. Under Richard Bellando's leadership, special sales events by invitation were arranged. An outlet was opened in a Lexington mall. A special arrangement was made in the wrought iron shop to set up the blacksmith as an independent craftsman with whom students would apprentice, solving a conflict of interest situation and giving him the incentive to be much more productive. He provided the college sales operations what they needed for their shops and catalog at less expense to the college, while prospering in his trade. As expected, the financial picture did not immediately change, but the industries were on the move. Then president Weatherford retired and there was a change in administration. A new vice president for business was hired and convinced the new president, John, that the industries should again be under the business office. Mim left Boone Tavern and the college, going back to graduate school and then eventually becoming president of Blackburn College in Illinois. The business vice president had some problems which became increasingly evident, and finally left, but it was a rough couple years while the new president discovered whom he could trust and who were just talkers. Meanwhile the labor program functioned productively and Bill continued to be active nationally in promoting student employment and service-learning.

*President Stephenson, and the presidents of some of the other work colleges with which we'd been in contact, exchanging visits and sharing experiences, made contact with the Ford Foundation. As a result, a proposal was prepared for a grant to further explore and share the work college model for higher education. The grant was approved and once again Berea was able to provide leadership in hosting conferences, sponsoring exchanges among the work colleges and self-examination. The other colleges involved at the time were Alice Lloyd College in Kentucky, Warren Wilson College in North Carolina, Blackburn College in Illinois and The College of the Ozarks in Missouri.*

## Issues of Childbirth and Senior Care

Rose had not lost her interest in childbirth education and was increasingly concerned with the advent of abortion as a means of birth control. The college had reached out to single mothers who wanted to continue their education and set up residence options for them. Bill was glad to provide these services but found they produced a mixed bag of results. Some young women moved on splendidly with their education and new responsibilities. Others seemed to find a comfortable place to continue the behavior that got them in the situation in the first place, while getting a lot of sympathetic attention in the process. Nevertheless it was right to try to help these women, even if some continued to make poor choices. In the community Rose joined with other concerned women to form a program called "MotherChild Mission" which would provide an information line for pregnant women seeking help. It would explain alternatives to abortion, like adoption or preparation for child care, and referrals to support systems. With Kathy Todd (daughter-in-law Eileen's sister), Roberta Schaeffer (wife of Doc Schaeffer of the college health service) and others, they joined with similar efforts in Richmond, with pediatrician son Stephen's help, to become a Madison County pregnancy center. Countless women have received help through the center which is now called the Pregnancy Help Center.

Grandpa John G. Ramsay was still living with Bill and Rose and walking to his senior citizens gatherings with his friend Virgil Griffith for fellowship and lunch. The leaders took good care of him and watched out for him, calling if he "escaped" looking for a candy machine. Patty and Earl sometimes took him for a visit to Columbus and brother John helped as he could.

*Patty and Earl had taken Dad to Columbus to be with them for a time and now John and I were going to meet them just south of Cincinnati to return him to Berea. We worried a little that he might be disoriented but he was in good spirits as we shared a meal at Bob Evans. He never lost his ability to eat anything he fancied. As we left Patty and Earl and headed south Dad, in the back seat, asked repeatedly where we were going and where he'd been. We*

321

*answered him patiently every few miles and he would comment that it sure was a long way. As we approached Richmond, not many miles from Berea, he asked if he could have some ice cream. He had always loved ice cream and we saw no reason not to stop at Baskin-Robbins in Richmond. John and I were still full from lunch so we did not get any but got him a cup of his favorite butter pecan which he happily ate in the back seat while we drove on in to Berea. When he finished, I asked him if he had enjoyed his ice cream and he replied quizzically, "Yes, but I don't know why we had to go so far to get it!" He never lost his gentlemanly ways and charm.*

*He was so agreeable and courteous that it was sometimes mistaken for understanding and this caused problems when he had to go to the hospital for surgery on his prostate. The hospital said it would be an outpatient procedure until we convinced them that he would not be able to care for himself during recovery. Once, when a nurse said she was going to need to give him a shot, he said, "If it makes you happy!" In the hospital they put a needle in his arm for a drip. He was pleasant and nonresistant. They had asked me to wait outside the room and I had warned them that he wouldn't understand but they thought they knew best. Having inserted the needle they came out and I said he would likely wonder why a needle was in his arm and try to remove it. Alarmed they re-entered the room and there he was trying to take the needle out. Another time after the surgery one of us had been staying with him in his room overnight and we were assured this wasn't necessary after the first day. They had sides on the bed and alarms if a patient got out of bed. We did not stay in the room that night. The alarm went off and they saw him standing in the doorway bleeding because he had stepped on his catheter.*

The hospital staff members were kind and tried to take good care of John, but were obviously not prepared for his condition. He "escaped" from his room on the fourth floor long term care ward and they found him wandering down on the surgical floor. They began to strap him in a chair and as a result he "became incontinent." Those were trying times and he finally came home to the Big House. Bill slept in the room with him as long as he had a catheter. As time went on caring for him and anticipating problems became more and more difficult. For example he rubbed himself with a caustic cleaning fluid, mistaking it for lotion. It was clear that he needed a more controlled environment with 24 hour observation available, so in late 1987 his transfer to the Berea Nursing Home was arranged. He enjoyed it there for several years. Wonderful caring nurses, aides and social staff helped him regain lost functions and he was treated almost as one of the staff, carrying towels and other supplies for the housekeeping personnel. Someone from the family visited him every day and he loved seeing his children, grandchildren and great grandchildren. Even though he couldn't remember who they were, he knew they belonged to him.

## Folk Circle

Shortly after John Stephenson had become president of Berea College a gentleman who had been to Christmas Country Dance School and knew John offered to make a donation to Berea College to build a folk dance hall. Russel Acton from Danville, Illinois was up in years and had never married. His "family" was fellow folk dancers and he went to gatherings in different states. He owned productive farm land in Illinois and had been an inventor. Reportedly, as part of the war effort in World War II, he invented the snowmobile for use in a possible invasion of Germany through Norway. At any rate he had acquired some wealth and wanted to leave a legacy for his beloved dancing. He had financed the building of a dance center in West Virginia and would like to see one in Berea. President Stephenson was interested but had just taken over and was involved in a major renovation of the science building and the fund raising that required. His response was that the college couldn't respond right then, but would be interested in the future. Russ Acton knew he was dying of cancer and had limited time left to see his dream come true. Bill and John suggested the formation of a nonprofit association to accept Russ Acton's offer and build a dance center. This was agreeable to all parties and Bill prepared the papers to incorporate the Folk Circle Association and obtain its tax exempt status. John served as president and Bill as secretary/treasurer of the board. As they explored the possibilities for location it occurred to them that it would be great if it developed as a community center for Berea rather than simply a dance hall in the area. The city was willing to grant a long term lease on land designated for recreational use on Jefferson Street just northwest of the college campus and close to the community school. Acton was willing if the Folk Circle Association could raise the additional funds needed.

*I had always heard jokes about something being built by committee being disjointed. In this case it was just the right thing. Russ wanted a log building. John, the dance expert, wanted an octagonal floor slightly pitched from the center to the sides. I had been impressed with the laminated arches in the folk school at Morse, Denmark, and suggested arches over the dance floor to avoid pillars. John Grossman, son of Dorothy, who was a faithful pianist for dances and on the Folk Center board, was an architect and visualized spaces needed for entry, dance floor, rest rooms, kitchen, etc. Peter Gott, the log builder from North Carolina recommended by Russ Acton, outlined the steps needed to create log structures. We visited the West Virginia facility Russ had sponsored and came up with a design that featured four log "cabins" with their fronts forming four sides of an octagon. The spaces between them defined the other four sides. The large interior space for a dance floor was to be spanned by laminated arches which would hold the roof of the interior. Each cabin had its own roof and housed rest rooms, a kitchen, an office/store area and a parlor or meeting room. John Grossman drew up an artist's sketch so we had something to show. We set out to raise funds and get started.*

Under John's leadership, volunteers were organized from people who wanted to learn to build a log cabin, to supplement Peter Gott's experienced crew. Pine logs were imported from North Carolina and hand hewn on site. The log building workshops went well and people were excited about the structure. J. Carroll McGill, a local architect, had been employed to prepare the construction drawings and secure necessary approvals. Lanny Simmons, an experienced contractor who added helpful and practical features, oversaw the erection of the main hall, provision of utilities, roofing and other construction details. McGill had introduced in the plans a foyer with an overhanging roof facing south to shade in the summer and let sun shine in during the winter. Emmer Harrison, a stone mason, constructed a beautiful interior stone wall between the foyer and dance hall to absorb heat and moderate temperatures year round. Laminated arches were ordered from a firm in London, KY, and it was the largest span they had yet done. All came together for an unusual and useful Russell Acton Folk Center.

Meanwhile fund raising was under way with the good assistance of Cecilia Wierwillie and other volunteers. The most popular gift option was "buying a log" for $100 and hundreds were sold. Plaques with the log number and donor were created to display. Others gave larger amounts and enough was raised to supplement the Acton gift and complete the structure with no public funds. When it was ready to be roofed, Russ Acton visited and was very pleased. He wanted a cedar shingles roof and offered the extra funds to accomplish this. He also agreed to make a special contribution to buy a small house at the corner of the property for a caretaker. Before the building was completed and equipped, Russ Acton, was again hospitalized and not expected to survive.

*John and I drove to Danville, Illinois to visit Russ at the Carl Clinic. He was frail but alert and we had a good visit. We also went over details of the project and his gift and he signed papers I had prepared to document his wishes and commitments. We didn't see Russ again but his name and memory are enshrined in the building he dreamed of in Berea.*

About a year before the death of Russel Acton, Bill and his campus activities staff conceived the idea of creating "the world's largest folk dance circle" in Berea. The idea caught on and on the appointed day hundreds of students and townspeople joined hands down the street through the campus and below the campus by the community school to make a circle almost a mile in circumference. John had arranged for the radio station to play a dance tune and broadcast his calls for a simple dance he created. With boom boxes and car radios around the circle everyone could hear. Police had stopped traffic through the campus and several people passing through simply parked their cars and joined the circle. Soft drinks were passed around. Balloons and colored t-shirts saying, "Largest Folk Dance Circle Ever," made everything look festive. The mayor and some members of the city council toured the circle in a convertible so they could make a report. A shirt was given to a pleased Russell Acton.

For the next years the care and maintenance of the new building fell to Bill and John, other volunteers and a part-time caretaker. White pine trees were planted on the western border of the property behind a grassy hill designed to seat people facing an outdoor stage. Folk Circle Association had offices and a small store in the front cabin wing. It became a place for many community activities besides folk dancing. Parties, weddings, family reunions and other gatherings were held there. It still lacked a finished floor and had some acoustical problems but was much used. As Bill and John approached retirement and contemplated leaving Berea, some other arrangement needed to be made. The city was planning to build a multigenerational facility, including head start and senior citizens center, and wanted to locate it behind the folk center on land included in the Folk Circle Association lease. They asked if this would be agreeable and it seemed like the right time to turn the facility over to the city. So agreement was reached to give the folk center to the city of Berea. The city agreed to honor the name for Russel Acton and folk dance as the primary purpose of the building. The city would install a finished floor and complete the outdoor stage. They would also purchase the caretaker's house. All this was ultimately accomplished and the Acton Center continues as a city facility.

*One humorous incident occurred at the meeting with the city officials to sign the papers when the city attorney said there was a problem with the caretakers house purchase. There was a tax lien on the house from before the Folk Circle Association had acquired it which would need to be paid before the city could make the purchase. I happened to have all the papers regarding the original purchase of the house with me and responded. "That is very interesting because I have a letter from our attorney at the time, who did a title search, declaring the property free of liens." The attorney who had signed the letter was now the city attorney. He wanted to see the letter and after perusing it said, "We'll take care of it!" The deal was closed.*

## NASEA

In 1986 the United Parcel Service Foundation gave a grant to the National Association of Student Employment Administrators (NASEA), later to be renamed National Student Employment Association (NSEA). UPS is a major employer of college students on a part-time basis, especially in holiday seasons and in summer. They pay well, provide benefits and insist on students remaining college. UPS wanted to encourage high quality student employment and relationships with colleges. The NASEA president at the time was Rick Kincaid from State University of New York at Brockport and he asked Bill to oversee the grant funds and report on their use. UPS Foundation continued to provide grants for years, allowing NASEA and the student employment movement to grow in effectiveness. Bill was elected president of NASEA in 1987. On sabbatical from Berea for six months in 1988, he devoted himself to strengthening the organization.

*NASEA and the regional associations had never had any extended time to plan and establish priorities. Annual conferences provided some time but, at these, the leadership was heavily involved in managing the conference, making presentations, and taking care of elections, budgets and other business. So we planned a retreat for leadership in Florida in early 1988, made possible by the UPS grant. Jennifer had completed high school and would be my assistant in making arrangements, taking care of reservations, registration and other meeting details. We traveled to Orlando and arranged for lodging and meeting rooms at a Holiday Inn at reasonable rates. We negotiated with nearby restaurants for special rates for meals including a dinner together at a Chinese restaurant. Then we prepared materials and sent packets to all participants. The meetings went very well; everyone enjoyed the accommodations and meals, and Jennifer became the NASEA mascot.*

The western association was hosting a conference in Claremont, CA, and Bill decided to drive across the states and back visiting student employment offices to encourage them, to learn their concerns and to promote the comprehensive values of student work or service experience. Rose and Jennifer accompanied him and they visited large universities like Tulane and Louisiana State, small colleges like Oakwood College in Alabama and community colleges like the one in Las Vegas, Nevada. The Las Vegas college had a problem of student employment peculiar to its location. Young men finishing high school could get jobs connected to the gambling industry that, with tips, paid really well, like providing valet services for parking, so they put off higher education. Enjoying a good income they often married, got a home and started a family. Then, in their thirties, they began to question whether they wanted to spend their lives parking cars. Going on to college as an older student with home responsibilities to become a teacher, a veterinarian, a businessman or other profession was not easy even with part-time work. A lot of counseling and support was needed.

Bill met wonderful colleagues on the trip. Sometimes he just toured their facilities and shared experiences about student employment programs. At other times he was treated like a visiting dignitary, meeting with presidents and deans and giving seminars on the educational and developmental values of student work beyond the financial benefits. Rose and Jennifer enjoyed sightseeing along the way. They all especially enjoyed driving up the Owens Valley on the east side of the Rockies in the morning with the sun shining on the peaks to the west. They drove through Tioga Pass and into the beautiful Yosemite National Park and they visited the giant sequoias. As they drove, Jennifer Rose sat in the back seat and practiced playing the guitar and singing. Her voice was maturing into a lovely soprano.

## Festival Dancers

Bill had asked Theresa Lowder, who worked in his office and had worked there as a student in earlier years, if she would take responsibility for the Festival Dancers while he and Rose traveled that year. Theresa was not an experienced folk dancer, but had been a cheerleader, had a sparkling personality and leadership abilities. She agreed. After all it was "just for the year". When Bill returned from his sabbatical Theresa agreed to continue. With the help of her husband, Bill, and sister, Jackie, she developed the group into an exceptional dance team which took trips all around the nation and world over for the next 26 years! Providentially, when she retired from her position in 2015 she passed the leadership on to Jennifer Rose, who had grown up in a dancing family and become a veteran dance leader and folk singer in her own right.

Back at work and at home life continued with increased grandchildren activity at the Big House, work at the college, and care of grandpa John at the nursing home. The family had added three more grandchildren in 1988 – Ralph Edwin Compton III to Ralph and Laura, Keith Romig Ramsay to Jim and Shawn and Adrienne Rose Ramsay to John and Eileen. The next year saw the arrival of Jonathan Moore Ramsay to Jim and Shawn and Samuel Osborne Ramsay to Stephen and Robin. The grandchildren now numbered 17 Beyond that, Martin and Charlie had added Joseph Earl in 1987 to complete their family of four boys. Child development was a primary subject of conversation in those days.

## Lord! Is It I?

In 1984 Bill had become involved in an annual dramatic production at Berea United Methodist Church of "Lord, Is It I?" based on the scriptural story of the Last Supper as portrayed in Da Vinci's painting of that name. The pastor, Clyde David Burberry, had introduced the play as a reading a year or so earlier and then the decision was made to do it as a visual drama. Bill became the director. The picture was recreated with men of the church playing the parts of the disciples. Each one steps out of the picture to tell his story. It is very moving to hear their thoughts from the other side of Easter. Laura helped with the music that accompanied the drama. Ralph both sang preparatory songs with a colleague and played the part of one of the disciples. Bill E. played a part some years, as did Jim. Some of the men played the same parts for the 25 years that the drama was presented but most changed over time. It was a very rewarding experience for all participating as cast, crew and audience.

Jennifer began college in the fall of 1988. She moved to the dormitory to experience college life more fully and began to receive expert coaching in voice as she took lessons with Dr. Steve Bolster and sang in the concert choir. She had become engaged to an older student and had marriage on her mind as Rose remembers.

*We had not been happy with some of the young men who had been paying Jennifer attention in her last years of high school so when a new college student*

329

*came to Berea, joined the country dancers, and began to notice Jennifer we were somewhat relieved. Gary was very polite, clean cut and pleasant. He seemed like a good alternative to some of the high school guys so when Jennifer responded to his attention we didn't discourage it. We didn't realize at first that he was not a new freshman, but had transferred to Berea and was a bit older. They shared a love of dancing and he became a frequent visitor in our home. We had purchased a time share at Abaco Island in the Bahamas in Jennifer's last high school year, anticipating Bill's retirement in a few years when we'd be free to travel. The time share deal offered us a free first trip and we took Gary and Jennifer with us to Abaco in the summer of 1988. Gary played one of the disciples in the annual church Easter drama. We worried that the relationship might be moving too fast for Jennifer's age and when they expressed the desire to set a marriage date after Jennifer graduated from high school, we said we would want her to have at least a year of college before taking such an important step, but if they were still of the same mind after the year we would be supportive. As she approached the end of her freshman year they began to plan a wedding in June. We tried to be helpful, although we began to have more serious questions about the differences in their ages, perspectives and experience. Gary was finishing college and ready for marriage, but Jennifer was just becoming an adult and beginning to explore the possibilities offered by the world. As the wedding date got nearer, it became obvious that she was not happy and finally she decided to call it off. It was hard but clearly the best decision and over the next months everyone moved on with new directions.*

Jennifer enjoyed the concert choir and other singing groups and toured with them. Rose helped arrange some of the opportunities for performances and on one trip to Oak Ridge and Florida, Bill and Rose accompanied the choir. Jennifer continued her voice lessons, her music studies, and her dancing. The summer after her sophomore year she went on tour with the country dancers to Denmark and fell in love with that country. Of course, she had grown up with Danes in her home through the Danish exchange program. No new grandchildren were added in 1990 but all the others were growing quickly and the Big House was usually busy. Bill and Rose had enjoyed their trip to Abaco in the Bahamas in 1988 and now were in the time-share system which gave them many vacation options. They went to French Lick, Indiana, in June 1990, with Bill E. and Anne joining them. In July they returned to Abaco with granddaughter Elizabeth and her cousin Mark.

*We had originally thought the time-shares would be for our post-retirement trips, but found them a great way to have special times with grandchildren and others. On the trip with Elizabeth and Mark we became better acquainted with Abaco and ventured outside the town of Marsh Harbor, where the resort was. Elizabeth, Mark and I had taken a walk outside the resort one evening and Bill had stayed behind to enjoy the activities the resort had planned for the evening, including a dance contest. Just as we returned the loudspeaker announced that Bill Ramsay had won the senior's limbo contest. We were stunned, but he had, in fact, wriggled under the limbo rod at a lower setting than anyone else of in his age bracket. His prize was a bottle of wine, which we gave to an appreciative couple from Switzerland. We had a good time with the children and determined to return with other grandchildren as they began to grow up.*

## Grandpa John Ramsay

Grandpa John was not doing as well in the nursing home. The wonderful head nurse, Emily, and the activities director, Val, had both left and personal care had declined. While he was helping a staff person, he stepped outside and fell off the walkway, cutting and bruising his cheek. He healed quickly but we suspect the home's owner was afraid of another fall and the possibility of a law suit. He had been so happy to be free to move about but now began to be strapped in a chair and have rails put on his bed. We were willing to take some risks to give him some freedom, but they were not. He would try to release himself by taking off his belt, untying his shoes or unbuttoning his shirt. Sometimes the attendants thought he was feeling hot and turned a fan on above his bed, which made him cold and miserable. One of us was there every day and tried to work with the staff, but the earlier days of social interaction with other patients and his sense of usefulness was never regained. Then he was afflicted with shingles and suffered from that, but he never complained and was always pleasant. Finally he contracted pneumonia and they moved him to the hospital where he died on February 26, 1991. He would have turned 89 in June.

*As with Mother Gertrude, I was the one there when death came. The hospital had called me at home. I let Bill know and went right over. Our pastor, Clyde David Burberry, also came and we prayed. Dad breathed his last and peacefully passed from this life but his gentle spirit lingered in the room and we felt it. Bill arrived moments later and he felt it as well. Laura came, too, and quietly recited Psalm 23. "God's Good Man" had gone home.*

Meanwhile, brother John had been struggling to care for Risse, who had been found to have cancer the year before. She underwent treatments to no avail and John took time off from work to care for her full time. She also died that spring on April 8, 1991. They had only been married five years. So it was a sad time. But two new grandchildren were born that year – Matthew Stephen to Robin and Stephen and Naomi Grace to Jim and Shawn. Also that year was one of anticipation of changes at work and in Jennifer's directions.

# CHAPTER 25

# WORK COLLEGES

Bill had been in contact with the other work colleges and discovering some of the difficulties all were having trying to maintain their programs while navigating federal financial aid and related regulations. For example, at one point Berea was told that it was getting more than its "fair share" by formula of work-study funds and would be cut back. The good news was that they would be eligible for more grant funds. Under federal programs work was the last form of financial aid, after grants and loans, since it was perceived as possibly interfering with education. The work colleges' philosophy was just the opposite, seeing work experience as part of the educational program and financial aid through self-help to be of primary importance, rather than being an add-on when grants and loans didn't cover costs. Berea considered loans, not work, as the last resort and most Berea students graduated with no or very little debt. After some effort, Bill was able to get an exception. At College of the Ozarks they had run into trouble with wage hour laws. They required students to work 15 hours per week in return for tuition room and board, which was a real bargain and they kept records of "overtime" and "undertime" for those who worked more or less hours so they could keep track of where students were in meeting their obligations. Students who graduated with more hours than required received note that they had contributed more than required but were not paid anything extra. The value they received for their labor was still greatly in excess of wage hour requirements. The Department of Labor found out that some students graduated with 'overtime' hours for which they were not compensated. Of course, overtime under federal regulations, was defined as more than 40 hours per week, not 15, but it took a year of struggle to get that point across to the bureaucracy. Since the rewriting of the tax laws, the tax liability of student "wages" was also in limbo. Bill was beginning to realize that some legislative remedy would be needed to give the work colleges the freedom to maintain their programs.

*I talked to President Stephenson about relieving me from the day to day duties of overseeing the labor and student life programs so I could work full time on legislative and policy matters and he agreed. I began to spend more time in Washington and at the other work colleges. With trustee approval, a new position was created and I was named Vice President for Policy Analysis and Planning which would include the office of institutional research. I moved to that office which was ably run by Susan Curtis Vaughn and had the services of a very capable secretary, Debbie Duerson. I still served on the administrative committee but was free to devote myself to issues important for the future of Berea and the other work colleges. In the summer of 1991 I spent some days in Washington and then, with Rose and Jennifer, went on vacation to England and Denmark, with a visit to Germany as well.*

# CHAPTER 26

# BACK TO DENMARK IN 1991

*Jennifer was planning to spend a term abroad in Denmark after she finished her junior year. Rose and I thought it would be a great opportunity in the summer of 1991 to return to Denmark after 18 years, help her make contacts for her study there, and also to visit relatives and friends in England and Germany. With all the Danish visitors who had stayed at the Big House, we had friends all over that country. We had gotten to know a young Danish man, Karl Iversen, who had been in Berea for a time, and he agreed to help arrange our visit.*

Bill, Rose and Jennifer drove to Columbus, Ohio, for an overnight with Patty and Earl. Then they drove to Washington where Bill had meetings with Don Eberly, the National Association of Independent Colleges and Universities (NAICU) and congressional offices. He also gave a presentation on student work at the National Association of Student Financial Aid Administrators (NASFAA), and met at the legal firm of Clohan and Dean with a legislative consultant named Buddy Blakey.

## First to England

They stayed with Don and Louise Eberly and left their car there when they flew out of Dulles Airport to Heathrow in England. They did some sightseeing in London, navigating the subway and bus and then took a train going north of London to the home of Dick and Shelagh Conner in Bedford. They learned from Dick that Bedford was the home of John Bunyan. He wrote Pilgrim's Progress while in prison there.

*Dick and Shelagh were cousins on mother's side of the family and they were Moravians. Dick Conner's mother was Josephine Romig, a daughter of Bishop*

*Benjamin Romig who married Samuel Connor. She was the younger sister of Elizabeth Romig who had married Theo Martin and was my grandmother on mother's side. Another of the Romig sisters, Emily, had married James Connor, a brother of Samuel so the Connor's were part of mother's family. Dick and Shelagh had been missionaries in Tanzania and were semi-retired and now were pastors at two Moravian churches in Bedford. They were marvelous hosts and we toured their part of England meeting some of their children.*

## Rose's Journal

Rose kept a daily journal of the entire trip starting each day with the devotional scripture text from the Moravian Textbook she carried with her. She shared her thoughts as well as recording the events of the day. For example:

*Saturday, August 3 -This morning at breakfast we read the Moravian text together. The verse in 1 Peter 5:6 was a message. "Humble yourselves under the mighty hand of God, that in due time He may exalt you." I think we cannot be all that we are meant to be if we are filled with pride and think we can always do everything ourselves. If we are humble and open to God's will, He can use us.*

*It is a lovely morning – so fresh and cool. Dick made eggs and we had fresh bread and tea. We are enjoying being with them. About 11:00 we left in their VW camper for Ely, where their daughter Anne and her family - husband John and boys, Jamie and Jack – live. Anne and John had visited us in Berea several years ago. The drive was wonderful – I love the English countryside – fields of wheat, golden brown, green meadows dotted with sheep, small villages with small houses and lovely flowers. We saw a sign that pointed left and said "Cambridge." I hadn't realized it was so close.*

*Ely is a charming little town with pretty little shops and tea rooms, small houses and flower gardens. Anne and John have a cozy house and pretty walled yard and garden. It was wonderful to see them and meet Jamie, 5, and Jack, 18 mos. Jamie reminds me of Benjamin – helpful and responsible and capable of adult conversation. Jack is sturdy and busy, almost two. We had a very good lunch. Then they took us to see the cathedral.*

*The cathedral and grounds were magnificent and grand. The stained glass windows are so beautiful, the stonework amazingly intricate. It seems unbelievable that such a structure could be built hundreds of years ago, before today's tools and machinery – but they were. Think of the skilled planning and craftsmanship. There has been a place of worship on that site in Ely for more than 1300 years and we felt connected to the hundreds of Christians who had worked and worshipped at Ely.*

Later Bill, Rose and Jennifer returned to London and took a tour bus across London Bridge, saw Big Ben and the Tower of London, and attended the play *A Midsummer Night's Dream* in London's beautiful Regency Park. On another trip they drove through Oxford and in the country they saw the ancient "white horses" carved into the chalk hills. They ate along the Avon River.

*We visited mysterious Stonehenge and Avebury on the Salisbury plain. Another day we took a train to a summer house near Ipswich for a visit with cousins on the Ramsay side, Martin and Jean Merrett and their son and daughter-in-law David and Mary. During the Nazi bombings of London before the USA entered the war my grandfather William had written to his English cousins, the Merretts, suggesting that the children be sent to be safe with him and his wife Jesse in Pennsylvania for the duration of the war. The children didn't come but the gesture was never forgotten and forged a special bond between these cousins and their families. It was great to make all these family connections in a new generation. We also took a day to visit Elaine and Martin Cole at Long Buckby. Elaine had been at Christmas Country Dance School teaching English clogging and she stayed with us at the Big House.*

## Across the North Sea to Denmark

Regretfully leaving the Conners on August 10, 1991, the Ramsays sailed on a ferry from Harwich, England to Esbjerg, Denmark. They were met by Karl Iversen and driven across beautiful countryside of southern Jutland to

Karl's home in Ammitsbol. Karl's mother, Margit, was a lovely, well-read woman and a kindred spirit who became a close friend. Karl and Margit had arranged for Jennifer and her parents to meet several school principals and teachers and leaders in the DDGU (Danish Dance and Gymnastics Society) like Henning and Bodil Andersen, who also became good friends. DDGU was the Danish sponsor of the exchange program. They also visited folk schools and met Danes who had stayed at the Big House over the years, like Hans and Karen Rosgaard. They visited Margit's daughter Ase, her husband, Michael, and little daughters at their pig farm.

*Ase and Michael lived in a long attractive building that had once been an inn and had all the outbuildings that go with an operating farm. We were amazed at how clean everything was, including the pigs. Their little girl got right in the pens with the pigs, her blond head barely showing above the pig's backs. She had no fear and the pigs were obviously used to her – perhaps even fond of her. We got a new appreciation for Danish hams. At dinner some conversation, with Jennifer as translator, triggered Bill to tell a joke that was a play on words. It made no sense in Danish but Michael laughed heartily. Jennifer asked if he understood and he said "No, but I knew it was a joke!" Now that is a gracious host.*

They visited nephew Loren and Ingelise, who had met at the Big House years before, married and now lived in Galten near Arhus, and other friends in Jutland. Jennifer had many supporters for her term abroad. They went south to Christenfeld, visited the Moravian church and saw the traditional flat gravestone of mother Gertrude's Uncle Frederick Martin. No monument type gravestones were in the graveyard because everyone was equal in death. They also enjoyed the wonderful honey cakes for which the town is famous. Then they went into Germany and had a good visit with Lori and Christian Poache in Herford. Lori had been a classmate at Berea during Bill and Rose's college days. Her parents had been German missionaries serving in India when Hitler came to power and when World War II started they were not welcome to come home to Germany. A Berea College trustee who heard of their homeless plight arranged for Lori and her younger sister Yuki to come to Berea. Lori had married Christian and they had served as missionaries but were now retired and living in a huge barn, built in the 1700's. They were restoring it as a family dwelling. Leaving Lori and Christian, the Ramsays visited a castle and other sites as they made their way to Frankfort for the flight home on August 26. Rose's journal records the last day in Germany.

*August 25, Sunday -Psalm 144: 15, "Happy the people whose God is the Lord!" We read the Bible together before we left and had prayer together. It is good to share with other Christians.*

*We had a nice breakfast together and a big gathering. Then Jennifer sang to the children and played her dulcimer and we sang in English and German,"Auld Lang Syne" and "Can You Count." That was nice. We said goodbye to the families and left about noon, following married children, Veronica and Peter for part of the way. They headed out on a country road, It was hilly and as we rounded a curve there was a lovely valley with patchwork fields and small clustered villages with red roofed houses – a lovely scene. Some of the villages had farm houses and barns right in the middle of the village. Our guides left us and we were on our own heading towards Frankfurt.*

*Veronica had suggested we stop and see a castle called Schloss Waldeck. We stopped to eat and Jennifer managed enough German to order us some lunch and get directions to the castle. We wound up a hill through a village and finally we were looking down on a lovely lake on either side. We drove along about 8 or 10 kilometers enjoying the views of the lake and sailboats. Then we rounded a curve and looked up – way up – and there was the castle. It looked like a fortress commanding the valley and the lake. It was an impressive structure. I wish we had time to go inside, but we were happy to have taken this road and seen this area of Germany. It's very hilly and the woods are cool with big trees. In Marburg there was a lovely cathedral on a hill overlooking the town. The bridges over the road had hanging baskets of flowers. We saw so many flowers. There are gardens by the houses and buckets of flowers on the porches and balconies and boxes of flowers underneath windows.*

*The last 80 or so kilometers were on the autobahn and so we sped on quickly. Even so cars flew past. The traffic moved along much better without the big trucks. No trucks allowed on the autobahn on weekends. We found the airport and circled around to the Sheraton Hotel entrance where a valet took our luggage and we took the lift to the 6th floor. Our room was large and comfortable with three beds and decorated in soft blues and lavenders. We enjoy having lots of ice for water and having great hot showers.*

*We are in Frankfurt, Germany, in an elegant hotel room after three wonderful weeks of travel. I can't think of anything I would change about our trip. Much more to see and I hope we can return soon.*

They had a pleasant and comfortable flight to Washington the next morning, arrived at the Eberlys' home, where they'd left their car, had tea before they packed and headed south. It was great to be able to read the road signs and newspapers and to understand the speakers on TV, waitresses at restaurants and people just passing by. One night on the road, a welcome fast-food meal at an Arby's in Virginia, and they arrived safely home.

# CHAPTER 27

# COMPLETING BEREA YEARS

What a year 1991 had been with the deaths of Bill's Dad and John's wife, Risse, the births of two new grandchildren, a new position at the college and a major overseas trip. Now they had to focus on Jennifer's plans, spend time with their expanding family, and see to tasks that needed to be accomplished before retirement which was expected to begin in 1993.

## A Big Snow

Bill continued to be active in the National Student Employment Association (NSEA) and attended a conference at Myrtle Beach in 1992 where they used a time share and shared a week's vacation with their dear friends, John and Martha Heneisen. That fall they returned to the Myrtle Beach area at Calabash with Jennifer, her Danish friend Karen Busk, who was visiting, and another college friend. They enjoyed wonderful seafood and fellowship. The next year, 1993, Bill shared responsibility for the NSEA national conference to be held at Hilton Head. They traveled there in March to make arrangements. Unfortunately they got caught in a blizzard around Asheville.

*We were driving the conversion van we had bought so Rose cold rest easily on the trip. She was recovering from a surgery that left her weak and feeling vulnerable. Our motel for the night was near the Asheville airport at Hendersonville and at the bottom of a hill where the road ended next Interstate 26. The blizzard conditions had been getting really bad. By the time we checked in, everything was covered and the wild wind still blowing snow. Most of the area had lost power but we never did, although it got very cold. Snow was being blown under our room door and we stuffed towels against the door to keep it out.*

*The TV said all roads were closed and reported power outages all over. I thought I'd better get the van up the hill while I could so I bundled up and drove it up hill in the snow. Almost at the top a person stepped in front of me and I had to put on my brakes and swerve. Of course, I ended up in the ditch with no possibility of getting out. I had some crackers and a heating coil for a coffee mug in the van and took those down the hill with the bad news about the van. Next morning I trudged up the hill against the wind, falling once on the slick ice, and got a couple hamburgers at a very busy Waffle House. I also got to a gas station with a convenient store and bought some canned chicken noodle soup. Back at the room we ate our burgers for lunch and were able to heat the soup in cups with the coil for supper.*

*After another night of being stuck there, I got back to the van and was able to start it but had no hope of getting out of the ditch in the deep snow. I saw a wrecker with a long tow cable pulling a car up from a steep hill that it had slid down and asked the driver if he could pull me out when he finished. He did and we had the van on level ground at the top of the hill a long block from our motel room. Traffic was still not moving and the entrance ramp to the interstate looked blocked by snow, but obviously the plows had cleared one lane on the interstate. When the day brightened we decided to give it a try. I made a couple trips to the van to carry our things and then helped Rose up the hill. Since the ramp to the interstate was downhill, we were able to maneuver it in spite of the snow and once we got there one lane was clear and there was no traffic. Just 40 miles further at the South Carolina border the snow stopped. If we had just made it that far two nights before we wouldn't have had the problem. There were signs of high wind damage all the way across South Carolina, but we made it to Hilton Head safely.*

In October they went to the NSEA conference, using another time-share week. In 1994 they returned to Abaco on a "bonus week" with Al and Sandy Osborne, daughter-in-law Robin's parents. This was the first of many travels with the Osbornes. Bill and Rose also made a visit to the College of the Ozarks and used a time-share at nearby Branson.

## Pine Mountain Settlement School

By 1992, John Stephenson was struggling with health issues. He had been diagnosed with a form of leukemia and, although it was a slow moving type of cancer, he was weak from the cancer and the treatments. In cutting back on the demands on his time and energy he asked Bill to move in to the position of president of the board of Pine Mountain Settlement School (PMSS). Tradition was that the president of the board was always the president of Berea College. PMSS, in its residential school days, had been a feeder of students from the mountains of eastern Kentucky to Berea College. The board had been agreeable to break with that tradition and have a Berea vice-president instead, so Bill was duly elected to the board and to the position of president. He served until he retired from the position in 2004.

Pine Mountain Settlement School is a very special place. It is nestled in the northwest of Harlan County, Kentucky and abounding in nature's beauty. Its historic buildings are built in the hillsides leaving open space on the bottoms where the clear waters run. For many years it had operated a residential school and then a day school, as well as serving as a community center with a variety of services for the area. When better roads and consolidated public schools made the residential school unnecessary, the directors, Burton and Mary Rogers, began to emphasize ecology and to use its beautiful surroundings to teach others to love and understand nature and live in harmony with it. Mary had died and Burton retired, although he still lived at the school. The director in 1992 was Paul Hayes, whose family had strong ties to Pine Mountain and to schools in Kentucky and Tennessee, which were the main source of students for the environmental programs.

*When I joined the board I found Paul to be a very careful manager and a person of great personal integrity. Working with the board he had stopped the "bleeding" of the school's small endowment which had been reduced under previous directors. The board included many members who had been students there during the residential and day school period and who had strong family ties to the area. Board meetings were like family or alumni reunions, interesting and enjoyable, but sometimes slow in conducting business. With the help of Paul, John Stephenson (who remained on the board for a time), and the board treasurer, Springer Hoskins, we established guidelines for investments and annual contribution of the endowment to realistic budgets and changed the endowment managing bank. We organized the board into six committees. Three were program committees – environmental education, heritage, and community programs - and three administrative – building and grounds, development and finance. All matters coming to the full board first were referred to committee. Each trustee served on two committees, one of each type. This way when three committees met at the same time three times as much talking could get done. The committees worked well and the board became more efficient. Under Paul's careful leadership, things were going well. The budget was sound enough to undertake a building project for the first time in years.*

*The old Far House needed to be replaced. The old deteriorated structure had no particular historical or architectural value but the patio at the side was the place where in 1917 Cecil Sharp, the noted British folklorist, had seen and recorded the Kentucky Set Running dance and recognized it as an early form of dance preserved in the hills of Appalachia from English roots and the forerunner of later country dances and the American square dance. We wanted to preserve the patio and incorporated it in the new building plans. I asked Jennifer to sing something appropriate for the dedication. She wasn't satisfied with the choices she explored and ended up writing an original ballad she called Pine Mountain Lullaby. She interviewed Springer Hoskins and others who had attended the old Pine Mountain school and was able to capture in her words and music the feeling of Pine Mountain. "When the world lies heavy on my mind; when I can't make sense of modern times; take me to Kentucky's hills and skies, and sing me a Pine Mountain lullaby." When she sang it on the old patio there were tears shed by many who love Pine Mountain.*

Unfortunately Paul Hayes contracted lung cancer and died, leaving a huge gap in the school's leadership. The board appointed an interim director and sought a new leader. Robin Lambert became the director and during her tenure Pine Mountain fought successfully to prevent a mountain top removal mining operation from destroying a mountain on the border of the school's property. Some board members owned property in the area and were divided on the matter so it was a tense time. Robin left the position and, after another interim, Nancy Adams was appointed. She was successful in introducing several historic preservation workshops which both improved the buildings and taught others the skills needed for caring for historic structures. Nancy served past the time of Bill's tenure. During the time he served Bill and Rose and some of their children and grandchildren had many enjoyable visits to this special place. When Bill retired from the board he was made "president emeritus."

## Work-Colleges Legislation

Bill was spending a good deal of time in Washington, with primary help coming from the office of Kentucky Congressman Chris Perkins, the son of the former Representative Carl Perkins. Bill's first priority was to gain recognition of the work-colleges and secure some legislative relief from regulations that were at odds with their programs. At first he was looking at the tax laws. The president of Blackburn, at the time, David Brown, suggested he talk with Buddy Blakey, a legislative consultant that Blackburn had employed in an unsuccessful attempt to gain special treatment of Blackburn's program. Buddy was a primary legislative representative of the traditionally black colleges and had excellent contacts in Congress, especially among Democrats.

*Buddy was great to work with and the work colleges retained him to assist in our efforts. We first looked at remedy through the tax laws, which had previously provided for special treatment of student labor payments at work colleges. Congressmen and Senators of both parties were very supportive of the work ethic among students and we drafted a technical amendment to the tax law of 1986, which was then under review, which would restore the older provision. There was no opposition to the amendment but there were so many technical amendments, some of which were controversial, that congress made the decision to avoid conflict by accepting no amendments.*

The chairman of the house Ways and Means Committee which handles budgets and tax laws was Dan Rostenkowski, a Democrat from Chicago, who had steered tax laws since 1981. He was sympathetic with the work colleges' attempt to restore the tax provision of the pre 1986 tax law and promised to write a letter of intent from Congress to the departments of treasury and labor saying that it was not the intent of Congress to change the way the work colleges treated their student labor payments. Chairman Rostenkowski came under investigation for fraud, was prosecuted, convicted and eventually went to prison in 1994, so the promised letter never got written. Bill and Buddy with Congressman Perkins staff and other helpful congressional friends decided that the higher education act, which was up for reauthorization, was the place to seek relief. The question posed was "What is a work college? There would need to be a legislative definition.

*The work colleges were all in agreement in philosophy and the universal work requirement, but varied widely on how their programs operated. Alice Lloyd, Berea and Ozarks served low income students exclusively. Warren Wilson and Blackburn did not. Some paid students partially in cash and some only credited work against board and room or tuition. Ozarks required some work during summers and the others simply employed students in the summer as part-time employees. The management of the programs varied from school to school. At all colleges and universities, the majority of students do some work while in school and in the case of low income students, part of their support came from the federal work-study program. My task was to write a definition and conditions for qualifying as a work college broad enough to include all the five (at the time) work colleges but distinguish them from other institutions. We would need to leave the door open for others to become work colleges so the legislation would not be limited to the five schools. Without going into details, which are now written into the higher education act, I drafted the definition and conditions and Buddy put it into legislative language and we wrote the special provisions that would apply to work colleges.*

Bill had gone to work on the legislation to get recognition for the work colleges and allow them to operate without impediments of regulations written for strictly financial aid purposes. That was achieved, but Buddy and congressional advisers insisted that to be effective there needed to be some provision for allocation of funds. So an amount was included to be authorized to implement the new provision. Bill is not sure but thinks the amount was five million dollars. Not only was the authorization successful but funds were appropriated, in a lesser amount, so the work colleges not only received regulatory relief but additional funds for their programs. At Bill's suggestion some of the new funds were set aside for the work colleges to use together as a consortium to promote and encourage the work college approach to higher education as provided in the new legislation. The achievement of the work college legislation was the result of positive help from many people in addition to supportive congressmen.

*Getting legislation passed requires that all bases be tagged, support organized and barriers avoided. Legislators listen to "interest groups" and those groups, rightly, keep track of what is going on in congress and the executive branch. We took care to inform and seek the support of groups who, had they not known of the proposal, might have tried to derail it. The independent colleges association NAICU was especially helpful in avoiding pitfalls in wording. The student employment association, NASEA, of which I had been president, was supportive. The executive director of NASFAA, the national financial aid association was a friend and helpful associate. In addition, we needed the understanding and support of the office of education and particularly those concerned with the administration of financial aid work-study funds, and I spent a lot of time with them. They offered no objections to the new provisions and their knowledge of the work colleges paid off when it came time to write regulations. On the political side we convened a meeting in Washington of the work program directors and representative students from each institution. They were brought up to date and then each visited their own congressmen and senators to inform them and seek support. In the end, there was no opposition and passage was smooth.*

*One amusing incident occurred during my Washington visits. This was after the 1960's when security in public buildings began to be provided, but before September 11, 2001 when homeland security became an obsession. I had given a presentation at a national financial aid conference on the values of student work and, as I often did, used role playing to make my points. I had learned that a small prop or costume helped people get over shyness and assume a character. With children if you use a wand, a cape or a crown they are quickly*

*transformed into a wizard, super hero or princess. So I had brought along*
*three items to help in the role playing. Every college has a food service so I had*
*brought a dish towel to drape over an arm for the role of a food service worker.*
*Likewise all colleges have athletes who are pressed for time between studies and*
*practices so I brought a sweat band for person in the role of the athlete. And*
*everyone has some sort of medical clinic where students might work so I brought*
*along a hypodermic syringe to symbolize the role of a medical practitioner.*
*We had fun with the session and those playing roles did well with their props.*
*Immediately after my session I had an appointment in a congressional office so*
*I dropped my props in the top of my briefcase and caught a taxi to the Rayburn*
*Building. Arriving a little rushed I went in and the guard pleasantly asked me*
*to open my briefcase. I obliged and there on top were a towel, elastic band and*
*syringe. His eyebrows went up under his hat. It took a little explaining, but he*
*was good humored and intelligent and let me pass. Now with tight security, I*
*may have ended up who knows where.*

Bill Stolte, who was Academic Dean and Vice President and also professor
of economics, suggested to Bill that they co-teach a course on the federal
budget in the January term. Bill agreed and a group of 10 students signed
up. They were exceptionally bright and motivated and quickly learned,
in the first week, the basic budget language and processes. Then the
whole group went to Washington where they were welcomed by budget
related agencies like the office of management and budget and the general
accounting office. Congressional committee staff members instrumental
in budget development and adoption and the congressional budget office
also gave of their time and information freely. It was a most enjoyable
adventure in learning and a pleasant visit to the sights of Washington for
students and their teachers. They ended the course in Berea as federal
budget "experts." This was the only course that Bill ever taught – or rather
co-taught – and he appreciated Bill Stolte for asking him.

## Jennifer's First Recording

Jennifer was preparing for her term in Denmark to study their use of folk
song and dance in schools. She had done some singing on the 1991 trip
and the Danes always asked her to sing and then asked if she had a tape.

When some Danish visitors had come to Berea, one of the young women was invited to stay at the Big House. She would coach Jennifer in her Danish and return to Denmark with Jennifer when she went for her study. She agreed and Bente Boisen became a sister to Jennifer and a daughter to Bill and Rose. By the time they went to Denmark Jennifer was fluent in their language and could sing in Danish as well as English. Her musical ear and training seemed to help her learn the language quickly. Jennifer would be staying with host families during her time there and decided to make a tape of her singing so she could leave one as a thank you memory gift. They located a young man in Lexington who had a recording "studio" in a closet and arranged to make a recording. Jennifer chose her songs and practiced them.

*The studio was definitely amateur but charges were inexpensive and it would suit our purposes. Occasionally the noise of traffic passing could be heard in the background of the recording but it went well. However the finished master was a disaster sounding very blurred and muddled. Jennifer cried when we listened to it. I noted that it seemed to be a problem of the mixing and not the recording itself. I talked to the recording technician and he agreed. He was able to fix the problem and the result was a very nice, if not perfectly professional, tape. Jennifer planned to order 100 copies but I said I would invest in more than that and we bought 300. She and Bente took 60 with them in their suitcases. Before the first month was over, Jennifer was calling for us to send more tapes. They had all been given away or sold. We sent a box full, and Jennifer's music career was under way.*

Jennifer had a wonderful time in Denmark, made many new friends and promised to come back. That was the beginning of her singing career. In fact she did return to Denmark for singing tours every year for about 15 years. She had to complete a final term before graduating from Berea in December 1992. Her senior recital was a final high point in her college experience. In the first half of her program, she sang traditional pieces for recitals like operatic arias and German love songs. She wore a formal gown and stood by the grand piano. It was lovely. But then at intermission she changed her costume and style. She dressed in calico, sat on a wicker love seat with her guitar and gave a report on Appalachian hymnody, singing

Old Regular Baptist hymns, spirituals, camp meeting songs, shape note hymns and other examples of the rich musical heritage of the region. She had the audience join in, singing choruses to familiar hymns. It was an outstanding and different recital and a fitting way to end her college program.

Bill planned to retire after the academic year ending in 1993 and for several years he and Rose had been making plans. They felt they should leave Berea, for a time at least, and Rose said she'd like to be closer to the ocean. She loved the beach, sun, breezes, palms, live oaks and sound of the ceaseless waves. They decided to look along the coast between St. Augustine, FL and Wilmington, NC, so they would be as close as possible to Berea and still be at the Atlantic. They began to travel when they could along the coast staying at different locations. They liked St Augustine Beach and Jacksonville Beach in Florida. St Simon's Island and the Savannah area were nice in Georgia. Myrtle Beach was too crowded but some beaches to the north in North Carolina were possibilities. But they used a time share at Edisto Beach, South Carolina, in 1989 and loved the Charleston area. They were especially attracted to the family friendly feel of Edisto as opposed to the country club feel of some other places. It was also the closest to Kentucky so they began to look at options there seriously. They arranged another time share in Fairfield Ocean Ridge at Edisto in 1993 and concluded that this was the place they wanted to be. They ended up deciding to buy a lot and build a house in the Fairfield Ocean Ridge Resort, which they completed in the spring of 1995.

## Berea College Years Come to a Close

*We hated to think of selling the Big House with all its memories but that would be necessary and we began to make plans and let people know. Laura and Ralph had been considering a move from their house on Van Winkle Grove, just a block away from the Big House. They decided to buy the Big House and their children were ecstatic, as were all of the rest of us. It would stay in the family. I was especially happy to have that family continuity and told Laura that she had to continue the annual Christmas Open House that had become such a tradition. She said, "Fine, as long as you will come to help!" It was easy to agree to that condition.*

The only problem was that Laura and Ralph wanted to move in before the Edisto house was even begun. So they did a house shuffle to the confusion of the Post Office. John had continued living in the log house on Adams Street after Risse's death in 1991, but had decided to move to the house he had lived in previously with Mother and Dad. He was planning to marry a beautiful dance partner, Berni Meyer, in spring 1994 and they would live in the house at 314 Estill Street. So Bill and Rose, with Jennifer, moved to the Adams Street house and Laura and Ralph moved to the Big House at 415 Estill Street. Grandchild number 20 had arrived with the birth of Stephen Patrick Blake Compton to Laura and Ralph in January 1994. Brother John and Bernie were married in April.

The college had a retirement party for Bill and many friends beyond the college, like Roger Lilly, came or, like Don Eberly, sent messages. Brother John presented a tribute called "Sibling Revelry" in which he observed that when Bill was born he was already one year old and thus infinitely older. By age two he was only twice as old and by age 10 Bill had come to be 90 percent as old as he, etc. Now, he said, with Bill retiring while he was still working, he thought his brother had passed him. President Stephenson presented Bill with a beautiful rocking chair, made in the student industries. But Bill's service to the college was not quite over.

John Stephenson had announced his own retirement, which meant the search for a new president needed to begin. The trustees asked Bill to serve as part-time secretary on the search committee as a nonvoting member. He would handle the notices of the opening, special invitations to apply, answer inquiries, collect applications and references, organize material for the committee and otherwise handle the business of the search. He would remain in his office with the excellent services of Debbie Duerson to do the computer and clerical work, filing and documentation.

*Rose and I had planned a September visit to Jennifer at Peaceful Valley Ranch in Colorado, where she had secured a job as singer and activities director. The owners were Karl Boehm, a college classmate, and his wife, Mabel, who was related to the Ambrose family. With the understanding of this commitment, I agreed to work with the search on a part-time basis. It was quite exciting. The search committee was made up of trustees, faculty, students, alumni and staff and worked very well together. I was pleased that they opened every meeting with prayer. A consulting firm had been retained to help find suitable applicants and advise on the process. We received a lot of applications and developed guidelines for responding, placing into categories and following up. We kept the college community informed of progress without divulging confidential information. Many of the applicants were in responsible positions and didn't want to have their interest publicized unless they were final contenders. After the committee had reviewed the serious applicants and done some more reference checking, a list of final candidates was developed. I was asked to arrange a meeting of these away from Berea for in-person interviews and meetings. We held the meetings in Cincinnati and it was like a high level seminar on higher education. All the participants were highly qualified, informed and articulate. From this session three finalists were chosen and I arranged for them to come to campus individually for a deeper orientation to Berea and to meet faculty and staff. Finally the search committee chose one candidate to recommend to the full board of trustees and Larry Shinn was offered the position. He accepted and one of my final acts was to welcome him and his lovely wife, Nancy, to Berea in June 1994. Now I was finally and fully retired.*

Meanwhile Bill and Rose were living in the log house on Adams Street. Risse had built her large modern log house on the front part of a lot on which her father Raymond Layne had moved an old two story log cabin. Raymond Layne had been a collector and teacher. The log cabin had originally been built in Bear Wallow (now Dreyfus) near Kingston by Thomas Shifflet in the early 1800's on land given to him as a reward for his service in the revolutionary army. Shifflet was an army buddy of a Layne ancestor and there was, reportedly, some connection by marriage as well. Raymond acquired the cabin and had it moved to Berea. He also acquired desks and other items form the old one-room school in the same area that he had attended as a child, and set up the second floor of the cabin as a schoolroom. Over the years he was alive and active, he would have local school groups come to experience how school used to be. By the time Bill and Rose moved to the big log house the cabin and its contents were dust covered, vermin infested and in general disarray. They undertook to clean it out and discovered some interesting memorabilia of farm equipment, World War II and furniture like a "rope springs" bed. In the short time Bill and Rose lived there they had groups come to see the cabin and schoolroom, once it was cleaned out and organized. One Christmas they decorated the interior with a tree having strings of popcorn, and lighted a faux fire in the old fireplace and then entertained groups of children from Christmas Country Dance School with stories, refreshments and a one-room-school experience. Later John, with agreement from Risse's daughter Becky, gave the Shifflet cabin to the city of Berea and it was moved to the tourism center at the old train station.

*Living at the log house Risse had built was different from living at the Big House. It was just a block away from the college track and I could walk there and go around the track often with friends I had walked with before. Sometimes Bill went too and jogged a little. It was good for us. The house had a nice porch and a spacious living room with a working fireplace. The first floor had a kitchen and dining room and three bedrooms – a master bedroom and two small bedrooms that Risse had built with her twin granddaughters in mind. Jennifer stayed in one of these. We had our bedroom upstairs where a large bedroom was next to an even larger room that Risse had used as a sewing and crafts area. Our bed had its headboard against a wall where the huge exposed hewed log beams that held up the roof came down to join the wall about five feet above the floor. One was close to Bill's side of the bed and if he wasn't careful he banged his head on the beam when he got out of bed. Usually he remembered to duck his head but too often he forgot. Finally after repeated contact of his head with the beam he wrote a rhyme and posted it on the beam as a reminder, The rhyme said, "To whom it may concern. Both now and ever after; whatever brains Bill Ramsay had, were dashed out on this rafter!"*

## Plans for Edisto

They had finalized plans for the house at Edisto and hired a contractor, Todd Babb of Walterboro. A lot of decisions were needed about cabinet styles and hardware, carpet types and colors, paint for various rooms, appliances and bathroom fixtures. They had decided to not take much with them but to start anew; Jennifer would be staying in the log house and would need furniture and appliances. She had finished her season at Peaceful Valley and had decided to see what she could do with a career in singing. She was ready to make more tapes or cd's and to schedule performances at festivals, retirement communities, schools, churches and community centers. Rose agreed to help her and for the next few years was essentially her agent, especially for winter tours in Florida.

The last memories of living in the log house are somewhat painful. Unfortunately Rose developed severe pains in her lower back and down her leg which turned out to be an attack of shingles. There was no way she could travel. Bill made several trips to Edisto alone to work with Todd Babb and purchase appliances. He would bring back samples of carpeting and paint chips for Rose to review and choose. After nights of no sleep for either of them, son-in-law Ralph, who was a physician, suggested using capsaicin to relieve the pain and it worked. Finally they got some sleep and recovery followed slowly.

*As Rose was feeling better enough to be up, we planned a trip to Edisto. We had purchased a conversion van that had a comfortable bed in the back where she could lie down. We had a camp style chemical potty she could use rather than having to stop at gas stations or restaurants. That was the fastest trip we ever made to Edisto. It worked out well bringing us closer to finishing the house and getting ready to move in. In February 1995, with the help of a couple young men friends, Jerry Houck and John Bowers, I drove a rental van to Edisto full of our first load of household goods. The house still had no heat and it was cold, but we could heat a room with a space heater and were comfortable. Later the boys and I made another trip and finally were ready to move. With the help of Melissa and Catherine we moved a lot of boxes of items in early March. The girls were so anxious to get to the beach hat they unloaded the van in record time. Rose and I, with perishables and the rest of our "stuff" in a U-Haul trailer arrived at our new home at Edisto Beach in March 1995. We consider the official date of the beginning of our Edisto home to be April 1995. Our Berea years were past and a new phase of life was beginning.*

# BILL AND ROSE RAMSAY TIME LINE

## BEREA YEARS: 1971 - 1994

| YEARS | FAMILY AND RELATED EVENTS | WORLD EVENTS |
|---|---|---|
| 1971 | Family moves to Dixie House on campus<br>Bill E. enters Berea College<br>Children join folk dance group<br>Jennifer is campus baby<br>Buy 130 acres on Clear Creek, Rockcastle Co | World Trade tower completed<br>Microchip invented |
| 1972 | Rose organizes Host Family program<br>Bill reorganizes labor and financial aid programs<br>Laura enters Berea College<br>Bill and Rose lead teen folk dance group<br>they later name Berea Festival Dancers | Strife in Northern Ireland<br>Olympics attack in Munich |
| 1973 | Stephen, John & Jim at Berea Community<br>Schools, active in sports and other activities<br>Bill and Rose take first group to Denmark to<br>begin teen exchange, Stephen & Martin go | SCOTUS *Rowe versus Wade*<br>strikes down abortion laws<br>Watergate scandal |
| 1974 | Bill elected to Berea school board<br>Stephen enters Berea College<br>Bill E dismantles Nursing Building and<br>starts building House at Clear Creek | Nixon resigns; Ford president<br>World population reached<br>four billion |
| 1975 | Bill becomes VP Labor & Student Life<br>Buy & move to 415 Estill St: the Big House<br>Bill E graduates, marries Anne Hylton<br>Jennifer starts school | Fall of Saigon, End of Vietnam<br>war |
| 1976 | Laura graduates, marries Ralph Compton,<br>move to Charlottesville, VA: Med School<br>John enters Berea College<br>Bill E and Anne to grad school in Florida | Ebola outbreak<br>American Bicentennial<br>Apple computer introduced<br>Interstate 75 completed at Berea |
| 1977 | Bill and Rose attend Carter inauguration<br>Rose and others begin to organize<br>Mother/Child Mission, pregnancy help center | Carter becomes president<br>Personal computers produced<br>Elvis Presley dies |

| | | |
|---|---|---|
| 1978 | Elizabeth Anne Compton born in VA | First test-tube baby born |
| | Jim enters Berea College | Minimum wage $2.30 per hour |
| | Stephen enters UK Medical School | |
| | Bill E and Anne return to Berea, Clear Creek house | |
| | John G & Gertrude Ramsay move to Berea | |
| | | |
| 1979 | John R, marries Eileen Ambrose | Smallpox declared eradicated |
| | Amber Rose Ramsay born in KY | Marg. Thatcher United Kingdom |
| | Jim spends 6 months in Denmark | Prime Minister |
| | Loren marries Inge-Lise | Mother Teresa receives Nobel |
| | John M & Winona divorce | Peace Prize |
| | | |
| 1980 | Stephen marries Robin Osborne | Poland freedom movement gains |
| | John graduates from college | Gas is $1.19 per gallon |
| | Laura & Ralph move to Clarksburg, WV | Bread costs 50 cents a loaf |
| | | |
| 1981 | William Joel Ramsay born in KY | Reagan becomes president |
| | Catherine Lois Compton born in WV | Assassination attempt fails |
| | John & Eileen go to U of Wisconsin | Iran releases American hostages |
| | John G & Gertrude M Ramsay receive | |
| | Mother Jones award in Bethlehem, PA | |
| | | |
| 1982 | Benjamin Gates Ramsay born in Akron, OH | Israel invades Lebanon |
| | Melissa Rose Compton born in WV | First CD players available to all |
| | Brian Cooney Ramsay born in WI | |
| | Jim graduates & goes to grad school in Utah | |
| | Dick marries Susana Espinoza in Texas | |
| | | |
| 1983 | BC Pres. Weatherford announces retirement | Beirut barracks attack |
| | Laura & Dr. Ralph move back to Berea | |
| | Jim returns to Berea; works at Goodyear | |
| | | |
| 1984 | Andrew Albert Ramsay born | HIV identified as cause of AIDS |
| | Colleen Aiden Ramsay born in WI | Indira Gandhi assassinated |
| | Jim marries Shawn Myers; works at ATR | |
| | In Danville, KY | |
| | Gertrude Eleanor Martin Ramsay dies | |
| | John Stephenson becomes president of BC | |
| | | |
| 1985 | Daniel Bowles Ramsay born in KY | First use of DNA "fingerprint" |
| | Rebekah Adair Ramsay born in KY | |

| 1986 | Work colleges conferences, projects & visits | NASA's Challenger explodes |
| | Jim & Shawn to Wilmore, Asbury Seminary | Mir space station launched |
| | John M marries Risse Layne McDuffie | Chernobyl nuclear incident in |
| | | |
| 1987 | Michael Aaron Ramsay born | Stock market crash |
| | Bill elected president of NASEA | World population 5 billion |
| | Jim & Shawn move to Junction City | |
| | John & Eileen move to Wooster, OH | |
| | John G to nursing home & happy there | |
| | | |
| 1988 | Keith Romig Ramsay born in KY | English Channel tunnel begun |
| | Ralph Edwin Compton born in KY | Air crash at Lockerby, Scotland |
| | Adrienne Rose Ramsay born in OH | |
| | Bill takes half year sabbatical for NASEA | |
| | First trip to Abaco Towns By-The-Sea | |
| | Jim & Shawn move to Danville, KY | |
| | | |
| 1989 | Samuel Osborne Ramsay born | GHW Bush becomes president |
| | Jonathan Moore Ramsay born in KY | Berlin wall is dismantled |
| | Bill E transferred by Hyster to Danville, IL, | Soviet bloc in Europe collapses |
| | He, Anne and family move | Liberian civil war erupts |
| | | |
| 1990 | Abaco trip with Elizabeth & Mark | Germany united |
| | John G situation in nursing home | Iraq invades Kuwait |
| | becomes difficult | First Gulf War begins |
| | | |
| 1991 | Naomi Grace Ramsay born in KY | Iraq driven out of Kuwait |
| | Matthew Stephen Ramsay born | Soviet Union dissolved |
| | John Gates Ramsay dies | Minimum wage is $4.25 per hour |
| | Risse Layne Ramsay dies | |
| | Bill, Rose, Jennifer to England-Denmark | |
| | Jennifer makes her first recording- a tape | |
| | for her term abroad in Denmark | |
| | | |
| 1992 | Bill is VP for Policy & Planning; | European Union created |
| | working on work-college legislation | Bosnian war begins |
| | Bill elected to board of Pine Mountain | |
| | Settlement School (PMSS) | |
| | Jennifer graduates from college in December | |

| 1993 | Bill helps with BC presidential search | Clinton becomes president |
| | Bill, Rose, Jennifer move to Adams St | World Trade Center bombed |
| | Laura, Ralph & family buy and move to | but not destroyed |
| | 415 Estill St: the Big House | |
| | Bill elected President of PMSS Trustees | |
| | Jim receives M Div from Asbury Seminary | |
| | | |
| 1994 | Stephen Patrick Blake Compton born in KY | Nelson Mandela elected in S |
| | Larry Shinn elected as BC president | Africa |
| | Bill retires from Berea College | English Channel tunnel |
| | Start to build at Edisto Beach, SC | completed |
| | Abaco trip with Sandy & Al Osborne | |
| | John M marries Bernice Meyer | |

THE FAMILY AT DIXIE HOUSE (LEFT) MOVED TO THE BIG HOUSE IIN 1975

JIM'S GRADUATION FROM
BEREA COLLEGE IN '82 WAS
THE 5th. JENNIFEER DANCES

BILL AND ANNE'S WEDDING WAS IN
1975. OTHERS FOLLOWED UNTILL ALL
THE CHILDREN WERE MARRIED

JIM & JENNIFER
AS LITTLE PEOPLE

## THE BEREA YEARS: 1970-1995

FROM A FAMILY OF SIX CHILDREN, AGES ONE TO 17, THE BEREA YEARS SAW SCHOOL
BEGINNINGS, HIGH SCHOOL GRADUATIONS. COLLEGE GRADUATIONS, WEDDINGS AND
GRANDCHILDREN ALONG WITH LOTS OF WORK, TRIALS AND FUN. WHEN THE BEREA
YEARS WERE FINISHED, ALL BUT JENNIFER WERE MARRIED AND THERE WERE 20
GRANDCHILDREN. THE FIRST WAS ELIZABETH (1978) SHOWN WITH MOTHER LAURA
AND COUSIN MARK (1977). BENJAMIN, MELISSA AND BRIAN ALL CAME IN 1982.

359

# REFLECTIONS 15

## "IT ISN'T FAIR!"

We often hear from children the phrase, "It isn't fair!" It is a common complaint of college students. Sometimes it simply because they didn't get what they thought they were due, or were asked to do more than others. I remember an international student who told me his professor in English class made him write more papers than his classmates. "It isn't fair!" I asked if he was having trouble with English and he said he was. I suggested that the teacher was trying to give him extra help because he had a greater need, coming from a different native language. But many times the complaints really did result from unfairness, for whatever reasons, and I always assured them I would investigate and follow up. I cautioned them that I had only heard their side of the story and would need to hear how others perceived the situation. Then I would suggest that if only everyone was as perfect as we were, we wouldn't have these problems. Of course they would immediately deny that they were perfect and we had a basis for discussion of living in an imperfect world. We would agree that justice was very important, but the thing most under our control was how we responded to incidents of unfairness. That is what defines our character.

I have noted that everyone wants justice, and that is a worthy goal, but in dealing with their own failures most people are more interested in mercy than justice. Seeking justice usually applies to the misdeeds of others. We will experience injustice and should try to find ways to confront it and remedy it, but we are first and foremost responsible for our own actions in response to it. Are we frozen in the old "an eye for an eye" or can we, with others, seek repentance and redemption? I like the definitions of justice, mercy and grace that I read somewhere.

*Justice is getting what you deserve.*
*Mercy is not getting what you deserve.*
*Grace is getting what you don't deserve.*

Let us pray for all three: justice, mercy and grace for ourselves and others.

# REFLECTIONS 16

## <u>LAUGHTER</u>

We laughed a lot. The boys were full of fun and made puns at any opportunity. We would share amusing stories. We did the skits at Christmas School in which we poked fun at ourselves, friends and our human condition. It is good to laugh together, not at each other but with each other. That was one of the joys of traveling with Al and Sandy Osborne. They liked to laugh and share a good joke. Al especially liked jokes in which the "bad guy" gets his come-uppence. Two in particular tickled him to the point that he could hardly finish telling them for laughing at what he knew was coming. We tell them here in memory of dear Al.

*A truck driver on a long haul stops at a truck stop for a break. He is not a large man and very mild mannered and courteous – the kind of trucker who doesn't speed and would stop to help a motorist in trouble. He notices three motorcycles parked in the lot of the truck stop and when he goes in to the café there are three bikers garbed in their usual black leather. He goes up to the counter and asks the waitress for a cup of coffee.*

*The apparent leader of the bikers, a big burly, bearded fellow, says loudly, "That's a mighty puny little fellow to drive such a big rig." The others dutifully laugh but the trucker ignores the comment. The waitress puts a cup of coffee on the counter in front of the trucker and the big guy reaches over and grabs it as if it were his. The trucker doesn't take the bait and object and the waitress quickly puts another cup in front of him. This time when he begins to drink the biker deliberately jostles his arm so his coffee is sloshed out of his cup. Not willing to play the game and get into a fight the trucker thanks the waitress, pays for the coffee with a nice tip and walks out. The waitress, distressed, goes to the window to watch him go and they hear the truck start and roar off.*

*The swaggering biker laughs and says, "He isn't much of a man, is he?" The waitress replies, "He's not much of a truck driver either. He just ran over three bikes on the way out.*

Al never tired of hearing that story. He liked another one with a similar twist.

*A farmer was laying fresh straw down in his milking stall in the barn when a new, sporty, Jeep Cherokee drives into the barnyard and a young man dressed western, but not looking like he was a working man, steps out with a clipboard under his arm. The farmer steps out and greets him and asks if he can be of help. The young man swaggers over and pulls out his wallet showing a card. Officiously he says, "I'm the agricultural inspector come to check your farm. See this card? This authorizes me to check everything. The farmer has nothing to hide and says, "OK, just let me know if you need anything, but don't go into that field over there, its …." Before he can finish the young inspector cuts him off and points to his card again, saying, "This card allows me to go anywhere on your farm." "Suit yourself," says the farmer.*

*Of course the inspector immediately goes to the field the farmer had pointed to, climbs the fence and starts up the grassy hill. The farmer watches as the young man gets about half way up the hill before the big bull sees him. The bull snorts tosses his huge head and begins to run down the hill towards the young man. He hears the snort and sees his doom rushing at him so he turns and runs wildly back down the hill towards the fence. The bull is gaining as the farmer shouts, "Show'm your card! Show'm your card!"*

We laugh with Al. Satisfying isn't it?

# REFLECTIONS 17

## CHANGING POLITICAL POSITIONS

Rose grew up in a household and community that were strongly Republican. East Tennessee had been that way since the Civil War. The Appalachian part of Tennessee was Union while the western part of the state was Confederate. The hill people were fiercely independent, not far removed from the pioneers, and didn't trust the government. They had strong family values and commitment to church and community. They gradually accepted help from government in getting properly located outhouses, roads, access to public schools and the benefits of electricity in their homes, but didn't want anyone telling them what to think or where or how they could live.

My grandfather, William Ramsay, was also a staunch Republican, but his son, my father John G. Ramsay, became allied with the Democrats who sought relief through government protections from oppressive conditions of the poor and the working class. But they also embraced freedom of choice, family values and mutual assistance through church, voluntary associations and local community. Big government was not to tell them what to do, but to give protection from oppression of the propertied class and provide opportunities for bettering themselves.

We both grew up in an environment of hard work, self-reliance, freedom to enterprise and to speak out, active citizenship and moral standards. We had a strong sense of right and wrong and helping each other. We did not depend on laws or government to provide for us, but only to protect us. We had a healthy resistance to those who felt they were superior and, in their arrogance, knew what was best for everyone. We weren't anti-authority and believed in the rule of law and democracy, but no group should set themselves up as better than others.

In our formative years it seemed that arrogance was most apparently expressed by the propertied class of people who held most power and dictated to others. They seemed to assume a sort of "divine right" of property. Those not so blessed should listen to them, since they obviously knew what was best. When Thomas Jefferson drafted the Declaration of Independence he borrowed from John Lock the phrase "life, liberty and the pursuit of happiness," but Locke's original phrase was "life, liberty and property." Jefferson reportedly didn't want to elevate property to the same level as the rights of life and liberty so he changed it to "the pursuit of happiness" which applied to all, not just the propertied class, and seemed more in keeping with democracy. In our early years it seemed to us that the Republican Party represented the wealthier, propertied class. The Democratic Party seemed more concerned with the workers, farmers and common folk having a voice and a share in the abundance of the nation. We allied ourselves with the Democrats.

We supported Adlai Stephenson against Dwight Eisenhower. To us Stephenson represented a voice for world peace and domestic programs to help the less privileged. Eisenhower was a military man which, we thought, boded ill for world peace and he seemed to represent the haves rather than the have nots. Yet it was he who warned of the "military/industrial" complex. He put people to work creating the interstate highway system. It turned out he, like most of our military leaders, wanted peace, not war, although he wanted strength. Under his leadership "In God We Trust" became the national motto and the words "under God" were added to the pledge of allegiance to the flag.

In the next election cycle we were in Oak Ridge and campaigned for Adlai Stephenson and Estes Kefauver against Eisenhower and Nixon. The tone of campaigns appeared to us to turn during that time from being "for" a candidate and platform, to being "against" the other side. This negative campaigning has persisted ever since, driven in part by the media, to the detriment of the process and an increasing loss of civility. We were happy when John F. Kennedy was elected four years later and pleased to hear him challenge, "My fellow Americans, ask not what your country can do for you, ask what you can do for your country." Lyndon Johnson followed, after JFK's assassination and significant legislative strides were made in civil rights. After the Nixon years ending in scandal we felt fortunate that Gerald Ford was a man of good will and integrity who saw the country through trying times.

My colleague at SREB, Mike Hart, had gone to work for Jimmy Carter, who was governor of Georgia so we got to meet and appreciate him. As a result we were invited to and attended his inauguration in 1977. By this time we were in Berea. He was the last Democratic candidate we actively supported although we continued to participate as Democrats in the election process until we felt the party had gone too far with its identity politics, pitting one group against another – black versus white, poor versus rich, labor versus management, women versus men, people versus police, secularists versus Christians. Their leaders were among the wealthy and "propertied class." They began to represent an "educational elite" who thought they knew what was best for everyone, expressing the same kind of arrogance we had objected to in the earlier Republican Party. Meanwhile the Republicans had broadened their base and represented the values we still held dear – self –reliance, freedom of expression, and enterprise, religious freedom and the Judeo/Christion values on which the country was founded. They seemed to have more concern for fiscal responsibility and less governmental intrusion into the lives of people.

We still like to think of ourselves as independent of party lines but now identify more closely to the platforms of the Republicans than the Democrats. We say that we didn't leave the Democratic Party but the party left us as it abandoned tried and true values, albeit in the name of equality and freedom. Equality and freedom are achieved because of those values and substituting "politically correct" values will eventually destroy the freedoms they pretend to promise. Some Democrat leaders seem to envision, in their arrogance, a version of big government that will control our lives – even limiting our freedom of speech and religious expression.

Ultimately the fate of our country will depend, not on political parties or government, but on the character of its people and its leaders. Lately leaders of high character seem to be missing or do not command the news.

Leadership makes a difference. It can call on fears, prejudice, selfishness and hatreds or can inspire hope, charity, civility and love of country and each other. We all have the potential for responding to either call. Our churches, our educational institutions, other organizations and government should be helping us as a people to seek God's will and obey his commands. If we don't we will suffer the consequences, individually and as a society. If we, like Adam and Eve, decide to gorge ourselves on the forbidden fruit of selfish desires and passions, deciding for ourselves what is true, what is good and what is evil, we will be lost. What arrogance to ignore centuries of civilization, inspired revelation and created order and think we can rewrite history, creation and morality. So, Democrat or Republican or Other, each of us will worship some god or gods. What will they be?

# PART EIGHT

*Edisto Beach*

*1995-2006*

# CHAPTER 28

# EDISTO YEARS I

*: Oh, what is abroad in the marsh and the terminal sea?*
*Somehow my soul seems suddenly free*
*From the weighing of fate and the sad discussion of sin.*
*By the length and the breadth and the sweep*
*Of the Marshes of Glynn.*

*Ye marshes, how candid and simple*
*And nothing-withholding and free;*
*Ye publish yourselves to the sky*
*And offer yourselves to the sea!*

(from *The Marshes of Glynn,* by Sidney Lanier)

*"My soul seems suddenly free"* expresses the feeling that comes with the crossing of the high McKinley Washington bridge from the mainland in Colleton County, South Carolina to Edisto Island. One can see the wide inland waterway flowing to the South Edisto River on its way to St Helena Sound and Atlantic Ocean. Beyond the waters lie the almost limitless expanses of marsh and low land underneath the open sky. One can smell the mixture of salt sea air and marsh gases and feel the vibrant life that grows and thrives there. One might see an osprey or an eagle soaring in the sky or gulls hovering over the water and egrets and herons standing in the marsh. Edisto Island!

## Edisto Island

*I never lost the special thrill of reaching the coast and the ocean. Bill would quote aloud the words from Sydney Lanier's poem as we crossed the bridge. The old drawbridge had been replaced by a new bridge, high enough for masted ships to pass under, so one can see for miles. Edisto Beach is still twelve miles further on but those go by quickly. We finally reached the ocean front by a causeway across a marsh where there might be water on each side depending on the tides. Then the road reaches the end of the land with only sand dunes between us and the waves breaking on the beach.*

*Turning right on Jungle Road, one block from Palmetto Boulevard at the beachfront, one drives past beach houses, with glimpses of the ocean to the left and marshes to the right and arrives at the entrance to Fairfield Ocean Ridge resort where Bill and Rose had built their house.*

*Our lot, on which the house was built, bordered the tennis courts. We had checked to be sure they were not lighted for night playing. It was hard to tell how many trees there were on the lot because of the vines, mostly poison ivy, that had luxuriantly engulfed trees and shrubs, but we could tell that there were palmettos and live oaks. Myrtle bushes, as big as trees, bordered the brackish lagoon at the back of the lot. The house was on pilings as required for flood protection, so we could park underneath and there was a large enclosed area for storage or activities. Up the stairs, which were deliberately built wide with a low pitch to each step, was a balcony and the door to the kitchen. The interior plan was what was called the "shotgun model." Kitchen, dining room and living room were in a row as one big room unbroken except for the counter between kitchen and dining area. Double French doors led from the living area to a sun porch beyond. On either side were two bedrooms with a bath in between. One of the bedrooms served as a study while the other on that side was our master bedroom. The other side had two guest rooms and the washer and dryer in the hallway. There was no wasted space. It was very convenient.*

Over the first months Bill worked on clearing the lot, often with the help of a young black man, Romano. Some of the vines were so thick they had to use a truck to pull them out of the trees. They wore long sleeves, hats and gloves to avoid getting poison ivy and washed thoroughly after each session. Only once did Bill get blisters. A particularly stubborn vine was resisting his pull but suddenly it came free and whipped him across the cheek and ear making a small gash. It took about a week for the blisters to weep themselves out.

*Once we were cutting brush in front of the house and Romano squealed, "There's a snake!" It had slithered under the pile of brush we had accumulated so I took a rake and carefully removed the branches one at a time, while Romano stayed well away. When I had removed the last branch, there was a copperhead coiled up by the trunk of a palmetto. I quickly brought the back of the rake down on its neck and killed it. When I lifted the dead snake dangling on the rake Romano came forward as proud as if he had won the battle all alone.*

By the end they had taken 17 truckloads of ivy to the recycling area where there was a bin for branches and vines. Now they could sit on the back deck and see the trees and the lagoon. They soon had birdfeeders set up and saw some lovely song birds. The beautiful and well named painted bunting was a favorite. Red bellied woodpeckers would come to the back deck where they had set a humming bird feeder on the railings. They drank the nectar with their long beaks and fussed if it ran out. Sometimes blackbirds came and chased the other birds away so Bill got a BB gun.

*Once I actually hit a blackbird and it fell dead to the ground. I picked it up and tossed it into the lagoon. Before long I saw the resident alligator glide over and gulp down the blackbird. Later I threw another blackbird in and the alligator was there almost before it hit the water. The gator had never before come up in our yard but now it did and I decided it was not a good idea to provide it any food. Once when Edie Weatherford Hunt and her family were visiting they discovered a bunch of little alligators across the lagoon by a culvert. Mama alligator had another batch later. We had an unspoken pact. We had great respect for her and didn't bother her and she didn't bother us, but we were careful not to tempt her with any potential food and warned friends with dogs about alligators' special appetite for them.*

Bill and Rose, and company if present, would go up the road to a larger lagoon where one could watch the egrets and herons fly in to an island to roost in the evenings. They are so light and graceful. After about a year the birds began to roost behind Bill and Rose's house and continued to do so for the rest of their stay. It was a special blessing to watch 100 to 200 white egrets and a few green and blue herons glide in to the myrtles every night at dusk. Usually the smaller ones arrived first trying to get a good spot but when the larger birds swooped in they chased the smaller ones to lower branches commandeering the higher perches for themselves. This was done with a lot of squawking and raised feathers on the heads, but finally all the birds settled in and were peaceful until they silently flew off at sunrise. Rose loved the birds. She loved the Spanish moss on the live oaks, the rustling of the palms and the beach itself. Bill had a running battle with squirrels which raided the bird feeders. He tried all sorts of devices over many months to prevent this – squirrel proof bird feeders, greased poles, suspended feeders, baffles on poles – but nothing daunted the greedy rodents for very long and he finally surrendered unconditionally and just provided more feed.

*Our house was about a half mile from the ocean so we were sheltered from the sea wind and salty air, but still had the breeze and we could hear the waves in the distance. I had never dreamed that we would live in a place where we could walk to the ocean. It was a long way from my childhood farm in east Tennessee. I loved to walk on the shore, to have the waves push the water over my bare feet and to hear the crash of breakers, sometimes soft and sometimes loud, depending on the weather. I found that, now that I was older, I could walk less easily than I used to on the soft sand and got tired more quickly. The hot sun, which I used to soak up with pleasure, sometimes made me feel breathless, but I never tired of watching the ocean and smelling the salt air. Sometimes we would drive to Edingsville beach, which was more remote with few people around, and find wonderful shells, including sand dollars, olive shells and conchs.*

Edingsville beach was the location of the older beach settlement that had been demolished in a hurricane around 1900. One still found an occasional piece of beach glass from china ware and glass ware that had been in houses destroyed by the storm and worn smooth by the action of wave and sand. The town of Edisto Beach developed after that storm so was relatively new. Its beaches are not as wide and sloping as some and are broken up by rock jetties at almost every block, but the beach is accessible from the end of every cross street. Around the southern end of the beach is St Helena Sound and there the waves are calmer, the beach wider and jetties are few so it is a great place for younger children. There are no high-rises and no hotels. Houses are mostly modest in size and construction. It is a family friendly place without the tourist atmosphere found at many beaches. Most the beach house owners were from Walterboro or one of the other towns not far away and a good many residents make Edisto Beach their year round home. The rest of the island is still quite agricultural with a few lovely old plantations from the days when cotton was king. Edisto long staple cotton had been highly prized and it was reported that much of it was presold to French clothiers before it was even picked. Marsh mud, rich in nitrogen, was used as fertilizer. After the Civil War and the boll weevil destroyed cotton as a viable crop, island farmers began to grow peppers, cucumbers and tomatoes. Way back, before the American Revolution and cotton, the island and area was a source of indigo and tea, mostly for British consumption.

A new house was built one lot beyond Bill and Rose's house and they got to know Bob and Beth Foster, who became their closest neighbors. They shared a love of watching the egrets come in at night to roost in the myrtles on the lagoon. Bill and Rose were able to purchase the lot between the two houses when the owners gave it back to Fairfield to sell. They got it at a fair price, ending up with a combined area of almost an acre in the resort. When they left Edisto in 2006, the Fosters purchased both their house and the extra lot, planning to sell the house and keep the lot next to theirs. The land had increased dramatically in value so Bill and Rose left Edisto with the ability to buy some land in Kentucky. Meanwhile, not thinking about the future, they simply enjoyed Edisto.

*We became friends with residents who had connections with the tomato plantations and were invited to pick tomatoes after the migrant workers had gone through and picked the ones just right for shipping. What they left were fully ripe and plentiful so we had wonderful tomatoes for eating and canning. Tommy and Ann Nease became very close friends and shared their bountiful pecans, and, better yet, the wonderful pecan treats that Tommy, a chef, had made. Tommy also collected crabs in a trap in a tidal creek by their house. He boiled the crabs and we stood around an outside table, broke open the claws and picked out the tasty meat. In addition, their display of azaleas was breathtaking. Their place became a regular stop on tours with any guests we had.*

## Edisto Island United Methodist Church

Bill and Rose had met Tommy and Ann Nease at the Edisto Island United Methodist Church and the Edisto Historical Preservation Society, both of which they visited and then joined. Tommy and Ann invited them to visit their home and see their azaleas and pecan trees. They lived on a beautiful piece of land bordering one of the inland tidal creeks. Visits to the Neases became a part of showing family members and visitors around Edisto. Tommy and Ann were always welcoming and gracious hosts, sharing their gorgeous azaleas and offering tasty treats made from their bountiful pecans. Tommy was a mild looking man with pale blue eyes and a peaceful face. He had worked in food service in the army in World War II and continued that trade in civilian life at colleges and other institutions. He was a great chef. Ann left the cooking to him. She had been a nurse and still had a wonderful caring nature. She was a petite, neat, smiling, grandmotherly lady, and the chief greeter at the church. Tommy often served as the acolyte, always with humble reverence. They were totally devoted to each other and had been so since their marriage some sixty years earlier. They never seemed tired of helping and sharing. For Tommy's 80th birthday, Bill wrote a little verse titled "The Energizer Bunny" about Tommy and gave it to him with a battery powered energizer bunny with its drum. Ann framed the poem and displayed the bunny with it on a shelf. Ten years later, after they had moved to Savannah, Ann asked Bill to write a sequel for Tommy's 90th birthday. This was done. Visits to Tommy and Ann continued years after they had had moved from Edisto. Sometimes Bill and Rose were accompanied by grandchildren. Ann knew each of the 22 Ramsay grandchildren by name. Tommy died after his 90th birthday, and Ann soon after. They were wonderful friends.

Bill and Rose learned that Edisto was named for the Edisto Indians who once lived there and gave their name to the Edisto River and Edisto Island. They had attended the Edisto Beach Baptist Church conveniently located near the beach front on earlier visits and intended to visit other churches as well, but they were invited to the Methodist Church by Marie and George Johnson, who also lived in Fairfield, and were welcomed so warmly that they just stayed. It was a new "mission church" supported by the denomination with supply ministers. The early ministers were Reverend Anderson and Reverend Jones, retired from a church in Walterboro which had helped get the Edisto church started. Both were fine pastors and preachers. Reverend Jones, by his own admission, couldn't carry a tune. Fortunately a talented pianist/organist and song leader supplied the need for a time. After attending a short while Tommy Nease asked Bill was to be chair of the administrative council. He tried to decline on the basis of his newness but everyone was new and they really needed someone with Methodist church experience. Tommy assured him that there were no issues and the job would be undemanding. Bill was experienced enough to know better than that but he agreed to serve. Before he had even taken office a controversy arose. Members who were residents wanted to become a full, self-supporting church while others, who lived on Edisto only part of the year and retained membership in their churches back home, wanted to remain a mission church. After a heated discussion at a church meeting someone made a motion and called for a vote. It was obvious that the church was split and emotions were high. A period of calm and study seemed more productive than a vote under the circumstances so Bill's role was thrust on to him a bit prematurely.

*I realized that a vote then would only accomplish a division and that the process of becoming a full church in the Methodist connectional system was not as simple as some seemed to think. So I suggested that the motion be tabled and the matter referred to a committee who would investigate the benefits and responsibilities of the alternatives and the process required to move ahead and then report back to the congregation. Everyone was relieved to avoid the impending confrontation and the motion to table and refer passed unanimously. Of course the idea that the task would be "undemanding" went out the non-stained glass windows.*

In due course information was gathered, contact made with district authorities, projections for potential growth prepared, a financial plan and budget constructed and a recommendation that the church be chartered was presented and passed. A few left the church, including the pianist and song leader. Rose remembers what happened to the church music.

*On a Sunday following the music leader's departure, Reverend Jones asked if anyone in the congregation played the piano. No one responded. He asked if anyone could lead the singing of the hymn, referring to his own limitations in this regard. Again no one responded. He told people to turn to the page number for the selected hymn and said, "We'll just read it together." That was too much for Patsy Cannon who had been a church organist and choir director but had vowed in retirement that she was not going to volunteer to do that again. Her husband, David, sitting next to her in the pew had been nudging her and she finally gave in. She went on to provide wonderful music for the church for many years as other talented singers and musicians joined her, so the church was never again without glorious music.*

## "Cair Paravel" and Hospitality

Granddaughters Catherine and Melissa had helped us move our household goods in when we made the final move in the March of 1995 and they were immediately anxious to go to the beach and to explore the area. Martin and Charlie with their boys had already made a visit and soon the other families and friends were visiting. Edisto became a very special place for family and friends as well as for Bill and Rose.

*We asked the grandchildren what we should name the house and they quickly agreed to call it "Cair Paravel." All of us had read, or heard read, the Narnia books written by C. S. Lewis and knew that Cair Paravel was the castle by the sea. It was not lost on the children, or on us, that this was where the children were kings and queens. So we made a sign and hung it at the entrance. It was fun to watch visitors notice the sign. You could always tell which children were familiar with the Narnia books because they would nudge their parents and their eyes would light up. At a reunion in 1996, Alfredo designed and printed t-shirts for everyone with a picture of the house looking like a castle and the name "Cair Paravel" proudly displayed. Each family at the reunion had rented a house but we had a big meal together and managed to feed 34 at Cair Paravel. For another meal, we had all the grandchildren while the parents went out on the town.*

The first year, 1995, saw visits from all of the children and their growing families along with Bill's brother John and wife, Berni. Cousin Ben Martin and his wife Bonnie and their two girls from nearby Summerville visited. English cousins, Dick and Shelagh Connor spent treasured time with Bill and Rose. Bente Boisen and Henning came from Denmark and took beautiful pictures of sunsets over St Helena Sound. Hans and Karen Rosgaard, another Danish couple who had stayed at the Big House in Berea, came for a visit. Al and Sandy Osborne, with whom Bill and Rose shared grandchildren and who became their frequent traveling companions, came to see them in their new environment. Former students who had become friends visited, including Don and Becky Rucker and Lynn and Robert Anderson with their small children, and singles Dan Sides and Jerry Houck.

The second year was a continuation of the first in terms of visitors. In addition to the family reunion and other family visits in 1996, Bill and Rose had visits from Sybil and Bill Nestor who had shared the work on childbirth education in Oak Ridge and Merle Ryan, a close friend from Boston who had shared NSEA experiences. Anne and Willis Weatherford visited and then their daughter Edie and her husband Mick with their young children. John and Marian Clarke, a cousin from Pittsburg stayed for a time as did Grace Price, one of Bill's closest cousins also from Pennsylvania. In the following years countless family members and friends visited and enjoyed the beach front, the sound, the sand, the waves and the many sights on Edisto and in the Charleston area.

*Not everyone lodged in our house, although many did, and we soon became proficient tour guides of Edisto and of the Charleston area. The oceanfront beach and sound were favorite places, but also the marshes with egrets and herons and sometimes an alligator were interesting. Also the plantations, tomato fields, majestic live oaks, azaleas and wisteria in season, were lovely to see. We would visit the Neases' beautiful place and look at some of the historic churches on the island. Going farther afield we'd go to the battery at Charleston Harbor with its wonderful old houses overlooking the harbor where one can view Fort Sumter at the harbor entrance. We'd stop at the old slave market and admire the sweet-grass baskets woven by local people. Sometimes we'd visit historic plantations in the area or go to the naval museum, including an aircraft carrier, destroyer and submarine, at Mount Pleasant and we'd tour Fort Moultrie on Sullivan's Island. We discovered Angel Oak, about 1500 years old, where John's Island meets Wadmalaw Island across the North Edisto River from Edisto. Eating seafood at Gilligans Restaurant became a family tradition, with an immediate serving of delicious hot hush puppies. The "low country" area is fascinating with its beauty, special foods, geography and history and we loved being part of it.*

Probably the most unusual visit was one from George and Elizabeth Deuillet from Dallas, Texas in 1999. Liz was one of the Sanborne children. Rev. Leon Sanborne had married them in Berea in 1952 and Liz was like a younger sister.

*We had kept up with Sandy and Marion, the two older children, Cathy and Liz, pretty regularly and with Nancy and David to a lesser extent. Liz had married George Deuillet and had two boys who were now grown. George had been raised on Long Island, NY, and he and Liz were seasoned sailors with a large sailboat. They had decided to visit us by sea and left Texas from the Houston area in their sailboat. They sailed across the Gulf of Mexico, around the Florida Keys and up the east coast to the inland waterways leading up to Edisto Island where they docked at the marina, about a half mile from our house. We had great visits both at Cair Paravel and on their beautiful boat. We had guests come to see us by land and air but never before or after by sea.*

As soon as they were moved in they began to get to know their neighbors and other residents of the Fairfield resort. Not surprisingly Rose became a part of the committee that arranged social gatherings for residents and soon they began their traditional open houses now at *Cair Paravel*, especially at holiday times, for new friends from church and community and any family or friends who happened to be visiting. Bill would usually make his refreshing punch and they would serve an array of goodies as they had in Oak Ridge and Berea during their years in those places. They continued their "no alcohol" policy. Bill remembers one incident in this regard.

*At one party a resident came who had a reputation as something of a character and a drinker. As people gathered and began to visit the table and punch bowl, he sidled up to me winking and asked where we had "the good stuff." I cheerfully told him we didn't serve alcoholic beverages but had a very good punch. He first looked incredulous, then like he might cry and then agreed to try the punch. After the first cup he said in amazement, "This is pretty good!" He had a second cup and didn't get far from the punch bowl all evening. He had a great time at the party without being in an alcohol induced fog – and no hangover!*

As if they didn't have enough company Bill and Rose joined a Christian bed and breakfast exchange club, later called "Wayside." They expected to use it on the travels they planned. They did use it over the next ten years and stayed with seven families in the program in various states. But being at the beach, the number of visitors to Edisto greatly outnumbered their own Wayside visits. They enjoyed a total of 36 visits to *Cair Paravel* by Wayside friends. They added another 21 Wayside visits after they had returned to Berea until they exited the program in 2012.

*The idea of sharing hospitality appealed to us and the exchange was sponsored by a Christian senior citizens association that was offering an alternative to AARP, to which we had belonged for years. We felt that AARP had become too much a self-serving interest group and lobby rather than an association for fellowship, sharing and service and the exchange program was an attractive manifestation of that approach. We met wonderful people who visited us or whom we visited. Staying in a home in most cases seemed preferable to a motel. Our first Wayside visit was in 1997 from Bob and Chris Anderson who lived in the Chicago area. Bob had helped set up the Wayside exchange and noted our listing on the South Carolina coast. He realized that he had not actually joined Wayside so he quickly remedied that and made the reservation. It was one of the first visits made under the program. We became good friends. They visited several more times at Edisto and later at Berea. They also hosted*

*Jennifer when she had a singing engagement in their area. Several other guests became family friends and came more than once and we visited them at their homes and exchanged Christmas cards every year. Having Wayside visitors made our home even busier than it was with family and friends but it added a dimension to our ever enlarging circle of Christian fellowship and enriched our lives.*

On one of the trips using a Wayside host, Bill and Rose drove to the northwest corner of South Carolina where Clemson is located, not far from the border with Georgia beyond which lies Toccoa Falls. They visited the Old Stone Church in Clemson and discovered a Ramsay section of the graveyard. They stayed in Salem with Stu and Pat Wright and discovered, near the Georgia border, the Ramsay Farm Road. They introduced themselves to Helen Ramsay who lived in an old family house there and told them stories of her deceased husband's family going back to early days. That Ramsay family held reunions at the historic Tougaloo Presbyterian Church and Bill and Rose were invited to join the group. Bill and Rose went on to visit Amber at Toccoa Falls College and the next year took Amber to the Ramsay reunion but never made a direct family connection; however, all went back to the same area of Scotland.

## Family Events

Bill and Rose were busy at Edisto but important family events were taking place that required trips to Kentucky. Jennifer and Alfredo Escobar were married on Bill's and Rose's 46th anniversary on September 7, 1996 at Union Church in Berea. A time share provided them a honeymoon at Abaco in the Bahamas. In November of that year Jim and Shawn, with their little family, left for their mission field in Kazakhstan. Bill and Rose saw them off at the Louisville airport.

*My brother Wayne had joined us for the occasion and we all said our goodbyes and watched as they started off on their adventure. I retain a clear picture of the little family heading to the gate. Each of them had a suitcase on wheels and they were pulling them in a line - first Jim with the boarding passes, then Rebekah followed by Keith and Jonathan striding along, and then little five year old Naomi, smiling as always. Shawn brought up the rear to be sure no one got lost. I prayed for each one and worried about their going to a foreign place. I received a sense of peace and the message that I should worry more about those grandchildren staying behind. Jim and Shawn and the children were in Karaganda, Kazakhstan for the next 10 years, although we saw them several times on trips to the USA and once on Denmark.*

Jim had put his house in Danville, Kentucky up for sale and asked Bill to follow up as needed. When the house sold they decided it would be good for Jim to have some real estate and that a beach house at Edisto would be a good investment and a place they could use in the future. They found a house for sale within a block of the ocean that the city owned and wanted to sell. They offered to buy it at a very reasonable price and the offer was accepted so Jim and family became owners of a beach house they named *"Chaika"* which is Russian for "seagull" and the name of a noted Russian hotel. Bill and Rose, with help from Edisto Realty when they were away, took care of the house and managed rentals.

## Florida Tours With Jennifer Rose

After a second period as a performer and activities person at Peaceful Valley Ranch in Colorado, Jennifer decided to make recording and performance her career. She began to sing in various venues and to produce recordings with the help of Bill Martin who had a recording studio near Winchester, KY. Ralph sometimes accompanied her in singing or on the guitar and for one recording Bill's old dorm mate, Homer Ledford, a wonderful musician and instrument maker, joined her. Jennifer had performed in Denmark while still a student and after she graduated she went back every year for a number of years on a singing tour. In the USA she found an annual tour in Florida in January-February was enjoyable and productive. She sang at retirement communities, churches, schools and community centers. In January 2000, Bill and Rose rented a time-share at Poinciana, FL which they shared with Jennifer and Alfredo as she did her tour. On subsequent years they continued this pattern and as Lydia and Isabel were added to the family, the annual Florida tour became a special way to spend some winter weeks with the two youngest grandchildren in the warmth of the

Sunshine State. In those early years of Jennifer's singing career Rose was the primary booking agent for *Jenifer Rose Music.*

*I made a lot of phone calls. I would call friends in Florida or contacts that Jennifer had to identify possible venues. Some of our Wayside visitors who had stayed with us at Edisto and other retired friends and family lived in retirement communities in Florida and would give me the names of places that might be interested in Jennifer's musical program. I'd follow up with calls, letters, and photos and publicity material.*

Jennifer had done special study of hymnody and could not only sing the old spirituals, camp meeting songs, shape note hymns and traditional church hymns beautifully, but could give history and context information. She could do the same with English ballads and Appalachian folk songs. She played and demonstrated the Appalachian lap dulcimer.

Once Jennifer had performed at a few places, with Alfredo manning the recording sales, and charming the people, the word got around among churches, schools and retirement center program directors and finding bookings became easier. Many places had her return annually for years. The family made enduring friends at the Villages and Plantations communities near Leesburg and other places. At the Villages former Edisto neighbors, Bud and Bonnie Dilman hosted them. Wilt and Marian Nelson at Plantations became like family. At Shell Point near Cape Coral, Ann and Al Parks adopted Jennifer and family and hosted them for many years. Churches at Davenport and Avon Park in central Florida had her back several times each. Some of her fans felt like grandparents as they watched Jennifer go through two pregnancies with the addition of two little girls to her family and her repertoire. Lydia and Isabel became seasoned performers as soon as they could walk and hold a microphone.

*Once on a repeat visit to a center in the Claremont area, little Lydia was singing a song with Jennifer standing in front of a fireplace in an assembly room when she suddenly stopped singing. Jennifer asked her what was the matter and Lydia pointed to the floor and said for all to hear, "There's a bug!" A script didn't have to be written for the girls to entertain an audience. The girls were not self-conscious about singing but were still little girls. I was carrying Lydia after a concert at Shell Point and a lady came over to compliment Lydia on her performance. Lydia hid her face in my shoulder and said, "I shy!" As soon as Isabel was ready to join them she really responded to the audience and sometimes didn't want to leave the stage when her number was over. Alfredo had to go get her. Of course the audience loved it.*

Rose and Bill would arrange a time-share or other rental in a central location to serve as a base from which to travel to performance sites. This became especially useful as Lydia and Isabel grew. Usually the base was in the Orlando, Kissimmee, or Haines City area. Sometimes they were at a resort with swimming pools, hot tubs and other amenities. Once they were on the same road as a petting zoo, which they all thoroughly enjoyed. Lydia especially liked to hold the chickens. And they were close to Sea World, Cyprus Gardens and the Disney complex.

*We always enjoyed the magic of Disney, the beauty at Cypress Gardens and the amazing creatures at Sea World. As Lydia and Isabel grew old enough to push on strollers through the attractions, a whole new dimension was added. What a wonder to see these things through the eyes of the children and to be able to share with them. The lovely lawns, shrubs and flowers of Cypress Gardens with the beautiful Southern Belles greeting us were enchanting and the water shows were exciting. In a fountain there was a statue which was really a live woman made to look like she was made of marble. She had water coming from her fingers as she moved in a slow motion dance making graceful water arches.*

*At Sea World we saw animal shows featuring trained cats, dogs, ducks, pigs and even a skunk and an eagle. Of course the big whale show was a favorite and the girls loved the penguins. They fed the seals with packets of fish you could buy. We sat and had an ice dream treat or ate sandwiches as we watched flamingos in their watery habitat.*

*Bill and I liked Epcot with its international themes and wonderful displays, but the girls, of course, preferred the Magic Kingdom. As they grew, Bill and I would stay at our vacation rental and Jennifer and Alfredo would take the girls. At about ages two and four they were into princesses and knew them all – Cinderella, Snow White, Sleeping Beauty, Belle from Beauty and the Beast and others. Lydia had a Cinderella dress and Isabel was Snow White. She called us from Disney where she had met and been befriended by the "real" Snow White. All she could say on the phone was to repeat over and over, "I saw Snow White! I saw Snow White!" It was truly a magic place.*

Bill and Rose had made contact with former classmates and cousins who had homes or vacation places in Florida and had many good times with them. Gwen and Hank Kulesa were especially close. Gwen had been one of the "Tab crowd" back at Berea and sang at their wedding in 1952. They enjoyed "unlimited" breakfasts at Perkins Restaurant with Marty and Bud King. They visited Bill's cousin, Marion Martin Kenner, in Sarasota and sometimes other cousins gathered there. They visited Marty and Julie Mariner (aunt Lydia's son and his wife) at Vilano Beach and, one year, enjoyed being with Aunt Grace's son, Fred Brandauer and his wife Marie, in their huge travel trailer. Rose's brother, Wayne, and his wife Carolyn began to spend winters in the Venice area and Bill and Rose, Jennifer and Alfredo and the girls often got together with them. They visited Rose's cousin Norma Jean and her husband Don Shell in Fort Myers and Bill's cousin Sarah Jane and Tommy Campbell in that area. Visits to Dick and Trilla Richardson in Lakeland gave them a chance to discuss shared grandchildren. Trilla is Shawn's (Jim's wife) mother. They also loved the succulent produce of Florida and became well known at one of the citrus orchards just west of Haines City. They ate plenty of oranges and grapefruit, drank fresh orange juice and took a load of produce with them when they left to have at home and to share.

*We had several favorite citrus places. One was best for oranges, grapefruit, juice and honey. Another had the best deals for buying in bulk to take home. Another was a favorite of the girls because it served orange ice cream that was so tasty and cold. But we also discovered the strawberry farms and indulged heavily in the luscious fruit. Sometimes we saw migrant workers in the fields, backs bent, picking the bountiful strawberries. What wonderful treats God has provided for his creatures. We used to be able to climb the Citrus Tower and see orange groves in every direction and we were saddened by the replacement of large orange groves in the Citrus Valley by enormous developments. Some years before a major freeze had wiped out many groves in that area and the land was more valuable for development than for orchards, but further south there are still acres of productive lands. We appreciate the people who tend them.*

Florida, with its retirement communities and tourism, is an interesting place. One must be careful with driving. Between the elderly who tend to drive slowly, the tourists, who don't know where they are, the workers who dart around going to work or making deliveries and the locals, doing their shopping and picking up children, there can be traffic problems. But the people are from all over and add to a fascinating mix of faces, cultures and backgrounds. Bill and Rose met some delightful folks.

*Jennifer sang several times at Penney Farms in north Florida, not far from Gainesville, and we went with her. We were interested in looking at retirement communities and were quite taken with this one. Several former Berea staff members had retired there and the director had a Berea connection. Like Berea, Penney Farms had a work ethic and all residents who could were expected to make some contribution to the community, whether it was volunteering in an office, visiting the incapacitated, helping with landscaping or whatever. Most residents were former pastors or missionaries. The community had been established some 70 years earlier by J. C. Penney, whose father was a minister. It was especially for church workers who in those days did not usually have strong retirement programs. Now it is open to all but still retains a mission spirit.*

*One of the staff members was showing us around and stopped before a door in the assisted living building and said, "This is probably our most famous resident, but most people don't recognize the name." The name on the door was "Meinhardt Raabe." We had no clue who he was, but just then this very small elderly gentleman rode up on a bicycle and we were introduced. He was one of the "little people" who had been tapped to play the Munchkins in The Wizard of Oz. In fact he was the Munchkin coroner who declared that the wicked witch was "really, truly dead" after Dorothy's house had landed on her. What fun to meet him! He told us about his experiences and also that his wife had for years been the bell boy with the pill box hat for the Phillip Morris advertisement who used to holler, "Call for Phillip Morr e e s!" We considered going to Penney Farms when we were ready to leave Edisto and we made a deposit to get on their list, but ultimately decided we would move back to Berea.*

*The years of the Florida tours were full and satisfying and a wonderful chance to continue our close friendship with Harley and Frances Patterson, be part of Jennifer's singing career and share in Lydia's and Isabel's early lives. Of course, we were always glad to get back to Cair Paravel.*

## They Grow Up

The Edisto years spanned a time of great changes in the children and grandchildren. Elizabeth graduated from high school in 1996 and that fall entered Berry College in Rome Georgia which gave Bill and Rose added incentives to visit the Heneisen's there. She finished college in 2000 and worked for a while at Brevard College where she met Ryan Sartor. Their wedding was in November 2001 at Montreat in the beautiful mountains of North Carolina. Bill's and Rose's first grandchild was now grown and married! Amber graduated from "home school" in an inspiring ceremony in Danville, Illinois, which they attended, in 1997. She went on to Toccoa Falls College in the mountains of north Georgia. They visited her there a number of times. Catherine finished high school and entered Charleston Southern University in 1999 and had four wonderful years close enough to Cair Paravel to visit weekly with her roommates over the years - Megan, Amy and Joy - and with other friends either at Edisto or in Charleston. Bill and Rose especially enjoyed meals together with Catherine and friends at Arby's or Fazoli's or the Chinese restaurant across from Citadel Mall. After four years of classes in Charleston, Catherine went to West Palm Beach, in 2003, to complete her required internship in music therapy at a Hospice facility. She graduated from Charleston Southern at the end of the year. She had met Chris Nielsen, from Jupiter, FL, during her internship in West Palm Beach and was married there in 2005.

In 2001 Brian and Benjamin entered Taylor University near Marion, Indiana and Melissa went to Flagler College in St Augustine, Florida. Bill and Rose had lovely visits to that early American (Spanish) town to see

Melissa and the historic sites and to visit Reverend Harley and Francis Patterson in Jacksonville. In the next few years Andrew, Colleen, and Adrienne all followed Brian and Benjamin to Taylor, so more visits were made there. They went to Brian's and Benjamin's graduation in 2005. Daniel had his college years at Berry College giving continuing reasons to visit Rome, Georgia. Rebekah enrolled in Houghton College, not far from Buffalo, New York and Bill and Rose were able to visit her a couple times. Once, in 2004, they stopped at Houghton on a trip through Wooster to see John and Eileen and on to meetings in Boston.

## CHAPTER 29

# WIDER TRAVEL

Bill and Rose had chosen to build in the Fairfield Ocean Ridge resort partly because they planned to do some wider traveling in their retirement years. They were not golfers even though they lived on Fairway Drive next to the golf course. The house in the resort would be secure when they were away and they always left their itinerary with the security office, as well as with family members. After the first year of getting established they were ready to travel beyond the Florida tours with Jennifer and Alfredo and many trips back to Kentucky, Ohio, Tennessee and Indiana visiting family and Pine Mountain. They planned an ambitious trip to Denmark and then to England, where they would be joined by the two oldest grandchildren, and go on to Scotland.

## Denmark and Great Britain

*The trip to Denmark, England and Scotland, from April 27 to June 13, 1996, was really two major excursions and a fulfillment of the dreams we had of travel in retirement from our Edisto base. Jennifer was already on a singing tour in Denmark and we would join her. Loren and Inge-Lise, who live in Denmark, were leaders of a folk festival in Silkeborg to be held in May and had arranged for a family get-together and performance at the festival to include Jennifer and us along with John and Berni, Patty and Earl, Fred, Susan and her daughter Andrea. In addition, I arranged two time-share weeks in England and Scotland and visits to English cousins. Granddaughters Elizabeth (just finishing high school) and Amber (in her last year of home school) were to join us for the England and Scotland visits.*

They started by driving to La Plata, MD, just across the Potomac River from Northern Virginia, where Rose's cousin Freda and her husband Richard Logsden welcomed them, kept their car and provided transportation to the airport, after a pleasant visit with them and their children for a couple days. They flew to Paris from Dulles airport. They had to make a hurried transfer to the flight to Copenhagen so saw nothing of France except from the air.

*It had been 23 years since Rose and I first saw Denmark when we took the teen group to begin the Danish American exchange and over the intervening years we had countless Danish youth and leaders at our Berea house – some for a meal, some for lodging and a few for longer stays. Some of the young people were now married and had families. When Jim, Bill Todt and then Jennifer spent time in Denmark and my brother, John, took other groups over, relationships were deepened and new friendships were made, so we felt like we had a bunch of Danish brothers, sisters, nieces and nephews and grandchildren. They had taken good care of us on our trip in 1991 to help Jennifer set up her term abroad, and they welcomed us with open arms on this trip five years later.*

## Arriving In Copenhagen

Rose remembers arriving at the Copenhagen airport, tired but happy to be back in this beautiful country.

*As we went through customs we saw two familiar smiling faces on the other side of the glass windows in the area. Bente Boisen and Henning Jensen had come to meet us. Bente had stayed with us in Berea for some months before Jennifer's term abroad and taught her to speak Danish. They were like sisters and she was like a daughter to us. Henning was a welcome addition to the family. They took us to their apartment where we rested comfortably for our time in Copenhagen and they took us to see the sights, their places of work and the wonderful Danish bakeries. What a special time we had with them.*

Bente and Henning drove them south to Nykobing, Falster, for a very pleasant visit and dinner with another Bente who had lived with us for a time in the big house. Bente Nielsen had attended Berea College, been a

391

country dancer and married Wayne Mabe, a fellow dancer and classmate from West Virginia. They had two boys in their family. Rose ad Bill enjoyed getting caught up with Bente and Wayne and meeting the older son, Malik, and holding baby Simon.

## **To Fynn and Jutland**

Jennifer was on the island of Fynn staying with Herdis and Erik Damkier. Herdis is the sister of Jennifer's good friend and host Birgit Hansen from Vejle. Jennifer had been loaned a car by Karen Busk Sorensen so she met Bill and Rose at Nyborg, which they reached by train and ferry from Copenhagen. They all had a very good visit with the Damkier family in their old farmhouse with a thatched roof in a beautiful area near Ringe. Then, on May 2, they drove to Amitsbol, near Vejle, on Jutland to the home of Margit Iversen, who had hosted them on their previous trip. Rose's journal reports:

*It was a delight to see Margit and her daughter Ase and her four charming daughters. While there we attended the confirmation of Birgit and Paul Erik Hansen's daughter, Meline. It was a lovely, very Danish service, followed by dinner and fun. Lots of friends and relatives made toasts to Meline, read poems written to her, gave gifts and speeches and shared delicious food. An accordion group arrived as a surprise for Meline. Birgit and her family and Jennifer had traveled to Austria with the group in the summer of 1994. The group did not know that Jennifer was present until she began singing with one of their numbers. It was a joyous reunion. The Danes know how to have a fun party ending with a traditional soup in the late evening at Birgit's home.*

The family visited other friends in the Vejle area and then traveled north to the home of Ole and Ingelis Sorensen in Jebjerg where they spent a few days. Ole and Ingelis and their two sons had cared for Jennifer like a daughter on previous trips and had arranged for a concert at their church. The organ was at the back of the beautiful, very old, vaulted sanctuary. Ole played a moving Bach fugue on his flugelhorn from the back and then Jennifer, unseen, sang *Ave Maria*.

*With the wonderful acoustics in that simple, solid, ancient setting one felt a connection to centuries of Christian worshipers. Then Jennifer came to the front and performed Appalachian ballads and other songs in English and Danish. The churches in Denmark are important for ceremonies and concerts. They are supported by the state and serve as community centers, but few Danes now attend regular Sunday services. Perhaps this dates back to Harold Blue Tooth, who when king declared Denmark to be Christian, so Danes became Christians by royal decree rather than by individual choice. But the Danes are very proud of their churches. Jennifer did most of her performances in the churches and always received a very warm and appreciative response.*

While Jennifer attended another confirmation of a friend, Ole and Ingelis took Rose and Bill on a tour of the area and an outdoor museum in the fields of heather not far from the North Sea. It was bitterly cold and the windmills were whirling madly. They all went shopping in Skive and Rose bought a pretty Danish dress. Bill and Rose drove by themselves to visit Ella Bidstrup at the Himmerlands school where they had taken the first teen exchange group 23 years earlier. They had a great time with Ella and visited Christian and Inge Holdrup who had been, as teens, on one of the first exchange groups to come to Berea in the 1970's.

## The Silkeborg Festival

Jennifer had concerts in the Vejle area and all went well. They did more sightseeing, including Legoland, and visited friends, always enjoying the wonderful Danish breads, cheeses and desserts. Bill thought of writing a journal entitled, "Eating our way through Denmark." Then they traveled to Rodkersbro where Hans and Karen Rosgaard lived. The Rosgaard family had lived with Bill and Rose in Berea for a time on an extended stay in Berea. They provided an apartment for the Ramsays while attending the nearby Silkeborg Festival. Jennifer stayed in Silkeborg and other family members had gathered there as planned by Loren and Inge-Lise. John had written a little play including dances portraying a sampling of life in Appalachia. Patty and Earl, John and Berni, Susan and daughter Andrea, Fred, Bill and Jennifer and friends performed for the festival and had a great time. Bente Mabe had come with her boys and Rose got to hold Simon again while Bente danced. Their journal reports a side trip.

*During the festival, on Sunday, we took a trip to Bugtrop to the farm of Bente Boisen's parents. Fred and Jennifer came too and Bente and Henning joined us for a beautiful tour of the farm, great eating and fellowship. Mrs. Boisen served five desserts, including two "lager" cakes. Yum!*

## Farewell Denmark – Hello England

When it was time to leave Denmark for England there were many goodbyes and promises to visit on both sides of the Atlantic. Those promises were kept. While at Edisto Bill and Rose enjoyed visits from both Bente's and their families, the Sorensens, Margit Iversen, Henning and Bodil Moeller Andersen (leaders in the Danish folk organization they had visited in Vejle), the Rosgaards and other Danish friends. Jennifer continued her Danish singing tours annually for many years and Bill and Rose returned once with three grandchildren. As the Danish part of their 1996 trip ended, Rose remembers the trip across the North Sea on Wednesday, May 15.

*We left Denmark on the overnight ferry from Esbjerg to Harwich, England. We had a little stateroom on one of the lower floors towards the front of the ship. The crossing was somewhat rough once we left protected waters and I felt a little uncomfortable. Being in the front of the ship, our cabin swayed with the rolls of the ship. Bill suggested I imagine I was in a hammock and go to sleep. This was so successful that I slept from 8:00 PM to 8:00 AM. In the morning, feeling better and able to see the horizon from the deck, we had a pleasant breakfast on the ferry.*

Dick Connor met them at the dock at Harwich and drove them, in the same Volkswagen bus they had used before, to his home in Bedford where Shelagh was waiting for them. It was so great to be with these dear English cousins again. On Saturday, Dick went with Bill by train to the airport at Luton to pick up a rental car. It was a dark green, sporty Daewoo sedan with a sun roof and very pleasant to drive once one got used to driving on the "wrong" side of the road.

*We left Bedford about noon with Bill driving and Rose praying and saying, "Think left," and helping watch for cars at the "roundabouts." We drove to Exton near Oakham, through lovely little villages and countryside to Barnsdale Country Club where we had a time-share week. Our unit in the Mews was on a hill overlooking rolling fields and a lake called the Rutland Water. Sunday Elaine Ford Cole came to visit with little Roseanna and we had a nice lunch and visit at the club restaurant.*

## Elizabeth and Amber Arrive

On Wednesday they were to meet granddaughters Elizabeth and Amber at Heathrow Airport so they did a practice drive on Monday to be sure they knew the way, the exits, parking places and where to be to meet the girls.

*Bill was doing better with driving and even occasionally passed a truck. I held my breath! On Tuesday we drove to Oakham to visit another of Bill's cousins, Rosemary Outram, whom Dick Connor had arranged for us to meet. Her grandmother and Bill's maternal grandmother and Dick Connor's mother were sisters, all daughters of Bishop Benjamin and Maria Wolle Romig. Rosemary shared pictures and memories from these ancestors, including a beautifully penned and illustrated account by Bill's grandmother, Elizabeth, of her sister's wedding. Later Rosemary sent the journal to granddaughter Elizabeth Compton, who was named for her great, great grandmother Elizabeth Romig Martin. We ate at a nice little restaurant in the village. I love the villages – so quaint, picturesque and English. Names of roads and towns made us sure we were in England – or Narnia.*

*On Wednesday we left at 5:00 AM for the airport and were waiting just beyond the customs area when two sleepy girls appeared. We were glad to see them and they were glad to see us. We left the airport and stopped at a "Little Chef" to have something to eat. We took them over some of the back roads we had discovered to show them the sights but they were too sleepy to be interested so we hurried back to our apartment and they had a long nap.*

The rest of the week at the Barnsdale Country Club was full of exploring and visiting. They saw Kenilworth and Warwick castles, ruins, bright fields of yellow rape, Oxford and a Shakespeare play at Stratford on Avon. They visited Rosemary Outram again and the girls enjoyed the journal of their great, great grandmother Elizabeth Romig. They read about Richard III. Leaving Barnsdale on Saturday they went to Ely to see the cathedral. They had received word from home that Willis Weatherford had died and were sorry they couldn't be with Anne and the family. They lit a candle in his memory at Ely Cathedral. They had lunch with John and Anne Connor Fanning and their two boys. They saw Cambridge and "punting on the Cam." Then they drove to Dick and Shelagh Connor's at Bedford where they spent a few days.

*On Sunday we went to church with the Connors. Amber played the piano and Elizabeth sang. The English church people were very friendly and interested in the girls. That afternoon we took a long walk along the river Ouise and saw some colorful houseboats. We passed John Bunyan's house remembering Pilgrims Progress. Amber and Elizabeth said they felt like they were living in a book or play.*

## York and the Merrets

They saw more sights and visited the senior Merrets (Ramsay cousins) in Croyden, just south of London. Then it was time to head north and they drove through the countryside to York. It was raining and a bit confusing but they found their bed-and-breakfast, Regency House. It was in a little alley close to one of gates in the old wall that still encircles the city. The landlady, Mrs. Podmore, with a decidedly Yorkshire accent, was a strong minded English matron who had opinions and advice on everything, but she was good-natured and an excellent hostess. They unpacked and then went to see David and Mary Merrett. David is the son of the older Merrett cousins they had visited in London. He is a railroad bridge engineer, member of the city council and history buff who was eager to show them York, but that day he took them to a little pub in what used to be a church for a delightful dinner.

At breakfast in the morning at the B & B they met the other interesting and congenial guests. Mrs. Podmore gave detailed instructions for each about what they should eat and how they should go about their day.

*We took a day to see the Yorkshire hills and moors. All of us had read James Herriot's books about being a veterinarian in the Yorkshire hills and we were excited to see the area. We went to the little town of Thirsk and saw the red door of Dr. Herriot's surgery. Then we saw stone walls, sheep, farmhouses, cattle and fields on the hills just as they had been described in the books. We saw some of chalk "drawings on the hillsides," many done hundreds of years ago.*

*The next day David took us on back streets and showed us remnants of walls and buildings from the times of the Romans, Vikings, Normans, Celts and other native English groups. We walked part of the old wall and went to Clifford's Tower built on a on a hill for defense of the city. We visited York Minster (teaching) Cathedral and again saw a time line of history in the names of the deans of the cathedral over the centuries – Angles, Saxons, Vikings, Normans and others who had conquered or settled at different periods. David took us by special arrangement to the Lord Mayor's house and we saw the ceremonial robes worn by the royal family and the mace carried in formal processions. The house reeked of history. It was a fascinating visual lesson in history led by a learned historian and local official, who happened to be a cousin. After supper at their house we bade a reluctant goodbye to our gracious hosts and guides, Mary and David.*

At breakfast Mrs. Podmore was very excited and anxious to tell everyone her news. She had been invited by a relative to come to London for an overnight visit. It was obviously a rare and important event in her life and she was overflowing with anticipation. Amber said she'd like to write a novel entitled, "Mrs. Podmore Goes To London!" The great times in and around York were ended and the foursome said fond goodbyes to Mrs. Podmore, wished her the best on her London trip, and headed north toward Scotland.

## North to Scotland

The countryside was picture-book material and the names reminded them of books they had read, ballads they sang and dances they'd done. They saw ruins of castles, monasteries and forts. They especially enjoyed walking along Hadrian's Wall and exploring Chester Fort. They were amazed at the extent, not only of Roman conquest, bur Roman culture that had reached the upper British Isles. They entered Scotland with rain off and on. Most showers were accompanied by rainbows. They arrived at the Moness Country Club at Aberfeldy in the Perthshire hills in the afternoon and were provided with a lovely condo with two bedrooms, two baths, spacious dining and living room area and kitchen. Outside were hills and fields with cattle and sheep. They walked to the quaint, friendly town of Aberfeldy and purchased goodies and other items at a a bakery for supper back at the condo.

*Scotland is truly beautiful with hills, castles, streams, misty rain and rainbows. Every time we took a drive we saw a castle and/or ruins. One misty day we drove to Loch Ness through the rocky hills. Amber was sure she would see the monster rising in the mist from the water. Then we drove to Loch Lomond and were treated with a double rainbow over the loch. I retain a mental picture of Amber sitting in a field of violets on the "bonny, bonny banks of Loch Lomond."*

Elizabeth had dreamed of seeing *The Phantom of the Opera* in London but they had not been able to arrange it, so she was quite excited when a brochure in their room announced that the Royal Scottish Company would be performing that play in Edinburgh at the Royal Opera House that week. They called and were able to get a student discount ticket for a matinee performance. Bill, Rose, and Amber planned to tour Edinburgh Castle while Elizabeth went to the play. Taking Elizabeth to the opera house and leaving her was a bit of a concern so Bill talked to the ticket clerk and she called the head usher who assured them that he would personally see that she was taken care of. She was. She was given a good seat and then at intermission was taken back stage to meet the cast. When the others picked her up after the performance she was on cloud nine and didn't stop talking for more than twenty minutes. Then she suddenly asked, "Oh! How was the castle?" Everyone laughed. Of course, the castle tour was great as well. Sitting atop a hill of solid rock it is impressive and full of history. As they entered the gate the last street passed was Ramsay Street. They bought Ramsay plaid hats for the girls and a tie for Bill.

On another day they visited Perth Castle where clan leaders gathered at times of change of leadership and brought soil carried from their home areas in boots and poured it on a mound signifying unity among the clans. The mound was called "boot hill." They saw paintings by Alan Ramsay in the castle. They visited a glassblowing plant making beautiful creations. They shopped for a birthday present for Amber who was turning 17 on June 3.

*We celebrated Amber's birthday at the condo and then walked up the burn to the Falls of Moness. We sat on the stone bench where Robert Burns sat when he wrote the poem The Birks (birches) of Aberfeldy" about that beautiful place. Another day we drove around the area, crossing narrow bridges and winding up narrow roads between rock walls, past a clan castle, through the little towns of Dull and Weem to Fortingall. The churchyard there boasts the oldest living vegetation in Europe – an ancient Yew tree estimated at 3000 years old. The tree wasn't impressive but the church had ancient relics from when it had been a hunting lodge and a monastery. We found a gravestone in the churchyard for a Marmaduke Ramsay. We also learned to our great surprise that this is claimed to be the birthplace of Pontius Pilate. A Roman delegation had come to establish a treaty with the clan leader and one of the wives gave birth to a son who, according to an old chronicle became the procurator of Judea. Later, Dick Connor expressed his doubts about that.*

## Goodbyes and Back Towards Home

On June 7 they left beautiful misty Scotland and traveled back to the Connors at Bedford. They were able to participate in a joint birthday party for several of the Connor children and grandchildren. They returned the rental car to Luton airport. They attended church with the Connors on Sunday and Amber again played the piano.

*We hated to say goodbye to these dear people but on Monday June 10 the Connors helped us get our luggage to the train and we headed back to London. We stayed at a motel near Hyde Park, and had a good time on a bus tour of London and a visit to Baker Street where everything was about Sherlock Holmes.*

*On Tuesday we said goodbye to the two lovely girls at Heathrow and sent them on their way home. The next day we took our flight via Paris to Washington and went to the Logsdens in La Plata. Reunited with our own car, we packed and drove on the right side of the road back to Edisto, thankful for a safe and wonderful trip.*

# CHAPTER 30

# MORE TRAVELS

Being back at *Cair Paravel* was great and Bill and Rose enjoyed the beach, their church and family and friends who continued to come and visit, but they also planned more travel. In 1997 they resumed a long tradition of trips to Williamsburg, Virginia, and looked in a new direction to Mexico.

## Colonial Williamsburg

Remembering their army days in Virginia, Bill and Rose began to visit Williamsburg regularly, almost every year from 1997 to 2011. Their friends Glenn and Reba McClanan lived nearby in Virginia Beach and they visited at their home or at the time-share in Williamsburg. Other family members often joined for the visit. Honeymoons there were arranged for some of the younger generation. A second cousin, and her husband, Susie and Malcom Reis, came several times from Pennsylvania and they all ate at Shields Tavern in Colonial Williamsburg in memory of her father, James Shields. Susie and Bill share a great grandfather in Morris Ramsay. The historical places have done a marvelous job in preserving the nation's heritage and portraying with historical integrity the values that heritage represents.

*Our love affair with Williamsburg and the surrounding colonial area goes back to the beginning of our marriage in 1952. When Bill was in the Army Medical Corps at Camp Pickett, VA and I was working in Richmond so we could be together on most weekends, we toured the Virginia area in Hedda, our 1939 Plymouth coupe. We loved to go to the James River plantations, like Berkley and Shirley, and to pretend that we were part of the elegant and romantic people we imagined had lived there. We walked the streets of Colonial Williamsburg, which was not highly developed back in 1952. We visited*

*Jamestown and Yorktown, immersing ourselves in the history of America's beginnings. During our child rearing years we seldom were able to visit but didn't lose our special feeling for the area and in retirement visited regularly.*

On various trips they went through the museum and re-enactment area of Jamestown, boarding the little ships replicated from those on which the settlers sailed from England. They drove the loop around the original Jamestown settlement, which is a national park, learning of the life of the times. They saw the statues of John Smith and Pocahontas and the foundations of the old church building in sight of the James River. They followed the movements of the armies and heard of the ships at the battle of Yorktown where the British surrendered.

## Talking With Colonials

*We listened to and actually conversed with Thomas Jefferson, George and Martha Washington, Patrick Henry, Gowan Pamphlet (the former slave and first black Baptist minister), Mrs. Peyton Randolph, the Marquis de La Fayette and others who were at Colonial Williamsburg in the form of "impersonators." They do a wonderful job – far more than entertainment but living history carefully studied and presented live with honesty, grace and humor. Once a gentleman in the audience asked Patrick Henry what he would think of an income tax. Patrick Henry looked incredulous and mused, "You mean a tax on a person's livelihood?" Addressing the young looking wife of the man, he complimented her for bringing her "father" to the meeting and suggested she take him to a physician who dealt in disorders of the mind. Another time a visitor asked Martha Washington about her dress, which was mostly black with some white fringes. She explained that she was just coming out of a period of mourning, and went on to observe that she and Colonel Washington were very attentive to what they wore. "After all," she said, "You are part of somebody else's landscape." Another colonial woman when asked about educating her young children at home seemed to wonder why the question was posed. She asked, "You wouldn't want to trust your young children's education to strangers, would you?" This made me think of our homeschooling children and grandchildren. We loved going to services or special programs at Bruton Chapel, which has continued as an "Anglican" church since colonial times.*

Bill and Rose become annual contributors through one of the "societies" of Williamsburg. When they sold their beach property, they tithed the net income and each made a charitable annuity contribution to Williamsburg. As donors they had the privilege of making visits to the St George Tucker House where one would get a cup of tea and cookie, see a demonstration of a colonial craft, or meet with one of the colonial characters. They would typically come in as their character and converse about life up to 1776. Then they would step out and return as themselves and discuss what it was like to portray their character.

*On one visit, with Bill E. and Anne, we all walked down the street chatting with George Washington after a session. On a visit with Alfredo and Jennifer, we attended a public meeting on the steps of the courthouse with colonials speaking and mingling in the audience. Alfredo, with his artistic talent, quickly sketched in color some of the colonials and then got them to sign their portraits, so his sketchbook includes signed portraits of Patrick Henry and others.*

## Visiting Friends

*In 2007, we went to the Walnut Hills Baptist Church, where our good friend, Rev. Tony Neal from Edisto days, was pastor, and had lunch with him and his wife, Danner. We were very pleasantly surprised to find a college classmate and his wife were members of the church and had good times with Iggy and Sue Cruz. We remembered Iggy as an international student from Guam. He had become a world expert on explosives and damage control, serving as a consultant on such matters as standards for lightning rods. We frequently had family members with us as well.*

*We liked to travel on country roads sometimes, starting with the ferry from Jamestown across the bay to Surry followed by the ever present sea gulls. Then we would traverse the width of Virginia through Lynchburg to Roanoke and down to Radford and then on to Kingsport in Tennessee. We sometimes took the ferry just for fun and ate at a little restaurant in Surrey. Once on a Veterans Day the proprietor asked if any diners were veterans. When I acknowledged having been in the Medical Corps, he gave me a free meal.*

*We visited friends en route to and from Williamsburg. We visited Charly and Tommy Sue Schindler at their home in Radford, VA. We almost always stopped in Kingsport, TN to see Juanita Walton, one of the few remaining older cousins of Rose. Then we would go to Baileyton and have lunch with Lizzie McAmis until she died at more than 100 years old. Lizzie had been a close neighbor of the Moore's when Rose was a little girl and used to hold Rosalba on her lap and tell her stories.*

In 2016 Jennifer, Alfredo and family, with the Berea Festival Dancers which Jennifer leads, performed at Colonial Williamsburg and they have been invited back. Bill and Rose hope the family tradition with Williamsburg continues.

### WILLIAMSBURG TIME-SHARE VISITS: 1997 – 2011

| Year & Week Begin | | Resort | Information |
|---|---|---|---|
| 1997 | Feb 7 | Powhatan Plantation | Bill & Rose |
| 2000 | Apr 9 | Fairfield Kingsgate | Bill & Rose |
| 2001 | Jan 16 | Patriots Place | Bill & Rose (McLanan's) |
| | Apr 7 | Kings Creek Plantation | B & R, Jen., Alfredo, Lydia |
| 2002 | Nov 8 | Kings Creek | Bill & Rose |
| 2003 | Nov 9 | Kings Creek | B & R. Jim, Rebekah |
| 2004 | Dec 10 | Kings Creek | Bill & Rose |
| 2005 | Oct 9 | Powhatan | Bill & Rose |
| | Oct 16 | Powhatan | Jen, Alf, Lydia, Isabel |
| 2006 | Oct 9 | Powhatan | Luke & Maggie Ramsay |
| | Dec 3 | Kings Creek | Bill & Rose |
| 2007 | Oct 20 | Kings Creek | Bill & Rose |
| 2008 | Sep 27 | Powhatan | Stephen & Robin Taylor |
| | Oct 4 | Powhatan | B & R, Bill E. & Anne |
| 2009 | Nov 13 | Powhatan | Bill & Rose |
| 2011 | Apr 3 | Powhatan | Bill & Rose |
| | Oct 22 | Powhatan | Bill & Rose |
| | Dec 26 | Powhatan | Jen, Alf, Lydia, Isabel |
| 2013 | Sep 22, | Powhatan | Laura & Ralph |

There were other visits not involving time shares but no dates are recorded.

# Puerto Vallarta, Mexico: 1997

Bill and Rose had been across the border into Mexico several times from San Antonio and El Paso. Several of their children had taken excursions, hosted by Dick, into the interior, but they had never been able to go along. Now with time to travel and a time-share they made plans to go to Puerto Vallarta along with Sandy and Al Osborne. The town is on the Bahia de Banderas on the west coast of Mexico at about the same latitude as Mexico City. Just to the north, the town of Nuevo Vallarta is a frequent stop for cruise ships. They left Lexington airport on September 5 flying to Cleveland, Houston and finally, Puerto Vallarta. Their time-share was the Royal Holiday Club at Los Tules, right on the bay. Across the road from the entrance was a grocery store called Gigante where they could get food and supplies, if they could translate the Spanish signs and labels.

*Our unit was on the lowest floor of a two story building, entered by going down steps below ground level. It was quite spacious with two bedrooms and a full kitchen plus sitting and dining areas. It was very close to the waterfront with lawns leading to a low wall before the sandy strip on the shore. An outdoor pool on the grounds included tables and chairs and a concession stand where one could order light food and have it served poolside along with chips and salsa. Palm trees and flowering shrubs abounded. A local bus stopped at the front gate and it was a short distance to the town with café's, shops and outdoor markets. It was very colorful and picturesque. The local people were friendly and helpful. There were vendors everywhere peddling their wares of jewelry, hats, blankets, trinkets and souvenirs. We bought some little Mexican dolls.*

There were opportunities for activities and tours offered by the resort. One day they signed up for a bus tour including a luncheon at an exotic jungle-like place on a hillside with a waterfall and charming pool in which one could swim. They saw iguanas, both held by locals, offering to take a picture of tourists holding one, and in the open along the roads. One lady passenger told a man with an iguana that if he came one step closer to her with that creature she would scream until he was sorry he'd done it. They saw luxurious vacation houses of the wealthy, with spectacular views of the ocean. Some of those perched right on the cliff wall supported by huge pillars 50 – 70 feet high. The town nestled on a narrow strip of land between the cliffs and the ocean.

## The Flood

*One day we took a boat ride out in the bay to see huge rock formations rising from the water, including tunnels through which the boat went. At one point of a cliff fronting the water there was a bungee jumping apparatus that we were invited to try. We declined. Back at the condo we ate well with food acquired at the Gigante and prepared by Rose and Sandy. We were living well in this beautiful place. Then it began to rain.*

It rained hard for a long time so they stayed inside. The rain caused streams to rush down the steep cliffs and wash over the strip between cliff and ocean. It did some damage to houses in the town. It also flooded the resort.

*We noticed that water was coming in the condo from somewhere. Most of it seemed to be coming under the front door so Al opened the door to see what was happening. The water had filled the stairwell and opening the door was like the breaking of a dam. Tons of water gushed in and soon we were ankle deep in water, frantically moving everything off the floor and on to the beds. There was a drain in one bathroom so Al and I got brooms and, laughing hysterically, we kept sweeping the water to the drain but it was more than the poor drain could handle. We reported the problem and were moved through the rain to a dry apartment.*

## Kentucky "Yee-Haw!"

One night the resort held a party and gave awards for various accomplishments. Bill and Rose, celebrating their 44th wedding anniversary on September 7, won the longest married couple contest and received a sombrero and serape. Not to be outdone Al got in line for the tequila drinking contest, though he didn't drink.

*They provided tall thin glasses of water with just a shot of tequila in it and the contestants were to take a drink and then give a cowboy yell. Most shouted*

*"Ye-haw" in cowboy fashion. Al announced to the crowd that he would do a Kentucky yell. He started off with a "yee" very low and slow, gradually increasing volume and pitch over a long, long, time. By the time he got to the high pitched "haw" everyone was laughing and clapping. He won hands down and received his sombrero. He was also given a bottle of tequila which he gave to the waiter at the poolside the next day. From then on we got nothing but the best of service as we snacked by the pool.*

They left Puerto Vallarta on September13 and made a three day stopover in San Antonio to visit old friends, Helen and Eric Telfer, and to revisit some memories of their army days there. Then they flew back to Kentucky. After a short visit in Berea they returned to *Cair Paravel* on Edisto with another collection of wonderful memories.

# CHAPTER 31

# EDISTO YEARS II

## Beach Fun

Everyone seems to love the beach and *Cair Paravel* was the base for many wonderful times for children and grandchildren and friends of all ages, often with children, who visited, sometimes lodging with Bill and Rose and sometimes renting Jim's house, *Chaika,* or another vacation house. Over the years patterns of fun were established. For the little ones the beach at the sound was preferable with its wide, gently sloping sand and mild waves. The first thing to do was to dig a shallow hole just above the water line so it would fill with water and the child could sit in it with a bucket and shovel. They could run to the water and fill the bucket and pour the water in their hole and sit in it pouring sand on their legs. Sunscreen was a must and usually they wore hats, but they could play happily for hours in their imaginary domain.

For the older children the beach front was more to their liking. They would dig a deeper hole or "slog mine" and a build sandcastle. Some sandcastles were works of art with sculpted towers, gates, steps and windows. The trick was to build it enough above the line where the tide was coming in to be able to complete it and enjoy it for a time, but then be able to watch the waves breach the walls protecting the castle, pass its moat and gradually, or sometimes instantly, demolishing the whole thing. But most the time was spent in the ocean. Bill remembers fighting the waves.

*The older children and their fathers, having reverted to childhood, liked it when the waves were a little rough with high breaking crests. They would get in inner tubes or on inflatable rafts and float over the waves at their highest point or ride the breaking wave all the way on to the beach and then run back in and do it again – and again –and again. Sometimes I would pull a whole line of tubes and rafts with each occupant holding on to the next, right up parallel to the breakers and try to position the line so all would be lifted up and over the wave just before it broke. When we miscalculated everyone was turned topsy-turvy in the water and came up laughing to try again.*

*Although they were all good swimmers, we did have to keep an eye on the children playing in the waves because the currents and undertow could catch them unawares. Once Keith was floating on a raft beyond the breakers and I realized that he was trying unsuccessfully to paddle in to shore. A current was taking him down the coast and out to sea. I was able to get to him before he was beyond reach, but it was a reminder that the ocean is big and powerful and can be treacherous.*

Rose remembers thinking ahead to have a supply of old bread, buns or biscuits on hand for beach excursions.

*The children and adults of any age liked to throw pieces of bread up in the air and watch the sea gulls swoop and pick their treats right out of the air. If just one gull was around at first it wasn't alone for long. The greedy avian acrobats came from all sides and soon a noisy white tornado of feathery creatures was swirling around. It was also fun to watch the pelicans go fishing. They would hover over the ocean and when they spotted a school of fish would dive into the water opening their bucket like beaks and turn a somersault in the waves, ending up with a mouthful of fish. In the evenings, we would count them as they silently flew in lines to their roosting places for the night. Sometimes there would be twenty, thirty or fifty gracefully riding the air currents in a line. We wondered how they decided who got to be the leader. Maybe they took turns. Occasionally we'd see a skimmer flying barely above the waves, and spoonbills or ibis on the beach*

*Shells were like treasure, especially the olive shells, conchs and occasional sand dollars. One had to be careful when finding a whole conch because it was likely inhabited by a hermit crab and couldn't be taken home. Once when Daniel and Ralph Edwin were visiting and we were having lunch at the Pavilion Restaurant at the beach front, the boys looked out the window overlooking the beach and saw a mass of shells stirred up by a storm and being deposited on the beach, They raced downstairs and came back wet and happy with their harvest. Daniel was especially adept at finding shark's teeth and collected something like 600 of various sizes.*

## Island Waterways

The grandchildren had enjoyed little excursions on Fran Averitt's boat from Live Oak Landing on Big Bay Creek - one of the Island waterways. It seemed appropriate that Bill and Rose should have a boat since there were abundant tidal creeks along the marshes to explore.

*We found a cheap older Aristocraft called "The Lazy Bee" and began our boating adventures. We decided to change the name to "Marsh Wiggle," following the Narnia theme, but never got around to changing the name on the boat. The boat was a 19 foot inboard/outboard model, really made for lakes rather than salt water, but we didn't know enough to let that worry us at the time. Someone had told us that a boat was a hole in the ocean into which unlimited amounts of money could be poured. This turned out to be the case, but we did have some memorable rides up and around St. Helena Sound, St Pierre's Creek and Big Bay Creek. Launching at a ramp from the boat trailer pulled by our truck or jeep was tricky, but not as tricky as getting the boat back on the trailer at the end of the ride. The water was never still and with the tides could flow in either direction. Once when our boat's motor had died and we were drifting backwards towards another boat at the dock on Big Bay Creek, Elizabeth shouted, "Grandpa, stop the boat." I answered, somewhat impatiently, "It doesn't have brakes!"*

Once launched, if the motor didn't quit, it was great fun. The sparkling blue water, the wide marshes, the shining sun and wind in the face were exhilarating. Everyone had a turn being captain, although only Bill had a captain's hat. At high tide one could go all the way up Big Bay and traverse the arteries crossing the marshes and come down St Pierre. If the tide began to go out, the boaters might have to pole through marsh mud in places. The biggest problem was that the motor wasn't always dependable.

*We had taken the boat initially to a marina on Wadmalaw Island to have it inspected and tuned up. We had several return trips to the marina and began to understand the "hole in the ocean" analogy. Besides its age, one of the problems was that the cooling system pumped water through the motor block. The salt water was, of course corrosive, and holes developed in the cooling chambers so the motor got overheated. Once Rose and I with Jerry Houck, were out on St Helena Sound, in sight of the Big Bay dock when the motor overheated, cracking and popping. I turned the motor off and waited for it to cool, but when started again it immediately got too hot. No problem, I thought, I was prepared with oars with which we could paddle back to the dock. The tide was with us but the wind was against us and in spite of our best efforts we made no headway, in fact were losing the battle. We threw out an anchor to keep from being blown down the sound to the ocean. Fortunately Rose remembered the phone number of the Fairfield office and was able to call them on our cell phone. They in turn called the little shop at the dock and a kind fisherman, about to embark, said he would go get us. We were very thankful that he did. I have the utmost admiration for those hardy souls who go out on the high seas with a boat.*

After a couple years of both fun and frustration, they decided they could do without the Lazy Bee.

## Turtle Patrol

Rose and Bill became interested in environmental protection efforts and helped with beach clean-ups, surprised at how much plastic, cans, glass and Styrofoam had accumulated, which threatened birds and marine life as well as being unsightly. They also joined the "turtle watch" and took training before being assigned a section of beach to patrol. Edisto is a nesting place for the large loggerhead turtles that are a protected species. The female turtles ready to lay eggs would crawl up the beach at night above the high tide line and dig a hole shaped like a light bulb with their hind legs, then deposit 75 to 150 eggs in it, cover up the hole and return to the ocean never to see their hatchlings.

*Our job on the turtle patrol was to walk our section of beach early in the morning to see if we could identify a "crawl." The heavy turtle would leave tractor-tire-looking tracks coming out of the ocean and then returning with the tracks a little less deep because of the loss of weight. At the top of the crawl would be a smoothed over area where she had covered her nest and tried to obscure it. We would take a pointed stick and probe lightly for the loose sand of the nest's chimney. When we found it we would put stakes and ribbon around it to mark its location and attach a sign to a stake identifying it as a legally protected site. Sometimes a nest was right on a path from the dunes where heavy foot traffic would be a problem and the nest would need to be moved. In these cases we would dig a new nest and then carefully excavate the original nest to transfer the eggs to the safer place.*

*The eggs were ping pong ball size and a little rubbery. A few might be ruptured but most were easy to move with care. We recorded and reported all crawls, relocations and numbers if relocated. We also reported false crawls where the turtle must have sensed danger and didn't make a nest. Once I actually saw a turtle on her way back to the ocean. She was as big as a semi-truck tire with legs and a head. What a sight!*

The turtle patrol would check the nest site from time to time for signs of disturbance. Occasionally a raccoon or some other animal would discover a nest and dig up the eggs and, in the past, human poachers would steal the eggs for eating. Some few people might ignore the protective signs and do damage. Then in about a month from the deposit of the eggs the patrol would watch for signs of hatching, usually at dawn. First a slight depression of sand might be seen as the eggs hatch in the nest and the sand above caves in on the disturbance below. Then a little turtle will emerge, soon followed by a swarm of brothers and sisters all instinctively heading for the water. The little hatchlings could fit into a serving spoon, but are perfect adorable miniatures of the big loggerheads. They face immediate dangers. Gulls may discover them and swoop down to have a feast. Ghost crabs may grab one and drag it into its hole for a snack. Once in the sea a variety of other sea creatures may find them a tasty breakfast. The survival rate is small but a few will make it and grow to the great size of their species. When it is the turn of the females who survive to lay their eggs they will return to the same coastal area to nest, no matter how far they have roamed through the oceans, and apparently they cover long distances in their lifetimes.

*The other danger to the little turtles is lights. It seems that they are drawn to the lightest horizon, which under normal circumstances is over the ocean, and so they head that way. But if there are street lights, or yard lights by beach houses, or bright windows in the early dawn when they hatch they can be disoriented and go the wrong direction. We have sometimes found them crawling across the dunes into the grasses and brush and even on to the beach front road. Many don't survive that misdirection, but those of us on the turtle patrol, and often others who want to help, will find them and carry them back to the beach. We put them down on the sand facing the ocean so they can crawl into the surf themselves, rather than putting them directly into the water. This may be important for their development and memory.*

The turtle patrol and other volunteers also take flyers around to the beach front houses explaining to those renting them about the turtles and the need to keep lights out during hatching season. Streetlights are not on during that time. If a light is seen to be on at the critical time the resident is asked to turn it off. Most people are very interested and cooperative and many come to watch when the little turtles are emerging from their sandy nest and heading for the sea.

## New Friendships

Rose became involved in the "homeowners association" and soon was taking leadership in providing opportunities for residents, especially new ones, to get to know each other. They learned what a "shrimp boil' was and thoroughly enjoyed it. Edisto had some very interesting people living there and they made many friends. At church Bill and Rose were helping to get the church chartered and became charter members. They developed close friendships with Joe and Annette Mole, Don and Francis Pate, Veda Godwin, Charles and Ethelynn Boozer, Tom and Lois Anderson, Bob and Angelle Beatty, Bob and Betty Davis, Bob and Betty Jo Warner and many other members of the little church. They hosted a Christmas luncheon for church members in December 1996. The church still had only supply ministers so the church leadership fell to the members, which is considered appropriate in the Methodist tradition. Bill and Rose represented their church on the island's ministerial association.

Not only did Bill and Rose have friends from their church but they joined with four other couples from other churches in a close fellowship for Bible study that lasted the whole time they were at Edisto. The friendships formed continued after they moved back to Kentucky in 2006.

*Bill and I had noticed a pro-life bumper sticker on a car that passed our house and wondered who the owners were. Later we saw the car parked at a house further down the road in Fairfield and we went up to the door and introduced ourselves to Frank and Carol Bremer. We were immediately kindred spirits and they invited us to join with others who were interested in a serious Bible study and prayer fellowship. Toni and Larry Mixon, who had built a house across the street from our house, were also involved. We usually met at the home of Gerry and Okie Murray out on the island surrounded by the fields and waterways of the old Murray plantation. The Murray's were an Edisto family going back many generations and we had met Gerry's mother Marion at the historical society, which she chaired. The fourth couple sharing the fellowship was Mike and Marianne Kaiser. We had great times of fellowship, worship, prayer and study along with tasty refreshments and, sometimes, a delicious meal. Others, including some of our guests, joined the group from time to time but the four couples were regulars. Larry Mixon would often lead the study, praise and prayer but sometimes Okie or another would provide leadership.*

Frank and Carol Bremer were of Lutheran background and long-time members of Gideon's International. They were very active in Bible distribution programs. For a time Bill and Rose joined them in attending Gideon meetings in Charleston and providing support. Gerry and Okie were members of the historic Presbyterian Church on Edisto. Toni and Larry had various church affiliations and were very charismatic and evangelical. Mike and Marianne had experienced miraculous healings and were deeply spiritual. All were serious about their faith and drew strength from the fellowship as they shared and prayed together.

# CHAPTER 32

# TRAVELS CONTINUE

The years 1998 and 1999 saw more special extended trips for Bill and Rose. They returned to Denmark taking three more grandchildren with them. They traveled up the east coast to Maine featuring lighthouse visits. They went across the southern USA to San Diego. They again visited Abaco in the Bahamas with grandchildren.

## Denmark 1998

Jennifer, continuing her annual singing tours of Denmark, had a full schedule of performances in the summer of 1998. She was now married to Alfredo Escobar and Bill and Rose decided to go with Jennifer and Alfredo; They would take along three teen age grandchildren - Will, Catherine and Melissa. Jim, Shawn and family had been in Kazakhstan for almost two years and planned to take a break and meet us in Denmark. They also would visit Danes who had hosted Jim years earlier.

The Berea travelers would fly from Cincinnati on June 8, 1998, to Chicago and on to Frankfurt, Germany, and then Hamburg. They had reserved two rental cars to drive to Denmark. Alfredo needed to come back before the full tour was over, but until then having two small cars for the seven travelers was the most convenient and reasonable way to go. They had reserved an Opal and a Volkswagen to be picked up at the Hamburg airport. Bill E., Anne and Daniel drove with them to Cincinnati and then took the cars back to Berea. They received a call from Laura at the airport informing them that Ralph Edwin, Melissa and Catherine's young brother, had been hospitalized with a serious kidney condition. She urged them to continue the trip but to pray, which they did.

The travelers flew to Chicago where they encountered a problem. An officious and unhelpful woman Lufthansa agent informed them that they had overbooked the flight and the girls would have to stay behind and be put on a later flight. Of course Bill said that was unacceptable and insisted that they all fly together. He had to walk miles across the airport to find the office and official who could overrule the agent and allow them to stay together. After that everything went as planned, and they arrived the next day in Hamburg. Their rental cars had been upgraded and they left driving a Mercedes and BMW. They drove to Kiel for the ferry ride to Langeland, then on to the home of their friends, Herdis and Erik Damkier on Fynn.

## Good Friends and Good Times

*Herdis - good friend, gracious hostess and wise woman that she is - was ready for us. After fond reunion greetings and introductions to those who were new to Denmark, she announced that she had prepared a bed for each of the seven of us and we were to take a two hour nap. She would wake us in time for supper and then we would be on Danish time. It worked beautifully. She also knew in advance from Jennifer, that it was Catherine's 17th birthday and had prepared a party. The Danes are great at decorations and it was a festive supper and party, with cake, candles, balloons and little Danish flags fluttering. A great birthday present was a call from home saying that prayers were answered and Ralph Edwin was out of danger and recovering well.*

The group visited Erik's parents' fairy-tale place, with arbors, ponds and bridges, and saw other sights before leaving for Copenhagen the next day. Bente Boisen and Henning Jensen met them and, once again, showed them the interesting city – ships in the harbor, the castle, changing of the guard, cathedral, round tower, and, of course, the little mermaid. They took a canal tour by boat and climbed the Round Tower. They went to Vartov, the headquarters of the DDGU folk association with its statue of Bishop Grundtvig. Rose and Bill lodged there with hosts, Kristen and Hans Grishauge and the others stayed with Bente and Henning. On June 12, they went to friends at Ronnede and a concert by Jennifer at Fenmark, followed by a dance.

*Denmark includes the peninsula of Jutland and a group of islands all connected by bridges and ferries. Leaving Ronnede we went to the ferry that connected to Jutland. A new long bridge had just been completed and we were on the last ferry to make the trip. The bridge opening was to be held that day and Queen Margrethe II had come for the ceremonies. We saw her yacht as we sailed past. We arrived on Jutland and proceeded to the Vejle area where Herdis' sister Birgit and Paul Erik Hansen and other friends live.*

Birgit and Paul Erik and Kirsten and Ewald Jensen each provided a summer house for the travelers to use. One would be used by Jim, Shawn, Rebekah, Keith, Jonathan and Naomi who arrived on June 14. They were pleasant little cabins in a lovely resort area on Vejle fjord and it was great to have a home base for a while.

*We enjoyed shopping at the little markets and bakeries and preparing meals. Bill found some bags of frozen soups which were delicious with the wonderful Danish breads and cheeses. Jennifer had a number of performances and everywhere we went we met friends who had been at our house in Berea. We loved the walking streets in some of the towns. It was great to see Jim, Shawn and the children and to go on outings together. We visited Margit Iversen, who had become a dear friend, and got to meet Karl's young wife and new baby. Henning Moeller Andersen and Bodil had us all over for dessert after a concert in Vejle and they were highly amused at a competition between Will and Melissa to see who could eat the most of the Danish cakes.*

They went to Legoland and saw the amazing structures made of legos and went on rides. Will was thrilled when he found a Burger King and was able to get French fries. They attended an exciting accordion festival in Ringe and Jennifer played and sang lively songs with some of the numbers. They spent time with Loren and Inge-Lise at their home in Galten near Aarhus. Martin and Charlie and boys were there as well and they all saw bonfires along the roads where "the burning of the witch" was being celebrated.

They visited Ole and Ingelis Sorensen and their boys again and went to more of Jennifer's concerts. Catherine and Melissa sometimes joined Jennifer in singing, adding to her concerts. They visited Karen and Hans

Rosgaard and their daughter Susan who was now married and had a baby. Alfredo had left, driving back to Hamburg with one of the cars and heading home.

## The Coast of the North Sea

Jennifer and the girls went with Karen Bertilsen (Rosgaard) to the far north of Jutland on Jennifer's tour and to see some sights. Bill, Rose and Will drove up to Viborg and had a lovely lunch with Frede Hansen and his wife. Frede's daughter had stayed at the Big House in Berea. He was manager of the gas company that serves central Jutland and showed us some of their facilities. Then they went to the Isle of Morse, and visited the school where the first group of teens had stayed 25 years earlier. Leaving Morse they went to the coast of the North Sea and drove south to Vejle.

*The trip down the coast was fascinating. The North Sea is rough and forbidding. All along the coast were ruins of German bunkers which had been built by forced Danish labor in anticipation of an allied invasion through Denmark. They were enormous cement structures which must have seemed invincible at the time but now had been tossed sideways and upside down by the power of the sea over the years and lay around like toys in a sandbox. Will darted in and out of their doorways and climbed on top of them whenever we stopped for a closer look. We crossed a ferry at a large inlet and found an unusual shell house. It was a large two story house totally and tastefully covered with shells. Inside one could buy all sorts of shells and crafts made from shells. We finally got back to Vejle proud that we had navigated all the way up and down the main part of Jutland, without getting lost.*

## Landstaevne

Jennifer and the girls also returned and all prepared to go to the major festival at Silkeborg, which is called Landstaevne. A very special event every four years in Denmark, it was held from June 25-28 in 1998. Groups from all parts of the nation came together for an extravaganza of dance, music, gymnastics and showmanship in a shared celebration of their folk culture. Jennifer and her friends had acquired tickets for all so they joined thousands at the spacious grounds where the events were held and marveled at the talent, creativity, color and joy exhibited by hundreds of participants. Some of their Danish friends were involved in groups from their home areas or folk schools.

*There was the inevitable and moving procession with the Danish flag and singing of the national anthem. The Danes know how to march and sing. Then the show was under way. I remember one large group surging on to the field dressed in black garbage bags like beetles swarming together in a fantastic dance. Other groups in beautiful costumes looked like fields of dancing flowers. The gymnastics were awe inspiring. Each act was introduced and announced with enthusiasm and appreciation. There was no sense of competition but rather a sharing of the best expressions of life in their country with each other. The music was spectacular and, again, very Danish rather than just a reflection of hyped up media culture. It was a special privilege to share the experience and mingle with the thousands who attended and a fitting climax to our Danish tour, which was coming to a close.*

## More Visits and Heading Home

They vacated the summer houses that had been so graciously provided, said goodbyes as they headed south, and spent the last week based in Falster with Bente and Wayne Mabe and Bente's family. Again a summerhouse had been provided for their use and also one for Jim and family who joined them there. They went to a medieval park and watched jousting, a blacksmith at his forge and other craftsmen and women showing how life was lived in the middle-ages. They went to a wildlife reservation and the young people got to hold lambs and chickens, feed ostriches and admire the giraffes and rhinos. In one area they drove through a gate, instructed to stay in their cars with windows up, and saw tigers. Some were bigger than the Volkswagens and other small cars visiting the park. Wayne was a vendor for Danish clogs and they acquired these comfortable and traditional footwear. They had wonderful meals and fellowship at Bente's and at her mother's home. They celebrated Rose's birthday on July 5. Finally it was time to go. They bade tearful goodbyes and drove away. They crossed the border into Germany and stayed at a B & B near Hamburg. It was called Hotel Schaefer.

*Mr. and Mrs. Schaefer were very welcoming and anxious to know about our group. They told us the name "Schaefer" meant shepherd. They not only raised sheep, but were good shepherds to us. When they found that Jennifer was a singer they quickly arranged for a private concert for themselves and other guests. Catherine and Melissa joined in for a lovely program. Will, who Mr. Schaefer had christened "Arnold Schwarzenegger," didn't join in. When we departed the next morning the Schaefer's gave each of the girls a little white sheep figurine. Then with a twinkle in the eyes gave Will a black sheep.*

The trip home was pleasant and uneventful and they arrived at Cincinnati airport late on July 7, weary but happy that they were back in Kentucky. Bill and Anne and Laura and Ralph met them and drove them home to Berea. After a Berea visit and thorough debriefing Bill and Rose made the trip back to Edisto. Another memorable retirement adventure in friendship and grand-parenting was ended.

## Up East and Lighthouses: 1998

Bill had been to NSEA conferences On Nantucket Island and in Portland, Maine, but Rose had never been to that part of the country. They decided to head for Maine, visiting in Pennsylvania and then seeing as many lighthouses as they could up the east coast. They arranged for a Wayside visit in Raymond, Maine with Paul and Priscilla Barber and would come back through Vermont, where Dick and Susana lived, and Wooster, Ohio to see John and Eileen and on to Berea for a work colleges meeting.

*We took off from Edisto on October 22, 1998 and drove to Petersburg, Virginia, remembering our army days in that area 46 years earlier just after we were married. Then we drove to Easton, PA and spent a day with my cousin Grace Price, remembering our childhood years in that area. The next day we crossed the Delaware River into New Jersey and headed for the east coast. The fall foliage was gorgeous in the hills and the weather warm. We stopped at some cranberry bogs and marveled at the growing and harvesting of this crop.*

## Lighthouses

Their destination that night was Hyannis, Massachusetts, from which they could take a ferry to Nantucket Island. They did this the next day and had a wonderful visit to this quaint island with its Cape Cod houses and other colonial style buildings. They traversed the length of the island and, read about its history, ate a lovely lunch and of course, saw lighthouses. Rose remembers being thrilled.

*I have always loved lighthouses. They are so solid emanating, not only light for guidance and protection from turbulence, but hope and safety. They always have a romantic air in the novels that feature their stories, and being a reader, I guess they symbolize nobility and stability to me. We had climbed the lighthouse on St Augustine beach with its bold black stripes and visited the candy cane striped tower at Cape Hattaras, NC. We had viewed the Atlantic from the one at Hopetown in the Bahamas. We had visited others on trips to Florida, St. Simons and Tybee islands in Georgia, Traverse City, Michigan and Assateague, Virginia. In South Carolina we visited the one on Sullivans Island, not far from Edisto and another at Charleston harbor. Now we were seeing a whole series along the rocky New England coast. It was marvelous. Some we walked to, some we climbed and some saw from a distance. We read about them all – Hyannis, Nantucket Nauset, Nubble, Three Sisters and others. Perhaps my favorite on this trip was the Nubble light on Cape Neddick near York, Maine. We walked across a causeway to the rocky point on which the lighthouse stood, unafraid with the sea futilely dashing its foaming waves against the rocks beneath.*

There are reportedly over 18,000 lighthouses around the world and about 1000 in the USA. Surprisingly Michigan is the state with the most at about 150. Bill and Rose saw only a small number but were amazed at the variety. They wondered what it must have been like to be a lighthouse keeper's family living in a home under and often attached to the lighthouse.

## Casa del Sol in Vermont

They also visited Plymouth and the Portsmouth area, seeing Plymouth Rock and a sailing ship like the Mayflower, which had brought the Pilgrims to these shores. They found that four children of a family named More sailed without parents or relatives on the Mayflower. They had apparently been shipped away as the result of a complicated family dispute. Three died on the journey or shortly after arrival, underscoring the harsh conditions of the trip and early settlement. Only Richard More survived and had descendants, but no evidence was found that he had any connection with the Moores of Rose's ancestry.

Leaving Maine they drove cross country to and through New Hampshire to Vermont. Dick and Susana were living in Putney at the time and had opened a restaurant, "Casa del Sol." They had a wonderful visit and great authentic Mexican food.

*It was great to be with my brother Dick and his lovely wife, Susana, see their restaurant and tour that area of Vermont. Both Dick and Susana are excellent chefs and we were fed well. They took us to see covered bridges, town squares, shops and lovely churches with white spires reaching heavenward. At one little bookstore I found a book I had been trying to find. Being in the low country of South Carolina where marshes abound, I wanted a copy of Sidney Lanier's poem "The Marshes of Glynn." I had looked in South Carolina and then in Georgia on a trip to Berry College, sure I could find a book of the "Georgia Poet," but to no avail. Then way up in Vermont in a little bookshop I find a collection on Lanier's poems including the one for which I was searching. It was an unexpected bonus of the trip.*

They went further south and visited Merle Ryan in Amherst, MA. Merle was a friend and colleague from NSEA connections. They had visited her several times when they were all in Florida. Crossing Massachusetts and driving west through New York they reached Ohio and turned south to Wooster and Columbus for visits with John and Eileen, and Patty and Earl. Driving back to Kentucky they had supper with Wayne and Carolyn in Louisville before arriving at Bill and Anne's home in Berea on November

3, 1998. Three days later Bill participated in a Work Colleges conference hosted by Berea College. On November 11 they left for home, stopping at Kingsport TN to see Rose's aunt Ruth Riggs. Finally, after 20 days of travel and visiting they arrived at *Cair Paravel*.

## Bahama Adventures

*Rose and I actually started wider travel a number of years earlier as we looked forward to our retirement years and after the children were grown up. In December 1987, Jennifer had graduated from high school and I took a half year sabbatical to work for NSEA in 1988 as its president. Jennifer, as my administrative assistant, had helped set up and run a conference for NSEA leadership in Orlando in January 1988. It included a behind the scenes tour of Disney which uses a lot of student employees. Then Rose, Jennifer and I traveled across country visiting colleges and universities and ending up at a national conference in Claremont, California.*

Bill and Rose had decided that he would retire in five years and they should be planning for life after retirement. They decided to buy a time-share based in the Bahamas so they could pay its basic costs while still working and then have it available when retired and ready to do some serious travel. They were thinking about the two of them, but as it turned out, they found it a wonderful chance to include others, chiefly grandchildren as they reached their teens.

## The First Trip

*Part of the deal when we purchased the time-share was a paid for trip to Abaco-Townes-By-The-Sea at Marsh Harbor on Abaco Island. In June, 1988, we went with Jennifer and her boyfriend of the time, Gary Curry. We flew in a very small airplane from West Palm Beach, FL. You know it is a small plane when you have to be weighed so total weight can be determined and distributed evenly and then the pilot loads your luggage in compartments in the wings and climbs on the wing to enter the cockpit through the window. The plane gave us fine views of the dark Atlantic dotted by an occasional ship, and then the azure coastal waters as we approached the Bahama Islands. We enjoyed the beautiful skies, white sand beaches, clear waters, and island atmosphere. We learned to snorkel, saw gorgeous fish and found wonderful shells. We ate conch burgers, grouper fingers, and other great seafood. We visited the lighthouse at Hopetown on Elbow Key, an old British settlement where Tories waited out the years of the American Revolution. Elbow Key is one of an arc of outlying keys about five miles off Abaco that form a protected part of the sea separated from the wider Atlantic. Regattas are held there and one sees lots of sailboats and other water craft. One comes to Abaco by plane or by boat. After our first visit, we quickly planned to return.*

Two years later, in July 1990, they returned with their first grandchild, Elizabeth, and her cousin, Mark. They were twelve and thirteen years old. Again they had a great time and explored the island further. Rose remembers a surprise on that trip.

*The children and I had gone walking while Bill stayed behind at the resort to meet other guests and participate in some of the activities. We got back just in time to hear the loud speaker announce that "Mr. Ramsay has won the Limbo dance contest." The children were impressed that grandpa had shimmied under the limbo bar lower than anyone else in his age bracket. His prize was a bottle of wine, which he gave to a grateful Swiss couple.*

## More Trips

In 1994, Bill and Rose made another Bahamas trip, this time with Sandy and Al Osborne. This was the first of several trips they enjoyed with Robin's parents.

*Al and I rented bicycles one day and brought back to our unit plates of the best breaded fried grouper we ever tasted. There was a little seafood shop we had discovered in walking around that offered ready-to-eat fish at the lunch hour only. On future trips we were sorry to find that this service had been discontinued.*

In 1996, Jennifer and Alfredo went to Abaco for a two week honeymoon. Later in the year, Bill and Rose went on a cruise from Fort Lauderdale to

Freeport with Sandy and Al. In 1999 John and Eileen had an anniversary trip to Abaco. Then Bill and Rose took two more grandchildren, Benjamin and Brian, for a week. By this time they were experienced tourists on Abaco.

*We took the ferry (a motorboat) to Hopetown on Elbow Key and climbed the lighthouse. We swam and snorkeled in the clear water over white sand. Back on Abaco we found we could walk from our resort to Mermaid Reef, an underwater park for beautiful snorkeling. We rented a car and added Treasure Key and the Blue Hole as places to visit. Treasure Key is reported to be one of the finest beaches in the world. It has soft white sand, extending for miles in a curved coastline, with gentle waves lapping on the shore. The water is clear but appears from a distance to be that lovely azure blue for which the Bahama waters are known. The Blue Hole is in a remote part of the island in the woods with no one around. It is a rock formation making a round pool of about 75 feet across and no one knows how deep. The first 25 feet or so of the water is fresh and then it is salty, apparently connected to the ocean by underground channels. Someone had hung a rope from a tree branch overhanging the pool so you could swing out and drop in the refreshing water.*

## More Grandchildren Travel With Us

*In 2002 with Sandy and All, we took four more teens – Daniel, Colleen, Andrew and Rebekah. The pilot of the eight seater plane let Colleen fly the plane for a spell but we made the trip safely. Daniel especially liked the Blue Hole. Rebekah liked Hopetown. Andrew kept us enjoying Moose Tracks ice cream and learned that grouper fingers tasted good. All four foraged way down the beach and came back with wonderful big conch shells. We read stories and played cards when it was too dark to be outside on adventures.*

In 2003 Robin went along with Bill and Rose and four more grandchildren - Michael, Ralph Edwin, Adrienne and Joseph (who is technically a grandnephew). They were a fun group. The boys stayed with Bill and Rose. Robin had another unit next door with Adrienne but they all ate and spent their waking hours together. The children especially liked to snorkel at Mermaid Reef with Aunt Robin and we visited some of the other surrounding keys, like Green Turtle and Man-o-War where boatbuilding and other crafts were found. Treasure Key and the Blue Hole were again favorites. They also discovered Long Beach where Robin reveled in the flowers dotting the dunes, the clear water and the expanse of white sand.

*That was our last trip to Abaco, ending our adventures there on a high note. The Abaco time-share was especially valuable to us because we could go on a "bonus week" at very low cost and bank our regular week to use elsewhere. It had great "trading power" and we used it in England, Scotland, Mexico and Canada as well as for western trips in the USA. But the annual "maintenance costs" had increased and large special assessments had been added. The resort was converting time-share units to condos for sale to the wealthy and was obviously driving out the time-share owners with offers to take units off their hands. We finally had to give up and accept the offer. For the 15 years we were Abaco time share owners we enjoyed very special times which we would never have experienced otherwise.*

## SUMMARY OF BAHAMAS TRIPS

| DATES | TRAVELERS | TRIP INFORMATION |
|---|---|---|
| 6/1988 | Bill, Rose, Jennifer Gary | 1st trip Marsh Harbor, |
| 7/1990 | Bill, Rose, Elizabeth, Mark | Abaco-Townes-By-The-Sea |
| 7/1994 | Bill, Rose, Sandy, Al | Discovered Grouper Place |
| 9/1996 | Jennifer, Alfredo | Honeymoon (two weeks} |
| 10/1996 | Bill, Rose, Sandy, Al | Cruise to Freeport |
| 3/1999 | John, Eileen | Anniversary |
| 6/1999 | Bill, Rose, Benjamin, Brian | Drove to Treasure Key |
| 4/2002 | Bill, Rose, Sandy, Al, Daniel, | |
| | Rebekah, Andrew, Colleen | Blue Hole, Hope Town etc. |
| 6/2003 | Bill, Rose, Robin, Adrienne, | |
| | Joseph, Michael, Ralph E | Blue Hole, Hope Town etc. |

# Southwest USA, 1999

Bill and Rose had been through the southwestern states on previous trips, but usually were on a tight schedule with business to do. Now, in retirement, they could be more leisurely and do more visiting and sightseeing, even if combined with conferences and meetings Bill still attended. The excuse for the trip, if they needed one, was a NSEA conference in San Diego scheduled for October 24, 1999. They left Edisto on October 8th and went first to Berea, staying with Bill and Anne. There was a president's dinner at the college, which they were able to attend. Then they headed west with the first stop at St. Louis.

*We had a very pleasant time with Doris and Bob Pohl at their home in Kirkwood. Doris was my roommate in college and maid of honor at our wedding. Bob was a consummate host and saw that we were well fed, entertained and housed for the night. It is so great to have friends like this all across the country and beyond.*

*We went on the next day to Abilene, Kansas and stayed with Ruth Dieter. Ruth was originally a Kentucky girl who went to Pine Mountain Settlement School when it had a residential program. She was now on the board with Bill and we had become good friends. She had a lovely home filled with dolls of all sizes. I love dolls!*

Ruth showed them the sights of Abilene including the Seelye Mansion which had been built by a man who made a fortune in patent medicine and invented some useful drugs in the early days of modern pharmacy. They also saw the town center, which included a performance hall named after Ruth, who was a patron of the arts and respected citizen. She had moved there as a young woman with on older physician for whom she was office manager when he left Kentucky and she stayed, becoming a very successful business woman.

*We left Ruth and made our way across Kansas. We stopped to see the ruts and tracks across the prairie made by the westward wagons on the Santa Fe Trail. What a trek that must have been across the grasslands with limitless horizon.*

*We read about other trails further north – the Oregon Trail and the Chisholm Trail. We stayed that night at a motel in Liberal, Kansas, in the middle of cattle country which could be clearly discerned by both sight and smell,*

## Further West

On October 14 they crossed into the panhandles of Oklahoma and Texas and into New Mexico.

*We remembered other trips that took us through Amarillo, Texas. We had especially enjoyed Palo Duro Canyon there. It is such a surprise. The country is flat and mostly barren and suddenly you come upon a canyon carved below the plain where there are streams and trees and beautifully colored rock formations. Since my student days at Berea College learning from Dr. and Mrs. Burroughs, I've always loved geology and here, as in other canyons you could see layers and colors and formations that spoke of the passage of time and the wonder of God's creation and laws. The water in the streams is green and gives a sense of springtime and freshness so different than the desert like terrain from which you descend. A magical place! We went on straight west until we could see Sandia Mountain at Albuquerque where our friends from Oak Ridge days, Bill and Virginia Busby lived. It was wonderful to visit them again and get caught up on their three grown children who had been little playmates of ours children years ago.*

The Busbys took them to Santa Fe to see some of the Spanish architecture and old mission churches and shops. It was interesting to see the end of the Santa Fey trail they had viewed on the plains of Kansas. They had planned to go from Albuquerque to Utah because they had never been to that state, but the weather forecast was for snow and so they cancelled their Utah trip and, instead, drove across the northern part of New Mexico and Arizona. They traversed the Three Mesas which have been the home of the Hopi Indians for centuries and then dropped down to Flagstaff, AZ. They went to Walnut Canyon and Bill went down the many steps to the cliff dwellings wondering how they managed with their back yard being the back of the cave and the front yard being an abyss. From Flagstaff, they drove down Oak Creek Canyon to Sedona.

*We stopped to look at, and to buy, some Indian jewelry displayed on blankets alongside the winding road on the canyon rim and then dropped down to Sedona marveling at the red rock formations and enjoying the warmer temperature. Sedona is most interesting and we wandered about shops and parks. We went on south to see Montezuma Castle and Montezuma Well. The "castle" is an impressive cliff dwelling that is not really a castle and has nothing to do with Montezuma but got that label mistakenly by early explorers. The well was a most mysterious place with cliff dwellings along the rim above the water below. One felt the ancient spirit of the place and could imagine the Indians living there. They had ingeniously channeled water from the well through tunnels and ditches to irrigate fields below.*

They continued their trip west. They had seen in New Mexico and Arizona spectacular rock formations caused by centuries of wind and water, sun and freezing. Going further west they saw mesas and cliffs displaying the bones of the earth. They took pictures of Church Rock and Ship Rock looking as if a giant had carved them. Bill took a picture of Rose with the background showing huge red rock with a hole right through the middle of it. The Saguaro Cactus, standing like sentinels with their arms raised, became familiar sights. They had a time-share in Scottsdale and enjoyed seeing that area and hearing the coyotes howl under the moon at night. In due course, on October 23 they arrived in San Diego. Bill attended the NSEA conference there.

*We had good visits with Martha Vickers and her daughters as well as NSEA friends. We visited the beautiful sailing ship, Star of India, at its dock and spent a day at the famous San Diego Zoo. We also took time to see Vera Kizer, whom we had known at Edisto, before Harry, her husband, died and she moved away.*

## Headed Back East

They visited other friends who had been fellow church members at Edisto as they began their return trip. George and Marie Johnson had moved to a retirement community below Tucson, almost to the Mexican border. Marie had been the person, when Bill and Rose first moved to Edisto, who invited them to come to the United Methodist Church there. While they were in the area they visited beautiful old missions and learned more about the holy friars that had traversed the west to minister to the Indians.

*We had seen the beginning of the San Diego Trail on visits to St Augustine. Florida and it was fascinating to have been at its end in San Diego and see missions at places across the width of the USA. We were reminded that there were all kinds of Indian tribes. Many were peaceful and had crops and domestic animals as well as being hunters of game. Other tribes were warlike and raided the lands that were productive, taking what others had produced. Protection was one reason for the cliff dwellings. The peaceful tribes welcomed the missionaries and were relieved to have strong buildings and walls and unity to protect them from the marauding tribes, as well as hearing that good news of the gospel and participating in the rituals of the church and having access to wider learning.*

While they were in the area they visited Tombstone. It has remained a western town with board sidewalks, saloons and cowboys with guns strapped on lounging along the streets. The OK Corral is still there. When mining played out it threatened to become a ghost town but was discovered by Hollywood and became a preferred site for films about the west. Being there is like being on a movie set.

Continuing east with a stop at El Paso they arrived at Dallas and had a fine visit with George and Liz Deuillet. They got back to Berea via Memphis to stay with Jennifer and Alfredo. Bill then went to a board meeting at Pine Mountain Settlement School. On Friday, November 12, he went to the David School in Prestonsburg, KY for a conference and service project of the work colleges. Then they left Kentucky for Edisto, arriving home on November 15 after a long trip and many new memories.

# CHAPTER 33

# EDISTO YEARS III

## Revival

In 1999, Larry Mixon in our Bible fellowship had an inspiration to call for a revival on Edisto and he proposed this to the ministerial association. The active leadership on the ministerial association at the time came primarily from the Edisto Beach Baptist Church pastor, Tony Neal, the Episcopal Church priest, Wey Camp, the historic Presbyterian Church minister, Chuck Klotzberger and the pastor of the New First Baptist Church (with an almost exclusively black congregation) Chick Morrison. Besides these four churches and the United Methodist Church, which Rose and Bill represented, there were nine other churches on Edisto Island. The priest at St. Frederick and St. Stephen Catholic Church was Father Bill. The Presbyterian Church USA (with primarily black membership) was pastored by Reverend McKinley Washington, for whom the bridge to Edisto was named. He had been a state legislator and government official in addition to being a minister.

There was another small black Baptist Church - Mount Olive - further up the island and three African Methodist Episcopal (AME) churches – Allen, Bethel and Calvary. Bethlehem Church was a reformed (RMUE) church with a black congregation. Zion Reformed Episcopal was another small black church. Finally the little Greater Galilee Church, with its black membership and pastor living in the Charleston area rather than on Edisto but with roots and a cemetery on Edisto, completed the list of 14 churches.

Every year the main churches jointly held an Easter Sunrise Service at the Pavilion parking lot at beach front. Alternating leadership and musical offerings the service was staged so the congregants sitting or standing outside on a brisk morning were facing east across the Atlantic and could see the sun rise on this holy day. It was a moving experience to worship and sing with others from various traditions. After the service the Pavilion restaurant offered donuts and coffee to all who wished to continue fellowship. The larger churches also cooperated in an annual Lenten series of worship services and a community Thanksgiving service held at a different church each year. Therefore planning together was not unusual, but many of the smaller churches were not involved.

The ministers active in the ministerial association were interested in revival but careful in their exploration of the idea. They had apparently had a revival some years before prompted by a drought and the need to gather to pray for rain. It had been deemed successful but did not directly involve all the churches. The decision was to spend a year praying and thinking about the matter. This was done and then the decision was to move ahead, but to take a year to plan. It was scheduled for February 2001. In February the island papulation would not include the vacationers and tourists that were present in the warmer weather. The locals said that after the vacation season they were "given back their island." It was decided to try to get every church involved and emphasize unity of Christians and renewal of vital faith. The scripture reference chosen for the revival theme was from Ephesians 4: 4-6.

*"There is one body and one Spirit... one Lord, one faith, one baptism, one God and Father of us all...."*

Each church prepared a banner using this scripture, and the 14 banners proclaiming this unity hung in the large auditorium of the historic Presbyterian Church. Bill and Rose drove around the island and took pictures of each church and put together a brochure of the Fourteen Churches of Edisto Island. Bill was asked to be in charge of publicity and prepared announcements, flyers, posters, a prayer calendar for the churches to use and articles for the newspapers. Rose was asked to serve on the music committee with Rev. Brown from Calvary AME Church and find a music leader. A choir was formed from all the church choir members who would join – and there were many representing very different styles of singing.

*We received several suggestions from ministers and others for contacts who might know of a potential choir director, song leader and pianist. We wanted the music to be the feature that held the revival together. The preachers would represent a different tradition each night but the music was to be a blend of styles. I made a lot of phone calls following up on leads. Rev. Brown was a joy to work with and we soon had interviews set up with possible candidates. We ended up choosing two musicians. One was a tall handsome black man whose experience was mostly classical hymnody. He was an excellent pianist who could play anything. The other was a shorter, younger black musician who had classical training but was a gifted song leader and had a flair for spirit songs. Together they made a formidable team and the music was just great. The choir had fun learning the different styles of singing, with the black singers teaching their white counterparts how to sway and clap properly with the music when it was from their tradition. The words to hymns were projected on a screen so no hymnals were needed and all were looking up as they sang together. To hear so many voices lifted up in unity was very moving.*

The planners and workers on the revival learned a great deal about each other and their ways of worship. When the Episcopal priest drafted an order of worship to guide those who were preparing for each night the Baptists observed that there was no "alter call." The priest explained that in their church congregants took communion each Sunday and that was considered an alter call as each came forward to seek forgiveness of sins and recommit themselves. An alter call was added to the order of worship. During the revival the Catholic priest explained that the use of icons or pictures of the saints was not a worship of idols or the saints but a remembering and honoring them, much as pictures of parents and grandparents on a person's mantle was a way of remembering and honoring those who were loved and had left a legacy. One of the black preachers instructed the congregation that their preaching was a joint endeavor requiring participation. The hearers were to respond with an "amen!" if they agreed with something or a "praise the Lord!" if they felt inspired. He said he was asked once what the response should be if he said something the person didn't agree with. His answer was, "Just say, 'Help him Lord.'"

*I can still see Father Bill from the Catholic Church on his night as he was leading the service and got mixed up. He had been ill and missed several meetings. He asked for forgiveness and pointed out that he didn't have a wife to keep him straight. "In fact," he said, "I live in a rectory; that is a home for unwed fathers." Each church, or group of churches from a shared tradition, had brought in a leader from their denomination to give the message on their night. The Methodists were represented by Bishop McClosky. All the "evangelists" were inspiring, full of wisdom and encouragement. They emphasized the theme of the revival – "One God and Father of us all!" Rose and I had planned to attend several times during the week but after the first night we didn't want to miss a single night. Others felt the same. The presence of the Holy Spirit and the joy of Christian fellowship were so strong that all wanted to be together and didn't want the experience to end. We felt that it was a foretaste of the Kingdom of God on earth.*

The revival did carry forward both in new relationships, particularly between black and white church members, and in practical ways. For a time, on one Sunday a month, an all-community worship service was held in the evening, moving from church to church so all could share in the different settings and styles. Bill and Rose got to know a wonderful couple of their age group from the Bethlehem Church and another couple whose families had lived on the island for generations. They had interesting stories to tell as Rose recalls.

*Richard and Ruth Brown are a highly educated, elegant but humble couple. He had been a teacher and superintendent of schools. She had been successful in business and with raising a family. Richard's ancestors had come to Edisto, not as slaves but as indentured servants and in due course had met their obligations and been granted land. They and other blacks were freeholders who prospered in the midst of a slave state. Richard served in the military in World War II. Ruth was one of five daughters from a tenant family in upcountry South Carolina. Her parents had taught their girls that they could achieve their goals in spite of discrimination and barriers. Ruth had done well in school and wanted to go to college and study business. The black college in South Carolina didn't have a business program but the state had a policy guaranteeing access to higher education for its black citizens, if not in the state then by arrangements with colleges in other parts of the country. Ruth was sent to Columbia University for her business studies at state expense and there she met Richard, just back from his service at the end of WW II. When he sought her attention, she told him she already had a boyfriend. He said to tell the boyfriend that he had some competition and that is what he had fought for in the war. Obviously, they ended up married and, after successful careers and family, had retired to the family land on Edisto. One member of the family was an Admiral in the US Navy. It was such a pleasure to visit them and share our faith and life experiences.*

## Special Edisto Times with Grandchildren

In addition to the many family visits there were times when one or two or more of the grandchildren would stay at *Cair Paravel* for extended periods. Those were special times. Bill and Rose took Catherine and John Paul on one such visit to a performance of *Serenade* in Charleston. It was a wonderful musical variety show.

*Once, when Jon and Keith and Naomi were staying, the boys saw a snake in our living room. It was bright green and had apparently climbed the palm tree by the back deck and got inside. We had seen another snake on that tree in a confrontation with a squirrel but never thought about one coming in the house. Bill captured the green snake and put it in a bucket with a lid over it. Then we called the Serpentarium which a reptile loving family had established on Edisto and they said to bring it on down. We had many interesting visits to the Serpentarium but I never became too fond of snakes.*

Another memorable time was on a visit from Martin and Charlie and boys when the "tall ships" sailed into Charleston harbor and gave tours of the graceful crafts. There were always visits to Fort Moultrie and the interesting houses on Sullivan's Island including some beautiful mansions, some built under the high dunes and some looking like a bowling ball or a piece of Swiss cheese. And usually a feast at Gilligan's was included or fresh grouper was grilled at *Cair Paravel*.

As the grandchildren grew into young adults they continued to love to come to Edisto. Catherine was at the College of Charleston from 1999 until 2004 and visited frequently. Melissa had entered Flagler College in 2000 and in the summer of 2001 stayed with Bill and Rose at *Cair Paravel* and worked for the recreation department at the Fairfield resort. She was an attendant at the swimming pool, check-out person for equipment and did other duties. The resort offered her a second and then a third summer of work and she accepted. Her artistic talent was discovered and she was commissioned to paint a mural on a wall just at the entrance to the resort and created a beautiful, colorful under water scene. She also began to make macramé bracelets, necklaces and anklets, ornamented with beads and/or shells to give to her friends. They were very attractive and popular. Melissa did such a good job that Fairfield was pleased to offer similar jobs to two more grandchildren the year after she had completed three years. So in the summer of 2004 Daniel and Colleen lived at *Cair Paravel*. Rose was pleased to have them.

*We had enjoyed the three summers with Melissa and found Daniel and Colleen delightful. They are both full of life, energy and charm. They liked it too. Where else could you have a paying job, get free lodging, and savor grandma's cooking all in the same summer? Daniel found the first couple weeks at work boring. He was attendant at a new swimming pool and it was early enough in the season that almost no one was around. He asked Bill what he had to read and Bill showed him the classics he had on the shelves. Daniel read War and Peace in that short interval but then got busy. Melissa had taught them how to make macramé items and Daniel and Colleen started to make them while they were at their stations at the pools. They used shells along with beads and sometimes incorporated sharks teeth they had found. The tourists were fascinated and soon wanted to buy bracelets, anklets and necklaces. The enterprising youngsters soon had a business going. The resort people were happy to encourage them since the guests were excited to buy inexpensive home-made souvenirs. They even let Daniel set up a display in the gift shop – bracelets hanging on a piece of driftwood with a sign announcing "Disto Dan's Creations." We would take Daniel and Colleen to Charleston to buy their supplies and they would come home and sit on the floor with twine stretched from their toes while they added the shells, beads and other items to create their wares. They ended up making* as much money from their enterprise as from their jobs and had a great time doing it. At the end of the summer the resort leadership asked if we had any more grandchildren who would like a summer job.

Bill and Rose, of course, had an almost endless supply of grandchildren, but not all were at the right age or circumstance. However the following summer, Rebekah filled one slot and the other was filled by her good friend from their mission time in Kazakhstan, Hannah Duggins, who was like a grandchild. So again *Cair Paravel* had two delightful young people in residence for the summer. They were also very good workers and they quickly learned the macramé tradition and continued that business, doubling their summer income. Bill and Rose were proud of their grandchildren and thoroughly enjoyed those five summers.

*We were blessed with so many opportunities to be with our families and they often scheduled times when all or most could be there at the same time, each renting a beach house and some staying with us. On one such family gathering in 1999, we carried on the family tradition in dramatics. For the reunion, Jennifer had abridged the script for the musical, Li'l Abner, taking out some of the bawdy humor and shortening it for family entertainment. The play, based on the classic comic strip by Al Capp, was produced by Paramount Pictures in 1959 as a spoof on society and politics of that time, but it lent itself to some good clean fun, especially for a family with roots in the hills of Kentucky. She assigned various family members roles and sent scripts. Some of the teens were a bit resistant at first but soon got in the spirit of the play. When family arrived on the weekend, we had the first read through on Sunday afternoon. By Wednesday, all had learned their lines and the songs and we put on a production at the unfinished fellowship hall at our church for a gathering of about 30 family and friends. Laura, on a keyboard, provided the music and accompanied the songs. Alfredo and Bill had created, from cardboard boxes, a statue of Jubilation T. Cornpone, who, according to the proclamation inscribed on it, almost singlehandedly lost the war for the South. The cast was a list of Ramsays, Comptons and Escobars. It was quite a production, strictly amateur, but fun for both those in the play and the family and friends watching it. Everyone wanted to know what, where and when the next production would be, but it didn't happen again on that scale.*

Another enjoyable series of events were visits from groups of students from Berry College. They were Bonner Scholars in a summer enrichment program. John Heneisen, who was Dean of Work at Berry, brought them to Edisto for a week's retreat for several years. Years before, Bill had helped get the Bonner Scholar's program started. He had accompanied Berea president John Stephenson on a visit to Mr. Bonner, who wanted to help young students who had limited funds have a chance at higher education and to learn the value of community service. Bill was able to give advice and counsel. Mr. Bonner and his wife endowed an enormous program to meet his goals involving a number of colleges, of which Berry and Berea were two. When the Bonner Scholars from Berry came to Edisto, Bill and Rose arranged housing and hosting and participated in some of their sessions on service-learning.

*Bob Warner, a friend from church had a portable gas fired boiler rigged up on a trailer which he used to do a shrimp boil wherever it was wanted. We contracted with him to provide the boiler and we purchased shrimp, potatoes, small sections of corn on the cob and other ingredients for the shrimp boil and sauces. The students and the rest of us enjoyed this low country specialty outside of one of their cottages. We also arranged for a black woman to come to give them a picture of the Gullah culture of the South Carolina and Georgia coastal areas. She was most informative and entertaining with her stories and humor, much of which had to do with the relationships of slaves or servants to their masters and mistresses and their shrewd observations. We also took the group to visit Ruth and Richard Brown to get a live history of a dignified and positive black experience which happened in spite of slavery and discrimination.*

## Events Away From Edisto

Bill had frequent trips to Pine Mountain for board meetings and to Middlesboro, Corbin, Kingsport, Berea and Lexington for meetings of the executive committee. On one trip to Berea in 1997 they were part of their college class homecoming reunion. Bill was given a special award from the Alumni Association for his services to Berea. That was the same year Pine Mountain dedicated their new Far House and Jennifer sang her composition, *Pine Mountain Lullaby*.

Bill and Rose traveled to Louisville in 2000 to be with Wayne when his wife, Velva, died. Velva had some mental issues and had been ill with cancer for some years and, finally, required full time care. Wayne was a faithful husband until the end and buried her in the family plot at Oak Dale in Tennessee. Laura and Ralph also attended Wayne at the time of death and the funeral. Wayne, though not yet retired, frequently visited Bill and Rose and they often met together in Greene County for decoration at Oak Dale cemetery which was held in May each year. They would always include visits to Lizzie McAmis, their old neighbor from early childhood, in Baileyton and often visited cousins Juanita Walton and Dorsey and Winnie Sproles in Kingsport. Three years after Velva's death Wayne met Carolyn, a lovely widow, in a church singles group and Bill and Rose went to their wedding in Louiville in November 2003. Many visits with Wayne and Carolyn ensued in Louisville, at Edisto and in Florida, where they acquired a vacation home.

In 1998, Bill E. and Anne had moved from Danville, IL to Berea, where Bill E. began work for Berea College.

*We visited Bill and Anne, Amber, Will and Daniel, helping them move into a college house to start their new Berea years. That winter, Berea had a record snow and we enjoyed playing with the various Berea grandchildren in it. Later Bill E. and Anne moved to a more permanent home on Holly Hill in Berea.*

## Anniversaries

*In September 1998, Jennifer and Alfredo invited us to come to Berea for our joint wedding anniversaries on September 7, our 46th year. They had chosen to be married on our anniversary and we subsequently shared a celebration whenever we could. They wouldn't tell us what they had planned but advised us to pack a suitcase, including some nice clothes, and said to follow them in our car. We drove from Berea to Knoxville and east, so we thought we were probably headed to the Smoky Mountains. But we drove past the exits to Gatlinburg and Cosby and headed into North Carolina, ending up in Asheville at the Albemarle Inn. It is a lovely bed-and-breakfast and we had spacious rooms and great food. We went out for dinner to the Richmond Inn.*

*We had a very special anniversary together, thanks to the thoughtfulness and careful arrangements of Jennifer and Alfredo.*

Bill E. and Anne, and Martin and Charlie were celebrating their 25th anniversaries in 2000 and Ralph and Laura the next year. Others were reaching anniversaries numbering in the 20 years, so Bill and Rose, with the help of their Berea children, organized a joint celebration of marriage for December 27, 2000. It was held at the Berea United Methodist Church and special married couple friends were invited to join the celebration, Doc and Roberta Schaeffer were there. Sandy and Al Osborne came. Rob and Susan Anderson, Alex and Debbie Carrick and others of the children's friends attended. Rev. Charles and Elizabeth Bertrand helped and participated. Rev. Clyde David Burberry, who had performed the wedding ceremonies of the first five of Bill and Rose's children, was present with his wife Susan. All together the number of married years represented was in the hundreds. Everyone shared stories and wisdom. Skits were presented exaggerating family lore to the amusement of all. Special songs were sung by those who could perform. Jennifer and Alfredo sang the song Jennifer had written for their wedding reception four years earlier. And everybody sang together. Prayers were offered. And, of course, there was "wedding cake" and lots of good food. It was a true *Celebration of Marriage.*

The Reunion Players Present

# L'il Abner

Edisto Island United Methodist Church Pavilion

7:30 PM Wednesday, August 31, 1999

Abridged and Adapted by Jennifer Rose Ramsay Escobar
Music Adapted by Accompanist Laura Ramsay Conpton

PICTURES

DAISY MAE SCRAGGS
ABNER YOKUM
EARTHQUAKE
MCGOON
MOONBEAM MCSWINE
MAYOR DAWGMEAT

PICTURES

MAMMY YOKUM
PAPPY YOKUM
MARRYIN' SAM
DR. FINSDALE
JACK S. PHOGBOUND
"SECRETARY" TWO

DOGPATCH IS ABOUT TO BE DESTROYED, BUT THE STATUE OF GENERAL JUBILATION T. CORNPONE IS DECLARED A NATIONAL TREASURE AND THE TOWN IS SAVED.

(Additional pictures and information on next page)

441

## L'il Abner

(page 2)

GENERAL BULLMOOSE HELPED BY HIS "PERSONAL ASSISTANT" APPASSIONATA WANTS TO GET THE TONIC THAT MAKES L'IL ABNER THE PERFECT SPECIMEN OF MANHOOD. HE IS THWARTED WHEN EVIL EYE'S "TRUTH TELLING WHAMMY" IS DEFLECTED BY EARTH-QUAKE MCGOON SO IT HITS BULLMOOSE INSTEAD OF ABNER.

GENERAL BULLMOOSE

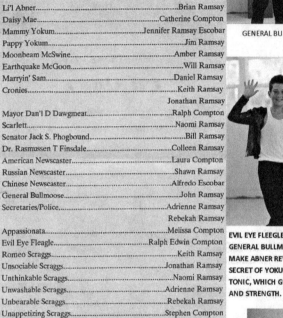

## CAST OF CHARACTERS

| | |
|---|---|
| Li'l Abner | Brian Ramsay |
| Daisy Mae | Catherine Compton |
| Mammy Yokum | Jennifer Ramsay Escobar |
| Pappy Yokum | Jim Ramsay |
| Moonbeam McSwine | Amber Ramsay |
| Earthquake McGoon | Will Ramsay |
| Marryin' Sam | Daniel Ramsay |
| Cronies | Keith Ramsay |
| | Jonathan Ramsay |
| Mayor Dan'l D Dawgmeat | Ralph Compton |
| Scarlett | Naomi Ramsay |
| Senator Jack S. Phogbound | Bill Ramsay |
| Dr. Rasmussen T Finsdale | Colleen Ramsay |
| American Newscaster | Laura Compton |
| Russian Newscaster | Shawn Ramsay |
| Chinese Newscaster | Alfredo Escobar |
| General Bullmoose | John Ramsay |
| Secretaries/Police | Adrienne Ramsay |
| | Rebekah Ramsay |
| Appassionata | Melissa Compton |
| Evil Eye Fleegle | Ralph Edwin Compton |
| Romeo Scraggs | Keith Ramsay |
| Unsociable Scraggs | Jonathan Ramsay |
| Unthinkable Scraggs | Naomi Ramsay |
| Unwashable Scraggs | Adrienne Ramsay |
| Unbearable Scraggs | Rebekah Ramsay |
| Unappetizing Scraggs | Stephen Compton |

APPASSIONATA

EVIL EYE FLEEGLE IS HIRED BY GENERAL BULLMOOSE TO MAKE ABNER REVEAL THE SECRET OF YOKUMBERRY TONIC, WHICH GIVES YOUTH AND STRENGTH.

THE DISCOVERY OF YOKUMBERRY TONIC IS NEWS IN USA, RUSSIA AND CHINA

DAISY MAE, AFRAID THAT SHE IS NEVER TO CATCH ABNER, PROMISES TO MARRY MCGOON IF HE WILL SAVE ABNER FROM BULLMOOSE. ALL WORKS OUT IN THE END. DAISY AND ABNER MARRY ATTENDED BY THEIR FAMILIES, INCLUDING DAISY MAE'S SCRAGGS COUSINS, ROMEO, UNSOCIABLE, UNTHINKABLE, UNWASHABLE, UNBEARABLE AND UNAPPETIZING.

EVERYONE SINGS A GRAND FINALE

# CHAPTER 34

# TRAVELING AGAIN

## Northwest Passage: Fall 2000

"Where are you off to this time?" Clint Williams asked as Bill and Rose drove out of the security gate at Fairfield Ocean Ridge and handed him an itinerary. They always let him know when they were leaving on a trip, how long they would be gone and where they were going. Clint, as head of security, would see that their house was watched and be aware of their being away. He already had met all of the family on their visits to Edisto and had their numbers to call on case of necessity. So Bill and Rose could leave with confidence and a happy send off. This time they were going on a long trip to the Canadian Rockies and then to explore Montana, and other areas of northwest. They would meet Sandy and Al Osborne, who were flying to Calgary to drive together to Banff in the mountains. It was September 23, 2000 and the first stop was Brevard College, near Asheville in North Carolina where first grandchild Elizabeth was working as a student residence counselor.

*Elizabeth showed us around the campus and introduced us to her friends. It made us feel proud that she had finished her college work at Berry and was happily employed. Then we drove on to Berea and stayed with Jennifer and Alfredo. They had a Danish visitor, Martin Hansen, staying with them and we had a lovely visit there and with other family members in Berea.*

On Monday they began their Northwest trip, stopping in Louisville for lunch with Wayne. It rained off and on all day with heavy showers at times until they got to their overnight lodging at Peoria, IL. The next day they drove through fields of wheat, corn and soybeans and saw big barns, silos, farm machinery and grain elevators. They crossed the Mississippi at Moline into Iowa. They met Frank Starr in Cedar Falls for lunch.

*It was wonderful to see Frank and his friend Veda Rasmussen. Frank had been one of the master science teachers in the first group of "traveling teachers" in Oak Ridge. He and his wife Eleanor became close friends and were at our house when Stephen was born in 1956. They were Stephen's godparents. Eleanor had died about a year ago. We all visited her grave. Veda was like a sister to Frank and Eleanor.*

## **Corn Country and National Parks**

They went on through Iowa seeing more farm country and had supper at Cherokee, wondering why the town was named that in the middle of Sioux country. At dusk they arrived at Sioux Center where they had a Wayside visit arranged. Their hosts, Gerald and Darlene Van Roeker, had recently moved into town from a large farm which they still owned with their son.

The Roekers took us on a tour of the farm and surrounding areas. We saw a pile of shelled corn higher than a two story house and visited a dairy owned and operated by the charming Roseblum family – Joe, Betty and three sons. It was harvest time and we learned a lot about large scale farming in the rich soil of the flat country, which is quite different from farming in the hills of Appalachia.

Leaving Sioux Center with thanks to the Roekers for their gracious hosting and touring, they headed north, crossed briefly into Minnesota and then crossed the Sioux River into South Dakota. At noon, they reached Mitchell, had lunch at Arby's and toured the Corn Palace. It is a town center and performance hall with the outside veneered entirely by corn – stalks, ears, kernels, tassels and leaves. Every year it is redone tastefully, especially for the birds that feed on it. They moved on to Chamberlain where a welcome center featured the Lewis and Clark expedition which had camped there on the Missouri River. Farm land gave way to drier ranch land with lots of cattle and a few horses. Then they reached the Badlands Park. Rose summed up her reactions in her journal.

*Incredible sights! We felt like we'd entered another world! The formations had been sculpted by wind and water erosion into designs and shape that are amazing. We are thankful for the people who had the wisdom to protect an area like this.*

Coming out of the badlands they visited the much advertised Wall Drug Store and related shops and went on to Rapid City where they spent two nights so they could see parks in the area. They took a steep drive into the Black Hills with its winding roads, lovely forests and great vistas. It was a fitting entrance to the magnificent Mount Rushmore.

*We first got glimpses of Mount Rushmore as we rounded curves in the hills. Then as we got closer had a better idea of the size and grandeur of the natural monument on which the faces are carved. The Visitor Center and Avenue of Flags are well done We received lessons in the courage, devotion and character of the men whose faces are carved there – George Washington, Thomas Jefferson, Theodore Roosevelt and Abraham Lincoln. It is a very impressive monument and, again, we were thankful for those who have created it and make it available to visitors in such a positive way.*

They drove winding roads, around corkscrew curves and over and under "pigtail" bridges on roads surrounded by deep green fir trees and golden maple and aspen. They went through tunnels carved right through solid rock. They saw sheer cliffs and beautiful views and then, when they reached the park were rewarded with sights of white tailed deer, buffalo, goats, coyotes, prairie dogs, burros and sheep. They visited Wind Cave in another lovely area. It was a full day and a surfeit of sights.

The next day, they went to Deadwood and Lead, towns of the late 1800s. Deadwood is full of casinos and slot machines in every establishment. Lead still has gold mining, now at 1800 feet below ground level. It was fascinating. They continued northwest into Wyoming and saw Devils Tower rising off the flat terrain like an enormous monolith.

*This huge rock with its vertical strata is a favorite challenge for rock climbers and we could see a few looking like ants clinging high above the ground to what appeared from a distance to be sheer sides. We didn't have any urge to try it and wondered about those who did. We went on into Montana driving across the Crow Indian Reservation and seeing farms and ranches, cattle and horses, but the ground was arid and the stream beds were dry.*

## On to Canada and the Rockies

After a night in Billings they wound their way to the top of a mesa and drove for miles along its rim. They saw huge tanks in the fields to provide water delivered by trucks for cattle. Water holes were dry and trimmed in white alkali dust. As they got further towards Great Falls and the Missouri River the land appeared more fertile and streams were running. They saw the small and graceful antelope along with horses and cattle in the fields and the now golden trees were bigger and more plentiful. They passed the Big Snowy mountain range and saw snow on top. The snow fences along the roads were silent testimony that snow was also part of life below the mountain top. It was windy and the golden stubble of harvested wheat moved in fields stretching to the horizon. Some fields had large round hay bales in evidence in preparation for winter. They crossed into Canada and the terrain was much the same. In the distant west were the outlines of high mountains. They stayed in Lethbridge that night and confirmed, by phone, the meeting with the Osbornes at Calgary the next day.

*We met the Osbornes at Calgary as planned and had a good lunch at their motel. Then we headed west for Banff. Al and Sandy are good company and our drive was very enjoyable. The countryside became more hilly, but still farmland. Then we saw the mountains, distant and towering. As we drew nearer they were breathtaking – huge snow-capped rocks, unbelievably enormous and beautiful, each one more amazing than the one before.*

They arrived at Rocky Mountain Resort and settled in a comfortable apartment. There were towering mountains on every side with little roads along the bases that led to Banff and to the marvelous lakes in the area – Minnewake with a few boats on sparkling water,, Two Jacks with a lovely picnic area on its pebbly shore and Johnson with its mammoth rocks. They drove around and enjoyed the scenery and went to "Melissa's" restaurant to eat. The menu had every imaginable hamburger combination including

446

cheeses, mushrooms, bacon, sauces and you name it. Sandy, always down to earth, found the most honest and cheapest, the "Plain Jane" described as "meat, meat, meat on a bun, bun, bun! She said it was good. We bought a shirt and hat with the restaurant's logo for our Melissa at home.

Bill and Al took several guided walking tours around lakes, sometime trudging through snow. They circled a hot springs marsh that steamed in the icy weather. Sandy and Rose prepared some meals at the condo and fixed a picnic lunch they enjoyed at Two Jack Lake. Other meals were at cozy, quaint restaurants in Banff. They drove to see Bow River and Bow River Falls and took a day trip to see Lake Louise.

*The scenery is unbelievably beautiful with towering rock mountains, some peaking at 9000 feet, tall pines, clear rivers and lakes. Lake Louise is a glacier fed lake tucked among the mountains. The powdered rock ground up by the glacier gives the lake a beautiful blue color. It was an icy walk from the parking area to the lake which was dangerous for Sandy who had recently undergone hip surgery, but we managed by hanging on to each other and got to see the glacier above the far end of the lake. We drove into British Columbia to see Takakau Falls tumbling and falling down from about 750 feet. Ice sculptures formed around its base from the water splashing as it hit the pool and stream below. The road there was so twisted that we watched a bus having to go part way around a corkscrew and back-up to make the curve. On the way back to Banff we saw more elk and a black bear.*

They took more tours of the area, revisiting some of the favorite lakes and just enjoying the cold, fresh, invigorating air and trying to get their minds around the grandeur of these mountains. They did laundry, talked and packed up for the return trip. They reached Calgary, had lunch and parted with the Osbornes at the airport. Rose and Bill continued their journey by car heading for the USA-Canada border.

## Back to the USA

Montana is a big state and one feels its space with fields, hills and distant, blue mountains. Towns are not close together. Gambling is legal and there are slot machines in almost every establishment which were not tempting to Bill and Rose, but seemed to be part of the culture there. They went back through Great Falls and caught up with family news by phone from their motel there. They went on crossing the Missouri River again several times and wondering at its extent and the Lewis and Clark travelers who had traversed it so many years ago when the northwest was largely unknown territory except to the Indian tribes in the area.

*Soon Bill and I were among the hills; then mountains of rock. We crossed the Missouri again. Water here is a deep blue. We took pictures near Craig and could see another bridge across the river. As we approached Helena the rocks were more layered and looked loose. They were a deep maroon red. We crossed Prickly Pear Creek. We stopped at an Arby's in Helena and I decided to have a "Montana" in Montana. It was a lot of meat but I managed to eat it all. We left Helena and entered a lovely valley. There was a blue lake and ranches and cattle and lots of red and golden trees. Always in the distance were the dark blue hills and misty, blue mountains. We crossed the Missouri again.*

They were headed for Yellowstone and the road ran along the Gallatin River. They had found a delicious bakery at Three Forks and supplied themselves with bread, rolls and pastries. About 20 miles from West Yellowstone where they were to stay a female or young male moose crossed the road in front of them. On October 10, they arrived at their destination and had four days to see this fascinating park.

## The Cauldron of Yellowstone

Yellowstone, established in 1872, and managed by the US Army before the National Park Service was established in the 1900s, is the world's first national park. It now includes over 3000 square acres with almost all in Wyoming and little sections in Montana and Idaho. It is considered an active volcano. More than 1000 earthquakes are recorded each year and there are numerous geysers, Old Faithful being the best known. Evidence of humans goes back thousands of years. Rose and Bill felt like they were on the fabled "journey to the middle of the earth" and very vulnerable as tiny insects on a thin crust above a boiling cauldron.

*We entered the park driving over and into mountains of sheer red cliffs and slopes showing acres of fire damaged trees. We learned that over 800,000 acres of forest had been destroyed by fire in 1988. We saw a buffalo herd by a stream where fishermen were standing in their high boots casting their lines. Thinking of the fires we saw "smoke" ahead but as we approached found it to be steam - lots of steam. Steam came out from boiling pots, from under the road, from the sides of hills. Obviously something was boiling beneath us. We saw Old Faithful shoot water and steam 40 to 50 feet into the air, on schedule, and other geysers that were not as spectacular or predictable. We saw blown out basins where earlier eruptions had occurred, blowing out rocks and trees and ground along with the steaming water and we wondered how safe we were. We drove to beautiful Yellowstone Lake and could see the Grand Tetons in the distance across the lake. Breathtaking country!*

They went to the visitor centers and read about the phenomenon that is Yellowstone. They walked on boardwalks over steaming streams and pools and saw bright colors on the rocks under the water, painted by minerals over time – yellow for sulfur, red for iron, etc. They drove the Firehole Lake loop and saw more boiling springs and more buffalo and elk. They learned that Steamboat Geyser had shot water 300 feet in the air in 2000 and they watched Echinus erupt, spewing a 15 foot geyser of water as acidic as vinegar. Each day was a new and exciting adventure. They drove through the park to the north entrance at Mammoth Hot Springs which takes you through forests, past steaming hills and down a long mountain.

*We saw two moose on the way and then two herds of elk lying on the grass of the visitor center like tame cattle. After a lunch at the center we went outside and I told Bill that I smelled snow and we'd better get back up the mountain before the road was covered. We got to the top before the snow but still had a long way to go and drove slowly through a wild snow storm with thunder and lightning. Just as we were approaching the west exit we saw a herd of buffalo right next to the road with their backs to the wind and their great shaggy dark bodies covered with snow. That night we looked out the window of our cozy room to see tall, snow decorated pines like a winter wonderland of Christmas trees. One night we heard a wolf howl and looked out the window to see a large moon shining on the snowy pines. It was beautiful.*

They shopped in West Yellowstone, enjoyed meals in their room or at a café in town, did laundry and wrote post cards. They read their Bible texts and wrote in their journal. They took a side trip through the snow further west to cross the state line into Idaho but it was snowing too hard to go far. Finally it was time to leave. About five miles from Yellowstone, still in the forested area, they saw an animal alongside the road and thought it was a large dog. As they neared it and slowed down they realized it was a gray wolf. It turned and gracefully trotted into the trees – so wild and beautiful – Mowgli's Grey Brother.

## Road to the Sun

As they headed further west towards Whitefish, Montana, it was cloudy and began to rain but they could see wheat fields as they came out of the mountains and into ranch country. They ate lunch with bread from home ground wheat at The Montana Wheat Bakery and climbed steadily higher seeing rocky canyons and flat topped buttes. They passed well named Butte, Montana and went through Missoula, then headed through the Flathead Indian Reservation. It appeared a prosperous area with nice houses, farms, country stores and small towns. They drove beside Flathead Lake and learned that it is the largest lake west of the Mississippi. They came to Whitefish, picked up some groceries and proceeded upward for about seven miles, with spectacular views, to their time-share called Edelweiss at Big Mountain.

*Being between the summer vacation season and ski season there were few people about. We had a lovely apartment with a great view. We settled in, made soup, called Laura and Jennifer and slept. We decided the next morning to go to Glacier National Park even though it was cloudy and breezy. The park was scheduled to close for the winter next week. The temperature was actually warmer than the girls reported it was in Kentucky.*

It was about 35 miles to the park entrance. There are a lot of fir trees and one, the larch, or tamarack, which has golden needles in the fall. There are birches, poplar and aspen as well with cool looking mossy areas underneath the trees. Lake Mc Donald, formed by the glacier is five or six miles long, fresh looking in its beautiful setting. Beyond that is the mountain with an inviting road leading up. "The Road to the Sun" it is called and it runs from the west side across Logan Pass to the east gate – a distance of about 52 miles.

*At one point, the clouds parted and we could see the rocky cliffs and mountain peaks high above us. I saw what I thought at first was a mountain goat and then realized it was a vehicle far up the winding road. The CCC had carved the road up the side of the mountain more than sixty years ago and it hadn't had much maintenance since. We decided to go up and regretted it many times on the way up as we negotiated the narrow belt of pavement with sheer rock on one side and sheer nothingness on the other. There was no place to turn around. There were no guard rails, no white lines. The surface was rough. Every once in a while the road widened enough for two cars to pass; otherwise someone would have to back up. To make matters worse, the clouds moved in and we couldn't see a car length in front of us. Rose, on the side bordering the abyss kept telling me to get further over. She had visions of falling down, down, down. I replied that there was a cliff of sheer rock on my left and no room to move over. Once in a while, a gap opened in the clouds and we could see other peaks in the distance and glaciers in the valleys between. It was spectacular but frightening as it revealed the extent of the abyss a couple feet to our right. To say Rose was on edge was true literally as well as figuratively. We saw warning signs showing a picture of rocks hitting a car. Prayer probably got us through to the top and when we reached it we were exhausted. The visitor center was closed but there were port-a-pottys in the parking lot. It was frightening using one with the wind rocking it and threatening to blow it off the mountain.*

While they were at the top, the cold wind dissipated the clouds and they were treated to spectacular views of peaks and glaciers. The trip down was not nearly as bad. They were grateful that they had met no other cars on the trip. Towards the lower reaches, they saw waterfalls, rushing streams and cold looking pools and then back to McDonald Lake. They saw a grouse on the ground and later four in a tree and were treated to a view of a mule deer and two fawns. They were glad to get back to their condo, but resolved to return to the lower areas of the park.

# Uncle Clarence and Aunt Dora: Pioneers

On Sunday, October 15, they went to a little Methodist Church in Whitefish. They were welcomed warmly and enjoyed the worship and fellowship afterwards. They packed a picnic lunch and went back to Glacier. The tamaracks' golden needles in the sunshine among the deep green of the firs and mossy trunks of other trees made for gorgeous scenery. They ate their picnic at Fish Creek on the border of McDonalds Lake with a stupendous view of the peaks above. Returning to Whitefish they had fine dinner at Pollo's, a restaurant recommended by people at church. The next day they went to an orientation and learned more about the area, being advised on what to do if meeting a bear. They decided to try to avoid meeting one. They drove to Flathead Lake and walked along its shores, saw lovely art work and crafts at little shops and had lunch at Swan Lake Café. They purchased huckleberry jam at Eva Gates Shop and smelled the delicious blueberry preserves they were making. That evening, they heard coyotes and saw one at the garbage cans in the parking lot.

*We had been in touch with my cousin Tim Martin who lived in nearby Kalispel and had arranged a visit to his father and mother, my Uncle Clarence and wife Dora, at their remote home at Star Meadows bordering a national park. We had a lovely visit and lunch in their cozy cabin and heard stories of the wild creatures, including the grizzly bears, that come to visit them. My mother's youngest brother, Uncle Clarence was a favorite of my generation. He would tell us fanciful stories in the old barn at Hidden Paradise, when he could get there from medical school. He wrote us post cards, sometimes with little funny verses. He always addressed me as "Eversogood" and signed them "Vootz." When I read Nathaniel Hawthorne's Wonder Book and Tanglewood Tales, a copy of which he gave me, I pictured Uncle Clarence as Eustace Bright, the story teller, but if I were casting him for a play, I'd have him be King David with his ruddy good looks, strength, courage and poetic soul.*

Tim and his wife, Irene, who is a physician, invited them to have dinner, along with Clarence and Dora, at the Grouse Mountain Country Club and they had a fine meal and good visit. Uncle Clarence is a pioneer sort as well as a physician so it was not a surprise that his sons Tim and Jonathan are involved in politics with the Constitution Party. Before they left Big Mountain, they took more wonderful walks, sent a multitude of post cards and prepared to go east. The mountains gave way to rolling hills and then the hills gradually gave way to flat lands and behind them on the horizon they were leaving the rocky, snow-capped peaks of the mountains. On their way east, they stopped to have a meal and visit with Clarence and Dora's older son Jonathan, his wife and charming three daughters in Great Falls. Then they drove a long, long way across Montana and spent the night at Billings. On Saturday, October 21, they left Billings for North Dakota.

## Eastwards Towards Home

*We left about 10:00 AM and were soon in North Dakota. We stopped at "Home On the Range," a home for juveniles who have been in problem situations. The Fraternal Order of Eagles and Knights of Columbus provide this ranch where young people can get a new start, working, riding, eating and having fellowship, with counseling as they get their lives together. We went through the Dakota Badlands, seeing a wind canyon and pink sandstone made bricklike by heat from underground burning coal beds. We drove through Theodore Roosevelt National Park, where we saw buffalo and elk herds and prairie dog colonies.*

They stopped at Painted Canyon and went north to Knife River Indian Reservation. They visited another Lewis and Clark center, crossed the Missouri River yet again and saw a beautiful sunset. They saw wild turkeys fly into trees for the night at Ft. Mandan before reaching Bismark, where they had supper and spent the night. Keeping in touch with family, they had enjoyable phone visits with Bill E., Wayne and Elizabeth. The next day they crossed the Red River at Fargo to Morehead, MN and had a good visit with Bill and Becky Todt and their lively family – Benjamin, Michael, Annalise, Pricilla and Chase. Chase is a foster child they are trying to adopt. Bill and Becky's oldest child, Kirsten was away at college. Bill took them around Concordia College, where he teaches. When Bill and Rose got to Minneapolis that evening they called Kirsten at Bethel College and invited her to supper. They had an interesting and enjoyable visit with this charming great niece.

Dropping down into Illinois the next day, they stopped for a day with Dev and Shashi Mandhyan. Shashi, who had lived with Bill and Rose at the Big House in Berea for some time, was a manager at Walgreens and Dev worked for State Farm Insurance. He showed them the company headquarters on its extensive campus. The next day, they crossed Indiana into Kentucky and arrived at Richmond in time to see their great nephew and godson, John Paul, play the part of Mortimer in *Arsenic and Old Lace*. Then, on to Berea, a trip to Pine Mountain for a board meeting, and finally home to Edisto, arriving on Sunday afternoon, November 4 after an absence of six weeks full of new pictures in the mind and again, many memories. Clint was glad to welcome them home.

## Golden Anniversary

The next year, 2001, Bill and Rose were a year away from their 50th wedding anniversary. Since Jim and Shawn and the children would be on furlough from Kazakhstan in 2001, but gone the next year, the children decided to celebrate the golden wedding anniversary early and arranged for a gathering at the Methodist retreat center at Lake Junaluska in North Carolina.

*We rented three cottages of varying size and close to each other. Bill and I had the upper floor of one of the smaller units. For our larger gatherings, the children had rented a hall in the retreat center. All six of our children and their wives and husbands were there and all 20 grandchildren. The 21st grandchild to be, Lydia Eleanor, was much in evidence with Jennifer, well into her eighth month of pregnancy. Elizabeth had brought her fiancé, Ryan Sartor, along since he would soon be part of the family. Catherine's friend and first college roommate, Megan, came with her. They put on quite a program to celebrate our coming 50th year of marriage with songs, skits, humor, memories, praise songs, prayers and testimonies. Jim acted as emcee but everyone contributed. Anne Weatherford came with her daughter Edie Hunt to share their memories and wisdom. The best thing was just being together as a family. We have been so blessed with our marriage, our children, grandchildren and friends.*

They enjoyed the gorgeous roses of the retreat center. Some went canoeing on the lake. One day, the whole group caravanned to Celo for a fun time at the cold waterfall up White Oak Creek in the Pisgah National Forest and swimming at the Hemlocks on the South Toe River. Another day, a group took advantage of being in the area and went white water rafting. Everyone had a wonderful time.

## The Emerald Isle, 2002

Since Jennifer and Alfredo shared their wedding date with Bill and Rose they shared anniversary trips and celebrations. The one on September 7, 2002 would be Jennifer and Alfredo's sixth and Bill and Roses 50th and they thought a longer trip was in order. Alfredo had found a trip package for Ireland that included air fare, lodging vouchers for B & B's and a rental car for a very reasonable price so each couple bought one. Lydia had been born the year before and was approaching her first birthday on August 22 and she was a good baby and traveler. The younger family would go a few days earlier than Bill and Rose. Then they would have a week together and Bill and Rose would stay a few days after Jennifer, Alfredo and Lydia flew home. It was a good arrangement and worked out well. Bill and Rose left Edisto on Saturday, August 31, 2002.

*We drove north into North Carolina and stopped in Raleigh for supper with Dan and Aimee Sides. Dan had been a Berea student and friend and we had attended their wedding a little over a year before. Now we got to meet their new baby, Megan. Going further that night just into Virginia, we spent the night at South Hill. We got off the interstate to take Route 301, which is a pretty drive through Virginia to Maryland where we stopped in Annapolis to pick up a cell phone Jennifer had left at the home of Charles and Gwen Rector when she, Alfredo and Lydia had gone through. We returned it to Jennifer in Ireland.*

They would leave from the Baltimore airport the next day, so they stayed overnight at a motel nearby that had a shuttle and was willing for them to leave their car parked on site while they were away. They found Baltimore airport a very pleasant and helpful place and boarded their flight to Boston where they could catch Aer Lingus to Shannon in Ireland. They arrived in Boston and were informed that the flight to Ireland would be delayed. They had seven hours to kill in the airport which was not as pleasant as Baltimore's.

*We went through security and found a sitting area close to our departure gate and then had a little soup and sandwich lunch there. Later in the day, we decided to have a pastry and tea. The pastry was delicious but in sipping their tea through the little sipper/stirring stick both of us scalded the roofs of our mouths badly. We immediately got ice water but it was several days before eating was comfortable. Finally, it was time to board with about 400 others but all went smoothly and soon we were cruising at 27,000 feet at 500 miles per hour. It was a pleasant flight but we slept very little. It seemed incredible to be landing at Shannon at 8:00 AM. What happened to the night?*

## On Irish Soil

*We went through customs and found our rental car. To our surprise and delight, there stood Jennifer and Alfredo wearing hats of Irish wool, holding Lydia, looking so sweet and dear in a green Irish cape. They had waited a long time. We got a little black Fiat and followed Alfredo in their silver gray Toyota to the inviting Clare Inn where we were to spend our first night in Ireland. Bill had to concentrate to keep on the left side of the road.*

They settled into their room and the Escobars went to their B & B at Bunratty so all could get some needed rest. For lunch, they all gathered again at the Clare Inn and enjoyed the dining room. Jennifer and Alfredo had made reservation for a medieval dinner and evening show at Bunratty Castle for that evening, but Bill and Rose offered to keep Lydia so her parents could have a night out. This suited everybody and Bill and Rose went to Gallows View B & B where the Escobars were housed to enjoy baby sitting with their precious grandchild. They bought cheese, yogurt and fruit for a picnic in the flower garden of Mary McKenna, the proprietress of the B & B. After a walk with Lydia in a stroller, they all had a good nap before Jennifer and Alfredo returned from the castle.

*We all drove down to a pub called Durty Nelly's near the castle. Jennifer and Alfredo had been there the night before and we were greeted like old friends by the locals who gather for music, song and drink. We had a wonderful time listening to music, singing along and chatting with new Irish friends. We found the Irish everywhere to be unfailingly warm, friendly and helpful.*

Next day they all checked out of their lodgings, saying goodbye to Mary, and visited the Blarney Woolen Mill. They enjoyed looking at the wares and bought a dancing Irish doll for Lydia. Nearby, they were impressed with the large, stone, square, Bunratty castle and heard all about the dinner and show Jennifer and Alfredo attended the night before. Then they headed south towards Cork. Rose reports in her journal.

*"The countryside is lovely – green pastures, sheep and cattle, cozy farm houses and barns and flowers everywhere. The smaller roads are narrow and lined with rock walls and thick hedges. There are no shoulders so as we drive on the left the passenger (me) feels very close to these walls. The motorways are wider and we took one of these most of the way to Cork. We stopped in Limerick and passed King John's Castle and went on to Adare. It is a very pretty town with nice houses and gardens and little shops and restaurants. We had lunch there and visited an old church which was formerly a priory. It was most interesting."*

They arrived at Carrigaline, near the southern coast and Greta O'Grady, their host at Chestnut Lodge B & B showed them to their rooms. The lawns were green and well-kept and the flowers in the garden were gorgeous with roses, hydrangeas, dahlias, begonias and dozens of other varieties. Flowers lined the fences and houses and circled the trees on the lawn. Fuchsias and lilies grew along the roadside. Heather and other wildflowers bloomed in the fields. In town, houses can be blue, green, pink or yellow and a city street lined with these bright painted houses is quite lovely.

## Celebrations

*Mel and John Crowley live near our B & B and came over to see us right away. They led a dance group that had come to Berea for an international festival Jennifer organized and had become friends. They planned a welcoming party for us that evening. We also had a call from Billy and Phyllis Walsh, who live in Cork and wanted to greet us and meet us. Phyllis is a relative of our daughter -in-law, Eileen, whose mother, Helen Cooney Ambrose, was Irish.*

*At the Crowley's party Mel and John had made a straw costume with a peaked hat and mask covering head and face and two garments of straw to wrap around the body. It represents an old Irish custom allowing an "uninvited guest" to appear at a wedding. They dressed Bill as the uninvited guest and had a lot of fun with it. Other members of the music group came and we had interesting conversations about culture and music and dance. Next day we went to visit Phyllis and Billy at their home in Cork. Not surprisingly, their garden was filled with flowers.*

*Phyllis made us feel like we were part of the family. She served a delicious lunch and we talked about our lives and families. They are looking forward to a visit from John Robert in January and from Brian for a spring semester in Ireland. I loved Phyllis' brown bread and asked her for the recipe. She gave me a bag of wheat flour with the recipe on the side. They showed us some of Cork as they took us back to our B & B. Then I rocked and sang to Lydia in the sun room and we both dozed.*

That night the Crowleys had arranged a dinner and music evening with their group at Robert's Cove Inn right on the water at St George's Channel. There were soft drinks and beer and wine and talk and laughter for almost an hour before dinner was served,

*Dinner was excellent and we enjoyed fellowship with new friends for us and old ones for Jennifer and Alfredo. Then John Crowley in costume – kilt, dress coat and knee socks – playing the bagpipes, came out and stood behind us. He played "My Old Kentucky Home" and Irish tunes to celebrate our wedding anniversaries. The waitress brought an anniversary cake and cards. Then they presented Jennifer and Alfredo with a memorial vase and gave to Bill and me a commemorative gold fringed plate for our 50th. What a lovely surprise. Other musicians joined in with their instruments. Jennifer joined the band with her dulcimer and sang some songs. The party was on. We took Lydia back to*

*lodgings before the party broke up and she fell asleep in the car. We put her to*
*bed and she didn't wake up until 7:00 AM, all smiles.*

## Through a Rainbow to The Ring of Kerry

The next stop on their itinerary was the Ring of Kerry where they had a
B & B reservation at Waterford. They bade goodbye to the Crowleys and
headed west. The first miles were through pleasant countryside and pretty
little villages. They went through Bantry, which was congested because of
some kind of flea market with booths all around. They ate at a pleasant
restaurant overlooking a river at Glengarriff. Then they were in the hills
and the views were breathtaking.

*We stopped now and then to take pictures, climb rocks and look around. The*
*blue sky with fluffy clouds and fresh air were wonderful. As we wound through*
*the hills the clouds played tag with the sun and then the sky got misty ahead of*
*us and we saw a beautiful rainbow wide and shimmering above the trees. As*
*you move towards a rainbow it always seems to recede so you never find the pot*
*of gold at its end. Well, as we descended into a valley the rainbow stayed right*
*where it was and suddenly we were in the middle of it. We stopped and rolled*
*down the windows. All around us was mist containing the rainbow colors like*
*we were enveloped in a blessing from God. It was a magic time, like nothing*
*we'd experienced before until it faded away.*

Shortly after the rainbow experience they saw a small shop by the road and
heard the tune *"Molly Malone"* playing. They stopped and had some tea
and apple crumb dessert. The proprietor, Stephen O'Sullivan told them of
a standing stones area nearby.

*We turned off the main road and went about two miles, parked and hiked*
*past an old cemetery and saw the stones. I had some doubts that they were*
*really authentic ancient monuments, but people have lived on this land for*
*thousands of years and there are all sorts of shrines, tombs, and runes and places*
*of worship in fields, villages and in the hills among the sheep. We continued*
*to drive through hills and valleys marveling at the different shades of green*

*that were displayed in fields, forests, lawns and shrubs. We saw why Ireland is called the "Emerald Isle."*

They reached the coast and Ballinskelligs Bay, with more gorgeous views and passed through Waterford to Kerry Way, where they found their B & B, Sea View.

Kerry Way winds along a rocky hill that slopes down to the sea. Houses are mostly made of native stone and some were obviously very old. Sea View, owned by Margaret and John Curan, was surrounded by flowers and had a spectacular view. Just across from Sea View was a smaller stone house where John had been born that had belonged to his family for eight generations. John, paralyzed from the neck down from an accident years before, was in a specially equipped wheelchair. He could communicate by moving his chin on a sort of joy stick and was very interesting and happy.

## Irish Hospitality

*Margaret is a fine person and a very good hostess. We enjoyed the rooms we were given and the comfortable chairs in the solarium with its plants and sunshine and wonderful view. I asked about a laundry and she immediately offered to do our wash. She refused to let me help and said she was doing some sheets anyway. She washed our white things, hung them out to dry, and folded them before returning them to us. This is a woman who runs a B & B and cares for a disabled husband, has raised four children who were young when the accident happened, and does it all with a smile and good will. What a saint.*

With Margaret's help John had written a book about his experience. It describes his hardships but is also filled with praise and joy. It was a pleasure to get to know them. Margaret provided great breakfasts and loved to visit and hold Lydia. John showed them the marvels of his chair and electronic devices. They were interested in Jennifer's singing, and Jennifer got her dulcimer and sang for them.

Margaret had suggested places on the rocky coast to go and they did go, finding striking rock formations, getting their feet in the water and picking up shells and stones as souvenirs. One day they had an especially pleasant adventure. Bill and Alfredo had gone to explore further down Kerry Way, which was a very narrow lane along the rocky hillside above the sea. Rose and Jennifer stayed at the B & B writing in their journals.

*Bill and Alfredo came back very excited. The views from Kerry Way were beautiful and they proposed to go get food for a picnic lunch on a rock at the end of the road. They got the food in Waterville and then we all went for our picnic in the Toyota. Lydia was delighted to be sitting between mommy and grandma. It is hard to describe the magnificence of the scenery. Each turn of the road brings yet another breathtaking scene. The water of the bay was deep blue, changing as the light changes to a gray blue. Clouds shifted across the sky over the green, rocky hills with sheep grazing about. Out in the bay two skelligs – rock islands – could be seen.*

They came to a gate across the lane and pulled to the side. There were some big rocks on which they could sit and spread their picnic lunch. They ate, took turns holding Lydia,, watched the water and listened to the bleating of the sheep. Then it started to rain and they quickly gathered up their things and dashed to the car. Alfredo turned the car around ready to leave when a pick-up truck came down the lane with a man and a woman in it. The rain had stopped. The man leaned out the window and asked if they needed help. They explained that they were visitors from the USA and had enjoyed a picnic but were just leaving.

*The man, with a distinctly Irish accent, introduced himself as John Brosnan and asked if we had gone to the end of the road. He said the views there were spectacular. We told him that we hadn't gone through the gate and didn't want to go into someone's private property. He informed us, "It's my property, and I'm inviting ya!" We followed him in and had a marvelous time at the point with ocean on both sides, waves crashing on the rocks far below us. A grassy hill rose behind and Jennifer, Alfredo and Bill climbed it for an even more extensive view while I sat on a rock with Lydia in the sunshine, which had reappeared. John Brosnan had gone up to a house he was building that fit into the landscape, with the woman who was an interior decorator, and then they left, saying goodbye to us. We marveled at the friendliness and charm of the Irish. After a time it started to rain again and we headed back to Sea View.*

The date was September 7, their actual anniversary date and later at a restaurant with a great view of the bay they had supper and cake (with a candle) and ice cream to celebrate. It was a memorable day and great that they could all be together. The next morning Margaret provided a good breakfast and they packed up and said their goodbyes. It was raining as they headed northwards to Lahinch. They stopped at Dingle, had lunch and shopped and then proceeded up the coast of Dingle Bay. They passed through Tralee to the ferry at Tarbert that would take them across the wide Shannon River to Kilmer in County Clare. Lydia loved to watch the water through the rain from the ferry windows. Once across they drove on to Lahinch, arriving at about 6:00 PM at Mullcar House, their next B & B.

*Our hostess was Klenagh Fawl and our rooms were very nice. It wasn't quite as homey as Margaret's house on Kerry Way, but pleasant. Bill and I stayed at the B & B with Lydia for a light supper of sandwiches and yogurt. Lydia is such fun. Jennifer and Alfredo went to town for a supper out. They had to leave the next day. Next morning parting was hard but it was a beautiful day for the Escobar's drive to Shannon and flight home. We prayed for a safe trip for them.*

## The Cliffs of Moher and The Burren

Bill and Rose, now on their own but accustomed to Ireland, went to the Kerry Woolen Mills shop and purchased a lovely blue cape for Rose and a colorful tam for Bill. Then they visited the spectacular Cliffs of Moher with the ocean's waves constantly assaulting the rocky base. There were vendors and singers around the visitor center and paths. They bought a tape from a sweet voiced young Irish singer named Tina Mulrooney. They drove through the area called the Burren with nothing but flat, cracked and scalloped rocks, like broken lava, stretching for miles. They stopped at visitor centers, went through little towns, saw castle ruins, an old abbey and a stone table monolith. Ireland has a long and colorful, and sometimes tragic history.

*Tuesday morning we left Lahinch heading for Ardmore, the area Helen Ambrose had come from and where relatives still live. Near Ennis we saw Clare Abbe ruins with a "for sale" sign posted. We decided we didn't want to* take on the repair of a building that size, but we hoped someone will. We went through Limerick and further on stopped at Celtic Heritage Park. It was most interesting and we had a pleasant walk ending at beautiful gardens. We had a picnic lunch and were on our way. Near Cahir we saw ruins of another ancient castle with the walls standing but the roof gone. We drove through Tipperary and were in rain for the rest of the trip to Ardmore.

## Irish "Cousins"

The land in County Waterford, to which they had come, is rich and productive with family farms and many dairy herds. The B & B was actually in Dungarvin near Ardmore and was called Summerhill, belonging to the Budd family. They have a dairy farm. The house was very comfortable with views of fields and ocean. Bill and Rose unpacked and called Eileen's cousin, Declan Powers, or "Dage" as he is called. He arranged to pick them up the next day at 1:00 PM. They took a drive around the area and saw St. Declan's Well. St Declan came to Ireland in 536 AD, before St. Patrick, and is especially honored in this area. Back at Summerhill they ate a little supper and Sheila Budd brought them milk and delicious home-made brown wheat muffins. After several unsuccessful attempts to call home, they received a message from Jennifer that they had arrived home safely and all was fine. They had a good night's sleep, woke to a promising day and had a good Irish breakfast.

We had a leisurely morning at the B & B. Bill took a walk and I wrote in my journal and visited with Sheila. We watched TV a while and saw some of the memorial services remembering the terrorist attack on this date, September 11, one year ago. We prayed for the families, especially the children, of those who lost loved ones in that tragedy. At 1:00 PM Dage came and we became acquainted with this charming Irish "cousin." He led us to the Round Tower Inn where we had lunch. He told us about his family, his farm and this area of Ireland. The TV was on in the dining room and we joined people in the USA, Ireland and around the world for a moment of silence for those killed in the September 11, 2001 attack. Then Dage took us to see the actual round tower, built in 600 AD.

The tower is 90 feet tall and was a place of refuge for the monks who were in the priory there when attacked by Vikings or other raiders. The entrance is at the second floor level with access by a ladder. Then there are stairs inside and, of course supplies kept for times of refuge. The monks would gather their books, writings and relics and take them into the tower, pulling the ladder up behind them. Beside the tower there is an old church ruin with some walls standing and some gone. Next to the church is a graveyard with many stones so weathered that reading inscriptions is impossible. Dage had recently cleaned the stones for his family graves – parents, grandparents, a brother, an uncle. Dage's mother Mary Cooney Powers was Eileen's great aunt. St. Declan's grave is in a little stone structure at the edge of the graveyard. He is honored and remembered for his efforts to bring Christianity to the people of Ireland.

*Dage showed us the Cliff Hotel with an incredible view of the ocean and took us down a very steep and narrow lane to the beach. Then he drove us to his farm which lies on top of a hill overlooking the ocean. It had been in his family for three generations. The buildings are close to each other on three sides creating a courtyard, very much like what we saw on the Danish farms. Dage grows parsnips turnips, carrots, potatoes and other vegetables that he sells to merchants and restaurants. The grass in the hayfields was thick and green. He buys feeder calves in the fall and feeds them hay through the winter. He enjoyed telling us stories of the time John and Eileen and family had visited while on a semester abroad in Ireland. He said they liked to drive the tractor, ride his horses and help in the garden, especially with potatoes. We found the view of his green fields with a rock wall border overlooking the ocean just enchanting.*

As they drove back to their B & B on very narrow winding roads they stopped to see the beach at Whiting Bay and Goat Island. Goat Island is an amazing rocky shore carved out by the relentless waves. The rocks are huge with caves worn in them. There are large boulders tumbled about. On the beach is a lot of heavy seaweed, like palm fronds, that the farmers collect for fertilizer.

*As we drove back up the hillside, I saw tall old stone walls and asked to have a look. There in the middle of hay and wheat fields was the ruin of an old castle. Dage said it was the McKenna castle and had been abandoned in the late 1800's. We saw fields of sugar beets and more fine farms and homes. We said goodbye to Dage at the inn, thanking him for a wonderful day. Tomorrow we head back to Shannon. Our time in Ireland is almost over.*

The next morning, they watched the cows come in for milking. The Budds have 60 very fine Holsteins and several pigs. Sheila provided a good breakfast and waved goodbye as they left in welcome sunshine. They stopped at Lismore on the Blackwater River and saw a restored castle – the home of the Duke of Devonshire. They learned that it was once occupied by Sir Walter Raleigh and a portion of it could be rented for $38,000 per week. They decided to stick with B & B's. They went to the Heritage Center and learned more about St. Declan who had come as a monk from Wales under the leadership of St. Carthage. He established a priory and school which, despite attacks, destruction and disappointments, survived and became one of the finest institutions in the world.

## Heading Home

They saw some other sites on their way back north through Limerick. They stopped at the woolen mill shop at Bunratty for a few gift items and went to their last B & B, the Golf View, across from the Clare Inn where they had started.

*It seems weeks ago that we stayed at Clare Inn, not 10 days. We met our hostess, Maureen Hogan and put our suitcases in the room. Then we took off for final sightseeing, We visited ruins of an old abbey at Quinn, where, as usual, the wooden parts of the structure were gone but the stone remained. It must have been fine in its day. We found Knappoque Castle, which had been restored and is very beautiful, but was closed that day. We went on to Dromoland Castle which was fully restored and open with lodging and restaurant. We went in and found it elegant. We went to New Market on Fergus for supper at The Weaver's Inn which featured Irish and Indonesian cooking. We had chicken and duck, Indonesian style for our last big meal in Ireland.*

The next morning, after a lovely breakfast served by Maureen, they drove through the sunshine to the airport. They returned their Fiat, a little sad about giving it up, and entered the nice roomy terminal. Check in was easy and the flight uneventful, with a change of planes at Kennedy in New York to a Baltimore flight. In due course they retrieved their own car at Baltimore. They drove to Annapolis for a lunch with former Berea classmates, Ed and Hilda Copeland, and headed south. They arrived at Edisto the next afternoon, Sunday, September 15. The last entry in Rose's journal says:

*"What a marvelous few days this has been. Some day we hope to return again to Ireland, truly the Emerald Isle."*

BILL AND ROSE'S 50TH ANNIVERSARY TRIP TO IRELAND WAS LIKE A DREAM. ALFREDO
AND JENNIFER, ALSO CELEBRATING AN ANNIVERSARY, WTH BABY LYDIA, MET THEM
THERE. GRANDMA ROSE WAS GLAD TO HOLD LYDIA. WITH THE HELP OF THE CROWLEYS,
THEY HELD A PARTY AT ROBERTS COVE. JOHN CROWLEY PLAYED "MY OLD KENTUCKY
HOME" STANDING BEHIND ROSE'S CHAIR IN HONOR OF THE ANNIVERSARY COUPLES

BILLY AND PHYLLIS WALSH.
COUSINS OF EILEEN

THE RING OF
KERRY (ABOVE)

THE TOWER AT
ARDMORE (LEFT)

A STONE TABLE
ON THE BURREN
(FURTHER LEFT)

THE EMERALD ISLE IS WELL
NAMED WITH ALL THE GREENS

SHEEP ARE PLENTIFUL AND THE
OCEAN ALL AROUND

THE CLIFFS OF MOHER ARE
SPECTACULAR

EILEEN'S COUSIN DAGE AT
ARDMORE, HER MOTHER'S
HOME AREA. ROSE AND
BILL SAT ON DAGE'S FARM
WALL ABOVE THE OCEAN

467

# CHAPTER 35

# EDISTO IV: LAST YEARS

## Paramount Chief

During his later years at Berea College Bill was involved with others in providing for Liberian students to attend Berea under a special program. Liberia was suffering from a useless civil war which was not so much a conflict over ideas or of ethnic groups as a battle between two men who wanted to be in power. The results were disastrous for the country and destroyed many good programs and people. Cuttington College was caught in the middle, geographically, and had to close its doors to protect its students as the two armies crossed the area, looted supplies and destroyed infrastructure. Its president, Melvin Mason, set up a "college in exile" and requested help from American colleges in admitting their students as guests during this time so they could complete their studies and graduate from Cuttington. Bill helped make the arrangements and, with Rose, assisted various Liberian students who came to Berea. One of these, Jerry Mowgbe, they then helped go to graduate school at Eastern Kentucky State University and he became a good friend. He had been caught in the civil war. He had gone to one of the warring leaders when his village was threatened to plead for its being spared devastation. Because he was educated and had skills in language and writing he was detained and forced to serve as a secretary for the leader. This made his position in the country dangerous as the conflict wore on and when he escaped to the USA he was given political asylum. After he had graduated and was working in Atlanta he was involved in a Liberian church there. They wanted to honor people who had helped Liberian refugees and invited Bill and Rose to come as honored guests.

*We had a fine time with Jerry and his Liberian friends at the church and found that we were to be honored along with some notable people. They gave us each an African name. Mine is "Muenda" which means "one who cares for others" in the Meru language of Kenya. Rose was named "Konwlor" meaning "kind heart" in the Kroa language of Liberia. They put me in a beautiful robe, which was four times my size, and installed me as a "paramount chief." It was a joyful and humbling experience, reminding us of how our small contributions can make a big difference in the lives of others.*

A number of the Liberian students and other international students that Bill and Rose had hosted over the years stayed in touch as they moved on, got married and had children. For some Bill and Rose had completed immigration papers of support needed to achieve residence status in the USA. Others went back to their countries to make their contributions to improving life there.

## Celo Reunion

Bill and Rose's children and their Ramsay and Todt cousins had such fond memories of Celo as they grew up that they took trips to share this beautiful spot with their spouses and children as they came along. In 2005 a family reunion was organized to be held at the Morgan School at Celo. Each family arranged for lodging close by or camped out at the school and they gathered to share memories, food and fellowship. Susan Todt and husband Dale Moody had met at the Morgan School years ago so it was special to them. Susan took the lead in arrangements helped by her daughter Andrea and others. Cousin Betty Martin Stauffer came from Pennsylvania and Dick and Susana were there from Mexico and with Patty and Earl, John and Berni and Bill and Rose, represented the now older generation. The next generation included young married adults as well as college students, teens and younger children, who had ideas and contributions to make.

Bill's brothers, John and Dick, shared a fascinating documentary they had prepared of their trip to Nicaragua tracing the places where Mother Gertrude Ramsay's parents, Theo and Lizzie Martin, had served as

Moravian missionaries. Mother had been born in Nicaragua in 1904. She and her siblings spent their early years along the coast where the Miskito Indians lived. John and Dick had visited the different locations they had served. They were able to go to the Moravian Churches and see some of the family references in church records.

*One story touched us especially since all our families still sing a Moravian song passed on by the Martin family at birthdays. After singing "Happy Birthday" we sing "Jesus bids us shine, like a clear pure light. Like a little candle burning in the night…." John and Dick arrived at a church on the Miskito coast just as the congregation was singing that song in English. It was probably taught to the singers' great grandparents by our grandparents a century earlier. It connected us with our mother and Martin grandparents and gave the younger ones an idea of their rich heritage.*

The reunion was a time to get reconnected with family members who were not together very often. Inge-lise, Loren and their boys were there from Denmark. Bill and Becky Todt and children came from Minnesota. David and Patsy Todt were present with daughter Megan and her husband Brad Sparks and their six months old Baby Noah. Good friends Mick and Edie Hunt and family came over from nearby Swannanoa. A trip to Mount Mitchell was organized and the enterprising younger ones hiked all the way up the mountain while the older generation and others drove to rendezvous at the tower on top. Some of the hikers were pretty tired by the time they made it but proud of themselves. Of course the waterfall and the Hemlocks were close by for shared enjoyment.

*We had arranged to use a pavilion at the Hemlocks for a special service and picnic. Catherine played her violin; Jennifer, Laura, and others sang and led group singing. Different ones offered thoughts and prayers for a very rich time of worship and fellowship. Before we all dispersed from the reunion we took the usual family reunion pictures. Looking at those pictures in view of subsequent events is sobering and thought provoking. Marriages, births, moves, medical emergencies and unexpected deaths were just around the corner. We learn to be thankful for our present blessings and live each day under God's care and guidance trusting Him for the future.*

## Church Struggles

Since their first arrival, Bill and Rose had been involved in the Edisto Island United Methodist Church and become charter members when it was changed from a mission church to a chartered local church. They had enjoyed the various ministers assigned as a mission church and those who came later after the charter church was established. They made close friends with other members who worshiped, studied, served and had fellowship together. They participated in the growth of the church in terms of numbers and physical facilities, adding a beautiful fellowship hall. They had helped each minister assigned to get oriented and settled and enjoyed the constant stream of visitors.

The Methodist Church is a "connectional" church. Each local church is connected to others as part of the wider church. Pastors are appointed to local churches by bishops after prayer and consultation and serve to give spiritual leadership, administer sacraments, teach and give guidance to the local congregation, who elect their lay leadership. The ministers are usually moved every few years so churches are encouraged to develop strong local leadership rather than depending on the minister. Ministers are responsible to the bishop of their region (or conference) and to God, rather than being "employees" hired by the congregation. The governance structure is somewhere between the more hierarchical Catholic and Episcopalian churches and the independent congregations loosely affiliated with the various Baptist groups or Pentecostal groups. Each local church pays "apportionments" to their district to support missions and other programs and administration of the denomination and to provide for ministers' pensions and insurance. In the Edisto church lay leadership had to be strong as various ministers were supplied when it was a mission church and then appointed when they became a regular chartered church.

*Rose and I had often discussed the various preachers we had heard and pastors we had known, representing all types and styles from very formal and studious to very emotional and personal. We had decided to learn from sermons, rather than evaluate them, whether they were well organized or not or well delivered or not. There was always something to learn, even if we disagreed with some interpretation or opinion, which helped us to examine and understand our learning and beliefs. Of course some were more inspirational and instructive than others and some preachers are more charismatic, entertaining or erudite, but each has a message. For example, I remember a sermon by one of the early supply ministers on the "mustard seed" parable. His admonition was to act on whatever faith we have, however small, rather than waiting until we think we have reached a level we consider high enough for us to have power.*

After several supply ministers and one "intern" the church was assigned a retired military chaplain, Stan La Torre who had roots in Charleston and seemed a natural fit. Bill helped him set up computerized membership and visitor data bases and mailing lists and assisted in any way he could. Stan's wife was very retiring, always wore black and if she came into the church at all it was briefly in the rear of the sanctuary. The church had no lobby. Some members began to see a pattern in sermons that disturbed them – no mention of Christ or of atonement and redemption. They did some research and found that he had been trained as a "Unity" minister after his military service and most of his sermons came from Unity material, with emphasis on "God in you" rather than Christ's sacrifice and our need of grace. Some members spoke to Stan and to the Methodist District Superintendent and for a while things seemed to improve, but Stan was dividing the congregation.

*We had been away a good deal and weren't as plugged in to what was happening as we should have been but we enjoyed the services and the fellowship. Meanwhile, Stan had been getting those who supported him unconditionally in leadership positions and been removing others who had questions. Stan asked me to be the second alternate delegate to the annual conference which puzzled me. I asked if he really needed a second alternate. He said he did and I assented. When we returned from a trip I found conference was coming up and that the delegate had declined to go to the conference and the alternate had likewise declined. I visited with them and urged them to go but they were adamant and I wasn't sure what was going on. I felt the church should be represented at the conference even though the representative had no particular role but to have one vote among many on issues coming before the body, so I went to Wofford College where it was being held. It was an inspiring conference and good to hear of all that South Carolina Methodists were doing but nothing particularly exciting happened. When I got back I found I was now on the black list and was asked "Why are you doing this?" I was perplexed but finally figured out that having no one attend the conference from our church was part of a plan to remove the church from the Methodist connection. In the Methodist system, this cannot be done but many of those who had given support to the idea of a separate church came from non-Methodist backgrounds and thought that if they had the votes they could just remove the church. They probably had the votes at the time but found it was not that simple. Now I was seen as one of the impediments to Stan's plan.*

Bill went and talked to Stan to try to understand what he was doing and offer advice, but was repulsed. Stan even made negative statements and accusations about wrong doing of Jim and his missionary connection with The Mission Society. It made no sense, but shortly after that Bill and Rose received an anonymous letter saying they were not wanted in the church. Since the contents reflected Bill's conversation with Stan, it was obvious the letter had come from him. Bill took it to Stan with no positive result and then they received an even more vitriolic anonymous letter. They shared the letters with others and all were horrified. To make a long story short, the Methodist hierarchy got involved and Stan left, taking a few members with him, to set up his own church. Later he was removed from the ordained ministry of the Methodists. Bill and others think he was having serious mental problems. Some years later they heard that Stan had Alzheimer's and had died. The church survived the difficulty and has prospered since with strong friendship ties remaining.

### Home to Berea

After Lydia was born, Jennifer and Alfredo began looking for a house of their own and ended up moving to a large house at Pilot Knob, east of Berea. There was a downstairs bedroom and bathroom that would be a good place for Bill and Rose to stay on visits. This worked out fine and visits were even more frequent as Isabel was added to the family in 2003. Then in 2004 a smaller house adjacent to their property was put up for sale and Bill and Rose thought about buying it as a more complete place to stay on visits and eventually moving there. Someone else bought it and they forgot about this idea, but then it came on the market again in 2005 and they looked at it seriously. They liked it and ended up making an offer which was accepted. Now they had houses at Edisto and Berea. They moved in minimum furnishings and stayed on a visit or two. Then in October, 2005 they had come to Berea for a visit, and for Bill to have a routine colonoscopy that Dr. Ralph had been recommending he do for some years. They would then leave for Florida to be at Catherine's wedding with Chris Nielsen. It sounded like a good plan, but the colonoscopy didn't go well and Bill ended up a couple days later with a ruptured colon requiring emergency surgery.

*I did the prep and went to the hospital expecting it to be quick and easy. Dr. Kent Kessler, a gifted surgeon, began the test but was unable to complete it because of unexpected kinks and twists. He decided that in this case a barium enema was a better alternative for a check-up of the colon. However for some reason I developed a spasm and the whole right section of the colon began to bloat until it became very distended and excruciatingly painful. When the radiologist looked at preliminary x-rays before a barium procedure, he, thankfully, decided it would not be a good idea. The next day my shoulders were hurting in addition to my abdomen and Ralph, my physician at the time, knew right away that my colon had ruptured and released gas to press on the diaphragm. He insisted I report to the hospital immediately and I didn't want to go. But he prevailed and tests confirmed his diagnosis. I would need immediate repair – right away!*

*My memory is somewhat foggy, blurred as it was by the pain and whatever they put through those tubes to which they quickly hook you up, and the general unreal sense of the situation. I recall that Rose and other family members were gathered around my gurney. Francis, a wonderful friend and nurse who had come in to help, and Dr. Kessler were all there. Rose said, "We'll be praying!" Francis said, "We can pray now!" All joined hands and Dr. Kessler said, "I'd like to start." He did and I felt a sense of peace and assurance as they wheeled me to the OR. He said his part was easy and it was the Lord who did the healing.*

Healing did happen and before long Bill was back on his feet. They had removed an eight inch section of his intestine to be sure they didn't leave any "dead" areas between blood supply connections. All reports were that the tissue was healthy and in due course they removed the staples they had used to put things back together. Bill's brother, John, learning of the removal of part of his intestine, said he was now a "semi-colon."

We were so glad that we had the little house next to Jennifer, Alfredo, Lydia and Isabel. When Bill was released from the hospital we stayed briefly with Bill E. and Anne on Holly Hill, and then moved to our own place until Bill was ready to travel. We decided that is was time to move to Berea from Edisto and bring to a close that wonderful chapter in our lives.

Back at Edisto they put the house on the market and began to ready things for leaving. There was immediate interest in the vacant lot they owned next to their house since land was getting scarce in the resort area and in Edisto Beach generally. Bill and Rose didn't want to sell the lot separately from the house, even though it may have been more profitable to do so. The neighbors, Bob and Beth Foster, really wanted the lot between their houses and decided to buy the house and extra lot and then sell the house and keep the lot. They made an offer and it was accepted so plans and preparations began in earnest. By spring of 2006 everything was accomplished and the move was made.

*The 11 years at Edisto were special for us, and for the family. Edisto continues to be a destination for visits by the extended family. Jim still has the house on Loring Street. Our memories of the ocean, sand, breezes, palm trees, live oaks, egrets roosting on the lagoon, good times and wonderful friends will last the rest of our lives.*

# BILL AND ROSE RAMSAY TIME LINE

## EDISTO YEARS: 1995 - 2005

| YEARS | FAMILY AND RELATED EVENTS | WORLD EVENTS |
|---|---|---|
| 1995 | Family moves to Edisto Beach, SC<br>Home is named *Cair Paravel* meaning<br>"Castle by the Sea" from Narnia books | Federal building in Oklahoma<br>City bombed by Timothy McVey |
| 1996 | Bill and Rose join Jennifer in Demark<br>Travel to England/Scotland with<br>Elizabeth & Amber<br>Jennifer marries Alfredo Escobar<br>Elizabeth enters Berry College<br>Jim, Shawn and children go to Kazakhstan | Taliban takes control in Afghanistan<br>Liberian war ends |
| 1997 | Purchase of house at Edisto for Jim, they<br>name it *Chaika*<br>Travel to Puerto Vallarta with Sandy & Al<br>Rose becomes ill on trip to Maryland and<br>returns to Berea for emergency treatment<br>Amber enters Toccoa Falls College<br>John & Eileen in Ireland on sabbatical | Princess Dianne killed in accident<br>Tony Blair PM of United Kingdom |
| 1998 | Trip to Denmark with Catherine,<br>Melissa and Will; meet Jim & family<br>Lighthouse tour to New England;<br>visit Dick & Susana in Vermont<br>Bill E accepts position at Berea College,<br>he and Anne move back to Berea | N Korea famine, 2.5 million die<br>Google started |
| 1999 | Catherine enters Charleston Southern<br>Abaco trip with Brian & Benjamin<br>NASEA conference in San Diego | Liberian civil war again<br>Columbine High School massacre<br>World population 6 billion |
| 2000 | Florida with Jennifer and Alfredo<br>Jennifer on annual Florida singing tour<br>Trip to Banff, Canada with Osbornes, then<br>Bill & Rose to Montana, Yellowstone, Glacier<br>Melissa enters Flagler College, Florida | International Space Station begins<br>Putin is president of Russia |

| 2001 | Lydia Eleanor Escobar born | GW Bush becomes president |
|---|---|---|
| | Abaco trip with Sandy & Al, Daniel, | Terrorists destroy World Trade Center |
| | Colleen, Andrew, Rebekah | and fly into Pentagon. Additional plane |
| | Revival with all Edisto churches | crashed in PA because passengers |
| | Jim & family on home leave in Danville | intervened |
| | Melissa works for Fairfield at Edisto | |
| | Brian & Benjamin enter Taylor University | |
| | Family gathering at Lake Junaluska, NC | |
| | Elizabeth marries Ryan Sartor in NC | |
| | | |
| 2002 | Melissa at Edisto for summer work | Rebellion in Georgia (Russia) |
| | Bill, Rose, Jennifer, Alfredo, Lydia go to | |
| | Ireland for anniversary celebration | |
| | | |
| 2003 | Isabel Lochiel Escobar born | Iraq war begins |
| | Abaco trip with Robin, Ralph Edwin, | Liberian war ends |
| | Adrienne, Michael, Joseph | |
| | Melissa again at Edisto for summer | |
| | Wayne marries Carolyn in Louisville | |
| | | |
| 2004 | Daniel & Colleen at Edisto for summer | Ronald Reagan and Yasser Arafat die |
| | Rebekah enters Houghton College, NY | |
| | | |
| 2005 | Rebekah & friend, Hannah Duggins, at | Hurricane Katrina hits Gulf coast |
| | Edisto for summer work | Angela Merkel elected in Germany |
| | Catherine & Chris Nielsen marry | |
| | in Florida | |
| | Bill has emergency surgery | |

BEWARE OF ALLIGATORS

PROTECT THE LITTLE TURTLES

FLOAT OF REVIVAL INCLUDING
ALL 14 EDISTO CHURCHES

LOVELY ISLAND WATERWAYS

JENNIFER AND ALFREDO
WITH LYDIA & OPIE AT
CAIR PARAVEL
(CASTLE BY THE SEA)

ANGEL OAK BELOW

DOC AND ROBERTA SCHAEFFER
MANY, MANY VISITORS HAD PCTURES
ON THIS BENCH OUTSIDE CAIR PARAVEL

MELISSA PAINTED A MURAL ON FENCE
ACROSS FORM RESORT ENTRANCE

LYDIA ENJOYING ST HELENA SOUND

LAURA AND YOUNG STEPHEN AT OCEAN

THE WHOLE FAMIY GATHERED MORE THAN ONCE AT CAIR PARAVEL
(Before Lydia and Isabel were born)

TRIPS TO CHARLESTON TO SEE THE BATTERY, THE OLD SLAVE MARKET, SHIPS AT PATRIOTS POINT, FORT MOULTRIE ON SULIVANS ISLAND, ANGEL OAK AND OTHER SIGHTS WERE OFTEN FOLLOWED BY A MEAL AT GILLIGINS SEAFOOD RESTAU-RANT, KNOWN FOR ITS HOT HUSH PUPPIES AND GREAT FOOD.

SHOWN HERE ARE BILL, ROSE AND CATHERINE AT GILLIGIANS.

AT PATRIOTS POINT WITH ROSE, ARE BENJAMIN, ANDREW, BRIAN AND WILL

## EVENTS IN SENIOR YEARS

RETIRED WITH TIME TO TRAVEL AND TO BE HOME FOR VISITORS, BILL AND ROSE ENJOYED BOTH.

BROTHER JOHN WAS HONORED IN ST LOUIS AS A "REMARKABLE SENIOR CITIZEN" AND HIS BROTHERS AND SISTER ATTENDED ALONG WITH SPOUSES AND COUSIN BETTY MARTIN STAUFFER. ROSE AND BILL VISITED KEN AND GLENDA AND WAYNE AND CAROLYN IN OAK RIDGE. JIM AND SHAWN AND BILL AND ANNE AND THEIR FAMILIES VISITED. BILL AND ROSE ATTENDED THE 100TH BIRTHDAY OF LIZZIE MCAMIS IN BAILEYTON. THEY VISITED WAYNE AND CAROLYN WITH JENNIFER, ALFREDO, LYDIA AND ISABEL IN FLORIDA. THEY WENT TO THE WEDDING OF DANIEL AND ERICA AT BERRY COLLEGE IN ROME, GEORGIA

LAURA

<u>ENGLAND!</u> ROSE, AMBER, ELIZABETH AT KENILWORTH CASTLE – COUSIN DICK CONNOR - AMBER AT EDINBURG CASTLE
ELIZABETH HOLDING ROYAL MACE AT YORK LORD MAYOR'S HOUSE—LONDON WITH RAMSAY COUSIN, JEAN MERRETT

<u>DENMARK!</u> COPENHAGEN: CANAL & MERMAID. CATHERINE AND MELISSA JOIN JENNIFER IN CONCERT AT VEJLE.
WILL IN A GERMAN BUNKER TOSSED ON BEACH BY NORTH SEA STORMS, JENNIFER IN CONCERT

BILL IN STOCKS
AT COLONIAL WILLIAMSBURG

ROSE WITH A COLONIAL
NEXT TO GOVERNOR'S PALACE

BILL AS A PARAMOUNT CHIEF

BILL AND ROSE WERE HONORED IN
ATLANTA FOR HELPING LIBERIAN
STUDENT REFUGEES DURING CIVIL
WAR IN LIBERIA

COLLEEN STANDS AT EDGE OF BLUE HOLE ON ABACO ISLAND
IN THE BAHAMAS. BILL AND ROSE VISITED ABACO NUMER-
OUS TIMES USUALLY WITH GRANDCHILDREN

COLLEGE OF THE OZARKS, MO
BILL AND ROSE CONTINUED
TO VISIT WORK COLLEGES
AFTER RETIREMENT

ST. AUGUSTINE LIGHT HOUSE
MELISSA WAS AT FLAGLER
COLLEGE

BILL AND ROSE TOOK A TOUR UP THE EAST
COAST TO MAINE VISITING LIGHTHOUSES,
INCLUDNG THOSE ON CAPE COD AND
NANTUCKET ISLAND. THEY ALSO VISITED
DICK AND SUSANA IN VERMONT WHERE
THEY HAD AN AUTHENTIC MEXICAN
RESTAURANT NAMED CASA DEL SOL

CANADIAN ROCKIES AT BANFF

ON A WONDERFUL EXTENDED TRIP TO THE NORTHEAST BILL AND ROSE MET AL AND SANDY OSBORNE AT CALGARY AND SPENT A WEEK IN THE CANADIAN ROCKIES. THEN THEY WENT DOWN TO MONTANA AND VISTED UNCLE CLARENCE AND DORA, ALONG WTH HIS SONS TIM AND JONATHAN NEAR WHITEFISH AND GREAT FALLS. THEY VISITED GLACIER NATIONAL PARK AND DROVE THE "ROAD TO THE SUN" WHICH ROSE REMEMBERS WITH TREMBLING.

THEY SAW "OLD FAITHFUL" AT YELLOWSTONE. ON THE WAY OUT AND BACK THEY SAW MANY SIGHTS AND VISITED FRIENDS INCLUDING BILL AND BECKY TODT AND THEIR LIVELY FAMILY.

ON ANOTHER TRIP THEY WENT SOUTHWEST TO CALIFORNIA SEEING SPECTACULAR ROCK FORMTIONS LIKE THE HOLE IN THE ROCK IN NEW MEXICO. THEY VISITED FRIENDS AND OLD SPANISH MISSIONS IN TEXAS AND ARIZONA.

483

# REFLECTIONS 18

## SHEEP AND GOATS

We have lived through some turbulent times and much of the strife we observe is because people confuse the separation of sheep from goats. You are probably familiar with the passage from scripture that says that at the end time the Lord will put the sheep on his right and the goats on his left.

*34 Then the King will say to those on his right, 'Come, you who are blessed by my Father; take your inheritance, the kingdom prepared for you since the creation of the world.*

*35 For I was hungry and you gave me something to eat, I was thirsty and you gave me something to drink, I was a stranger and you invited me in,*

*36 I needed clothes and you clothed me, I was sick and you looked after me, I was in prison and you came to visit me.'*

*37 "Then the righteous will answer him, 'Lord, when did we see you hungry and feed you, or thirsty and give you something to drink?*

*38 When did we see you a stranger and invite you in, or needing clothes and clothe you?*

*39 When did we see you sick or in prison and go to visit you?'*

*40 "The King will reply, 'Truly I tell you, whatever you did for one of the least of these brothers and sisters of mine, you did for me.'*

*41 "Then he will say to those on his left, 'Depart from me, you who are cursed, into the eternal fire prepared for the devil and his angels.*

*42 For I was hungry and you gave me nothing to eat, I was thirsty and you gave me nothing to drink,*

*43 I was a stranger and you did not invite me in, I needed clothes and you did not clothe me, I was sick and in prison and you did not look after me.'*

*44 "They also will answer, 'Lord, when did we see you hungry or thirsty or a stranger or needing clothes or sick or in prison, and did not help you?'*

<sup>45</sup> *"He will reply, 'Truly I tell you, whatever you did not do for one of the least of these, you did not do for me* (Matthew 25: 31-45, NRSV)

It is obvious that the sheep and goats represent those who do good and those who do not – the righteous and the unrighteous. That is where the line is drawn by God, but we have seen the line between people drawn between black and white, between rich and poor, between police and protesters, between one culture and another or one religion and another. It is "us" against 'them." and this tension has been furthered and exploited by politicians and others seeking power and by media seeking sensation and fundraisers seeking contributions. Do we fall into the trap?

We know in our hearts and minds that there are good and bad people in all races, all economic circumstances, all cultures. There are good and bad black people. There are good and bad policemen. There are good and bad people who call themselves Christian or Muslim, Democrat or Republican. Why can't we draw the lines between what is good and what is not good regardless of the group represented? Why do we call those not of our group or persuasion names like bigot, homophobe, trash, idiot, or worse? That doesn't achieve anything but enmity and response in kind.

In addition to seeing good and evil around us we also know that we have within ourselves both good and evil. We like the story of the wise old Indian chief who told his grandson that every man had two wolves in him fighting for control. One represents love, courage, honor, peace, generosity, justice and other good things. The other represents hate, war, greed, dishonesty, cruelty and other evil things. The boy asks, "Grandpa, which one wins?" The old man replies, "The one you feed, son. The one you feed." We should acknowledge our misdeeds and potential for misdeeds, repent, forgive others and accept forgiveness and the redemption offered to us by a loving God. We should recognize our human condition of being capable of both good and evil, which is shared with others who may not be like ourselves.

No one is all good or all bad. No one is beyond reproach or beyond redemption. Let us stop drawing lines that separate people. We don't want to play the game of "us against them." The separation of sheep from goats is up to the Lord. Let us draw lines between behavior that is good and behavior that is harmful. We don't want to join in or enable destructive behavior. We seek to join with others of all races, conditions and places who are trying to live lives of honor and righteousness as God would have us do.

We want to be numbered with the sheep and not the goats when our time of accounting comes. We also know we fail if we depend only on ourselves. We pray for God's help. We want His justice but rely on His mercy and grace. We can claim His redemption. Otherwise we are lost.

# REFLECTIONS 19

## SEPARATE BUT EQUAL?

We act as if the separate but equal matter was settled when the Supreme Court overturned *Plessy vs Ferguson*. The problem is not resolved yet and it is much more complex than it appears. First let us examine the idea of "equal."

We know everyone is not equal in physical stature, health, economic condition, talents, etc. Even "equal opportunity" can be misleading since we are not all equipped to respond in the same way. Equal opportunity in art for me leads nowhere, since I have no talent in that area. Equal access to a seafood feast is of no value to a person allergic to fish. Equal opportunity in pro football is of no value if I am five foot five and weigh 130 pounds. If we try to make everyone equal in every way it is not only impossible but leads to despotism, not freedom. This was communism's major flaw. Equal does not mean sameness. Freedom is to be valued more highly than the kind of equality that reduces everyone to sameness. So where is "equality" important? It is important in **valuing people** and it is important **before the law.**

The truth about the basic value of all people is explained by the apostle Paul:

> *There is no longer Jew or Greek, slave or free, there is no longer male and female, for all of you are one in Christ Jesus.*
> (Galatians 3:28, NRSV)

What a revolutionary idea that must have been with Roman rulers, Jews not allowed to eat with Gentiles, citizens with rights and noncitizens without rights, with slaves and women viewed as property. Paul tells us that under God all are equally valued. Almost two thousand years later that truth, that all are created equal, found its way into the American Declaration of Independence. Even then, it took more than another century before it became a reality in respect to the law for slaves, women and black citizens. But now America makes the claim that all citizens are equal before the law. It has taken even longer for society to reflect that commitment to equality that values each person and the struggle still goes on.

So equality before the law, however faulty in administration, is established in America, without loss of freedom for individuals to enterprise, express themselves, discover their callings, achieve and be different. There are always those who would want you to sacrifice those freedoms for their ideas of reaching utopia through social engineering and conformity to their agendas. Equality before the law and under God is to be valued and expressed in our lives and institutions and need not restrict the freedom to be different.

What about the "separate" part of "separate but equal"? It always bothered me a bit that Berea College's motto, *God has made of one blood all peoples of the earth,* leaves off the rest of the verse which says *and has determined their preappointed times and the boundaries of their dwellings...* That sounds like "equal but separate." Berea's founders were strongly abolitionist but more fundamentally, seeking "to promote the cause of Christ," and opposed to anything that separated people and valued them differently, be it race, sectarianism, economic position or other division. I agree with their view, but am also aware of the case for separation. Each race, each ethnic group, each culture has its own beauty, customs and contributions and to homogenize them loses some of that richness in humanity. Is it wrong to identify oneself with a racial, ethnic or cultural group? It is wrong if it divides us into conflicting camps, based on ethnic or racial lines and not on righteousness, justice and truth.

The idea of each group living in its "appointed dwelling" on earth, has long since been given up, although most of the wars and strife the world suffers are still because of conflicts between groups. None of us today are racially or ethnically "pure." A visit to the British Isles doesn't support the idea of WASPS at all. White-Anglo-Saxon Protestant just won't stand up to the history of Angles, Saxons, Jutes, Scots, Irish, Picts, Normans, Vikings and who knows how many others who came there and mingled. The same is true in Africa. The Zulus, the Bushmen, the Hottentots, the Ibo and hundreds of other tribes are quite different in appearance and culture. And in South Africa the white presence came through the Boers who were basically settlers rather than conquerors. Add to that the mingling of races and groups in America, and the idea of African American or Native American becomes suspect along with the WASP stereotype. Asia and the Middle East are also a mixed bag of peoples. I'm reminded of a joke about prejudice that puts it in perspective.

*A Jewish pilot is preparing to take off on an international flight and sees that his copilot is Chinese. They both do their professional task of getting the flight off the ground and to a cruising altitude. Then the Jewish pilot says, "I don't like Chinese!" The copilot asks why he doesn't like Chinese and the Jew replies, "Chinese bombed Pearl Harbor!" The Chinese copilot replies, "Chinese didn't bomb Pearl Harbor. It was Japanese." The pilot says, "Japanese, Chinese, Korean ... all the same." After a while the copilot says, "I don't like Jews!" The pilot asks why he doesn't like Jews and the copilot replies, "Jews sank the Titanic!" The pilot objects saying, "An iceberg sank the Titanic." Whereupon the copilot says, "Greenberg, Goldberg, Iceberg... all the same!"*

Prejudice is not rational and stereotyping leads to falsehood, yet our society does it all the time. I remember a female colleague remonstrating with me that there were only males on the administrative committee at the college. It needed to have a female presence. I had no doubt that a woman could serve well but not just because she was a woman. It struck me that she was grouping me with all the other males even though she and I were in much more agreement on issues than I was with some of my male colleagues. There is value in having different perspectives represented, but that is not achieved automatically by racial or gender stereotyping and forced "proportional" representation.

Can we be separate and still be equal? A little historical perspective is in order. After the Civil War the Southern states were under military supervision and were required to rewrite their constitutions to include provisions for prohibition of slavery and for citizenship for blacks. I listened to a radio series when we were living in South Carolina and learned some interesting history. In South Carolina, the establishment political leadership followed a strategy intended to thwart the writing of a new constitution by boycotting the constitutional convention, denying it a quorum. However, enough forward thinking leaders filled in the gaps to achieve a quorum and so the old guard was essentially cut out and a rather progressive constitution resulted. The question of equality of the races was debated in terms of education, social interaction, and government services. At that time neither black nor white leadership wanted "integration." For the blacks it could mean assimilation and the disappearance of their culture. For the whites a mingling of the races was not desired either. So the idea of separate but equal arose. In theory it made sense. Equal education, equal services, equal treatment under the law was contemplated. I don't know the history in other states, but that idea of maintaining separation with equality seems to have been widespread. It was in this environment that the Plessy vs Ferguson case came about, which officially accepted "separate but equal" as a national standard.

Louisiana, following the principal of separate but equal, had passed a law in 1890 requiring separate railroad accommodations for blacks and whites. This was not the railroads establishing a policy but the state telling the railroads what they must do. In fact the railroads were opposed because it meant more problems for them and they would have to buy more cars. A group of citizens of New Orleans recruited Homer Plessy to deliberately violate the new law. He was seven eighth white, but by Louisiana standards considered black. The group even hired a detective with arrest powers to go with him and make the arrest so Plessy wouldn't be charged with a different violation like vagrancy. He purchased a ticket, got on the "white" car, was asked to move and refused. He was duly arrested and charged and tried in the local court with a ruling for the state by Judge John Howard Ferguson. Plessy was ordered to pay a $25 fine. He had achieved the group's goal of having a test case in the judicial system and they appealed the ruling. The case became Plessy vs Ferguson.

At the Louisiana Supreme Court, he found no sympathy for his plea. In ruling against him the court cited precedents from Massachusetts and Pennsylvania courts that found no prejudice or implied inferiority in providing separate accommodations or services. Clearly the idea of separate but equal was not peculiar to the South.

On appeal to the Supreme Court in 1896, the ruling was again in favor of the state by a vote of seven to one. The majority rejected the view that the Louisiana law implied inferiority and affirmed that it simply reflected a public policy separating the two races. The court ignored what by this time was quite evident, that public facilities provided for black citizens were clearly inferior.

Almost all the justices were from "Union" states. The lone dissenter in the case was Justice John Marshall Harlan from Kentucky. He first lamented the tendency of courts to substitute their opinions in matters that are the prerogatives of the people through their legislatures and asserts his view that the courts should defer to the intent of legislatures, whether or not they agree, unless there is a clear constitutional question by strict interpretation.

*There is a dangerous tendency in these latter days to enlarge the functions of the courts, by means of judicial interference with the will of the people as expressed by the legislature. If the power exists to enact a statute, that ends the matter so far as the courts are concerned.*

He comes to the conclusion that there is a constitutional problem with the Louisiana law and therefore the state did not have the power to enact this statute. He goes on to state his objection to the Louisiana law and the courts judgment. Following are excerpts from his dissent.

*The white race deems itself to be the dominant race in this country. And so it is in prestige, in achievements, in education, in wealth and in power. So, I doubt not, it will continue to be for all time if it remains true to its great heritage and holds fast to the principles of constitutional liberty. But in view of the constitution, in the eye of the law, there is in this country no superior, dominant, ruling class of citizens. There is no caste here. Our constitution is color-blind, and neither knows nor tolerates classes among citizens. In respect of civil rights, all citizens are equal before the law. The humblest is the peer of the most powerful. The law regards man as man, and takes no account of his surroundings or of his color when his civil rights as guaranteed by the supreme law of the land are involved. It is therefore to be regretted that this high tribunal, the final expositor of the fundamental law of the land, has reached the conclusion that it is competent for a state to regulate the enjoyment by citizens of their civil rights solely upon the basis of race.*

*We boast of the freedom enjoyed by our people above all other peoples. But it is difficult to reconcile that boast with a state of the law which, practically, puts the brand of servitude and degradation upon a large class of our fellow-citizens, our equals before the law. The thin disguise of 'equal' accommodations for passengers in railroad coaches will not mislead any one, nor atone for the wrong this day done.*

*I am of opinion that the state of Louisiana is inconsistent with the personal liberty of citizens, white and black, in that state, and hostile to both the spirit and letter of the constitution of the United States.*

*For the reason stated, I am constrained to withhold my assent from the opinion and judgment of the majority.*

Seventy two years later in the case of *Brown vs Board of Education* the court ruled that segregation in the public schools was unconstitutional and then, in 1964, the Civil Rights Act made "separate but equal" no longer legally acceptable.

But what happens among the different ethnic and racial groups in America? Do they lose their identity in society as well as before the law?

When I was growing up amidst the labor union struggles in Bethlehem, PA, I was aware of ethnic, if not racial differences. Workers at Bethlehem Steel represented all sorts of national and cultural backgrounds. There were Italians, Poles, Asians of various kinds, English, Irish, Scottish, etc. Each group had their own special foods, customs and, even languages. Many of the older generation in their families spoke little English. Yet they had in common their desire for better working conditions and more voice in their workplaces. This desire overcame their differences. They were Americans whatever their families' places of origin.

To be an American is different than being a Frenchman, or Pole or Chinese. I heard a preacher talking about an experience in China that sheds light on what is means to be an American. He is a white man who would shop at the "Big and Tall" section of a clothing store, and was teaching a class of Chinese. One of his students asked him about race relations in America. He responded, "If I asked you what nationality you were and you said 'American' that would be no shock. There are all kinds of races and ethnic groups in America." He paused and then went on. "If you asked me my nationality and I said, 'Chinese'…" He stopped as they all laughed incredulously. The point was that being an American is not a matter of ethnicity or race but subscribing to the American ideals of democracy, rule of law, Constitutional protection of individuals and freedoms. You may be called "un-American" if you are thought to not agree with its principles, but no one would call a native of China "un-Chinese" or a citizen of France "un-French." America is different. I thought as a youngster, and still think, that the image of "melting pot" was a good one. Not that everyone is reduced to sameness or loses their special heritage, but that they are all part of a unified people "dedicated to the proposition that all men are created equal." *(from Lincoln's Gettysburg Address)* Separateness gives way to unity.

Somewhere in the 1960's or 1970's "pluralism" became a buzzword. This has evolved into "diversity" and "multiculturalism." "Inclusiveness" and "transparency" are other buzzwords in current popular lexicon. I prefer the old fashioned words like "brotherhood" and "honesty." I dislike buzzwords because they usually imply a simplistic definition of a more complex matter. If you don't use them or take issue with them you are "unenlightened" or "deplorable" or branded by other buzzwords like reactionary, racist, bigot or worse. I am all for recognition of the variety of cultures represented in our country and the world. I am amazed at the variety in creation. Not even two snowflakes are identical, much less two human beings. I am also aware of the history of man's struggle, in every land and time, to find meaning and purpose and ways to get along and flourish. We are all the beneficiaries of that struggle which results in "civilization" instead of simply animal existence. I have studied western civilization, including the contributions of Greeks and Romans and Jews and the Judeo-Christian insights that have shaped this country. I also studied English History, Far Eastern History and civilization, Latin American History, Russian History and found in all of them the same elements of the search for justice, freedom and meaning. We are all of one blood, after all.

I think studying other cultures and peoples is important, but not to the exclusion of the rich heritage that shaped America. Jennifer attended public schools ten years after her brothers and sister and by that time academic faddism had taken hold. She learned a whole lot about the Native Americans and very little about the founding fathers. Now Women's Studies and Black History are in ascendance in the academy and Gender Studies is coming. There is nothing wrong with these studies if they are kept in the perspective of their place in the wider history of the world and not used to promote a particular world view or political agenda. In other words, we should not promote the old idea of "separate but equal." We know it doesn't work. It becomes a battle between groups. Some politicians and demagogues have found it effective to play identity politics pitting one group against another – male versus female, black versus white, citizens versus police, wealthy versus poor, old versus young. Most the solicitations I receive, and they are a constant stream, are cast in the "us versus them" mode. Can we not work together in the struggle between good and evil, between right and wrong, between justice and injustice, between want and plenty, between love and hate? Those issues cut across racial, gender, economic and social lines and are the important ones. My parents were friends of Reverend Dr. Martin Luther King before he became a national figure and I'm sure this is what he meant when he said "I have a dream!"

We know that not every path leads to what is beautiful, just, wholesome and helpful, in spite of the apparent promise of "multiculturalism" that all paths are equally valid. Hitler's path wasn't valid. Hirohito's wasn't. Stalin's wasn't. The path of ISIS isn't. We have to choose our paths together based on what is good for all, as one people sharing the earth rather than as each group seeking to dominate others or to get its share – separate but equal.

Should there be groups that celebrate a common heritage? Certainly. Should there be associations of senior citizens, homemakers, blacks, Irish for St Patrick's Day, etc. etc? Of course. But they should not have an agenda of "my group first" but rather "how does my group contribute to the whole." Our groupings should in no way impair individual choice. If a mixed race couple wants to marry that is up to them. If a person chooses to preserve racial identity by marrying someone of the same race, it is up to her or him, not the government and not the social group. We are all unique, but also all part of the same humanity. When we separate ourselves in the wrong spirit it leads to conflict that serves no one well. Let us live out the scriptural message that "God has made of one blood all peoples of the earth," and treat each other with respect and love as brothers and sisters, children of a loving and just Father.+

# PART NINE

*Back Home in Berea*

2006 - 2017

# CHAPTER 36

# FORT BREEZY

The move back to Berea in 2006 seemed right and natural for Bill and Rose. When they had left eleven years earlier they weren't sure that Berea would remain the "home place," but Laura and Ralph had continued in the Big House, Bill and Anne had settled in, Jennifer and Alfredo and the girls were established there, Stephen was close by and John and Eileen had roots there on both Ramsay and Ambrose sides of their family. Martin and Charlie and their four boys had chosen to stay in Berea. Bill, Rose and all their children and most of their children's spouses had gone to college there and been married there. No other place could compete with Berea as the family home area. So they moved into their little house at Pilot Knob and were settled in by May 2006.

The house was close to the Pilot Knob Baptist Church at the top of a hill and just an eight to ten minute drive to Berea and not much more to Richmond on US 421. It had a nice view of the mountains and pinnacles, with lovely sunsets. Even though it was on a hill it was in an area called Jackson Hollow with high points of the hollow about three miles to the north and to the south, so it was somewhat protected from storm activity. Even so it always seemed to get a good breeze. When they bought the house it had a large back yard enclosed by a privacy fence so it looked like a fort. They decided to name it Fort Breezy. Their road was called McKee Road but later was changed to Battlefield Memorial Highway, which fit with the Fort Breezy name.

*We had sold the Edisto property at a good price and had owed very little on it. We had paid for the Berea house when we bought it, so we had the funds to make some improvements, and we wanted to get some family land in the Berea area. First we took ten percent of our net gain on the Edisto sale and put it aside for charitable giving. For one charity Rose and I each made an annuity donation to Colonial Williamsburg. Twice a year it would pay us an amount from the annuity which we would use for additional charities.*

*The house was like a brick shoebox with no porch or entrance foyer and had no family room. We made a plan to add a family room and a porch and an entry from the porch, which would change the roof line and give the place a more gracious appearance as well as being more useful. We also did a lot of landscaping. We contracted with Albert Powell to help us with the plans and do the work. Albert had done good work for Martin and Charlie and was wonderful to work with. Rose and I became good friends with Albert and his wife Judy. It was Albert's sister, Frances, who was the so helpful nurse when I had my surgery the previous fall.*

Albert Powell is a well built, strong featured fellow with working man's hands and a genial manner softening a no-nonsense approach to life and work. A genius at building and anything mechanical, he could tell the square footage of a house by walking through it and knew just how to make things come out right, When Bill had ideas or problems about building, maintenance or equipment he'd discuss them with Albert who would respond with knowledge, wisdom and good humor, saying which ideas would work, making suggestions for improvement and rejecting those that weren't sound.

He and Bill became close friends, sharing a love of work, gardening and caring for others. Albert and Judy are pillars of their little church and share a deep faith. They became an important part of the Ramsay and Escobar families and a favorite of Lydia and Isabel. A visit to "Papaw" Albert's home in rural Rockcastle County was a treat. The girls loved him and nagged him to stop a lifetime habit of smoking because they wanted him around for a long time. After several attempts and some health issues he did stop smoking.

## Tragedy Strikes

Bill and Rose continued to travel, but not as far and wide as during their Edisto years. During their first year at Fort Breezy They got back to Edisto, made their annual pilgrimages to Williamsburg and Kingsport, went to Andrew and Cindy's wedding in Indiana and went to Branson, Missouri to enjoy a time share and to visit the College of the Ozarks. While they were on their way back, they received terrible news.

*It was November 15, 2006. We had left Branson and Bill was driving on a dark and rainy night through Missouri and Illinois towards Mt. Vernon, IL where we would spend the night before going home. My cell phone rang and it was our son John with bad news. Two of Stephens' boys, Michael and Samuel, had been killed in a car wreck. They had left their job at a Richmond car wash and were driving in the rain when their car hydroplaned into the path of an oncoming car. Both were killed instantly. We couldn't believe it! We got to Mt Vernon, made phone calls and tried to get a little sleep. We drove to Kentucky as soon as we could get away the next morning.*

*We suffered through the ordeal with Robin and Stephen, their other three boys and the rest of the family. The outpouring of love, sympathy and support from the church and community was heartwarming and we got through it, but it still seems unreal. We had not had to deal with this kind of personal family tragedy before. Michael and Samuel were just 17 and 19.*

Life brings heartaches and sorrow, but life goes on. Earlier that same year, in addition to Andrew and Cindy's wedding, Bill and Rose had attended the weddings of two great nephews (who are like grandchildren) John Paul, who married Kristin Giner in Ohio and Luke, who married Maggie Storm in Richmond, KY.

# Chapter 37

# Happiness Hills

Bill, with son-in-law Alfredo, started looking at possibilities for some land.

*We assumed that we'd have to go a few miles out to find acreage at a reasonable price and we looked in neighboring Jackson, Rockcastle and Estill counties. We wished to find land not subject to development which had some water on it and wasn't too hard to get to. Nothing seemed to fit. I had noticed a "for sale" sign on property just down the hill from Pilot Knob church, basically across the road from us and not half a mile distant. Because of the road frontage I thought it would be expensive and grabbed up by developers, but it wasn't selling, so I inquired and found out that the road frontage was located below a flood control dam and couldn't be developed. Furthermore there was an ill-defined tenancy on the property which had been established years before and passed on to heirs. The property was lovely with open fields, the lake, a running stream, hills with great views of Pilot Knob, and it bordered the Berea College forest. It had everything we wanted and was practically in our back yard. We were able to purchase it at a reasonable price and clear up questions about the tenancy. Mrs. Elva Lamb and her family had lived in the tenancy house for 40 years. Her children were grown but she remained and we were glad to have her on the property. We closed in January 2007, and suddenly owned 79 acres right across the road from our house. What could be better?*

The farm had an old barn which had housed sheep years ago and then was converted for tobacco. It was leaning to one corner, as old barns do when they are falling down, but upon closer examination the roof and superstructure seemed to be in reasonable condition. The posts supporting it had buckled and the lower siding was rotted but, with the help of Albert Powell, they decided it could be salvaged. Rose, who loves old barns, was happy but they knew it would take a lot of work. First they would have to have electrical service and water. These were available along the road. They decided to first fix up the old block "stripping shed" with the needed utilities. They would use it as a bath house to go with the barn. They cleaned it out and Albert fixed the roof, poured a floor and covered the blocks outside with a cement/paint mixture. They put in a septic tank, hooked up electricity and water. Inside they insulated it well, including a ceiling, and put bead-board panels over the walls. They put in a kitchenette and bathroom, a space heater in the wall and air conditioner in the window. It turned out so well that they decided to make it a cabin rather than just a bath house, and put in basic furnishings. By the end of 2007, it was ready for use and a pleasant cozy little place. Later they added a front porch with a swing. Meanwhile they had started to work on the barn, a much larger project, and they began to think of how it could be used as a gathering and activities place.

*I began to think of a retreat facility and felt guided to provide facilities without worrying about uses. We needed a name and I was thinking about Heritage Hills. Jennifer said that sounded like on old peoples home and suggested Happiness Hills, which was more upbeat and reflected the earlier family place at Celo which we had called Happiness Hill. We agreed and Happiness Hills was established.*

# CHAPTER 38

# CHURCH AND FELLOWSHIP BIBLE STUDY

Bill and Rose returned to their church of many years, Berea United Methodist. They had looked forward to being in a Sunday school class with Elizabeth Bertrand, wife of a former, but now retired, minister. Unfortunately Elizabeth succumbed to cancer and they never got to enjoy her class. She had also taken over the direction of the annual Easter drama, *Lord! Is It I?*, which Bill had directed for many years before moving to Edisto. Now Bill resumed that duty for a couple years completing 25 years of continuous performances of the play by the church. Laura and Ralph had continued to be part of the church over the years, with Laura taking leadership in music and other ways. She got Bill and Rose involved in Bible fellowships within the first year or so.

*We were so blessed to again become part of a group of Christian brothers and sisters who loved to study, pray and have fellowship together. Bill served as facilitator. He insisted he was not the teacher, and everyone contributed to preparing and presenting lessons. We first met at the home of David and Maxine Snively in Berea. Members at first fluctuated but then settled down to a group of sixteen who were regulars. Besides Bill and myself and the Snivelys, the regulars were Dorothy and John Chrisman, Edna and Preston Hill, Wanda and Leonard Lombardo, Jackie May, Barbara McDonald, Roberta and Everett Schaeffer, Jean Abney and Gary Williams. They called themselves the Fellowship Bible Study. Anyone was invited and they often had visitors from their families and other church members.*

*By 2008, we had studied several Bible subjects and books and the group decided to follow a study guide using reruns of the Andy Griffith show to illuminate scriptural values. The Chrismans offered to host the group in their*

504

*family room with a big screen TV and plenty of seating. John was especially fond of the Andy Griffith show and Barney Fife. Everyone eagerly accepted and the weekly fellowship moved to the Chrisman's home. We never moved out, although we did move upstairs to the living room, with its grand piano which John played beautifully, and then to their dining room where they had a wonderful table big enough for everyone. After sharing, prayer and study all would gather in the kitchen for treats different ones prepared.*

*We studied sects and cults, the sermon on the mount, minor prophets, prayer and fasting, the churches of Revelation, what happened to the apostles, prophecies and other scriptures and issues, with everyone taking turns leading and making contributions. We were studying the book of James when John Chrisman had his 90<sup>th</sup> birthday and was dealing with a serious heart condition. In 2011, he passed from this life – the first of our fellowship to go. A few months later his beloved Dorothy joined him. Leonard Lombardo died and then Roberta Schaeffer and later Doc Schaeffer so our fellowship was sundered but the experience remains a high point in our lives since coming back to Berea.*

# CHAPTER 39

# MORE TRAVELS, WEDDINGS AND THE NEXT GENERATION

In 2007, they spent time in Florida with Jennifer and Alfredo and the girls on Jennifer's annual singing tour. They also visited Williamsburg and Kingsport and spent a wonderful week with Lydia and Isabel at Lake Lure n North Carolina. The next two years again included trips to Williamsburg, Kingsport and Florida. Two grandchildren, Elizabeth and Catherine, were married before the move back to Berea, and after the move, weddings blossomed starting with the three in 2006 (Andrew/Cindy, John Paul/ Kristin and Luke/Maggie) followed by Melissa and Vito and Colleen and Cason in 2007, Daniel, who had graduated from Berry college in 2007, married Erica the next year and grandnephew Mark married Clarissa. The following year, 2009, saw Benjamin and Amanda's wedding in Indiana and Brian and Michelle's in Florida, and two more followed in 2010 - Amber and Eric in Berea and Adrienne and Matt in Wooster, OH. (A chart in the Appendix includes marriage names and dates.)

*In 2010, we traveled to my home area in east Tennessee to attend the celebration of 100$^{th}$ birthday of our dear old neighbor and friend, Lizzie McCamis. It was a fine occasion with her family and friends at the Sulfur Springs Methodist church near her home. Our travels were becoming more difficult and limited because of my health issues but we still enjoyed our trips.*

They made a trip to Fairfield Glade in Tennessee for a time-share week and visited Ken and Glenda on the way home. Then, they took a trip to Elon College in Burlington, NC.

*During the years when we organized and administered the service-learning internships, first in Oak Ridge and then Atlanta, we had kept good records and copies of every intern report. Sometime in the 1970's SREB sent the reports to me and I stored them at Berea. When I retired, the boxes were moved to the library archives. Then in 2010, I received a call from the archivist at Elon College informing me of a new collection of material on service-learning based on papers donated by my colleague Bob Sigmon. There would be a dinner honoring Bob and Marian and we were invited. I thought of the intern reports and called both Bob and the archivist to see if they were interested. They were and the Berea library had been wondering what to do with the reports so we arranged to transport them, along with other papers I had kept, to Elon where they now reside in the Sigmon and Ramsay archives on service-learning. We had a fine time at the occasion and a good visit with the Sigmons.*

# CHAPTER 40

# HAPPINESS HILLS FARM
# AND RETREAT CENTER

With the help of Albert Powell and his good associates in the construction business, the barn had been not only raised upright and stabilized, but renovated with a cement floor, running water and sinks in a kitchenette with electricity. It provided a space of about 40 x 60 feet for activities of various kinds. They added a campfire site down from the barn above the creek.

*When we cleaned out the barn, which was a mess, with dust, dirt, tobacco and straw remnants and other detritus including numerous empty cheap whisky bottles, we found hundreds of tobacco stakes. Some of them were the old hand-hewn variety and some were more recent and sawed. We made piles of the unbroken ones and used them for fences, garden stakes, railing on the barn balconies, trim on shutters, trellises and other uses and still had many to give away mostly for garden stakes. Some of the fences were modeled after the Williamsburg fortifications, although much smaller. The appearance of those got a lot of attention. They were useful because they were in eight foot sections and movable. The straight fences served as a border for flower plantings and we had a row of beautiful gladiolus between Gate House and the highway. We also put in a small garden, fenced with garden wire and tobacco stakes.*

Meanwhile, Gate House had become a popular get-away for couples, small families or individuals looking for inexpensive and rural lodging, so Bill and Rose were now doing a lot of cleaning and laundry as well as reservations and accounting. They decided to build a larger guest house to become a retreat center for family reunions, church groups and others wanting something informal and outdoors oriented, larger than a motel room but smaller than a convention center. So Albert built Hill House just beyond the barn on the hillside looking over the open fields above the creek. They completed Hill House in early 2009. The only serious problem they encountered during construction was the theft of copper pipes just at the moment they were ready for installation. The thieves knew the right moment and also cut all the exposed copper wire. The various contractors were most helpful, thoughtful and generous in providing replacements and making repairs.

*Hill House was just completed and ready for occupancy but no one had yet stayed there. We had gone to Florida where Jennifer, Alfredo and the girls would join us but they were still in Kentucky getting ready for her annual Florida tour. They called to tell us that a very cold and windy storm had frozen and burst pipes in the attic of Hill House and as it thawed the plumbing had dumped quantities of water on the second floor ceiling over one bedroom. The ceiling dropped onto the bed and water damaged the carpet and floor dripping on down to the ground floor. Fortunately Alfredo had driven by and noticed something and got the water turned off. What a mess. Between the very cooperative insurance company and Albert and his good coworkers we were able to handle the problem long distance. Our first rental of Hill House was April 1, 2009. After that rentals took off with many wonderful guests and groups. Our washer and dryer were very busy, but we got help with cleaning.*

In 2009, they held a dedication of the farm committing it to Christian hospitality and God's glory. They had invited their minister, Gary Rowan, previous minister Charles Bertrand, and prayer warrior Debbie Carrick to join them and Alfredo and Jennifer with Lydia and Isabel. Annette and Eddie Eckart were visiting and joined in. They lead a worldwide healing ministry called Bridge for Peace. The dedication referred to scripture passages, and included prayers songs at various points of the retreat center and farm. For example:

> *"Use hospitality one to another without grudging.*
> *As every man has received the gift, even minister the same to*
> *one another, as good stewards of the manifold grace of God."*
> 1 Peter 4:9-10, NRSV)

*"Here let the weary one find rest,*
*The troubled heart thy comfort blest,*
*The guilty soul a sure retreat,*
*The sinner pardon at thy feet."*
(How Blessed Is This Place, Ernest E. Ryan 1886)

*"The earth is the lords, and everything in it,*
*The world and all who live in it."* (Psalm 24: 1, NRSV)

*In preparation for the dedication, I had done some reading in scripture and reports of Jewish tradition and found that once something is given to God it can't be taken back. This sobered me as I realized what a profound commitment we were making while having the assurance of Gods provision and care. Another interesting coincidence was the presence of the Eckarts related to the bridge across the creek which was one of the stations of the dedication event. When the electric company had hooked up our electricity they put in new poles shared with telephone and cable and informed us that the old poles were ours. Albert pulled the old poles across the creek at a narrow point and made a bridge. It was a pretty spot on the creek under the trees but I said we weren't sure what it was for. Annette immediately dubbed it the "bridge for peace" in Kentucky. It became a lovely entrance to the retreat center from the fields next to the highway.*

Bill and Rose had expected the retreat center to be closed during the winter but reservations kept coming, especially for Gate House. One guest was a mathematics professor on sabbatical working with colleagues on robotics, one of whom was at Berea College. He stayed for a week and later returned for additional time. He liked to tell that he had started his sabbatical at a penthouse in Manhattan and ended at a stripping shed in Kentucky. He said he preferred the stripping shed because he could step out and see the stars.

*In addition to some lovely families and small groups we sometimes had larger groups who wanted the space and flexibility offered, Chrissy Davis-Camp brought her group of twenty some teenage folk dancers every year to attend the Berea Mountain Folk Festival and they were a delight. Probably the largest group was the leadership of Campus Crusade from Eastern Kentucky University and Berea College. These were about 60 students who had become leaders on their campuses and got together at the beginning of a new school year to get oriented, make plans and just have fellowship with each other. They brought sleeping bags and slept on various floors as well as occupying all the beds and couches. Talk about a lot of wash to do after they left!*

The barn, not being sided and insulated, was uncomfortable when the weather was cold. They were considering another structure with temperature control. Jennifer and Alfredo had decided they would build their dream home at the farm and were thinking of a lower floor that would serve as an alternative to the barn for open space. Bill advised against that and suggested they put up a modest structure, perhaps a prefab barn, to serve that purpose. Albert said he could build a block hall with bath and kitchen for little more than a prefab so they started on Harmony Center. Completed in 2010, it turned out to be better than just open space and became a very useful hall with kitchen and bathroom that served well for family gatherings, parties, receptions, dances, workshops year round.

*We had become acquainted with a young woman, through buying produce from her, who turned out to be the daughter-in-law of John Bowman, the farmer who cut hay on the farm. Lydia Bowman also did cleaning and had a number of relatives who could help so she became part of the crew at Happiness Hills. She wanted to have a birthday party at Harmony Center before it was finished and talked to Bill as he was getting the interior ready for painting. She offered to help paint in exchange for the party and a deal was made. Lydia and her sister Edna did a beautiful job of painting walls. Alfredo installed tobacco stick trim attractively below the chair rail and hung some of his "Hands" paintings framed with tobacco sticks. The hall was so attractive that we put in a laminated wood floor which really dressed it up.*

Later, they dropped in a ceiling to help control temperature and provide improved lighting. Richard Carter and his sons, David and Jon helped paint the ceiling and they became important parts of the crew. Even later, they added central heating and air conditioning. What started out as an idea for a rough "shed" had become a really nice addition to the retreat center.

## The Garden and Rose's Incident

They had moved the garden from its original location which was too small, too shaded and too near the creek to manage the raccoons who feasted on it. A larger fenced garden was made in the field between Hill House and Harmony Center and became very productive. They had less trouble with coons but caught several and transported them to a wildlife area. They found that at critical times, leaving a radio on in the garden kept the coons out. Bill was afraid they might like the late night music and have a dance. Zucchini and yellow squash did particularly well and one year when the sun and rain came in perfect combination they picked over 400. They gave a lot to friends and family and the Berea food pantry. Bill and Rose also became experts in making zucchini bread, zucchini relish, zucchini/apple pie, squash casseroles and all kinds of soup. They especially liked the zucchini curry soup and the yellow squash soup with tarragon. They ate well and filled their freezer each year with vegetables, casseroles and soups.

*One morning, I think it was June 2009, Rose and I had gone down to the garden to pick spinach before breakfast, while it was still cool. Rose picked a basket full while I hoed in the potatoes. She stood and said, "I think we'd better go have some breakfast" I agreed and leaned my hoe against the fence, but she picked up another one and began to hoe the beans. I asked her if we weren't going home and she looked blank and said, "I don't know how I got here!" That was alarming and it was obvious that she was disoriented. I got her to the house, called Jennifer and Laura and fed her some breakfast. She regained cognition, but was still disoriented and had no memory of the last half hour, and she was feeling weak. With the girls help we got her to an urgent treatment center where they found nothing wrong other than her body had gone into shock, perhaps from a blood-sugar problem, having exerted herself before eating anything. To make a long story short, her doctor, Sarah Little, ordered all kinds of tests and sent her to specialists, to check heart, neurology, and other body systems. No clear cause was found but her body fatigue continued for about a year and she never was able to remember the events of that morning.*

# CHAPTER 41

# MORE WEDDINGS, DEATHS AND BIRTHS

Weddings of grandchildren continued with Ralph and McKenzie in 2011, Jonathan and Katie in 2012, Matthew and Kendall in 2014 and Keith and Sarah in 2015. Over the same period, Bill and Rose saw the passing of many dear friends. In addition to members of the Fellowship Bible Study and other church and former college friends, they grieved over the passing of Al and, later, Sandy Osborne who had been such delightful traveling companions. Rose's college roommate and maid of honor at their wedding, Doris Pohl had been in a care facility for some years after a stroke and now was gone. She was a brilliant concert pianist and teacher and had suffered the loss of her ability to play and even to talk. Anne Weatherford also departed this life and with her passing it seemed like the end of an era for Bill and Rose. Lizzie McAmis and Rose's cousin Juanita Walton from her home area in east Tennessee both left this life, so trips to the Kingsport area were no longer scheduled. Bill and Rose shared in the struggle with brain cancer of Eileen's brother and John's close friend, Kelly Ambrose, who was also their neighbor. He was the age of Bill and Rose's children and had always been so positive, healthy and vigorous that his cancer and death seemed out of order. They went to a lot of memorial services. But a new generation was beginning as the older one dwindled.

*It is hard to get used to our children being grandparents. When Bill's dad became a great grandparent, he said not to call him "great grandpa" but "grandpa the great." We generally settled for Grandma Rose and Grandpa Bill. The first of the new generation was Noah, born to our great nephew and godson, John Paul and his wife Kristin in 2007. Then in 2008, Isaac, our first great grandchild, was born to Elizabeth and Ryan Sartor. Also that year, Noah welcomed a little sister named Lily. The next year was quiet but then the flood gates opened and before we knew it we had 28 great grandchildren and Martin and Charlie had 12 grandchildren bringing the total for the next generation of close family to 40 in a decade. We love each one and like to speak their names so they are listed here by year:*

| | |
|---|---|
| *2007* | *Noah* |
| *2008* | *Isaac and Lily* |
| *2010* | *Abram, Eleanor, Penny, Nina and Annabelle* |
| *2011* | *Gabriella Rose, Jacob, Rosaline and Rose May* |
| *2012* | *Graham, Lucy, Cashel, Vito, Elise, Simon and Audrey* |
| *2013* | *Grover, Alister and Mercy* |
| *2014* | *Acacia, Bridget, Blaise and Grace* |
| *2015* | *Harrison, Gabriel, Lorelei, Joel, David and Patrick* |
| *2016* | *Felicity, Ramsay and Eleanor Rose* |
| *2017* | *Heidi, Micah* |
| *2018 (Jan,)* | *Cora Rose and Junia Aiden* |

*With only 14 of our 20 grandchildren married, and the married ones still of childbearing age, the numbers and beautiful names are bound to increase. We pray for them and the world in which they are destined to grow up.*

## Changes and Aging

Jennifer, Alfredo and the girls assumed more and more of the responsibility for the retreat center and had begun to build their house. Beginning with 2015, Jennifer took over management, schedules, records, etc. Bill and Rose transferred the property on which the retreat center buildings were situated and the Escobar house was being erected to Jennifer. It was about 13 acres. The remainder of the farm, about 66 acres was retained as a family place with Bill and Rose the legal owners. Plans are to put it into a family trust. In 2016, the Escobar family moved into their new house, continuing to do some of the interior finishing themselves. They had instituted a pot luck gathering every Tuesday night from spring until cold weather in the barn. Anyone was invited and some friends, guests and family became regulars with numbers ranging from ten to forty. Alfredo would grill chicken, hamburgers, hot dogs, pork chops and sometimes fish on a large grill and others would bring sides and desserts. It was great fellowship and food with room in the field beyond the barn for children to run and play. Some would play in the creek below the bridge in warmer weather, catching crawdads and minnows.

*We continued to help as needed but it was a relief to pass on the responsibility to Jennifer and family. Rose was not getting around as well and tired easily. The year after her "incident" in the garden she was bending over the low picket fence sections of a flower bed unable to resist pulling out a few weeds when she fell forward and stabbed one of the pickets into her abdomen. Nothing was broken or bleeding and a doctor visit revealed no damage other than bruising which healed soon. But we think it must have dislodged some gall stones which had been lurking in her gall bladder because the next year, 2011 she was having symptoms of gall bladder problems.*

She was referred to surgeon Dr. Shields, who upon examination and tests immediately put her in the hospital. Gallstones had clogged the ducts and the pancreas had become inflamed. The inflammation had to be taken care of before the gall bladder could be removed so she was put on intravenous antibiotic. That had the desired result and the gall bladder was successfully removed laparoscopically. However the surgery, which apparently had been difficult, could not remove stones in the ducts and the incision where the gall bladder had been severed from the duct could not be satisfactorily sutured. Dr. Shields arranged for Rose to go to St Joseph East hospital in Lexington while still a patient at Berea to have the stones removed and repair done by endoscopy. Dr. Martin, using her computer and tubes down the throat, through the stomach and up the ducts was able to accomplish all this. Rose remained in the Berea hospital another day while still getting antibiotics intravenously.

*I sat in the back seat with Rose while Bill E. drove us to the Lexington hospital. We were so relieved when it was over and the doctor declared that she was done and Rose could go back to Berea. She had put a stent in the duct so the incision inside could heal. She would need to see Rose again in a week or so to have the stent removed. The small holes through which the laparoscopic surgery had been done healed quickly and in due course the stent was removed along with a remaining stone. We celebrated by having a late breakfast at a Waffle House in Lexington on our way home.*

Shortly after all these procedures Rose began to experience extreme weakness in her muscles and joints. She was diagnosed as having polymyalgia rheumatica, or PMR; perhaps it was an immune reaction to all the antibiotics she had received. The doctors put her on prednisone and that helped. She was a regular visitor at the Berea hospital clinic where Dr. Hardy, rheumatologist and Dr. Elkinson, gynecologist, came once a week from Lexington. She was still not back to full strength and reducing prednisone dosage, when in 2012 she began to have severe pain in her lower back.

*I had several nights when the pain in my right lower back and hip was so bad that I not only couldn't sleep but couldn't be still. The pain eased off at morning and the days were not so bad. I had been given medications but they didn't stop the pain every night and then one morning the pain didn't stop. I begged Bill to do something, poor man. He suffered along with me, rubbed my back and called for help and advice. Jim and Shawn were in town and came over. Bill had called both Ralph and Stephen, who were physicians, and they agreed that I needed to go to a hospital with more depth of resources than Berea. Ralph was out of town but between them they arranged for me to be admitted through the emergency room at St. Joseph East in Lexington. Shawn had been rubbing my back and praying and things were a little better. I thought I could make the trip to Lexington and that afternoon we left.*

Bill drove and Jim and Shawn followed them in their car. Bill and Anne met them at the hospital. After a long wait and some tests and procedures Rose was admitted and taken to a room. They waited until late in the night before the attending physician came. He administered heavy doses of steroids and pain medication and got control of the pain. He ordered an MRI for the next day. Being denied any breakfast because of the ordered MRI, Rose was weak and groggy from medication. Then they found out that MRIs were not done at that hospital on weekends so there was no technician available. Some food was provided but it made Rose nauseous. Phone calls were made and a generous technician agreed to come in and provide the MRI. They gave Rose medication for nausea and to relax her for the test and she went into a drug induced sleep. Stephen and Kathy had come over that day and just stayed with them.

*When it was time to take Rose to the MRI room we woke her up and she was very confused. She kept asking who she was and wanting reassurance that I would stay with her. Because the MRI unit was not open that day and no one else was around the helpful technician allowed me to go in with her and keep talking to her. Between us, we managed to get through to her that she must remain motionless and she was very cooperative. When it was over and we got her back to the room she was still talking in short phrases like, "Me Rose" and, You Bill" trying to make sense of what was happening. We teased her about reverting to Indian talk because of her Cherokee ancestry. Then she asked, "How deep?" I knew she hated confined places and thought she wanted to know how far the machine had been above her head and body. I answered estimating the distance as four or five inches, but she insisted to know "How deep?" We finally figured out that she had the sensation of being put in a tube and lowered into a pit in the earth and being afraid the ground would collapse over her and she'd be buried alive. A really bad nightmare. Gradually she regained her ability to think clearly and express herself coherently. Stephen and I went out and got frozen yogurt for everyone to celebrate the survival of a long day.*

They put a patch on her back that night which allowed her to sleep without pain and then discharged her the next day with instructions for reducing the steroids and prescriptions for more patches and pills. They only had to use one patch that first night home and then no more. The spasms seemed to be over. Later, as arranged by the doctor, she went for more x-rays and consultation with an orthopedic surgeon. He explained three possibilities of problems in her lower vertebra and nerves in the area that could have caused the episode and recommended exercises and avoidance of strain on that area. Dr. Hardy continued to see her in regard to PMR related weakness and oversaw her gradual reduction of prednisone until she was off it completely.

*For the next few years the only problems I had were some nights when sleep escaped me, some fatigue, especially after a night of little sleep, and some loss of memory which has no particular pattern. I exercise every morning, eat well the food that Bill provides and visit on the telephone or with guests at home from time to time. It is an ordeal to get dressed up and go out so I prefer to sit in my chair and do crossword puzzles. Bill and I read out loud every night from scripture and entertaining books. I put eye drops in his eyes and rub his feet where arthritis threatens. We are blessed to be able to live independently in our own home and have so many family members and friends around.*

Bill had some loss of clarity in his vision and had various eye examinations which are ongoing. Cataract surgery was performed in 2016 successfully but didn't eliminate the "smudge" in his left eye's vision. With three sets of glasses for driving, reading and computer work he does well enough. He has done a lot of writing, so he uses the computer word processing regularly.

## "ScripturePicture Plays"

*Ever since I had been involved in the Easter drama, "Lord. Is It I?", I had toyed with the idea of other dramatic presentations based on a visual scene or tableau with the characters in the picture stepping out to tell their stories. With no dialogue and little business it is a simple but powerful way to present a story. I wrote one sketch called The Innkeeper's Wife which was performed at church by Jennifer and went over well. I also wrote a script for a play to tell the story of our church for its centennial year. But in 2014 and 2015, I got serious about the idea and wrote more.*

*Martin suggested I do twelve so I ended up with 12 "ScripturePicture Plays," each with a picture of a miracle, parable or event in the Gospels. The characters give their accounts and their thoughts so it is like hearing Jesus's words and actions from those who were there. Writing them was a Bible study in itself as I tried to present a cohesive story and remain true to scripture.*

The plays each needed a picture as a base for the drama. They considered using illustrations but ultimately decided to create live tableaus to be staged and photographed at Happiness Hills. Bill and Jennifer, with the help of Richard Carter and others arranged the settings, props and instructions for the 12 scenes. They recruited family and friends to play the parts. Laura organized costumes for everyone. A friend, Elisabeth Skeese, did the photography. On a beautiful Saturday in October 2015 everyone gathered, got costumed, received instructions and shared a lunch. Then the scenes were staged and pictures taken all within a few hours. They turned out great and are included in the resulting book.

*In 2016 I had it published through iUniverse and made the plays available to churches, Bible study groups or others who are interested. They are meant to be dramatic and interesting, but are serious Bible studies and not just entertainment.*

## The Drama of Our Lives

*It has been great to have time in retirement to do such things as write plays and memoirs. Rose and I are trying to record the drama of our lives to share with our children, grandchildren, great grandchildren and future generations and anyone else who is interested. While we write life goes on so there is always more to write. In June 2017, at our college class's 65th reunion Rose was honored with an honorary degree of Bachelor of Arts in Theater, making up for the diploma she almost got in 1952, but didn't because of her mother's death that year.*

*Everyone has a unique story to tell. Our lives, scripted by a higher power, tell of a good heritage, an enduring marriage, a wonderful family and a blessed long life over a time of great changes in the world. The story goes on.*

# BILL AND ROSE RAMSAY TIME LINE

## BACK HOME IN BEREA: 2006 - 2017

| YEARS | FAMILY AND RELATED EVENTS | WORLD EVENTS |
|---|---|---|
| 2006 | John Paul & Kristin Giner marry in OH | Saddam Hussein executed |
| | Luke & Maggie Storm marry in KY | |
| | Andrew & Cindy Robinson marry in IN | |
| | Bill & Rose move back to Berea | |
| | Jim, Shawn & family return from Kazakhstan | |
| | and move to Atlanta | |
| | Michael and Samuel killed in car accident | |
| 2007 | Bill & Rose purchase "Happiness Hills" farm | Global recession |
| | Bill & Rose join "Fellowship Bible Study" | Spike in food prices |
| | Stephen and Robin divorce | |
| | Melissa & Vito Rinaldi marry in KY | |
| | Colleen & Cason Wittig marry in KY | |
| | Noah born to John Paul & Kristin | |
| 2008 | Happiness Hills barn renovated | World stock market plunges |
| | Hill House constructed | |
| | Stephen marries Kathy Potter | |
| | Daniel & Erica Doss marry in GA | |
| | Mark & Clarissa Davenport marry in KY | |
| | Isaac born to Elizabeth & Ryan in Canada | |
| | Lily born to John Paul & Kristin in KY | |
| 2009 | Rose has "incident" in garden and | Obama becomes president |
| | momentarily loses memory | Boko Haram terrorizes Nigeria |
| | Brian & Michelle Lightbourne marry in FL | |
| | Benjamin & Amanda Harsy marry in IN | |
| 2010 | Rose falls and bruises abdomen | Haiti earthquake kills 230,000 |
| | Attend Lizzie McAmis' 100th birthday | "Arab Spring" begins |
| | Amber & Eric Wilson marry in KY | Turmoil in Middle East |
| | Bill & Rose travel to Elon College for opening | |
| | of "Service-Learning" archives with Sigmons | |
| | Adrienne & Matt Harrell marry in OH | |
| | Abram born to Luke & Maggie in KY | |

Eleanor born to Elizabeth & Ryan
Penny born to Catherine & Chris in FL
Nina born to John Paul & Kristin in KY
Annabelle born to Mark & Clarissa in KY

| 2011 | Rose has gall bladder surgery and later diagnosed with PMR (auto immune) | Earthquake & tsunami in Japan Fukushima nuclear meltdown |
|---|---|---|

2011    Rose has gall bladder surgery and later    Earthquake & tsunami in Japan
diagnosed with PMR (auto immune)    Fukushima nuclear meltdown
Ralph E. & McKenzie Robinson marry in KY    Iraq war ends for USA
Jacob born to Daniel & Erica
Gabriella Rose born to Melissa & Vito in FL
Rosaline born to Luke & Maggie in KY
Rose May born to Brian & Michelle in FL

2012    Rose has serious back pain & treatment    World population 7 billion
Jonathan & Katie Carter marry in OH    USA Embassy in Benghazi
Graham born to Brian & Michelle in FL    attacked, ambassador Stevens
Lucy born to John Paul & Kristin in KY    killed
Cashel born & adopted by Colleen & Cason, KY
Vito William born to Melissa & Vito in FL
Elise born to Amber & Eric in KY
Simon born to Mark & Clarissa in KY
Audrey born to Andrew & Cindy in IN

2013    Grover born to Catherine & Chris in FL    Boston Marathon terrorist attack
Alister born to Elizabeth & Ryan in KY    Terrorist attack in Ankara,
Mercy born to Amber & Eric in KY    Turkey

2014    Matthew & Kendall Miller marry in KY    Ebola epidemic in West Africa
Acacia born & adopted by Colleen & Cason, KY
Bridget born to Brian & Michelle in KY    ISIS begins conquests in Iraq
Blaise born to Colleen & Cason in KY
Grace born to Adrienne & Matt in IL

2015    Jennifer & Alfredo take over Retreat    Boko Haram massacres 2000 in
Center, build house & begin to move    Nigeria
Bill completes writing scripture plays    Earthquakes in Himalayas kill
US-Cuba relations resumed    10,000
Keith & Sarah Elrod marry in KY    SCOTUS decision in Obergefell v
Harrison born to Mark & Clarissa in KY    Hodges requires states to allow
Gabriel born to Andrew & Cindy in IN    same sex marriage

Lorelei born to Luke & Maggie in KY
Joel born to John Paul & Kristin in KY
David born to Jonathan & Katie in KY
Patrick born to Daniel & Erica in NC

2016    "ScripturePicture Plays" published          Terrorist bombings in Brussels,
        Felicity born to Amber & Eric in KY          Orlando, Berlin
        Ramsay born to Melissa & Vito in FL          UK votes to leave European
        Eleanor Rose born to Daniel & Erica in NC    Union
                                                     Clinton/Trump campaign in US
                                                     ugly. Trump & Republicans win

2017    Veronica Ruth born to Mark & Clarissa        Trump begins presidency
        Heidi Pearl born to Catherine & Chris in FL  in a divided nation.
        Jennifer & Lydia travel to China             Persecution of Christians and
        Rose receives honorary AB degree in theater  wars continue in mid ease
        Jennifer, Alfredo & girls travel to Denmark  causing refugee problems in
        with festival dancers, Jennifer sings national many countries.
        anthems at Independence Day celebration
        in Denmark.
        Micah Gabriel born to Jon and Katie in KY

2018 (Jan,)  Cora Rose born to Adrienne and Matt in IL
             Junia Aiden born to Colleen and Cason in KY

**FORT BREEZY**

BILL AND ROSE MOVED BACK TO
BEREA IN 2006 NEXT TO JENNIFER
AND ALFREDO. ALBERT POWELL
ADDED A PORCH AND FAMILY
ROOM. THEY SETTLED IN WITH LOTS
OF TIME FOR GRANDCHILDREN
LYDIA AND ISABEL

## HAPPINESS HILLS FARM, BEREA, KY

IN JANUARY 2007, BILL AND ROSE PURCHASED 79 ACRES BORDERING THE BEREA COLLEGE FOREST IN THE PIILOT KNOB AREA EAST OF BEREA VERY CLOSE TO THEIR NEW HOME. IT HAD HAY FIELDS, WOODS, A STREAM AND A FLOOD CONTROL LAKE. THEY FIXED UP AN OLD SAGGING. BARN AND AN OLD STRIP-PING SHED, BUILT HILL HOUSE AND HARMONY CENTER AND CREATED A RETREAT CENTER NAMED, BY JENNIFER, "HAPPINESS HILLS." IN 2016, JENNIFER AND ALFREDO BUILT THEIR DREAM HOME ON THE SITE AND THE RETREAT CENTER PORTION BECAME THEIRS. MANY FAMILIES AND GROUPS HAVE ENJOYED HAPPINESS HILLS FARM AND RETREAT CENTER.

ROSE WITH LYDIA AND ISABEL

(ABOVE) GRANDCHILDREN AT THE BIG HOUSE IN 1986

(BELOW) GRANDCHILDREN'S CHILDREN A GENERATION LATER

ROSE WITH CATHERINE AND PENNY

BILL WITH ACACIA

BILL AND ROSE
WELCOME BABY
ELISE NICOLE
WILSON TO THE
LIST OF GREAT
GRANDCHILDREN

BY SEPTEMBER 2017,
25 GREAT GRANDCHIL-
DREN HAD BEEN BORN
AND THREE EXPECTED

GREAT GRAND
NEPHEWS AND NIECES
IN BEREA ADDED 12
TO THAT GENERATION

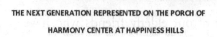

THE NEXT GENERATION REPRESENTED ON THE PORCH OF

HARMONY CENTER AT HAPPINESS HILLS

525

# REFLECTIONS 20

## AGING WITH GRACE, DISCOMFORT AND HUMOR

During our Florida trips with Jennifer Rose we often went to retirement homes or communities. We saw older people in all stages of the aging process from independent living to full care, from alert activity to wheelchair-bound unresponsiveness. The great majority live a good life in their twilight years. We noted that elderly folks in retirement communities not only enjoyed Jennifer's beautiful singing of folk songs and hymns, but responded, gleefully, to the humor which she included in her programs. One of the favorite stories which she claimed was told her by a nurse as truth, recognized the fact that women in retirement centers outnumber men. We won't speculate on the reasons.

*Three elderly women are sitting at their usual table in the dining hall of the retirement home. A nice looking elderly gentleman approaches and asks if he may share their table, using the fourth seat. Of course they invite him to sit there and he sits between two and across from the other. They are naturally curious about him and the one across from him says, "We haven't seen you before. Are you new here?" He tells them he has just arrived. She goes on to ask "Where are you from?" "Well ma'am," he says, "For the past 20 years I've been in the penitentiary." She is a bit taken aback and doesn't know what to say, but the woman on the one side picks up the conversation and asks, "Why were you in the penitentiary?" He replies, "I killed my wife, ma'am." Startled, she leans away. The woman on his other side gets all bright eyed and clutches his arm saying, "Oh, then you're single!"*

We know and have known a number of our elderly friends who have remarried after losing spouses years before. Usually they never intended to remarry but as time passed they met other singles and the desire for companionship was strong. When our good friend Maxine Bowles met someone years after Joe had died and she felt herself attracted to a single gentleman, she at first resisted. She had never even thought of remarriage, But she found that life goes on and she and her friend, Bill, were ready for a more than casual relationship. He was such a considerate man that he asked Judy, Maxine's daughter, for her permission before asking Maxine to marry him. Judy was delighted. Then Bill, who was retired from the Air Force, in which Joe had also served, researched Joe's World War II service and wrote a history for Maxine and Judy. He wanted to get to know Joe since they both shared love for Maxine. We've known other successful elder marriages, and a few not so happy, but Rose says she'd never remarry and would haunt me if I did.

Whoever said "aging is not for sissies!" got it right. As your body starts to decline you can't do the things you used to do. You give much more attention to basic bodily functions. You are careful to take the various medications and supplements designed to keep you going. You use rubs for back ache and joint pains. You don't want to get too far from your chair or bed. Your social life is structured around visits to doctors, dentists and physical therapy, but you have less and less desire for social activity. Phones that take pictures, answer questions and text others in a new language are incomprehensible. Hearing is diminished, not just requiring more volume but slower, distinct speech. Vision is no longer sharp and you need glasses for reading, computer work and driving. You no longer like to drive and at some point it becomes unsafe. A feature of Florida retirement areas is traffic problems. Old folks, with their diminishing reflexes and vision, are cautiously going here and there. Tourists are not sure where they are and are looking at the sights. Commercial vehicles are darting to and fro. Local residents are picking up kids or groceries or going to or from work. No wonder there are billboards advertising legal services for accident victims.

Daughter-in-law Anne related this tale.

*Grace and Mable are finishing up lunch at the retirement home on the edge of town and Grace says she'd love to go to the mall on the other end of town and do some shopping. Mable likes the idea and says she has her car in the parking lot and will drive. Grace observes that she hasn't driven for a while but Mable assures her it will be fine. It takes Mable a while to remember where she had her keys, but finally they get in the car and head through town. When they come to an intersection with a light that is red, Mable cruises right through as if it weren't there. Fortunately there was no cross-traffic, but Grace tensed up a bit. They came to a second red light and the same thing happens, again with no problems. But Grace thinks she'd better say something. It happens a third time and Grace gently says, "Mable, dear, do you realize you have run through three red lights?" Mable looks at her and blinks and says, "Oh, am I driving?"*

We find ourselves not wanting to acquire anything else but wanting to get rid of some of our accumulated possessions. We are blessed to be able to live together independently in our own convenient home with family and friends around. We don't know how anyone without family and friends manages. We love having family and friends visit but even that stimulation takes its toll on physical and mental energy. One mistake we probably made when we were caring for elderly parents was not to recognize this.

When our grandchildren came along we felt a direct connection with them and a need to be involved in their lives – and we were. With great grandchildren the connection is more remote although we love them all dearly. We enjoy hearing the stories of their adventures with their grandparents – our children who are now senior citizens themselves.

We have considered moving to a retirement facility but leaving the comforts and security we have in our familiar home is daunting. Most retirement homes have apartments where an elderly couple can continue to live together as they adjust to not having their own home. Whatever the housing, being together is important with many shared memories.

*An elderly couple is lying on their bed remembering former times. The wife asks her husband if he remembers how they used to cuddle and he would nibble her ear.*

*He remembers and she says, "You want to do that?" He jumps out of bed and heads for the bathroom. Alarmed, she asks, "Where are you going!" He responds in a rush, "To get my teeth!"*

Growing old has its challenges, but, as they say, "it's better than the alternative."

# REFLECTIONS 21

## KINDRED SPIRITS

We have been blessed throughout our lives by the lives of others with whom we've shared time and experiences. Someone said, "I know who I am because you called my name!" We do realize our identity as a reflection of our friends and family – especially those who we discover to be "kindred spirits." We remember that phrase from the *Anne of Green Gables* books as Anne responded to and was responded to by others in more than a superficial way. The importance of finding and being open to finding kindred spirits can't be over stated. These are people who share our feelings, who laugh and cry with us, who love us for ourselves and not just for what we do. What a blessing it is to find kindred spirits.

We have found these special friends in all aspects of life and among all sorts of people. The young woman who helps in the house and yard is a kindred spirit as have others been who did tasks for us. The employer-employee relationship and the financial arrangements are much less important than the personal feeling we have for each other. The man who keeps our yard mowed and trimmed does it as a ministry and we provide support for an extended ministry he provides to young men. In our community service – civil rights, childbirth education and literacy – we shared a special feeling with people of other faiths, races and political positions. On the job, certain employees shared, not only work related tasks, but life itself with its hopes, joys and sorrows. We have been fortunate to work in environments that made this possible. Neighbors, cousins, check-out clerks, waitresses, bank tellers, seatmates on a plane or in a theater, teachers, students, all are potential kindred spirits. They are everywhere.

The strongest sense of connection seems to happen in church, Bible study or prayer groups. We certainly found many at the revival we enjoyed at Edisto in which people from all 14 churches came together to sing, worship, learn and have fellowship together. Our Bible study groups over the years and most especially at Edisto and in Berea upon our return in 2006, have yielded strong friendships – more spiritual than social. A good number of these kindred have left the earth now but their spirits still remain with us. Kindred spirits enrich your life. Seek them.

# REFLECTIONS 22

## WORDS AND LABELS

Words have power. Our thinking would be difficult without words. In our media culture words and phrases are especially potent. We regularly see words like "jaw dropping" or "bombshell" or "scandal" as the media tries desperately to get the viewer to look at their article or story or website. When words have a consistent meaning understood by people in the same way they are the most important means of communication. Unfortunately, words have been twisted and meanings altered so that one can no longer be sure communication is reliable. We have seen the word "discrimination" change in popular understanding from indicating a thoughtful selection of value such as "a discriminating taste" in food, music or art, to an accusation of racism or bigotry. Most notoriously the word "gay," once meaning happy or joyous, has come to mean a homosexual lifestyle.

Labels are slapped on people simplistically, especially to put someone down or write them off as racists or bigots or parasites or sexists or homophobic or fascists, socialists or terrorists or fanatics or "deplorables." There are many other words often applied, dare we say, "indiscriminately" to persons or groups one wants to discredit or marginalize. Too often in our media culture we live by these labels and thereby cut off any real understanding or civil communication. Groups resort to protest signs, slogans, yelling obscenities at each other rather than trying to listen with respect and understand each other. The sensational media loves it and, unfortunately, many people respond.

# REFLECTIONS 23

## MARRIAGE AND FAMILY

Since this is the story and record of a marriage and family it seems appropriate to reflect on these institutions. We want to look at marriage and family from natural, spiritual, social, economic and civil perspectives. We know we have been blessed in our marriage and family and we haven't experienced the kinds of brokenness many have, although we've had ups and downs, high points, frustrations and tragedies. Some guests at the big house in Berea, when the children were still at home, said we were like the Waltons in the TV series. Having sons named John and Jim the boys would play on this and call out at bedtime, "Good night John Boy" and "Good night, Jim Bob." Our experience may not be typical of modern marriages and families, but we've seen a lot in our eighty some years and observed what is going on in our society and other people's lives, as well as in our own.

### The Nature of Marriage

Humans are created in two sexes – male and female. The male and female forms are exquisitely designed to complement each other. The sexual union of male and female is natural and the mating instinct is strong. The natural result is the conception of children and continuation of the race. Marriage is the institution which gives order to this mating of man and woman and provides for the care and rearing of children. A woman carries the developing child in her body until it has reached the stage of development for living independently of the umbilical cord which has nourished it from the mother's body. Even then, she is equipped to continue to provide nourishment through breast feeding. Substitutes for sustaining the child outside the womb during developing stages have been designed and substitutes have been found for feeding the new born child but that is what they are: "substitutes."

Mankind has learned how to interrupt conception by devices or drugs or other procedures, but the mating instinct is still the driving force and the use of contraception clearly acknowledges that conception is the natural result. The female form is especially designed to attract the male and females are aware of this and instinctively promote the attraction by dress, posture, cosmetics and other devices, especially during the prime mating years. Advertisers have long discovered this and use it relentlessly for all kinds of products and services many of which have nothing to do with mating. Marriage provides an essential framework for mating and child rearing and without it chaos results and people, especially children, get hurt. Marriage is much more profound than just two humans loving each other and deciding to share their lives, although that is an important part of good marriages. Accordingly, marriage since the beginning of human history has been a basic institution provided by the Creator for the benefit of mankind.

## The Spiritual Dimension

First and foremost we see marriage as a sacrament and family as a sacred trust. God created man and woman to be as one, commissioning them to participate in creation by having and raising children. The traditional marriage ceremony, which has been distilled beautifully over centuries, has many variations but is centered on vowing "before God and these witnesses" to care for each other and be faithful "as long as you both shall live," not just until it no longer satisfies your needs or moods. When couples take these vows we have no doubt that they mean them, but we also know that too often the vows are broken. We are not perfect people and we fail and can be redeemed, but the model and the intentions are still the ideal and what was intended in creation. So marriage is instituted by God and family is expected to be a result. Some may be called to remain single or have no children and find their ways to serve God and their fellow men, but marriage is the norm and the coupling of man and woman is essential for continuation of the human race, as God intended.

The birth of children is a miracle as new life is created, each unique and full of potential. Parents are blessed with children as a sacred trust, not as property. The child does not "belong" to them but is entrusted to them. Parents are responsible to their Creator for the care and instruction of children, not to the state or to themselves or to others, although each of these has some responsibility to hold parents accountable. Again, we are faulty and sometimes fail, but that doesn't change the ideal for which we strive.

At the marriage ceremony of one of our former students, the minister referred to the song *"Love and marriage go together like a horse and carriage"* and suggested that we get the cart before the horse when we put "love," meaning "feeling", before "marriage" meaning "commitment." Commitment is essential and love will grow bigger and deeper as that commitment is kept. Marriage becomes more than a man and a woman meeting each other's desires and needs. It is a new entity, with a spirit of its own, capable of being more than the man and woman can be alone.

You don't lose individuality in marriage, but a dimension is added to your life because you are now connected to another who is an integral part of your life. You want what is best for the other rather than seeking primarily to have your own needs met. "Greater love has no one but this: that he lays down his life for another." Being careful to respect and support each other's individuality, you both grow together, not just as equal partners, but as parts of each other. We like the story of the elderly gentleman who was at a doctor's appointment and said he'd have to leave in a few minutes to go see his wife. His doctor inquired where she was. He replied that she was in a long term care facility and had Alzheimer's. "Does she know who you are?" asks the doctor. "No," the man replies. "Then why is it so important that you go see her?" the doctor asks. The man replies, "Because I know who she is!"

Marriage and family have important social and economic dimensions and civil laws have been established to recognize and respond to them, but at its root, marriage is a sacred institution and part of the plan of creation.

## The Social Dimensions

In our years of schooling we were taught that marriage and family are the basic building blocks of any civilized society. They provide order in relationships, protection of the vulnerable, safe environments for the bearing and rearing of children. They are the strong fabric of communities and an essential economic and social unit for the whole society. We are not sure what is now taught, but we believe what we were taught is true. Every society has rituals, rules and customs reflecting the special place of marriage and family. Without these rituals, rules and customs, chaos would reign. The apostle Paul advised that Christians stay single so they could devote themselves fully to following their faith unencumbered by responsibilities for a partner and children. He thought end times were upon them. But time did not end and life has gone on for thousands of years since then. He was right, though, about marriage and family imposing responsibilities on people. This makes for a stable, productive society, which would not be the case in the absence of marriage and family. Rose's mother watching young singles trying to navigate their lives would say, "I'm glad my fortune's done told!" She was settled and a dependable community contributor. What would youth programs in sports be without "soccer moms?"

One shouldn't need studies to inform us that a stable family with father and mother is far, far more likely to produce successful children as they become citizens in their own right; however, studies do underline what common sense tells us. Children without stable home situations are much more likely to suffer. Statistically, they do not do as well. Of course, there are other factors involved and many children from difficult homes do become mature, productive adults and some from stable homes make bad choices and become problems. But in general the likelihood of success is much greater where children have the advantages provided by a two parent, stable family.

We noted when we came back to Berea after graduating almost twenty years earlier that many more students came from difficult or dysfunctional home situations. In our generation, we were economically poor because of the economy and limited opportunities, but we came from stable families and communities. Twenty years later a larger pattern was that being poor is related to problematic home situations and fractured communities. As our children interacted with classmates they realized that they didn't carry the same burdens that many others carried. Fortunately there is a Berea to provide all the opportunity to achieve, but it is a lot harder for those who carry the baggage of dysfunctional families.

Since World War II, the family has changed dramatically, largely due to the changing role of women. Women make important contributions in the workforce and it often requires two incomes for a family to provide for themselves and their children. One mistaken view that grew along with these changes is that being a homemaker or a stay at home mom or dad has less of a job than one that pays a wage or salary. Rose bridled when a form required a choice between "employed" and "unemployed." The implication was that a housewife was "unemployed" and she knew from personal experience that this was a misconception.

From our perspective, it seems that many of the problems in our society, and in other societies, result from the breakdown of the traditional family. As the family weakens or is marginalized, the fabric of communities and society loses stability. Other institutions and government programs just can't provide an adequate substitute. Care of children, care of the infirm and elderly, community volunteer services, church programs, and community cohesiveness all suffer. We were created to live in communities, to marry and have children, to take our places in society and this can best be accomplished in a society that honors and protects marriage and family.

## The Economic Dimensions

In an earlier (primarily agrarian) society, the family as an economic unit was assumed. It still is true in numbers of farm families and families with small businesses, but to a large extent, the family as a working unit to provide food and income has given way to having a breadwinner or both parents working outside the home. The family is still an economic unit in terms of sharing costs for housing, food, transportation and other life essentials and activities. The shift away from families having to work together as an economic necessity has contributed to the fracturing of families, although it need not happen. Rose's family depended on each member to help manage the farm. Bill's family had a wage-earner but still worked together doing needed home and garden tasks. Children's work doing odd jobs and delivering papers provided cash for school lunches and other expenses.

The most significant economic dimension of families is in the costs of raising children. Children depend upon someone else to provide for them until they can provide for themselves. This is usually parents – family. The costs of raising children, from an economic perspective, can be seen as an investment. When children grow into responsible, productive adults the investment pays off. When they continue to be dependent, for whatever reason, they not only fail to return the investment, but actually continue to be an economic burden to family or to society. The social and economic costs of children who grow up dysfunctional are enormous. Prisons, rehabilitation centers, medical care and other costs brought about by drug and alcohol use, criminal activity, reckless driving, pregnancies outside of marriage, and other social problems must be paid for by others.

Consider social security as an example of the importance of investment in raising children into productive adulthood. We all pay social security taxes over our working years, but these payments are not simply an investment account to pay for our retirement. They are used to pay those who are already beyond working age. We paid into social security for forty some years and have been recipients of social security payments for twenty. Our children began to pay into social security as soon as they completed college and were employed and now have been paying into the system for forty years (plus or minus) themselves. We don't have the actuarial tables or compound interest formulas, etc. to do a precise economic analysis, but it would appear to take two wage earners paying in to the system to cover the payments for our social security income. We paid for those who preceded us and our investment in raising six children is more than covering our cost. Suppose we had raised no children, or that they had become burdens on society rather than contributors? The lesson is clear. The wage earner contingent must be large enough relative to those who are not working to cover their costs and the way to keep the wage earner group large enough is to resupply it through the rearing of children in stable productive families. When this doesn't happen on a large enough scale, social security and the economy in general is in trouble and disaster looms.

Other countries have realized this in recent years as they have seen the population of productive citizens drop. Denmark has a program to encourage more children. China offers premiums for second children whereas a few years ago they discouraged more than one. Russia also is offering incentives to have more than one child. The handwriting is on the wall. If we don't provide a next generation of productive citizens our economies and our societies will fail. The family is at the heart of this matter. We should be doing all we can to encourage, support and protect marriage and the family, not weakening these basic institutions.

## Civil Dimensions

Every nation has laws regarding marriage and family. They reflect and give structure to these institutions, but did not establish them. After all, marriage and family long preceded any government and is present in all societies. Because of the importance of marriage and family the laws generally provide protection and support. When Bill was in the army, he received a dependency allowance because he was married and part of the cost of his service was support for Rose and children as they were born. Marriage is certified and recorded by the state. The marriage "covenant" or "contract" has legal standing. Marriage partners have rights and responsibilities recognized and incorporated in laws. Most marriages are performed in churches or synagogues and officiating ministers serve as agents of the state as well as of the church. For those who choose not to marry under the blessings and obligations of religious faith there are civil alternatives. Marriage and the resulting family are recognized as a basic unit of society.

Once, at a talk by the "impersonator" of Thomas Jefferson at Colonial Williamsburg, a gentleman asked Jefferson what he would think of giving the vote to women. His thoughtful response was that that would appear to be redundant. After all the woman was part of a family unit in which the man cast votes for the family. By and large a woman was part of her father' household until she was "given" in marriage to a husband to establish a new household. This didn't make the woman property but emphasized the unity and importance of family. In due course the rights and benefits of women suffrage were recognized, but the perception of marriage as a unity was so strong at the founding of America that, at that time, women voting seemed "redundant." Women expressed themselves as part of a family. The tradition of the father "giving the bride in marriage" persists in traditional marriage ceremonies. The point is that marriage and family were recognized and treated as an entity to be fostered and protected by the laws and customs of the land.

This special treatment of marriage and family has served America well over many years. Government support includes help in education, child care, tax relief and spousal benefits. Unfortunately, as more and more marriages ended in divorce, laws were needed to establish rights and responsibilities in those situations, especially where children were involved. However beneficial these state programs are, they sowed the seeds of the notion that "marriage" exists by state action, as if the state created marriage rather than having recognized it as a centuries old institution, defined long before the modern state.

Because there are benefits conferred by the state on marriage some have claimed that these benefits should be granted to others who want to share their lives with another in the same kind of relationship as marriage. Some states agreed with this view, enacting laws permitting "same sex marriages." Other states held to the traditional definition of marriage as between a man and a woman. Some states established a category of relationships called "civil unions" providing equal benefits to same sex unions as to traditional marriage. Conflict was inevitable and finally came to the Supreme Court to sort out the differences among the states when some same sex couples were married in states where it was legal and then moved to states where it was not recognized.

The generic definition of marriage for hundreds of years has been the union between a man and a woman, This definition prevailed as the legal definition as well for hundreds of years, but the legal definition in modern times was broadened in some states to include other two person unions. The state has a right to establish legal definitions in relation to the law. For example, a corporation is treated as a 'person' for legal purposes. Everyone knows it is not a person, but in regard to its legal standing to own property, sue and be sued, interact with tax laws, etc. it is treated as one. This seemed to be the intent of the states which established civil unions in regard to same sex couples – to give them status before the law as if it were marriage. This didn't satisfy those who wanted to be called "married" even though it isn't marriage in its full definition. But instead of recognizing these unions as "like marriage" before the law some states enacted legislation redefining marriage to include same sex couples. Other states continued to define marriage as between a man and a woman. Presented with the differences the Supreme Court by a five to four opinion supported a redefinition of marriage and declared the basic and historical definition unconstitutional. As chief justice Roberts asked in his dissent, "Who do we think we are?"

Justice Roberts and the other three dissenters pointed out that the decision violated the courts role as interpreter of laws and not legislator, disregarded the rights of states whose laws were not in accordance with the decision and found a constitutional guarantee where there was none. Justice Roberts said, "The majority's decision is an act of will, not legal judgment. The right it announces has no basis in the Constitution or this Courts precedent. The majority expressly disclaims judicial 'caution' and omits even a pretense of humility, openly relying on its desire to remake society according to its own 'new insight' into the 'nature of injustice.... As a result the Court... orders the transformation of a social institution that has formed the basis of human society for millennia. For the Kalahari Bushmen and the Han Chinese, the Carthaginians and the Aztecs."

We observed in another reflection that often decisions are reached because of feelings, biases, political agendas and other subjective reasons and then rationalized in an attempt to make it appear the decision was reached by careful study of the facts, logic and reason, That seems to be the case in this decision. It ignores the basic and unique relationship of the two sexes and reduces marriage to a relationship between any two individuals. No one has been denied the right to marry, but since the definition of marriage is the relationship between a man and a woman, this excluded same sex or other relationships. The court found it necessary to redefine marriage and then claim a constitutional right to this newly defined marriage. This opens the door to all kinds of redefinitions and has quickly led to the whole transgender mess where it is considered wrong to try to help a person deal with conflicting feelings about their gender but not to mutilate their bodies in a vain attempt to change their gender. No way has been found to change DNA.

The effect of all of these "new insights" about humans is to weaken the institutions of marriage and family that are basic to society and to the human race. We are afraid it will get worse instead of better. Earlier, damage to the foundations of marriage and family was the widespread choice of divorce as a solution to marriage problems. Ease of divorce made "living together" outside of marriage seem like a rational thing to do. Beyond that sexual activity as a form of recreation or self-expression apart from the protection and obligations of marriage or any committed relationship has grown. This all with the worship of individualism gave rise to growth of abortions. Legalization of abortion by the Supreme Court was another case of finding a constitutional right where there was none and embracing a practice contrary to nature and to God's plan for humankind.

We are not comfortable with the state intruding on people's choices, although it must establish limits when it affects others or the well-being of society. If the state can prohibit abortions it can also require abortions. But the problem is that an abortion is not just about what a woman does with her body (as if she created herself); it is about what is done to a new body. This new creation is not part of the woman, although it depends on her for development. It is not her property to be disposed of as if it were a dress that doesn't fit. It is a human being with life and potential and has its own value as such. The choice to kill it is wrong morally and the state has an obligation to give it protections, not encourage its murder. Ancient pagan societies sacrificed children to Molech or some other god and we consider that barbaric. Our society is sacrificing innocent life to the gods of selfishness, undisciplined sex and material possessions and we justify it as a right.

You and I have life because of the union of a man and a woman, hopefully in the blessed institution of marriage, and our mother's willingness to nurture us as we developed in the womb and then after birth, rather than arranging for our murder before we were born. Marriage is meant to be the sacred institution in which a child is conceived and grows in a loving, nurturing and protected environment. Nothing else does that job as well and we all reap the consequences. We pray for a return to a view of marriage as sacred, a commitment to the sexual union of man and woman as unique and meant to be reserved for marriage. We pray for the valuing of the gift of new life as a trust to be cherished, and for care and help to those who find themselves suffering outside of those precepts. Our laws and policies should support and foster those values.

# REFLECTIONS 24

## SEX AND GENDER

The topics of "sexual preference" and "gender identity" are so volatile and confusing today that it is difficult to speak about them honestly and rationally. Everyone seems quick to misinterpret any opposite views as immoral or as bigoted or as intolerant or licentious. We are bewildered by the rhetoric, the passion, the featuring "homosexuality" as noble on one hand and depraved on the other. Obviously homosexuality is a mixed bag of behaviors as can be seen in the length of initials adopted by the LGTBQIA movement. Add to that the whole transgender miasma and it is no wonder there is confusion. We will try to sort out our understanding, feelings and experience for our own benefit. Let us admit from the start that our views are colored by our conviction that God created male and female as complementary for the continuation of humanity and charged them to be fruitful and multiply. With a marriage of 65 years, six children, 22 grandchildren and soon to be 28 great grandchildren, we have lived out our convictions.

First, we will deal with the difference between sex and gender. Although the terms are sometimes used interchangeably they really mean different, but related, things.

Sex has to do with our physical nature or the way we are made. Males and females have different body forms and parts. They have different concentrations of body chemistry. They have chromosomes particular to their sex and either male or female DNA. That can't be changed, although alterations can be made chemically and surgically to give appearances of change. So sex is fixed at conception and the person develops accordingly as a male or female. There are a very small percentage of births in which the sexual traits are mixed up, but this is very rare, and even then the DNA seems to be fixed.

The term gender is more fluid and culturally established. We learned in Latin class about gender in regard to words, especially describing objects. Words are masculine, feminine or neuter. This system still prevails in some languages and has remnants in English. For example a ship is always feminine - "her." In general gender assignment seems to follow cultural perceptions of traits identified as more feminine or more masculine. Females were seen as nurturing, care givers, home makers, preferring silk to coarse material, etc. Masculine traits were often associated with hunting, fighting, protecting, muscle strength, etc. Looking at King Arthur's Knights of the Round Table one sees the ideal of manhood being the strong protector of the weak, having courage and honor. As roles changed through the centuries these cultural perceptions have changed, but there are still many remnants of the perceived and real differences between men and women. That is one reason there is pressure to have "equal representation" to assure that women's unique perspectives are represented.

A male may exhibit what are perceived as feminine traits and be termed effeminate. A woman may engage in traditionally masculine activity and be called a tomboy. This doesn't change their sex. Gender doesn't determine sex, but, in general, sex determines gender and most people are comfortable with gender and sex identities being one and the same. A person who "feels" at odds with his or her sexual reality in terms of preferences, mannerisms, and self-identity essentially sees their gender as different from their sex. Until recently the response in such situations was to help the person with the feelings. Today some think that feelings are more real than reality, and attempt to change anatomy and physiology to conform to these feelings. So there are now men who claim to be women and women who claim to be men and have changed their appearances accordingly. We have heard of some who change back and forth, wanting to act and be treated as women or men depending on their feelings at the time. This seems to us to be ridiculous, although we don't question the persons' sincerity in regard to their feelings.

This elevation of the right of persons to put their feelings or desires above natural or moral laws is a mistake. No matter how much we want to fly if we jump off a building flapping our arms, we will fall to the ground.

Putting feelings and desires above natural and moral laws is evident in the matter of "sexual preference." This phrase has been used to cover a multitude of sexual relationships that deviate from the natural union of male and female for which human bodies are specifically designed. Male and female are designed for mating. Anyone with farm experience knows the fundamentals of the essential mating between the male and female forms of any species, be it cow and bull, rooster and hen, sow and boar or even drone and queen bee. There is no mating between same sexes. Sexual stimulation between same sexes is just that – sexual stimulation – and not mating. This is why we discard the notion of same sex marriage. Same-sex relations may be exploitive as in the case of men using young boys for their sexual gratification or it may be mutually satisfying as with same sex couples who want to share their lives in a loving relationahip, but it is not marriage.

Our experience with those who call themselves homosexual and those who engage in homosexual acts shows us that there are many different kinds of such activity. We have known men who do not call themselves homosexual who engaged in homosexual activity seeking a new thrill. We have been approached by others who do not consider themselves homosexual seeking to satisfy their fantasies on us because there were no female partners available. We have seen those who find hook-ups at gay bars but have no further relationship with the partner. We have known friends who were successfully married for years and had children and in later life left their families for a homosexual lifestyle. One such close friend died bitterly of AIDS. We know friends and relatives who have chosen to share their life with another person of the same sex and consider themselves as married. So to talk about homosexuality without refining the discussion by the type of relationship intended is futile. To say "I'm Gay!" is meaningless unless one explains what they mean. Our definition of a homosexual is a man who has chosen to engage in a lifestyle of homosexual behavior. Were our friends who were married and had children and then entered into homosexual lifestyle heterosexual or homosexual? We have heard nor seen no evidence that it is a genetic condition. All of us are physically capable of such activity. The choice is ours. To say "I'm just made that way" is a denial of free choice and a convenient escape from any responsibility for our choices. We do well to seek guidance for our choices from natural and moral laws rather than our feelings and desires of the moment.

Years ago when considering why students (and others) behaved and thought as they did, I read of an observation attributed to Jean Piaget, the French child development researcher. Summarized, it suggested that behavior preceded belief as children develop. That seemed profound to me and a good reason for rules to govern behavior as children grow up and develop their beliefs. This observation is opposite of thinking that people's behavior **proceed**s from their beliefs, which is probably also true. I began to notice how children and others often construct or adapt beliefs to accommodate their behavior. When Jennifer was little she had imaginary playmates who were not just entertaining but convenient for her excusing herself. Idom, Adam and Odem were three favorites. Idom was the mischievous one and if she did something against the rules she simply said, "Idom made me do it." When Rose's brother's wife, who had married at 16 felt that she had missed out on life, she got involved with a young man. She left her husband with three children saying that she wasn't a fit mother and Rose could raise them better than she could. This kind of rationalization of behavior is not at all uncommon. Why is it that we are so reluctant to simply admit our misdeeds, seek and accept forgiveness and move on, but would rather change our beliefs and world view? I suspect this is what goes on in the case of sexual deviations, resulting in the effort to change other people's world view to conform to one's own.

The LGTBQIA lobby has been quite successful in convincing many people that homosexuality is a condition rather than a choice. Then following in the wake of racial discrimination they have given the impression of also being a minority group suffering from discrimination. Of course anyone who looks at this claim honestly can see that it is not the same thing as racial discrimination. No one asks your sexual orientation for admission to a national park, a restaurant, a barber shop or beauty salon. They are not denied the vote. They are welcomed in churches. They don't have separate water fountains or schools. They are not forced to move to the back of the bus or to a separate train car when they cross into a southern state. In fact many are in high position. Many are wealthy. They have the same citizen rights as anyone else. However, when they ask for endorsement of their lifestyle or try to promote their views or agenda they will find resistance. So do members of the Ku Klux Klan or anti-Semites or other groups who would promote views others hold to be wrong. They seem to want not just tolerance but affirmation and are not tolerant of anyone who disagrees.

We come to our own conclusions with no hatred of those who choose differently, and we do not support persecution or demeaning of others. We are not "homophobic" or "bigoted" or even "unenlightened." We simply try to be true to our faith, follow our conscience and treat everyone as a brother or sister under God. We know there can and should be loving relationships between people across sexual, racial, ethnic and religious lines. While we all have our own tendencies and temptations we do not believe that "sexual orientation" or "sexual preference" is an unalterable condition like color of skin or eyes or hair. We believe people have the right to choose their friends, their living arrangements, and their beliefs. But we believe that sexual activity outside the sanctity and protection of marriage is wrong and does not lead to the highest good for individuals or for society. We subscribe to the official position of our church about sexuality.

*"We recognize that sexuality is God's good gift to all persons.*

*Although all persons are sexual beings whether or not they are married, sexual relations are only clearly affirmed in the marriage bond. Sex may become exploitive within as well as outside of marriage. We reject all sexual expressions that damage or destroy the humanity God has given as a birthright, and we affirm only that sexual expression that enhances that same humanity. We believe that sexual relations where one or both partners are exploitive, abusive, or promiscuous are beyond the parameters of acceptable behavior and are ultimately destructive to individuals, families and the social order.*

*We deplore all forms of the commercialization and exploitation of sex, with their subsequent cheapening and degradation of human personality*

*Homosexual persons no less than heterosexual persons are individuals of sacred worth.... although we do not condone the practice of homosexuality and consider the practice incompatible with Christian teaching."*

Our only exception to the Methodist statement is in the reference to "homosexual" persons compared to "heterosexual" persons. It is our contention that these assignments are meaningless as respects to the human condition. We are all capable of being homosexual or heterosexual or both. The designation arises from behavior, not condition. A plumber, a philanthropist, a thief, a murderer, a singer are designated as such because of their behavior. Homosexuality or other sexual variations derive from behavior. They are choices. To consider them conditions beyond a person's control leads to erroneous conclusions.

# PART TEN

*The Last Chapter*

# CHAPTER 42

# ANOTHER JOURNEY

*Someone asked the old codger in the hills if he had lived there all his life. His answer was, "Not yit!" Our story to date has been told as best we can remember and what the future holds is unknown. We do know that our physical and mental abilities are declining. We are not going to regain our youthful stamina, strength, clarity of vision and hearing, or the ability to do all we want to do. We have aches and pains, weaknesses and blemishes that are not going to go away. We have joined others in the mixed sorrow and celebration for many friends and colleagues of our generation who have departed this life. We are blessed with family and friends who care for us and we enjoy their stories, thoughts and achievements. We are thankful for each day and the little pleasures of life: like great grandchildren who bring us presents of their art work; granddaughters who sit at the foot of the bed or on the floor and rub their grandmother's feet as they share their lives and memories; friends who clean house or mow the lawn but also share their lives and love with us; children, nieces and nephews who visit and bring special food or desserts. We also enjoy just time alone, together, caring for each other, reading scripture and light fiction, and remembering good times and sometimes difficult times we have shared. What is ahead?*

*Many friends and family have gone to retirement communities and care facilities and this may happen to us. While we can live independently in our own home now it is likely that will change at some point. A fall, a stroke, heart problems or other medical conditions can strike at any time and require a change in living patterns. Will we live to see our youngest grandchildren grow to adulthood? Lydia is now 16 and promises to become our chauffeur. Isabel is 14 and a natural caregiver who promises to take care of us. Our oldest great grandchild, Isaac, is now almost 10. Is it conceivable that we will see great, great grandchildren?*

*Having enjoyed involvement in dramatics we often think of lines from plays that speak to life's issues. We remember the line from the great drama Macbeth. By William Shakespeare;*

> **"Tomorrow, and tomorrow, and tomorrow,**
> **Creeps in this petty pace from day to day,**
> **To the last syllable of recorded time;**
> **And all our yesterdays have lighted fools**
> **The way to dusty death. Out, out, brief candle!**
> **Life's but a walking shadow, a poor player,**
> **That struts and frets his hour upon the stage,**
> **And then is heard no more. It is a tale**
> **Told by an idiot, full of sound and fury,**
> **Signifying nothing."**

*We know that we have had our time on stage in a wonderful drama and that our act is coming to a close, but we don't agree that our lives signify nothing. We look at our children, our grandchildren and great grandchildren and feel the continuity of generations. We know that the blessings of those who love God and try to live under his laws and guidance will be passed on to many generations, as promised in scripture. We have been blessed by the lives of our parents, grandparents and those further back in time. We also know that we are but a speck in this great universe and occupy only a moment in time. But this is the time and place allotted to us and we have tried to play our roles well, true to the script written for us.*

*Rose sometimes says that we should take all our aches and pains and weaknesses, lock them in the bedroom and leave the house to take another journey. That is what will happen someday. We don't know the departure dates or the means of transportation. We don't need to pack any suitcases since all will be provided. We have full confidence in our travel agent to have arranged everything and we know our destination.*

# REFLECTIONS 25

## ETERNITY

We have been intrigued by notions of time travel expressed in various books and plays. Mark Twain's *A Connecticut Yankee in King Arthur's Court*, and H. G. Welles *The Time Machine*, along with various King Arthur stories like *The Once and Future King*, by T. H. White are fascinating. We enjoyed the play, *Berkley Square*, which was the last major production in which we were involved during our college years, where a young man goes back in time and falls in love with a girl of an earlier time. It is interesting to speculate about being freed from our limitations of time and space. We are time and space bound and it is hard to conceive of concepts like eternity. We tend to think of it as an unlimited future, but it must also include the past. Eternity goes in both directions. Someone observed that our present is our ancestors' future and our descendants' past.

Are our limited years a part of a continuum of life that doesn't end but continues forever? Are all the events of our lives still there in another dimension for eternity? A "cloud" that retains information from thousands of computers and the endless stretches of space makes one wonder. When our souls are released from our time and earth bound bodies will we be able to "revisit" our past not just in memory, but in actuality, in another dimension? There are many moments of our lives we'd love to enjoy forever and others we would like to have erased. And we'd enjoy a "new" body free of weaknesses and blemishes. Is this what is meant by the "new creation" where we are washed clean of our misdeeds and sinful thoughts and there will be no sadness, pain or death? If we were aware that our deeds and even our thoughts in this life never go away would we be more careful of what we do and let into our minds?

Perhaps the Kingdom of God is not some future place and time but another dimension to which we can relate even during our lives. We have known people who seemed to have a connection with the transcendent and divine. They have a glow or aura about them. We were at the hospice bedside of a dear friend and had the distinct impression that she was partly still with us and partly already in heaven and we were aware that she was loved in both places and at peace. Can we be part of the "kingdom" before we are completely released from our time and space bound lives?

# APPENDIX

## DESCENDANTS OF BILL AND ROSE RAMSAY
## AS OF JANUARY, 2018

# DESCENDANTS OF BILL AND ROSE RAMSAY
## Births, Deaths and Marriages as of January 31, 2018

WILLIAM ROMIG RAMSAY - ELVA ROSALBA (ROSE) MOORE

August 19, 1931 – PA          July 5, 1931 – TN

married Sep 7, 1952

### Children, Grandchildren and Great Grandchildren

WILLIAM EDWARD RAMSAY - ANNE MARSHALL HYLTON

November 15, 1953 – GA          December 3, 1953          married Nov 23, 1975

AMBER ROSE RAMSAY - ERIC WILSON

June 4, 1979 – KY          February 19, 1979          married Mar 27, 2010

ELISE NICOLE WILSON

October 21, 2011 – KY

MERCY MARIE WILSON

September 10, 2013 – KY

FELICITY ANNE WILSON

July 19, 2016 - KY

WILLIAM JOEL RAMSAY

March 27, 1981 - KY

DANIEL BOWLES RAMSAY - ERICA DODD

April 24, 1985 – KY          September 19, 1983          married Jun 14, 2008

JACOB DANIEL RAMSAY

November 1, 2011 – GA

PATRICK DODD RAMSAY

February 14, 2015 – NC

**ELEANOR ROSE RAMSAY**
November 9, 2016 - NC

**LAURA ELIZABETH RAMSAY - RALPH EDWIN COMPTON, JR**
December 23, 1954 – AL          April 11, 1954                    married Aug 22, 1976


**ELIZABETH ANNE COMPTON - RYAN SARTOR**
July 14, 1978 – VA              November 10, 1975               married Oct 21, 2001


**ISAAC JAMES SARTOR**
May 27, 2008 - BC


**ELEANOR DAWN SARTOR**
April 13, 2010 – BC


**ALISTER RYAN SARTOR**
August 1, 2013 – KY


**CATHERINE LOIS COMPTON - CHRIS NIELSEN**
June 9, 1981 – WV               September 9, 1982               married Nov 5, 2005


**PENELOPE CATHERINE NIELSEN**
April 23, 2010 – FL


**GROVER BENJAMIN NIELSEN**
April 9, 2013 – FL


**HEIDI PEARL NIELSEN**
May 16, 2017 – FL


**MELISSA ROSE COMPTON - VITO RINALDI**
October 11, 1982 – WV          August 5, 1980                  married Aug 12, 2007


**GABRIELLA ROSE RINALDI**
January 21, 2011 - FL


**VITO WILLIAM RINALDI**
October 9, 2012 – FL

RAMSAY VINCENT RINALDI
September 22, 2016 – FL


RALPH EDWIN COMPTON III - MCKENZIE JADE ROBINSON
February 22, 1988 – KY          August 19, 1989          married Aug 13, 2011


STEPHEN PATRICK BLAKE COMPTON
January 17, 1994 – KY


STEPHEN GATES RAMSAY - ROBIN OSBORNE
July 18, 1956 – TN          April 27, 1959          married Dec 21, 1980
                                                    divorced 2007


BENJAMIN GATES RAMSAY -AMANDA MARIE HARSY
October 4, 1982 – OH          November 7, 1984          married Jul 3, 2009


ANDREW ALBERT RAMSAY - CINDY ROBINSON
June 25, 1984 – OH          August 9, 1983          married Jun 15, 2006


AUDREY LAURIE RAMSAY
December 24, 2012 – IN


GABRIEL MICHAEL RAMSAY
March 17, 2015 – IN


MICHAEL AARON RAMSAY
May 2, 1987 – SC -- November 15, 2006 (automobile accident)


SAMUEL OSBORNE RAMSAY
January 18, 1989 – KY – November 15, 2006 (automobile accident)


MATTHEW STEPHEN RAMSAY- KENDALL JOYCE MILLER
April 12, 1991 – KY          March 2, 1995          married Jun 20, 2014


STEPHEN GATES RAMSAY - KATHY POTTER
(repeat)          July 28, 1964          married April 19, 2008


561

JOHN ROBERT RAMSAY - EILEEN AMBROSE

May 30, 1958 – TN          February 7, 1959                          married May 26, 1979


BRIAN COONEY RAMSAY - MICHELLE LIGHTBOURNE

December 7, 1982 – WI          July 14, 1983                          married Jan 31, 2009


ROSE MAY RAMSAY

March 17, 2011 – FL


GRAHAM ROBERT RAMSAY

August 9, 2012 – FL


BRIDGET COLLEEN RAMSAY

July 15, 2014 – KY


COLLEEN AIDEN RAMSAY - CASON WITTIG

December 24, 1984 – WI          December 14, 1984                          married Dec 15, 2007


CASHEL AMBROSE WITTIG

August 28, 2012 (adopted at birth)


ACACIA GRACE WITTIG

February 19, 2014 (adopted at birth)


BLAISE RAMSAY WITTIG

October 22, 2014


JUNIA AIDEN WITTIG

January 19, 2018


ADRIENNE ROSE RAMSAY - MATTHEW HARRELL

April 25, 1988 – OH          November 11, 1985                          married Jun 26, 2010


GRACE COLLEEN HARRELL

December 1, 2014


CORA ROSE HARRELL

January 9, 2018

JAMES MOORE RAMSAY - SHAWN ADAIRE MYERS
January 25, 1960 – TN        July 22, 1964 – IL                          married Aug 18, 1984

REBEKAH ADAIRE RAMSAY
December 14, 1985 – KY

KEITH ROMIG RAMSAY - SARAH ELIZABETH ELROD
February 12, 1988 – KY        February 4, 1990                          married Jan 17, 2015

JONATHAN MOORE RAMSAY - KATIE LEIGH CARTER
June 14, 1989 – KY                August 21, 1986                        married Jan 14, 2012

    DAVID JAMES RAMSAY
    November 25, 2015 – KY

    MICAH GABRIEL RAMSAY
    December 7, 2017

NAOMI GRACE RAMSAY
February 11, 1991 – KY

JENNIFER ROSE RAMSAY - JOSE ALFREDO ESCOBAR
February 12, 1970 – GA April 29, 1962 - Chile                            married Sep 7, 1996

    LYDIA ELEANOR ESCOBAR
    August 22, 2001 - KY

    ISABEL LOCHIEL ESCOBAR
    August 3, 2003 - KY

Printed in the United States
By Bookmasters